Literary Taste, Culture and Mass Communication

Volume 2

MASS MEDIA AND MASS COMMUNICATION

Literary Taste, Culture and Mass Communication

Volume 2

MASS MEDIA AND MASS COMMUNICATION

Peter Davison/Rolf Meyersohn/Edward Shils

CHADWYCK-HEALEY CAMBRIDGE
SOMERSET HOUSE TEANECK, NJ

© Chadwyck-Healey Ltd 1978

Chadwyck-Healey Ltd
20 Newmarket Road
Cambridge CB5 8DT

ISBN 0 85964 037 X

Somerset House
417 Maitland Avenue
Teaneck, NJ 07666

ISBN 0 914146 45 9

Library of Congress Cataloging in Publication Data
Main entry under title:

Mass media and mass communication.

(Literary taste, culture and mass communication; v.2)
    Bibliography: p.
    1. Mass media – Addresses, essays, lectures.
    2. Popular culture – Addresses, essays, lectures.
    I. Series

    AC1L79 vol.2 (P91.25) 301.16'1 77-90610

British Library Cataloguing in Publication Data

Literary taste, culture and mass communication.
    Vol.2: Mass media and mass communication
    1. Arts and society – Addresses, essays, lectures.
    I. Davison, Peter II. Meyersohn, Rolf
    III. Shils, Edward Albert IV. Mass media and
    mass communication.

    700   NX180.S6

Contents

Introduction

This second volume of *Literary Taste, Culture and Mass Communication* is devoted to general and theoretical, rather than specific and detailed, considerations of mass media and mass communication. The volume opens with Morris Janowitz's contribution on 'The Study of Mass Communication' to the *International Encyclopaedia of the Social Sciences* and the bulk of the volume is made up of three important issues of two journals, the *Journal of Social Issues* and *Daedalus*. The first of these was published thirty years ago when the mass media deemed most significant were film and radio; the other two were published in the same year, 1960, and make an interesting contrast in the way two important journals treated the analysis of mass culture and the society which produced it — or for which it was intended. The volume also contains two short articles: a relatively early analysis — it was published in 1937 — of the growth in circulation of newspapers and journals in America over a period of 120 years and the effect that might have on education and democracy; and an editorial from one of the most important scientific journals in Britain, published just after an Act of Parliament had reached the statute book establishing independent — that is, commercial — television in Britain (a country until then without any form of commercial television or radio).

Professor Janowitz's account of how mass communication is studied was published later than all the other contributions in this volume, but it provides a valuable perspective for the readings that follow, and for much that is in other volumes. The differences, for example, in estimates of 'the effectiveness of potency of the mass media' (p.3) will be apparent from much that is reprinted in these volumes or referred to by contributors, but a preliminary overview will prompt the reader's discrimination without, one hopes, unduly directing it. Professor Janowitz also provides certain essential bases in the course of his analysis. Thus, on p.4, he refers to Harold Lasswell's key questions, formulated in 1932, for analyzing the mass communication process: 'Who says what to whom with what effect?'. These questions he then uses as a convenient framework for a lucid analysis of approaches to problems posed by mass communication. Implicit is a fourth question, and one that might usefully be included with those asked by Lasswell (and, indeed, conventionally asked in Shakespeare context questions for many decades), 'in what context?'. As can be seen from the last section of the article by S. S. Sargent and Gerhart Saenger, 'Analyzing the Content of Mass Media' (*Journal of Social Issues*, 1947, pp.60-61), the context in which something is said is particularly important (and see also the earlier article in that issue, 'Ego-Involvement and the Mass Media', by Muzafer Sherif and S. Stansfeld Sargent). Also particularly lucid in Professor

Janowitz's contribution is his account of the three basic approaches to discovering the effects of mass communication: laboratory and quasi-laboratory experiments; surveys based on interviews and questionnaires; and intensive case studies. As he says, the findings of such studies are strongly influenced by the research method used.

The first of the two issues of the *Journal of Social Issues* reproduced was published in 1947. It can be dated in one sense by its concern with radio and film, rather than television, and by the seeming surprise in the footnote to p.2 of Professor Fearing's introduction, where it is adduced that the publication in the United States and England of '50 odd magazines' devoted to serious aspects of motion pictures is (rightly) taken as evidence of concern with film as a social force. It was then still possible to be slightly taken aback that films could be discussed seriously on any scale (though one should not, perhaps, pin too much on the omission of a hyphen from '50 odd'!). But though the articles were written a long time ago (as time is measured in this field of study), they contain a great deal that is well worth reading for what it has to say now, as well as in the context of the development of such scholarship. Questions of social responsibility asked by Professor Fearing are still inadequately, if at all, answered and even more striking are Professor Lazarfeld's remarks on the role of the mass media in 'so-called tolerance propaganda' – improving relationships between racial groups by means of propaganda in the media. There is no doubt that his analysis of the question, 'if we can sell soap in this way, why shouldn't we also be able to sell good interracial relations' (p.40) is still instructive. It is particularly usefully juxtaposed with Sherif and Sargent's article on ego-involvement and the part it may play in the adoption of new forms and values (p.33).

I suppose we are now a little more suspicious of the possibility of being 'realistic and objective' in 'serious' films, and not quite so anxious about the undesirability of escapism as was the case when Professor Gundlach wrote on 'The Movies: Stereotypes or Realities?', but the pervasiviness of the stereotype and the prejudice that can be implied from it is well caught. Indeed, one might even suggest that it is illustrated, doubtless unwittingly, by Professor Gundlach himself when he states that 'An effete British author made the classic remark that nature imitated art' (p.51). Is there a stereotype lurking here? How does it affect the statement made? What will an American – a British – reader make of the statement? Why not name the author or simply make the whole thing impersonal, 'It has been said that . . .'?

The last four articles are concerned with analyzing the content of mass media (and in particular, how much agreement there is between analysts and on what needs to be done), assessing film audience response, and measuring radio audiences. Professor Fearing rounds off the symposium.

The second issue of the *Journal of Social Issues* to be reproduced was first published in 1960. It takes the form of a detailed analysis of mass society and mass media in America by Raymond A. Bauer and Alice H. Bauer, which serves Professors Talcott Parsons and Winston White as a 'springboard' for additional contributions on this theme, as well as for certain refinements, and as the basis for a vigorous, indeed, heated debate between the Bauers and Professor Lewis A. Coser. Their differences clearly reveal the issues involved but they should not detract from the Bauers' solid analysis of research findings in mass communications, something to which Professor Coser himself points.

Much of the Bauers' analysis is of work done and conclusions reached (with notable succinctness, if with a certain cynicism, in listing the alleged effects of mass media, p.107). They were also concerned to categorize the particular stances of theorists of mass society – that they are elitists, intellectuals, and opposed to the Protestant Ethic (and it was with this aspect of the study that Professor Coser particularly took issue). In the Spring of that same year in which the Bauers' study appeared, 1960, *Daedalus* devoted a special issue to mass culture and mass media. In the light of the Bauers' categorization of the attitudes of theorists of mass society and mass culture, there was a certain irony in the fact that among the contributors to *Daedalus* was James Baldwin, offering, as Norman Jacobs put it in his Introduction, 'personal testimony to the plight of the creative artist' (p.179). The debate in *Daedalus* is every bit as vigorous (if not quite so heated) as that in the *Journal of Social Issues* but it is orientated differently, about three basic positions: what Norman Jacobs calls 'optimist', 'pessimist', and 'meliorist' (p.177). This collection of papers arose from a two-day conference (and some important points made by those who took part in the conference discussion are mentioned by Professor Jacobs in his Introduction). Later the issue became the book, now out of print, *Culture for the Millions?*, 1961. One paper from this collection has been brought forward to volume one, Professor Shils's 'Mass Society and its Culture'; it has not been printed a second time here but an excellent summary is given by Professor Jacobs in his introduction (pp.177-81). Professor Jacobs introduces most of the papers reproduced but a word might be said about two or three of them. First, I would point out that in this volume we have the first two contributions in the series by creative writers: Randall Jarrell and James Baldwin. Discussion of the role of the creative artist, as he sees it, in a society dominated by a mass culture, is an important facet of this series. Secondly, a counter statement to those of Baldwin and Jarrell – or, at least, a much more optimistic point of view – is offered by James Johnson Sweeney, 'The Artist and the Museum in Mass Society'. He starts his contribution very firmly indeed: 'One should put aside at the outset the notion that there is any essential threat in the mass media to the genuinely creative artist or to genuine art' (p.245). Stanley Hyman and H. Stuart Hughes disagree as to whether America has or has not retained 'a vision of the good society' and discuss the part mass culture plays in this. Although Hyman is the more optimistic of the two, believing that 'We are not a good society, but we do have a vision of it', he does concede that mass culture can be no more than 'a kind of shabby poetry' (p.285). Hughes 'could scarcely disagree more strongly. I believe we have lost that vision: most of us are quite satisfied with the ugliness of our cities, the waste in our economy, the cheerful incompetence of our leaders, the meaninglessness of public discourse, the general insensibility to the overwhelming danger that threatens us' (p.294). The disgust and disillusion are plain; but whether what is described as being lost amounts to the vision for America expressed by Cotton Mather in *Magnalia Christi Americana* is another matter.

This issue of *Daedalus* contained two interesting documents: de Tocqueville on 'Democracy and the Arts' (Alexander Pope would surely have approved of what he has to say of 'The Trade of Literature', p.314), and what Norman Jacobs calls, 'a rare glimpse of how and where much of mass culture is being produced, and by whom' (p.319).

Volume two is completed by the reprinting of a leader from an eminent British scientific journal and by a relatively early study on 'Cultural Change and Changes in Popular Literature'. This, and especially its 'two direct implications' (pp.341-42), should be read in conjunction with Sherif and Sargent on 'Ego-Involvement and the Mass Media' (pp.31-39, especially 'Mass Media and Social Change', pp.38-39) and Herbert Gans's 'Popular Culture in America' in volume one.

The editorial from *Nature* was written in reaction to Parliament's decision to permit commercial broadcasting in Britain. As does Harold Punke in his article, the editorial concludes by expressing concern about the educative function of the media and it refers to fears that had been expressed that 'the most significant influence of the popular Press is now on what [Sir William Haley, Director-General of the BBC 1944-52; editor of *The Times*, 1952-66] calls morals, whereas the influence of British broadcasting [till then exclusively BBC] has been mostly on manners' (p.348). These remarks, it should be stressed, were made in a scientific journal. Indeed, the first two paragraphs were printed in a column adjacent to the list of contents, which included articles on 'Principles of Experimental Physics', 'Problems of Water Supply', 'Acoustics of the Singing Voice', 'Localization in the Cerebral Cortex', and, perhaps somewhat nearer to 'Mass Communication, Power and Influence', an article on 'Beliefs and Society'.

PETER DAVISON.

Further Reading

Morris Janowitz's study is one of five on mass communications in the *International Encyclopaedia of the Social Sciences*. The others are 'Control and Public Policy' by Wilbur Schramm; 'Television and Its Place in Mass Culture' by Richard Hoggart; 'Audiences' by Leo Bogart; and 'Effects' by Joseph T. Klapper. A bibliography to Professor Janowitz's study is reprinted in this volume and the study by Raymond A. Bauer and Alice H. Bauer is, of course, in itself an annotated bibliography. Particular reference might be made to the three studies of the effects of mass media listed on p. 108.

A conveniently available anthology with the title, *Sociology of Mass Communications*, 1972, edited by Denis McQuail, has been published in Penguin Modern Sociology Readers. This contains twenty articles grouped under six headings: General Perspectives; Mass Media and Mass Society; The Audience of Mass Communications; Mass Communication Organizations; Structural Analysis of Mass Communications; and Issues of Policy or Social Control. Macmillan has published in its Student Editions series, *An Introduction to Mass Communications: Problems in Press and Broadcasting*, 1971, by Martin D. Carter.

The fullest summary of issues and reviews of research undertaken, complete with bibliographies and name and subject indexes is *Handbook of Communication*, edited by Ithiel de Sola Pool, Frederick W. Frey, Wilbur Schramm, Nathan Maccoby, and Edwin B. Parker, Chicago, 1973. See also Melvin L. De Fleur and Sandra Ball-Rockeach, *Theories of Mass Communication*, 1975, (3rd edn), especially ch.7, 'Mass Media as Social systems'; and *Mass Media and Communication*, edited by Charles S. Steinberg, New York, 1966, which contains twenty-six articles in ten sections and three appendixes listing the canons of journalism and film and television production codes. Among the contributions is the classic study of stereotypes by Walter Lippmann from his *Public Opinion*, 1922.

For those who wish to take further a particular event to which reference is made in the editorial reproduced from *Nature*, the coming of commercial broadcasting to Britain, the following are recommended: *The Report of the Committee on Broadcasting*, 1960 (The Pilkington Report), 1962; H. Henry, ed., *A 'Sunday Times' enquiry* [into public opinion and the recommendations of the Pilkington Committee], 1962; and 'Difficulties of Democratic Debate' (on the reception of the Pilkington Report), by a prominent member of the Pilkington Committee, Professor Richard Hoggart; this last is reprinted in volume nine of this series.

PETER DAVISON.

Literary Taste, Culture and Mass Communication

The Study of Mass Communication
Morris Janowitz

from

International Encyclopaedia of the Social Sciences, vol.3   David L. Sills (ed.),
Macmillan, New York, 1968.

THE STUDY OF MASS COMMUNICATION

Urbanization, industrialization, and modernization have created the societal conditions for the development of mass communications. In turn, these processes of social change produce societies that are highly dependent on mass communications. Mass communications comprise the institutions and techniques by which specialized social groups employ technological devices (press, radio, films, etc.) to disseminate symbolic content to large heterogeneous and widely dispersed audiences. In other words, mass communications perform essential functions for a society that uses complex technology to control the environment. These functions of mass communications include the transmission of a society's heritage from one generation to another, the collection of information for the surveillance of the environment, and the correlation of the various parts of the society in response to changes in the environment. Social science research on mass communications seeks an objective understanding of the institutions that fashion mass communications and the consequences of communication and mass persuasion for human society.

The social scientific perspective. In surveying the extensive research on mass communications, one finds that there are great gaps between the orientations of social scientists and those of mass media personnel and their critics. First, there is a great difference in estimates of the effectiveness and potency of the mass media based on the findings of social scientists as compared with the viewpoints of those directly involved in operating the channels of mass communications. Mass media personnel, as well as their critics, tend to contend that the mass media are all-pervasive influences and powerful agents of social change. Thus they point to the individual and dramatic impact of specific programs and campaigns, such as the publication in Germany of President Woodrow Wilson's Fourteen Points early in 1918, or Orson Welles's dramatization of H. G. Wells's *War of the Worlds* over the CBS radio network in 1938 (for which see Cantril 1940). They point to the long-term consequences of the mass media in fashioning tastes and moral standards and in creating images of political leaders. While social scientists continue to differ in their particular inferences and conclusions, in general they tend to view the impact of the mass media as circumscribed. They see the mass media as limited agents of social change and as only one element among others, such as technological progress, organizational controls, cultural and ideological forms, and the processes of socialization and personality development.

In part, this gap is due to the different questions being asked by mass media personnel and by social scientists. Professional practitioners in the mass media are seeking specific and pragmatic answers to practical communications problems, while research workers are more concerned with general principles and hypotheses. In part, this gap is due to the weaknesses and limitations of social science research on mass communications, which, because of its highly fragmented character, is often not cumulative and therefore unable to supply valid answers to basic issues.

Second, the mass media have been subjected to uninhibited social criticism by some intellectuals and practitioners who see them as contributing to the demise of civilization. These critics hold the view that the growth of the mass media, in and of itself, deteriorates moral and intellectual standards. This point of view stands in contrast to the aspiration of intellectuals at the turn of the century, who hoped that with the proliferation of the mass media, modern society, however large and complicated, could yet fulfill the requirements of the democratic process. It was in the mass media that hopeful thinkers saw a new opportunity for mass education and the elevation of men's minds. Modern political history has undermined such intellectual hopes, and in the contemporary world the mass media are seen by critics as speeding up the development of a mass society and the destruction of individuality. But the social scientific point of view must reject the notion that the growth of the mass media necessarily produces an undifferentiated society with a general lack of articulation and an inability to make collective decisions. Researchers must see the mass media as instruments of social control and social change that may have either positive or negative consequences, depending upon their organization and content.

Popular images of the pervasive effects of the mass media were generated by the use of propaganda during World War I, by the growth of mass advertising in the United States during the 1920s, and by the use of mass techniques of agitation in the rise of European totalitarian movements. Thus, it is understandable that the first results of empirical research were to challenge such perspectives and to debunk popular notions. For example, although the pioneering studies on the impact of the movies carried out under the auspices of the Payne Foundation (Charters 1933) showed definite and discernible consequences of moviegoing for youth behavior—often socially undesirable consequences

—the over-all conclusions hardly attributed a pervasive influence to the film in shaping youth culture. Specific studies on totalitarian states conducted during World War II and thereafter also revealed that after the seizure of power by dictators mass persuasion became less important as a basis of control in these political systems. The image of limited communication effect was, in particular, reinforced by research on the basis of civilian and military morale in Germany and Japan (see, for instance, Shils & Janowitz 1948), which showed that ideology was of limited significance and that hostile propaganda could operate only within specific confines. In addition, laboratory studies on the impact of the mass media, as well as studies using the sample survey technique, also tended to produce findings that highlighted the limitations of mass effects, especially since these research procedures were used mainly to study specific messages and short-term effects.

Nevertheless, students of mass communications recognize that available research describes only part of a complex process and that the findings of specific empirical studies need to be evaluated and integrated by means of a more systematic frame of reference that takes into consideration the fundamental nature of personality and the broader process of social change. This frame of reference includes, first, the assumption that the mass media both reflect the social structure and social values of a society and operate as agents of social change. Because of the diffuse nature of communications processes, the mass media are both causes and effects; or, in the language of social research, they are both independent and dependent variables. Therefore, the full range of effects can only be understood by making inferences about causal processes. Second, the analysis of mass communications involves not only a study of the continuous process of transmitting symbols and their effect on audiences but also the equally complex and subtle process by which the audience communicates with and influences the communicator. In fact, this assumption implies that the analysis of mass communications is incomplete unless this two-way process is included. Third, mass communication systems invariably involve an interplay with interpersonal communications. Again, a comprehensive analysis requires the study of how interpersonal communications condition the communicator as he produces messages and content and, in turn, how interpersonal communications negate or increase the impact of mass communications on audiences.

As a result of the complexity of the mass com-

munication process, most research has been oriented toward probing one or another phase of the total process. Harold Lasswell's phrase, "Who says what to whom with what effect?" has been the general format in which specific research proceeds: The "who" question includes the study of the organization and personnel of the mass media; "what" refers to the content of the mass media; "to whom" points to the structure of the audience and various audience characteristics; and the "with what effect" aspect has received attention in the studies of mass media impact and audience response. Although this format was coined over thirty years ago (Lasswell 1932), it still presents a highly useful approach for integrating the large number of diverse approaches to the study of the mass media of communications and their effects. But the study of each element must be thought of as a step in understanding the total process and especially in estimating the long-run consequences of mass media.

Personnel and organizational structure

The "who" question has been investigated through two different but highly interrelated approaches. First, who are the people—the managers, directors, writers, performers—who produce and transmit mass communications? This is the sociology of an occupational and professional group. What are the social origins, educational backgrounds, career lines, and professional organizations of mass media personnel? What type of personalities are attracted to work in the mass media, and what are their self-images and social perspectives?

Second, since mass communications must inevitably be produced by large organized collectivities rather than by individual persons or small groups, what are the decision-making processes in mass media enterprises? How are these enterprises structured in terms of status, power, and other elements of social control? What consequences do the technological characteristics of the various media have on their internal organization? How does the control of the mass media relate to the economic and political organization of the society?

Personnel and professionalization have been the least explored aspects of the mass media. However, two comprehensive studies by Leo Rosten—one on the Washington corps of correspondents (1937) and the other on the Hollywood movie colony (1941)—reveal several central issues. The Washington correspondents represent a case of the highly developed but informal type of professionalization, where rules and regulations concerning standards of performance have evolved and are enforced by colleague pressures so as to raise the level of performance. On the other hand, Hollywood, as a movie colony and subsequently as a television center, represents an extreme case of the type of media establishment that has a high level of social and interpersonal tensions; in such communications enterprises the demand for spontaneity and creativity necessarily outruns human energies. The popular stereotype of Hollywood as a frenzied, schizoid community staffed by persons with constant fears of failure and frequent feelings of self-hatred is a caricature that is apparently not without support in fact.

The limited number of studies of the sociology of the creative arts in the mass media, together with astute observations of participants who have written on the subject, such as James T. Farrell (1946), suggest that one major source of discontent and "alienation" among mass media personnel derives from the organizational need to bureaucratize creative effort. The result is a divorce of creative workers from control over and identification with the end products of their work. The term "bureaucratization" must be used with reservation, for a considerable number of productive activities in the mass media have not become rationalized. Therefore, sociological observations about alienation among the producers of mass aesthetics are difficult to translate into precise conclusions. These notions apply to the very small numbers of truly creative personalities and not to the vast bulk of symbol handlers and technicians. Moreover, it would appear to be an error to assume that inevitably the essence of creativeness is lost in organized group effort. We need merely to recall the corps of assistants who worked with Michelangelo and Rubens or the monuments to collective artistic creativity such as the Sainte-Chapelle and the cathedrals of Chartres and Milan.

The significant point is not that artistic and creative work has been collectivized in the mass media for the first time in human experience, but that it has been extensively collectivized on a scale never before possible. The technological requirements of the mass media and the exaggerated pressure to create rapidly under deadlines force a high degree of specialization and a detailed review of each person's efforts. In the setting of a massive and complex organization, as is to be found in many of the mass media, it is not difficult for the individual worker, whether artist or not, to lose or otherwise abnegate his sense of personal responsibility for the quality of the work eventually produced. Nevertheless, against this response must be weighed the pressures of creativity or of profes-sional responsibility to maintain areas of individuality even in these large-scale organizations. One of the reasons that such pressures continue to exist is that the pervasive demand for new ideas and new content insures a constant and ever increasing search for talent.

It is also important to distinguish between genuine creativity and professional responsibility among mass media personnel. Social research has little to say about the conditions under which genuine creativity appears, but it is clear that the organization of the mass media has tended to inhibit or at least dampen the development of professional responsibility. It is very difficult to apply the concept of professionalism to the mass media personnel in a one-party state, while in nations with multiple-party systems and relatively autonomous communications institutions, the status of mass media personnel is more that of employees of a large-scale organization than that of practicing professionals. Even in Great Britain, where the organization of journalists is highly developed, the professional associations are more concerned with conditions of work than with professional standards. In democratic societies there are no bodies for enforcing professional standards among journalists or even quasi-public bodies for reviewing and evaluating their performance. Professionalization therefore takes the more limited form of an emphasis on more adequate educational preparation (a topic about which there is little agreement), a concern with informal relations among specialists, and the development of devices such as the increased reliance on the "by-line" in order to identify mass media products with individual producers and writers [see JOURNALISM].

The absence of higher levels of professionalization in the mass media is a result of the structure and process of decision making within the mass media. Because of the presumed importance of the mass media as instruments of social and political control, these institutions become fused with the basic control structure of any society. In a totalitarian state, this control is comprehensive but not without inherent limitations. If the media of such political systems are to serve more than merely to reaffirm basic societal loyalties, and if they are to disseminate information and contribute to collective problem solving, then some limited degree of independence is required. Alex Inkeles, in his *Public Opinion in Soviet Russia* (1950), a research study that describes the organization of the Soviet mass media, points to such devices as letters to the editors and reports of self-criticism as efforts to increase the validity and acceptance of mass media content. In some one-party socialist societies there have been modifications of central party controls, including the development of limited areas of professional responsibility for mass media personnel. Often the modification takes the form of creating specialized periodicals with limited circulation to reach specialized groups without disturbing the larger process of mass media control via precensorship.

In multiparty states with mixed forms of media ownership and control, the historical development of the mass media shows a trend toward greater freedom from government control. In such states there is typically an emphasis on the necessity of an independent and competitive mass media system. However, political theorists have come more and more to recognize that the removal of governmental interference does not necessarily, or in fact, produce mass media systems that meet all the requirements of a free society. There have been a small number of penetrating studies of the control structure of the mass media in the United States and Great Britain. Most of these studies were undertaken by foundations, universities, and, in a few notable cases, governmental agencies. They all concluded that certain technological, economic, and organizational factors may prevent competition from supplying an effective basis for high levels of mass media performance. One of the most important of these studies was conducted in the United States under the aegis of a quasi-public sponsor, the Commission on the Freedom of the Press. It is noteworthy that the principal financial supporter of this commission was Henry Luce, head of the Time–Life publishing corporation.

The work of the commission included historical surveys of the radio, motion picture, and book industries, as well as a comprehensive review of the role of the government in the mass media process. The policy recommendations of the commission (Commission on Freedom of the Press 1947) were afterward closely paralleled by the findings of the British Royal Commission on the Press (Great Britain . . . 1947–1948). In short, while government interference was rejected by both reports, the view they set forth was that traditional conceptions of competition would not guarantee adequate media performance. Instead, it was recommended that the mass media accept public responsibility for presenting a comprehensive and meaningful interpretation of contemporary events and that the government would have to take a positive role in this process.

Underlying these recommendations was a series of empirical observations that were documented in the 1940s and have been repeatedly confirmed by subsequent research. For the United States, these studies point to a drift of the major media toward increasing centralization in their decision-making processes, but none has even suggested that complete monopolistic control is or will be the outcome in any of the mass media industries. The evolving pattern is rather that which appears to obtain in many other areas of mass production, namely, that a limited number of very large units dominate a wide sector of a particular medium or even a combination of media. That a degree of competition has characterized the relations among these organizational giants cannot be denied. This competition is to a considerable extent enhanced by the fact that the audience can choose between various media.

Moreover, technological changes do not inherently move in the direction of supporting more and more concentration. For example, frequency modulation (FM) radio has introduced a new network of decentralized units; and even in the newspaper field in the United States, the trend toward consolidation has leveled off as new reproduction techniques have been introduced. Equally apparent, however, is the fact that the large producers of mass communications have often cooperated with each other in generally successful efforts to fend off attempts by other, supposedly countervailing, power groups (such as the government, the churches, and other public or private interest organizations) to influence decisions regarding the structure and content of the mass media.

In assessing the consequences of this drift toward power concentration, simple stereotyped conclusions are not warranted. For the United States, there is considerable evidence that the larger and more all-embracing these industries become, the more they come to resemble public institutions and the more sensitive they grow to the shifting imperatives of public opinion, public relations, and public responsibility. Of course, the mass media have developed codes of performance to protect themselves from the extreme excesses of public pressure. These codes have tended to be negative in outlook and to neglect the needs of specialized audiences. It has been suggested that in some circumstances the fewer the units of mass communications the less they are susceptible to the dictates of particular outside vested interest groups. Thus it is argued, for example, that publishers in a community with only one newspaper are relatively immune to the pressures of advertisers, inasmuch as the latter have no recourse to the threat of taking their business elsewhere.

To make these observations is not to suggest, however, that where mass media are operated as business enterprises a community of interests with other business enterprises fails to operate. Nor is it to argue that the mass communicators' growing consciousness of the attitudes of the public means that the control of the mass media is inevitably becoming more responsible. The meaning of public opinion and public responsibility may be read and interpreted in different ways. Recourse to the dictates of public taste and opinion may quite conceivably mean little more than the misuse of survey data to justify existing tastes, rather than stimulate new and more enlightened interests. Furthermore, an easy acquiescence to the amorphous and often ambiguous desires of the audience may simply reinforce those pressures and opportunities for the abdication of leadership responsibility for change.

If in the democratic societies the issues of media control focus on professional and organizational responsibility, throughout wide sectors of the world the basic issue is still the establishment of greater autonomy of the press. Raymond Nixon's investigation of the freedom of the press throughout the world indicates that there is a gradual trend toward broader freedom. He linked this development to higher levels of education and economic development (Nixon & Ward 1961). However, there is no reason to believe in the inevitability of such a trend or to assume that specific variables are at work. This issue involves the most fundamental and complex processes of political development.

Content of mass communications

The symbols and messages of the mass media are available for widespread consumption. The sheer availability of mass communications content has stimulated a considerable body of research into the "what" aspect of Harold Lasswell's four-faceted question. Research into mass media content, or content analysis, as it has come to be called, has been particularly influenced by the recognition that such content is amenable to quantitative treatment (see especially Lasswell & Leites 1949; Berelson 1952). As a result, content analysis procedures, both quantitative and qualitative, have been applied to all types of media content, most frequently for descriptive purposes and to a lesser extent as an analytical tool for analyzing the communications process and its impact. First, content analysis has been an effective instrument for describing both short-term and long-term trends in media content. The range of topics covered by descriptive trend studies is indeed broad: for example, such studies have traced the decline in prophetic religious themes in popular sermons (Hamilton 1942), the growth of scientific authority as a basis of child-rearing advice in women's magazines (Mead &

Wolfenstein 1955), and the trend in propaganda, from World War I to World War II, toward a less emotional, less moralistic, and more truthful orientation (Kris & Leites 1947). Second, content analysis supplies an approach for comparing the same material as presented in different media within a nation or the contents of the same media as between different nations. For example, Asheim (1949) found that in converting dramatic fiction into movies the result was not to produce "happy" ends but rather indeterminate endings. For cross-national purposes, school textbooks have supplied a convenient device for revealing societal differences (Walworth 1938).

Third, the procedures of content analysis are also particularly appropriate for comparing media content with some explicit set of standards or abstract categories. For example, studies have been done to determine whether newspapers conform in their content to particular standards. In this vein, content analysis is also used as a form of propaganda detection or propaganda analysis. The objective may be to identify the use of particular propaganda devices, such as simplification, glittering generalities, testimonials, and the like. Alternatively, the objective may be to uncover propaganda strategies by the use of such analytical categories as distortion, parallel presentations, or patterns of imbalance. Propaganda analysis can be based on comparing a suspect source with a set of categories derived from a source identified as representing a biased or propaganda outlet. This particular technique was applied during World War II by the Organizations and Propaganda Analysis Section of the U.S. Department of Justice to compare native fascist publications in the United States with Axis media content. Findings based on these procedures were admitted in court trials of Nazi agents and native fascists and had the consequence of absolving many suspect newspapers and radio stations from charges that were based on only a few examples of bias in their presentation of news or in their editorial comments.

Fourth, content analysis offers a relatively precise technique for describing the diffusion of scientific and scholarly knowledge and for observing the process of popularization of scientific materials. A leading example of this aspect of content analysis is the readability test (Flesch 1951); such tests have been developed to help editors and publishers judge the difficulty of a particular communication and to estimate the type and size of audiences that can readily understand the message.

On the basis of the existing body of quantitative and qualitative research, several broad generalizations may be made about the contents of mass communications. First, what is communicated by the mass media is a highly selected, nonrepresentative sample of all that is available for communication. Likewise, the content that is received and consumed by the potential audience is a highly selected sample of all that is communicated. Second, considerably more communications content is entertaining than informative; there is more of the sort that distracts and diverts attention and less of the quality that stimulates consideration of the central social, economic, and political problems of living. However, notwithstanding the demonstrable difference between the contents of mass communications and the contents of human existence, there remains in the mass media a quantity of the sober and serious, the educational and informational, so considerable that it has served, in the view of some experts (see, for instance, Schramm 1954), to confound and confuse rather than to educate and inform segments of the mass audience. Third, because mass communications are commonly aimed at the largest possible audience, most of them are simple in form and uncomplicated in content. In their desire to be understood by the overwhelming majority of their audiences, mass communicators have tended to de-emphasize intricate presentations, the meanings of which may be unclear and may be misinterpreted. However, with the growth of mass literacy and with ever larger segments of the population receiving college-level education, counter trends have developed. As a society enters the phase of advanced industrialization, there is a trend within the general mass media toward devoting a portion of their content to high-level material, just as there is a trend toward higher quality in those media, such as FM radio and certain publishing houses, that cater to more specialized audiences.

If content analysis procedures are to produce more than descriptive findings, it is necessary to address the simple but basic question, "What does the content of mass communications mainly reflect —the characteristics of the mass audience or the characteristics and intentions of the communicator?" Undoubtedly, the contents of most mass communications reflect both of these elements. In any particular study it is difficult to separate out the relevant importance of each element, and therefore the significance and validity of content analysis remains decidedly problematic. But it is precisely by making assumptions about the conditions under which the contents of the mass media serve either as indicators of the intentions of the communicators or as reflections of the interests and values of the audiences that content analysis

is transformed from a descriptive tool to a device for analyzing the process of mass communications.

The use of content analysis in order to infer the intentions of the communicator is best applied to highly purposive communications such as political content. Nathan Leites (1951) speaks of the "operational code," that is, the basic assumptions and directives underlying the communications of political elites. The more knowledge an analyst has about the organizational setting of political communication the more feasible is such content analysis. Thus, Gabriel Almond, in his study *The Appeals of Communism* (1954), is concerned with the contrast between the pattern of internal communications among Communist party leaders and their core members, on the one hand, and the content of their communications to larger external audiences, on the other. Leo Lowenthal and Norbert Guterman, in *Prophets of Deceit* (1949), analyze the content of fascist output in order to probe its underlying intentions and to assess the limited extent to which these agitators propose an explicit program. This approach also makes the assumption that agitational propagandists have the ability to reflect the repressed aspirations of their particular publics. While their format and appeals may be extreme and their audiences small, their content reflects a measure of potential political desires of the larger society and therefore warrants the closest scrutiny.

By contrast, if content analysis is to be used as a measure of the underlying values and sentiments of the audience, it is appropriate to use mass media content with wide appeals and to trace changes through time or to make comparisons between different countries. We are dealing here with the notion of the "focus of attention." One of the earliest efforts in this regard was that of Hornell Hart (1933), who studied changes in social attitudes and interests through analyses of selected popular magazines published from 1900 to 1930; he found a general decline for this period in the status of religion and religious sanctions, which he took as a measure reflecting changing attitudes toward religion. Leo Lowenthal (1961) has reported on the change in the heroes of popular magazine fiction from idols of production to idols of consumption. Martha Wolfenstein and Nathan Leites (1950) have used the movies as an indicator for the comparative analysis of sexual attitudes in Great Britain, France, and the United States, while McGranahan and Wayne (1948) studied dramatic plays to compare the *Zeitgeist* of the United States with that of Germany. Content analysis of the mass media has become an element in the cultural analysis of traditional societies that are in the process of modernization. Because of the problems involved in making inferences about causality in content analysis, the burden of the task of analyzing the impact of mass media has shifted to the direct study of audience structure and audience response. [See CONTENT ANALYSIS.]

Audience research

One aspect of the direct investigation of the impact of the mass media is the description of the size and structure of the audience for each particular medium of communication. There is a large amount of material, especially from the industrialized nations of Europe and North America, but also increasingly from all the nations of the world, that describes the "to whom" of mass communications in terms of gross characteristics and media preferences. The Department of Mass Communications of UNESCO has an active program for collecting basic statistical data on the development of the mass media and the size of audiences throughout the world. These world-wide reports rely mainly on statistical data about the number and circulation of newspapers, radio receiving sets, movie theaters, published books, and other measures of audiences that derive from production figures. Important aspects of audience size can also be measured from such "built-in" or automatic measures of consumption as ticket sales, newsstand circulation, or subscription sales. However, a basic impetus to audience research has come from those media, such as radio and television, which lack such simple measures; the managers of these media frequently want to know more about the social characteristics of their audiences and to find out what particular segments of their output receive the greatest attention.

Interest in audience research is particularly strong in the United States, where the mass media are heavily supported by commercial advertising revenues. Paul F. Lazarsfeld has been one of the leading experts in the development of such research. Although various mechanical and electronic devices as well as self-reporting questionnaires and diaries have been used, the standard approach is to make use of sample surveys to measure audience size and composition. Frequently these surveys are conducted by telephone and involve elaborate and rapid field work in order to measure the relative position of leading mass media performers. For the United States, Handel (1950) has summarized movie audience research, and Bogart (1956) has done the same for television.

In countries where radio and television are operated by the government, audience research is carried out for the purpose of understanding audience reactions and as an aid to program planning. Thus, for example, the British Broadcasting Corporation and the various West German regional networks have extensive audience research programs. Even in such one-party socialist states as Poland, radio audience research is undertaken both for scientific purposes and in order to take into account consumer preferences and tastes.

A summary of the more quantitative findings of audience surveys will show some of the changes that have taken place as the content and roles of the media have changed. Although American audiences are by no means typical, they do reflect the pattern existing in those countries where there is an increasingly high level of mass media penetration together with some choice between alternative offerings. In the United States television has emerged as the dominant medium, and national surveys in the mid-1960s reveal that the typical American family watches as much as four hours of television daily. Despite this extensive exposure to television, 85 per cent of the families read one or more newspapers regularly, and 60 per cent read one or more magazines regularly. As newspapers have transformed themselves from essentially political journals to purveyors of news, human interest features, and amusement materials, their readership ranks have been broadened to become more representative of the whole population. Television has captured large segments of the former radio audience; however, radio broadcasting of music and news has re-emerged in response to more specialized demands. The movies have suffered the most from the impact of television; but film attendance is still extensive among young people, and "super-features" attract mass adult audiences. The number of comic books sold each month exceeds the number of children in the country. Clearly, the term "mass audience" is no misnomer.

Researchers have also devoted energy to the question of whether mass media exposure is competitive or cumulative (Columbia University . . . 1946). Is exposure to one medium associated with exposure to others, or does one medium crowd out the next? No clear-cut answers are available, for at least two patterns can be discerned. In one sense, exposure is cumulative: with an increase in level of education, persons who are exposed to one medium (including television) are likely to expose themselves to newspapers, magazines, and books. In other words, as a person's field of interest is broadened by more education, his interests in the mass media also grow. However, there is a point at which competition sets in, for even with the growth of leisure there are limits to available time. Especially among better educated persons, extensive involvement with television reduces the time spent on and interest in other mass media. For these groups, there appears to be some competition between the printed media (newspapers, magazines, and books) and the electronic media (television and radio).

By contrast, the development of the mass media and audience exposure in the so-called new nations reflects limited levels of literacy and scarcity of technological facilities. However, most of these nations make large investments to increase literacy and to expand the mass media as part of the processes of economic development and the formation of central political control. In many of them literacy has risen at a faster rate than was the case for Europe during the nineteenth century. While these new mass media systems are not developed in depth, after a country achieves independence there is characteristically a striking increase in the capacity of these media to disseminate messages from the central political authority. In these nations the media and audience structures that develop are different from those of Western industrialized nations. Newspapers and magazines supply crucial but limited channels of communication between elite groups, especially in the urban centers, while radio emerges as the national mass medium because of its low cost and because it does not depend on the prior development of literacy.

Audience research has developed in the direction of seeking to describe more precisely the social and psychological characteristics and the specific content preferences of the persons who make up the audiences of particular media. Routine surveys of audience structure, especially those sponsored by commercial groups, proceed in terms of basic categories such as age, sex, education, occupation, and income. But these categories are not refined enough to capture the complexities of contemporary social structure. Nor do the categories focus sharply enough on the web of group and associational life through which a person is integrated into the larger society. As a result, the explanatory power of conventional research into audience structure is not very great.

Emerging lines of research are reflected in the work of university-based scholars, such as Harold Wilensky (1964), who have sought to classify audience membership in terms of more refined categories, such as career patterns and work settings. This approach focuses on the content as well as on the amount of education. Emphasis is placed on the bureaucratic setting in which the person follows his profession or occupation and on the role of voluntary associations in conditioning media exposure.

Audience research has also come progressively to concentrate on social-psychological and personality characteristics. Both from a theoretical point of view and in the practical application of research findings, it is not enough to know the gross characteristics of those persons who are exposed to a particular channel of communication. It is equally important to isolate those social-psychological predispositions that can be appealed to in order to mobilize new audiences or to change the exposure patterns of existing ones.

Walter Lippmann's classic book, *Public Opinion* (1922), in which he developed the term "stereotype," still remains a basic point of departure for the analysis of audiences. Human personality has a powerful capacity to simplify social reality and to select congenial elements from the media content. The oversimplification of social reality, especially when it is rigidly rooted in personal and social needs, is the essence of the process of stereotyping. Following up on these basic insights and broadening the perspective to include the observations of psychoanalysis resulted in a series of brilliant studies by Herzog (1943), Warner and Lunt (1941), and Henry (1947).

In recent years, advertisers have shown considerable interest in the study of the motive structures underlying exposure to various types of sale messages. The term "motivation research" has been loosely used to refer to studies that seek to understand the social psychology of audience exposure to advertisements. Popular accounts of these developments (see, for instance, Packard 1957) have attracted widespread public attention, but they have not answered the question of the extent to which such audience research has increased the power of advertising beyond that produced by forceful and imaginative practitioners operating without benefit of systematic research.

At some point research on audience characteristics blends with the direct study of audience reactions and media impact. Audience research includes studies of media preferences, interest in particular types of content and messages and in the mass imagery of the media, and the level of confidence and trust that the audience places in different media sources. These dimensions are not only audience characteristics but also indicators of the ongoing impact of the mass media. Thus in the United States, for example, surveys indicate that popular trust in television as a news source has gradually risen to a level comparable to that for newspapers. The increased confidence in television as a news source is concentrated among young people who have grown up in a television culture and thus accept this channel with fewer reservations than their parents.

In the United States audience research sponsored by commercial television companies also documents extensive audience criticism of television content, including complaints about the great amount of violence and the heavy emphasis on advertising. While such criticism reflects a popular culture that encourages critical remarks about television, and while this criticism does not lead to marked resistance to television exposure or articulated demands for changes in programming, these attitudes are noteworthy. These findings underline the conclusion of careful observers that television no longer has a single mass audience but, like the film audience, is becoming more specialized. According to Steiner (1963) there are at least two major segments in the television audience. On the one hand, there is the mass audience that is satisfied with a common fare and that exercises little or no selectivity in its viewing habits. On the other hand, there is another segment that consumes massive dosages of television but that actively searches for a more subtle media fare. (The distinction is between the viewers of the nondescript westerns and those who require westerns that have historical, revealing, or thoughtful contents, such as "High Noon" or "Gunsmoke"; another example is the distinction between the viewers of an anthology of light drama and those who watched the "Play of the Week.") Nevertheless, these same findings on audience structure indicate that as the national levels of education rise, there are marked changes in the mass media, but that because of the economic and organizational reasons described above in the section on media control, a lag persists in the capacity of the mass media to supply the demands of more discerning audience tastes and standards.

Communications effects

The findings of studies of communications effects are strongly influenced by the research methods that are employed. The three basic approaches are experimental studies, both laboratory and quasi-laboratory experiments; surveys based on interviews or questionnaires; and intensive case studies employing participant observation, informal and group interviews, personal documents, and other sources of documentation. While the technical aspects of effect studies have been greatly refined and improved, these methodologies were already employed in the Payne Foundation studies of films which were completed during the early 1930s.

The first two methods are the most extensively utilized because of their presumed quantitative precision. In the experimental technique, persons are given controlled exposure to a communication, and the effects are evaluated on the basis of the measurement of attitudes before and after such exposure. This method also requires comparison with a control group that is not exposed to the message. In the sample survey method, data are collected by means of questionnaires or interviews dealing with media exposure and attitudes, opinions, and behavior. The goal is to derive conclusions from correlations obtained between the degree or conditions of exposure to various communications and the measured attitudes and behavior. A sample survey can be a type of field experiment if the interviews are repeated during the period in which the population studied is exposed to the mass media. The third approach, that of the case study in depth, has emerged less as a specific method of research than as a strategy of evaluation and synthesis of material from a variety of sources.

From the thousands of laboratory experiments, it has been demonstrated that under contrived conditions even brief messages can produce measurable changes in attitudes among selected groups. Because experiments deal with persons removed temporarily from their social group attachments, it is understandable that experimental findings are formulated as psychological and social-psychological propositions without regard to the cultural and social setting. Under the stimulation of Carl Hovland and his associates (e.g., Hovland et al. 1953), this form of experimentation has become highly sophisticated, and the theoretical assumptions have been made explicit. This approach has generated some illustrative findings with regard to the conditions under which communications tend to be effective, for example: communications are more effective when they seek to alter peripheral rather than central attitude patterns, when they are cumulative, and when they seek to reinforce rather than to convert existing attitudes. However, it is recognized that there are limiting conditions that are not included in the experimental design.

Experiments have demonstrated a "sleeper" effect, namely, that the consequences of exposure to even a brief message can be delayed and become manifest some time after the exposure. Considerable research has been done on such topics as the credibility and prestige of the source, the order of presentation of items, and the manner of presentation of controversial issues. For example, experiments have shown that among better educated persons the presentation of both sides of an issue produces more attitude change than the presentation of only one side, while less educated persons are more influenced by communications that employ one-sided arguments (Hovland et al. 1949).

Investigation of the question of whether attitudes are changed more by arguments that diverge a little or by ones that diverge a great deal from a person's opinion has led to contradictory findings. The importance of the issue or its salience to the person may be an intervening variable; that is, for important issues arguments that diverge slightly may produce more change in attitudes than do marked differences (Hovland et al. 1957). Psychologists have been particularly concerned with the role of anxiety in producing or inhibiting the receipt of information and modifying attitudes, since a great deal of mass communication makes use of "scare" techniques. Laboratory research indicates that there is a point at which the anxiety produced by such appeals becomes so great that it actually inhibits attitude change (Janis & Feshbach 1953).

The findings from experiments seem to show evidence of attitude changes that are greater than those reported by survey research studies. This discrepancy is due to the differences in the research technology and the research objectives, for neither approach supplies definitive and comprehensive answers. Experiments deal with specific delimited messages, while surveys must of necessity focus on broader flows of communications. The experimental situation is seen as contrived, and therefore the results have been labeled by some specialists as unreal. In particular, because the experimental situation deals with specific messages, it rules out those contradictory messages that a person encounters in the real world of communications. In other words, because the subjects are "forced" to be exposed to a message, the process of self-selection of content is weakened. It is precisely this mechanism of self-selection of material congruent with one's existing opinion that reduces the impact of mass communication. Sample survey findings are better able to cope with this process of self-selection. Moreover, experiments generally tend to deal with immediate reactions to mass communications, while surveys cover a longer period of time and therefore include the extinction effect.

Experimental studies tend to deal with relatively unimportant issues as compared with surveys.

Again, this would lead to uncovering greater impact in the case of experiments, but there have been efforts to introduce important substantive issues into experimental work. Perhaps the most important difference between the two methods is that in experimental work the salience of social group affiliation is eliminated and the audience is reduced to a collection of individuals, a form of mass so to speak, and therefore becomes more liable to persuasion. Some experiments have built-in group process variables and have found that communication effects are therefore reduced. An alternative formulation of the issue is the contention that most experiments deal with university undergraduates in an educational setting, that is, a population and a setting predisposed to change, and that this is not an adequate representation of social reality.

Nevertheless, the experimental approach has important advantages because of its precision and ability to focus on specific variables. In contrast, because the survey approach cannot focus on specific messages, it may overlook particular forms of mass media impact. For example, survey work on the impact of television has followed the same pattern as the earlier work on the impact of movies. In Great Britain, Hilda Himmelweit and her associates (Himmelweit et al. 1958) found that television did not have a profound effect on children's behavior and academic achievement; its effect was more discernible on a small minority of overexposed children for whom there was reason to believe that television served as a form of defense, as a result of social and personal difficulties. However, experimental studies of exposure to television programs containing aggressive materials give a clearer indication that exposure to such content produces disruptive and socially undesirable effects. It is as if the experimental approach operates as a magnifying glass in revealing subtle reactions that become obscured by more diffuse research tools.

If the experimental method is subject to criticism because of its contrived and oversimplified character, the survey approach has the pervasive difficulty of adequately analyzing the host of intervening variables between the communications "input" and the resulting attitudes and social behavior. However, the strength of the survey method rests in its concern with group process, that is, both with primary group structures and the role of the opinion leader. Mass communication research has been influenced by observational and case studies, particularly in industrial sociology, which have underlined the crucial importance of primary groups (face-to-face intimate associations) in fashioning attitudes and morale. The impact of research findings on military morale during World War II served to refine and extend this type of sociological analysis. In particular, Edward Shils and Morris Janowitz (1948) observed that the German *Wehrmacht* was relatively immune to Allied propaganda appeals because of the effectiveness of primary group cohesion, which protected the rank and file from the appeals of outside sources. The hard-core noncommissioned officers constituted a cadre of "opinion leaders" who supported the control structure; direct attachment to and trust in Hitler served as the basis of secondary attachments. Only when the primary group structure was disrupted were German military personnel accessible to the symbols of Allied propaganda.

There has been a variety of survey researches that have elaborated the importance of primary groups and of rank-and-file opinion leaders in conditioning the impact of the mass media. Preoccupation with these concepts has led to an interpersonal or "two-step" theory of mass communications. As set forth by Elihu Katz and Paul F. Lazarsfeld (1955), this theory asserts that the mass media have influence through informal leaders who have high exposure to the mass media and who in turn make their interpersonal influence felt on their close associates. In this view, the innovation of new practices takes place because the mass media supply ideas to these opinion leaders, who then rely on face-to-face contact as the mechanism of diffusion [see DIFFUSION, *article on* INTERPERSONAL INFLUENCE].

Undoubtedly this is one process of audience response, but there are other processes through which the mass media have an impact. First, there is considerable research evidence that some persons are directly accessible to the mass media because they have weak rather than strong group attachments (see Daugherty & Janowitz 1958). These are persons characterized by a high degree of "anomie" and a limited degree of social integration. Often these individuals verbalize their distrust of societal institutions and the mass media; nevertheless, they come to depend heavily on selected channels for their opinions and social support. Second, on certain issues, certain persons will find themselves under conflicting primary group pressures, especially during political campaigns (Janowitz & Marvick 1956). These persons are likewise more accessible to the mass media than those persons who live in a politically homogeneous culture. Third, there are both temporary and more chronic social and psychological conditions, especially during periods of stress and crisis, that weaken the effectiveness of informal face-to-face pressures and controls; under such circumstances the mass media

can more directly impinge on the individual's attitudes, values, and behavior [see BRAINWASHING; PERSUASION].

The two-step theory of communication is neither precise enough in its conceptualization of opinion leaders nor detailed enough in the accumulation of empirical materials. The term "opinion leader" might best be reserved for the limited number of top-level figures in journalism, politics, economic, and professional life who are strategic in the introduction of new ideas. For the United States, the number would be in the hundreds at most, and such persons are not to be located by sample surveys. In addition, one can speak of mid-level and local community level opinion leaders of increasing numbers but of decreasing influence. Even local community level opinion leaders are limited in number and not identifiable by conventional sample surveys. Forms of sociometric and reputational designation have been used to describe these leaders, especially in studies of community power structures. These researches indicate that, while there are general opinion leaders, leadership can vary on the basis of the specific issues involved. Moreover, formal office and official position also have elements of opinion leadership, since power to influence opinion is not confined to informal and interpersonal networks [see COMMUNITY, *article on* THE STUDY OF COMMUNITY POWER].

The persons identified in sample surveys as opinion leaders might best be described as local "activists." They do have higher levels of exposure to the mass media and greater involvement in local community affairs than other people. These activists also tend to be better educated and of higher socioeconomic status than the population in general. Therefore, one important research task is to understand the dynamics of opinion formation in low income groups and in marginal groups, where the penetration of local activists is incomplete and fragmentary. There is reason to believe that for these groups such functionaries as trade union officials, teachers, and political party officials are more crucial than informal "opinion leaders." Moreover, because lower income people characteristically have weak networks of social contact outside their familial settings, their incomplete views of the larger social order tend to be fashioned by the mass media.

Mass media and social control

The emphasis on discovering specific reactions and changes generated by media content tends to produce a basic distortion or limitation in their findings. The bulk of the content of the mass media is not designed to challenge or modify the social and political structure of a nation, either in a one-party state or in a democratic society. This is not to underemphasize the ability of minority groups to have their points of view presented in the mass media; rather, this is to emphasize that a fundamental impact of the mass media is to contribute to the patterns of social control. Therefore, the impact of the mass media must be judged not only in terms of the changes in attitudes and behavior produced but also in terms of the *reinforcing* effect on social norms and social behavior.

To study mass media as a system of social control, it is essential to encompass all of the elements of Lasswell's formula. This requires the use of the case study, despite all of its scientific limitations. W. I. Thomas' and Znaniecki's classic study, *The Polish Peasant in Europe and America*, includes one of the first major theoretical and empirical analyses of the functional significance of the press as an instrument of social control (1920). Thomas demonstrated that for the submerged Polish community under alien rule in Europe or in minority status in Chicago the native language press supplied an important element of group integration and a linkage to the wider community. Robert E. Park continued this sociological perspective in his study *The Immigrant Press and Its Control* (1922). Lasswell and Kaplan (1950), in their analysis of political power, also assigned to mass communications a crucial role in maintaining and fashioning the symbols of legitimate government.

Theorists with such widely diverse formulations of contemporary social structure as Louis Wirth and Talcott Parsons have emphasized the importance of mass communications systems as instruments of social control (see Wirth 1948; Parsons 1942). Within this general frame of reference, research studies of the structure of industrial societies have taken various forms. For example, Riley and Riley (1959) have sought to probe peer group structure and the consumption of the mass media as elements of normative structure among youngsters. In his study *The Community Press in an Urban Setting*, Morris Janowitz (1952) sought to fuse within a single work analyses of several aspects of the press: its historical development, ownership and control, the social role of the publisher, the image of the community as reflected by the contents of the press, and the functions of the local press for its readers. This research viewed the community press as one of the social mechanisms through which the individual is integrated into the urban social structure. Harold Wilensky (1964) has traced out the role of the mass media in leisure in order to distinguish those occupational groups for whom the mass media operate to strengthen their associational integration and those for whom the mass media serve as a substitute for group membership. This perspective has also penetrated studies of political communication. The emphasis of such research is less on the study of audience reactions to specific messages and the specific political decisions that are presumed to be generated than it is on the role of the mass media in defining the political issues of the day and in fashioning the relevance of politics for the individual (see, for instance, Lang & Lang 1959).

The social control perspective also supplies a basis for the development of the comparative analysis of mass media systems, a research theme that is likely to grow in importance in the years ahead. The first of such analyses were case studies of the Nazi social system by Harold Lasswell, Ernst Kris and Nathan Leites, and others, who analyzed the declining role of mass communications as the Nazis shifted to a heavier reliance on organizational pressure and terror. Alexander Inkeles and Barrington Moore have studied the Soviet Union during different periods of political control and have emphasized the manner in which the elites have utilized the apparatus of mass agitation, not only as propaganda devices but also as imperfect and fragile channels for informing themselves about popular attitudes and loyalties [see PROPAGANDA].

In the comparative analysis of mass communications, the use of mass communications in the rise to power and the consolidation of power by the Chinese Communist party present fundamental issues for communications research. Historians will debate the question whether the Chinese communists' seizure of power and their consolidation of power took place with less terror than in the case of the Russian Revolution. If there was less resistance to their consolidation of power, and consequently less need for terror, this may have been the result of the greater decay of the traditional Chinese social structure. But in the process of political revolution, mass agitation and effective propaganda of the deed appear to be important techniques. While the rise of "thought reform" (brainwashing in popular jargon) is not confined to China, it has been practiced in China on such an immense scale that it has contributed to common understandings and therefore has effectively articulated with organizational controls. As a result, during the first fifteen years after their seizure of power, the Chinese communists were able to rule without the mass purges that characterized the Russian Communist party.

Social scientists have made efforts to integrate the study of the mass media as instruments of control with the study of political and economic developments in the so-called new nations of Africa and Asia. For example, Daniel Lerner (1958) has emphasized the general pattern of increase in standard of living, urbanization, literacy, and exposure to the mass media during the process of transition from traditional to modern society. Social research must guard against the danger of imposing categories grounded in Western experience on these mass communication processes. While there is a heavy emphasis on the expanding of the mass media in developing societies, the penetration of the central authority into the daily consciousness of the mass of the population has to overcome profound resistances. In this process of modernization, the resulting forms are not inevitably Western or European but are likely to include important neo-traditional elements, especially in the area of mass media and mass culture.

The responsibility of social scientists

Finally, research into mass communications has led to extensive debate about the moral implications of social research and the professional responsibility of social scientists. A minority of social scientists, as well as outside observers, have expressed concern that the findings might create the basis for extensive mass manipulation that would weaken and destroy democratic freedoms and values. By contrast, the typical opinion among social scientists working in this field is that knowledge accumulates slowly and that this fear is greatly exaggerated. They rest their position on the historical observation that even without the benefit of scientific research political agitators intuitively have succeeded in the worst imaginable forms of mass manipulation.

A more careful and reasoned defense is to be found among those social scientists who are concerned with a "sociology of knowledge" position. These persons hold that the pursuit of scientific knowledge is a valid and legitimate human goal, provided the research procedures are carried out with due regard for human dignity. They accept the notion that agitators have succeeded without scientific knowledge, but they do not claim that this observation relieves the social scientist from both personal and professional responsibility about the use of his findings. Obviously, in a free society there is a limit to his control over the use of his findings, but he must take reasonable steps to protect both himself and society. These steps involve seeking to insure that his findings are accurately reported in both the professional and popular media and that his research is not made the permanent private property of a particular group or sponsor. He must also seek through professional associations to establish and enforce adequate standards of performance.

The "sociology of knowledge" position rests not merely on personal and professional responsibility but also on a theory of knowledge as well. In this view, the accumulation of knowledge is designed to assist understanding of the power, and therefore of the limits, of mass communications. It assumes that a deeper understanding of social and political processes can serve to reinforce a pluralistic society. In fact, research into mass communication has served to reduce the image of the omnipotence of communications. Mass communications operate within definable parameters, and when mass manipulation becomes excessive, although the results can be disruptive and disastrous, there are other social processes at work as well. In short, research into mass communications has served to emphasize the underlying issue that "institutional building" is required for effective social change. There is no logical or demonstrated reason that it must of necessity create a basis for mass manipulation.

BIBLIOGRAPHY

The amount of monographic research literature on mass communication is vast and will doubtless continue to increase. A number of comprehensive bibliographic volumes have been prepared on the available scientific and semi-scientific literature: for instance Smith, Lasswell & Casey 1946; and Bureau of Social Science Research 1956. As convenient guides to the analysis of mass communications, a series of research and source books has been published for use by students and practitioners. Among them are Berelson & Janowitz 1950; Schramm 1954; and Society for the Psychological Study of Social Issues 1954. Joseph T. Klapper's The Effects of Mass Communication 1960, and Wilbur L. Schramm's The Science of Human Communication 1963, supply convenient bibliographic essays.

ALMOND, GABRIEL A. 1954 *The Appeals of Communism.* Princeton Univ. Press.

ASHEIM, LESTER 1949 From Book to Film: A Comparative Analysis of the Content of Novels and the Motion Pictures Based Upon Them. Ph.D. dissertation, Univ. of Chicago. → Partially reprinted in Berelson & Janowitz (1950) 1966.

BARGHOORN, FREDERICK C. 1964 *Soviet Foreign Propaganda.* Princeton Univ. Press.

BERELSON, BERNARD 1952 *Content Analysis in Communication Research.* Glencoe, Ill.: Free Press.

BERELSON, BERNARD; and JANOWITZ, MORRIS (editors) (1950) 1966 *Reader in Public Opinion and Communication.* 2d ed., rev. & enl. New York: Free Press.

BERKOWITZ, LEONARD; CORWIN, R.; and HEIRONIMUS, M. 1963 Film Violence and Subsequent Aggressive Tendencies. *Public Opinion Quarterly* 27:217–229.

BOGART, LEO (1956) 1958 *The Age of Television: A Study of Viewing Habits and the Impact of Television on American Life.* 2d ed. New York: Ungar.

BUREAU OF SOCIAL SCIENCE RESEARCH, WASHINGTON, D.C. 1956 *International Communication and Political Opinion: A Guide to the Literature,* by Bruce L. Smith and Chitra M. Smith. Princeton Univ. Press.

CANTRIL, HADLEY 1940 *Invasion From Mars: A Study in the Psychology of Panic.* Princeton Univ. Press.

CHAFEE, ZECHARIAH 1947 *Government and Mass Communications.* Univ. of Chicago Press.

CHARTERS, W. W. 1933 *Motion Pictures and Youth: A Summary.* New York: Macmillan.

COLUMBIA UNIVERSITY, BUREAU OF APPLIED SOCIAL RESEARCH 1946 *The People Look at Radio: Report on a Survey Conducted by the National Opinion Research Center.* Chapel Hill: Univ. of North Carolina Press.

COMMISSION ON FREEDOM OF THE PRESS (1947) 1958 *A Free and Responsible Press: A General Report on Mass Communication* . . . Univ. of Chicago Press.

CONFERENCE ON COMMUNICATION AND POLITICAL DEVELOPMENT, DOBBS FERRY, N.Y., *1961* 1963 *Communications and Political Development.* Edited by Lucian W. Pye. Princeton Univ. Press.

DAUGHERTY, WILLIAM E.; and JANOWITZ, MORRIS (compilers) 1958 *A Psychological Warfare Casebook.* Baltimore: Johns Hopkins Press.

DEUTSCH, KARL W. 1953 *Nationalism and Social Communication: An Inquiry Into the Foundations of Nationality.* Cambridge, Mass.: M.I.T. Press; New York: Wiley.

DOOB, LEONARD W. 1961 *Communication in Africa: A Search for Boundaries.* New Haven: Yale Univ. Press.

FARRELL, JAMES T. 1946 *The Fate of Writing in America.* New York: New Directions.

FLESCH, RUDOLF F. 1951 *How to Test Readability.* New York: Harper.

GREAT BRITAIN, ROYAL COMMISSION ON THE PRESS 1947–1948 *Minutes of Evidence.* 1–38. London: H.M. Stationery Office.

HAMILTON, THOMAS 1942 Social Optimism and Pessimism in American Protestantism. *Public Opinion Quarterly* 6:280–283.

HANDEL, LEO A. 1950 *Hollywood Looks at Its Audience.* Urbana: Univ. of Illinois Press.

HART, HORNELL (1933) 1934 Changing Social Attitudes and Interests. Pages 382–443 in President's Research Committee, *Recent Social Trends in the U.S.: Report.* New York: McGraw-Hill.

HENRY, WILLIAM E. 1947 Art and Culture Symbolism: A Psychological Study of Greeting Cards. *Journal of Aesthetics and Art Criticism* 6:36–44.

HERZOG, HERTA (1943) 1950 What Do We Really Know About Day-time Serial Listeners? Pages 352–365 in Bernard Berelson and Morris Janowitz (editors), *Reader in Public Opinion and Communication.* Enl. ed. Glencoe, Ill.: Free Press.

HIMMELWEIT, HILDE; OPPENHEIM, A. N.; and VINCE, PAMELA 1958 *Television and the Child: An Empirical Study of the Effect of Television on the Young.* Oxford Univ. Press.

HOGGART, RICHARD 1957 *The Uses of Literacy: Changing Patterns in English Mass Culture.* Fair Lawn, N.J.: Essential.

HOVLAND, CARL I.; HARVEY, O. J.; and SHERIF, MUZAFER 1957 Assimilation and Contrast Effects in Reactions to Communication and Attitude Change. *Journal of Abnormal and Social Psychology* 55:244–252.

HOVLAND, CARL I.; JANIS, IRVING L.; and KELLEY, HAROLD H. 1953 *Communication and Persuasion: Psychological Studies of Opinion Change.* New Haven: Yale Univ. Press.

HOVLAND, CARL I.; LUMSDAINE, ARTHUR A.; and SHEFFIELD, FREDERICK D. 1949 *Experiments on Mass Communication.* Studies in Social Psychology in World War II, Vol. 3. Princeton Univ. Press.

INKELES, ALEX (1950) 1958 *Public Opinion in Soviet Russia: A Study in Mass Persuasion.* 3d printing, enl. Russian Research Center Studies, No. 1. Cambridge, Mass.: Harvard Univ. Press.

JANIS, IRVING L.; and FESHBACH, SEYMOUR 1953 Effects of Fear-arousing Communications. *Journal of Abnormal and Social Psychology* 48:78–92.

JANIS, IRVING L.; and HOVLAND, CARL I. (editors) 1959 *Personality and Persuasibility.* New Haven: Yale Univ. Press.

JANOWITZ, MORRIS 1952 *The Community Press in an Urban Setting.* Glencoe, Ill.: Free Press.

JANOWITZ, MORRIS; and MARVICK, DWAINE (1956) 1964 *Competitive Pressure and Democratic Consent: An Interpretation of the 1952 Presidential Election.* 2d ed., Michigan, University of, Governmental Studies, No. 32. Chicago: Quadrangle Books.

KATZ, ELIHU; and LAZARSFELD, PAUL F. 1955 *Personal Influence: The Part Played by People in the Flow of Mass Communications.* Glencoe, Ill.: Free Press. → A paperback edition was published in 1964.

KLAPPER, JOSEPH T. 1960 *The Effects of Mass Communication.* Glencoe, Ill.: Free Press.

KRIS, ERNST; and LEITES, NATHAN C. (1947) 1953 Trends in Twentieth Century Propaganda. Pages 278–288 in Bernard Berelson and Morris Janowitz (editors), *Reader in Public Opinion and Communication.* Enl. ed. Glencoe, Ill.: Free Press.

LANG, KURT; and LANG, GLADYS E. (1959) 1966 The Mass Media and Voting. Pages 455–472 in Bernard Berelson and Morris Janowitz (editors), *Reader in Public Opinion and Communication.* 2d ed. New York: Free Press. → This article was first published in 1959 in *American Voting Behavior.*

LASSWELL, HAROLD D. 1932 The Triple-appeal Principle: A Contribution of Psychoanalysis to Political and Social Science. *American Journal of Sociology* 37:523–538.

LASSWELL, HAROLD D.; and KAPLAN, ABRAHAM 1950 *Power and Society: A Framework for Political Inquiry.* Yale Law School Studies, Vol. 2. New Haven: Yale Univ. Press. → A paperback edition was published in 1963.

LASSWELL, HAROLD D.; and LEITES, NATHAN 1949 *Language of Politics: Studies in Quantitative Semantics.* New York: Stewart.

LEITES, NATHAN C. 1951 *The Operational Code of the Politburo.* New York: McGraw-Hill.

LERNER, DANIEL 1958 *The Passing of Traditional Society: Modernizing the Middle East.* Glencoe, Ill.: Free Press. → A paperback edition was published in 1964.

LIPPMANN, WALTER (1922) 1944 *Public Opinion.* New York: Macmillan. → A paperback edition was published in 1965 by Free Press.

LOWENTHAL, LEO 1961 *Literature, Popular Culture and Society.* Englewood Cliffs, N.J.: Prentice-Hall.

LOWENTHAL, LEO; and GUTERMAN, NORBERT 1949

Prophets of Deceit: A Study of the Techniques of the American Agitator. New York: Harper.

McGranahan, D. V.; and Wayne, I. 1948 German and American Traits Reflected in Popular Drama. *Human Relations* 1:429–455.

Mead, Margaret; and Wolfenstein, Martha (editors) 1955 *Childhood in Contemporary Cultures.* Univ. of Chicago Press.

Nixon, Raymond B.; and Ward, Jean 1961 Trends in Newspaper Ownership and Inter-media Competition. *Journalism Quarterly* 38:3–12.

Packard, Vance O. 1957 *The Hidden Persuaders.* New York: McKay. → A paperback edition was published in 1958 by Pocket Books.

Park, Robert E. 1922 *The Immigrant Press and Its Control.* New York: Harper.

Parsons, Talcott 1942 Propaganda and Social Control. *Psychiatry* 5:551–572.

Personality and Persuasibility, by Irving L. Janis et al. Yale Studies in Attitude and Communication, Vol. 2. 1959 New Haven: Yale Univ. Press.

Riley, John W. Jr.; and Riley, Matilda W. (1959) 1962 Mass Communication and the Social System. Pages 537–578 in American Sociological Society, *Sociology Today: Problems and Prospects.* Edited by Robert K. Merton et al. New York: Basic Books.

Rosten, Leo C. 1937 *The Washington Correspondents.* New York: Harcourt.

Rosten, Leo C. 1941 *Hollywood: The Movie Colony, the Movie Makers.* New York: Harcourt. → See especially Part 2.

Schramm, Wilbur L. (editor) 1954 *The Process and Effects of Mass Communication.* Urbana: Univ. of Illinois Press.

Schramm, Wilbur L. (editor) 1963 *The Science of Human Communication: New Directions and New Findings in Communication Research.* New York: Basic Books.

Shils, Edward A.; and Janowitz, Morris (1948) 1966 Cohesion and Disintegration in the Wehrmacht in World War II. Pages 402–417 in Bernard Berelson and Morris Janowitz (editors), *Reader in Public Opinion and Communication.* 2d ed. New York: Free Press. → First published in Volume 12 of the *Public Opinion Quarterly.*

Smith, Bruce L.; Lasswell, Harold D.; and Casey, Ralph D. 1946 *Propaganda, Communication and Public Opinion: A Comprehensive Reference Guide.* Princeton Univ. Press.

Society for the Psychological Study of Social Issues (1954) 1962 *Public Opinion and Propaganda: A Book of Readings.* Edited by Daniel Katz et al. New York: Holt.

Steiner, Gary A. 1963 *The People Look at Television: A Study of Audience Attitudes.* New York: Knopf.

Thomas, William I.; and Znaniecki, Florian (1920) 1958 The Wider Community and the Role of the Press. Volume 2, pages 1367–1396 in William I. Thomas and Florian Znaniecki, *The Polish Peasant in Europe and America.* New York: Dover.

United Nations Educational, Scientific and Cultural Organization, Division of Free Flow of Information 1959— *Professional Association in the Mass Media: Handbook of Press, Film, Radio, Television Organizations.* Paris: UNESCO.

Walworth, Arthur C. Jr. 1938 *School Histories at War: A Study of the Treatment of Our Wars in the Secondary School History Books of the United States and in Those of Its Former Enemies.* Cambridge, Mass.: Harvard Univ. Press; Oxford Univ. Press.

Warner, W. Lloyd, and Lunt, Paul S. (1941) 1950 *The Social Life of a Modern Community.* New Haven: Yale Univ. Press.

Wilensky, Harold L. 1964 Mass Society and Mass Culture: Interdependence or Independence? *American Sociological Review* 29:173–197.

Wirth, Louis 1948 Consensus and Mass Communication. *American Sociological Review* 13:1–15.

Wolfenstein, Martha; and Leites, Nathan 1950 *Movies: A Psychological Study.* Glencoe, Ill.: Free Press.

Mass Media: Content, Function and Measurement
Journal of Social Issues, vol.3, no.3, 1947.

Vol. III   No. 3

SUMMER

1947

Mass Media:
Content, Function, and Measurement

Issue Editor: FRANKLIN FEARING

CONTENTS OF ISSUE

Preface

The challenge to the social scientist and social leader — the maintenance of peaceful group relations and the stimulation of a fuller more productive individual and group life — seems to come into focus as one reads this issue of *Social Issues* in sequence with the previous number, "Social Therapy", by Dr. Jaques and his co-workers. The central problem emerging from the two issues seems to be the question of how the face-to-face techniques of the educator, group worker, social therapist, and social leader can be most effectively integrated with the mass communication techniques discussed by Dr. Fearing and his colleagues. Teamwork of the two types of methods of releasing social energy and influencing social change is surely the main hope of a successful democracy. It is exciting to visualize situations where groups working with adequate leadership and social scientist consultants are prepared to utilize effectively the resources of the mass communication networks, and where the needs and requests of these groups in turn serve as the basis for the content communicated through these widespread channels. Certainly we can predict that the release of human potential, in terms of creative intelligence, group productivity, and individual happiness which would result from such efforts would be beyond the bounds of our experience to date.

It seems imperative that the social scientists working on the two types of problems collaborate in joint research explorations. It also seems clear that such research calls for partnership with social practitioners who work with the mass media and with primary groups.

RONALD LIPPITT,
General Editor

Some Sources of Confusion

FRANKLIN FEARING

There seems to be very general agreement that radio and motion pictures should and do play a tremendously significant role in our society. People of good will generally are deeply concerned about the character of this role and its potentialities for the future. This is true of many of those who are directly concerned with the production of pictures and radio programs, as well as those persons whose professional activities bring them into contact with this multi-phased, many valued, human enterprise. Altogether a very large number of persons— social scientists, educators, members of various creative crafts, writers, directors, musicians, animationists, and (some) producers—are conscious that these media have a meaning for a democratic culture which is at least as important as their significance as a business or industry. Whether this sense of social responsibility derives from the professional code of the creative craftsman, or from the intelligent layman's need to understand the forces which shape his world, it is persistent and real, and reflects a healthy human intent to understand a great social instrument.[1]

This intent is frustrated or at least impeded by the array of contradictory assumptions and hypotheses, and conflicting systems of values as regards the basic character and effects of films and radio. This confusion is found not only in popular attitudes towards these media, but in the more sophisticated attempt to construct systematic conceptualizations and working hypotheses.

It is not the intent of the present discussion to suggest a formal theory as a happy resolution of these conflicts. In part these conflicting ideas and assumptions reflect existing disagreements regarding the part which the great mass media play, or ought to play, in a democratic society. In part they reflect outmoded notions about the nature of collective behavior and the supposed differences between the behavior of the *individual,* and the behavior of the *masses.* In any event, it may be useful to set forth some of the focal points around which these confusions seem to center as a first step towards clearer thinking.

---

[1]Evidence of this concern with radio and motion pictures as social forces is found in the increasing number of scholarly and semi-scholarly journals in the field. In the current issue of the recently founded *Hollywood Quarterly* (published by the University of California Press) Arthur Rosenheimer (*A Survey of Film Periodicals*) lists 50 odd magazines published in the United States and England which are devoted to the serious aspects of motion pictures.

Motion Pictures and Radio as Entertainment

The first source of confusion has to do with the basic function of the media themselves. It seems to center around the meaning of the term "entertainment." It is sometimes assumed that radio and films, especially commercial films, are primarily vehicles for "pure entertainment" and that injection of any "serious" content is a perversion of the high mission to provide "escapist dreams." The argument in support of this states that in a world of stress and strain that motion picture theater offers almost the last refuge where the harrassed citizen can for a time forget his troubles. The ambiguity of the term "entertainment" and "escape" is in this context obvious. In a sense all dramatic presentations— story-telling, Greek tragedy, medieval morality plays, the modern novel—are escapist insofar as they afford the individual an opportunity to get away from the world of his personal experience and escape into a more ordered and hence more meaningful world. It may be true that a substantial proportion of commercial entertainment via the mass media presents a picture of life which is oversimplified, unrealistic, and in marked contrast to the way of life as actually experienced by most of the audience. This fact, if it is a fact, should be evaluated in the light of trends in our society. It is not a basis for equating motion picture "entertainment" with escapism or daydreaming. As a matter of fact the great function of the teller of tales psychologically and historically has probably never been merely to provide escapist dreams. His role has been a dynamic one. He has interpreted, explained and psychologically structured the world of his audience.

Whatever the character of pictures or radio programs may be—gay, frivolous, realistic, unrealistic, comic, tragic—the term "entertainment" as commonly used is constricting in its implications and confusing in its assumptions. Its use when coupled with the term "escapist" subtly devalues both the media and their audience.

The "Mass Audience"

A second source of confusion has to do with the nature and make-up of the vast audience which is exposed to radio and films. The enormous complexity of this audience, its diversity, as regards make-up, psychological backgrounds and needs is pretty consistently ignored. No audience like it has ever before existed. A single motion picture may be seen by ten million persons and a radio program heard by twenty million. All this means psychological complexity rather than simplicity. The term "mass audience" as commonly used is a stereotype which conceals this psychological complexity.

In its most extreme form this stereotype presents the audience as made up of featureless robots with blank minds and low intelligences. As regards this last, we continue to be relentlessly pursued by the average-mental-age-is-13-years idea. Psychiatrists comment on the peculiar "suggestibility" and "passivity" of the motion picture audience. Social psychologists familiar with the "crowd mind" fallacies will recognize the familiar LeBonian pattern in some of the current theorizing regarding the mass audience.

But it is not the fallacies, long exposed, of the "crowd mind" concept with which we are here concerned. It is the use of these concepts to rationalize a policy which confines motion picture "entertainment" to a restricted type of content on the grounds that the "mass audience" doesn't "want" or can't understand anything else.

The Question of Effects

A third source of confusion concerns the nature of the *effects* of the mass media. Perhaps the core of this difficulty has to do with the *relation* of content to audience reaction. The question around which this confusion seems to center might be put this way: "What does the audience 'get out of' a film or radio program?" It is what the producer or script writer intended? This last question concerns the critical discrepancy, apparently unrecognized or ignored, between what is *put in* the content of the film or radio program, and what *comes out* in terms of its meaning to the audience. The recently revived controversy regarding the effects on attitudes towards the Negro by the film, *Birth of a Nation,* illustrates the point. In a letter written to *Sight and Sound,*[2] D. W. Griffith, the producer of this film, states:

> "I am not now and never have been 'anti-Negro' or 'anti'-any other race. My attitude towards the Negroes has always been one of affection and brotherly feeling. I was partly raised by a lovable old Negress down in old Kentucky, and I have always gotten along extremely well with the Negro people.
> "In filming *The Birth of a Nation,* I gave to my best knowledge the proven facts, land presented the known truth, about the Reconstruction period in the American South. These facts are based on an overwhelming compilation of authentic evidence and testimony. My picturization of history as it happens requires, therefore, no apology, no defense, no 'explanations.' "

For Mr. Griffith, *Birth of a Nation* is an historical film based upon adequate historical documentation. When this film, along with a number of others, was the subject of experimental study in 1933, by Thurstone and Peterson[3] it was

---

[2]*Sight and Sound,* vol. 16, 1947, p. 32.
[3]Peterson, R. C. and Thurstone, L. L. *Motion Pictures and the Social Attitudes of Children,* 1933, Macmillan, New York.

found that it *did* significantly influence attitudes towards Negroes and in an adverse direction. Mortimer J. Adler[4], a severe critic of the Payne Fund studies, of which the Thurstone-Peterson investigation is one, comments: "The power of Thomas Dixon (author of *The Clansman,* the novel on which *Birth of a Nation* is based) as a propagandist is thus confirmed." It is not necessary to question Mr. Griffith's sincerity or integrity of purpose to recognize the discrepancy between what is put into a film and what its effects may be. This question must be clarified, not merely argued, before the educational and social potential of the mass media may be fully realized. The most serious intent of a socially conscious and responsible maker of films may misfire. A recently released film, *Crossfire,* intended to deal constructively with anti-Semitism, may fail as badly as did *Birth of a Nation.*

It is questionable if the current techniques for appraisal of audience response, valuable as they may be for certain purposes, will provide the clarifying data for this problem. For example, the results of these studies are usually expressed in the simple like-dislike dimension. This dimension of appraisal may correlate only slightly, if at all, with the true significance of the film's (or radio program's) content for the audience, or the long-term effects of such content. Interpretations of motion picture content and effects in terms of the more sophisticated rubrics of Freudian or near-Freudian psychology—*vide* Kracauer[5] and Parker Tyler[6]—do not contribute much to this problem either. Kracauer's analyses of the film in pre-Hitler Germany as a reflection of the German collective unconscious contains many useful insights, but it tells us little regarding the extent to which these films actually *did* communicate the content which Kracauer's analyses now reveal. Nor do we know whether the motifs which Kracauer now finds in these films—motifs which, according to Kracauer, were premonitory of the rise of Hitler—actually reflected the insights on the part of the films' makers into the state of the German mind. If these motifs were the results of judgments "unconsciously" made by the makers of the films the situation is even more confused. Formulations which state that the collective unconscious of the makers of films communicate to the collective unconscious of the audiences who see them, are not very satisfactory to most contemporary social psychologists.

It is worth noting, in passing, that these confused conceptions regarding the supposed specific effects of films or radio programs are related to the emo-

---

[4]Adler, M. J. *Art and Prudence,* 1937, Longmans Green, New York.
[5]Kracauer, Siegfried. *From Caligari to Hitler,* 1947, Princeton University Press, Princeton, New Jersey.
[6]Tyler, Parker. *Magic and Myth of the Movies,* 1947, Holt, New York.

tionally loaded question of "propaganda" in these media. It seems almost impossible for the layman to discuss propaganda without moral indignation. In the context of film or radio this indignation is frequently directed towards those who supposedly add "propaganda" to an otherwise innocent "entertainment." It seems difficult for the layman to realize that even the most innocuous "entertainment" is about *something*. Wittingly or unwittingly, attitudes are indicated with emotional loadings. If they get through—always an uncertain matter—they are "propaganda."

Who is Responsible?

There is, finally, the confusion of values which centers around the question of social responsibility. Many films and radio programs are planned with the intent to say something which will affect behavior. Whether these effects are achieved is beside the point. Who is to assume responsibility? At this point. the question of censorship is apt to rear its ugly head. This writer shares with the most militant defender of freedom in the arts a profound distrust of institutionalized censorship expressed in formal codes. There is a question, however, of the film which, regardless of the intent of its makers, does increase interracial tensions or perpetuate harmful ethnic stereotypes. What is to be done? Whose freedom is transgressed if the film is "banned," or is permitted to be shown? The whole question of social responsibility of the creative workers and others professionally concerned with the mass media is a confused state. It is tied up with opposing systems of values of the creative artist, the mass media as a business enterprise, and the vested interests of particular pressure groups. It is possible that in some measure this confusion arises out of the failure to recognize the communicative character of radio and film and the fact of the immensity of the audience to be affected. This may mean that standards and techniques of evaluation will have to be developed for films or radio. The status of these as "art", at least in the commonly accepted sense, may be of secondary importance.

These are some of the areas in which there is much confused thinking and inadequate analysis. Outmoded assumptions about the nature of human nature, the forces which condition human behavior, including thinking, as well as conflicting systems of values, centering around opposing group interests, seem to have created many of the difficulties. There is need for a large amount of clarifying research, particularly on the crucial problem of the relation between content and meaning as apprehended by the mass audience. It is startlingly true that if a group of socially minded makers of film, together with an equally socially minded group of social scientists, operating with an unlimited budget with unrestricted facilities, wished to make a film to alleviate, say, interracial tensions, they would not know precisely what to put in it. At present, about all such a hypothetical group could do would be to utilize whatever odds ands ends of armchair psychology they happened to possess plus their social good will and hope for the best. This is a sad state of affairs. Until we have such clarifying data, together with sharper conceptualizations about human communication and the mass audience, it will be difficult to deal constructively with most of the confusions which have been discussed in the foregoing paragraphs.

Ego-Involvement and the Mass Media

Muzafer Sherif and S. Stansfeld Sargent

The mass media of communication are products of the revolutionary technological developments of modern times. As such, they are subject to control by those who own the means of production and transportation. As the Report of the Commission on Freedom of the Press quoted from William Allen White: "Too often the publisher of an American newspaper has made his money in some other calling than journalism. He is a rich man seeking power and prestige. He has the country club complex. The business manager of this absentee owner quickly is afflicted with the country club point of view."[1] The content of newspaper columns, movies, or radio broadcasts is not determined solely by news value or intrinsic newsworthiness or entertainment value. It is significantly affected—in some cases selectively chosen—in accordance with the personal involvements, conscious or unconscious, on the part of the publishers, owners, producers and their friends. The work of Doob and other students of propaganda gives detailed evidence of this point.[2]

Therefore an adequate social psychology of mass media should start by determining the personal involvements of publishers, owners, producers, etc. Only in this way can the content, direction and effects of mass media become really intelligible. Usually researches into the effects of mass media concentrate on the readers or listeners—their attitudes, prejudices, personal involvements, etc. The selective processes of the recipient and those of the originator of the stimuli do not operate independently; they act and react upon each other. Unless the one-sided stress upon the reader and listener is broadened to include study of the predilections of the originator, the social psychology of the mass media is doomed to remain academic and sterile.

The two features of the situation which are of particular significance to the social psychologist are (1) mass media replace, to a great extent, *face-to-face* contacts in shaping attitudes, identifications and the subsequent "public opinion"; (2) mass media reach millions of people with their message almost simul-

---

[1]Report of the Commission on Freedom of the Press, University of Chicago Press, 1947, pp. 59-60.
[2]Doob, L. W. Propaganda: Its Psychology and Technique. Holt, 1935.

taneously. These two features are already forcing us to revise our provincial views of social psychology based on social stimulation mediated solely through the actual presence of other individuals. The radio, movie and newspaper have become *institutions,* each with its own prestige halo. The printed word, the broadcast announcement, the star on the screen, appearing with this stamp of prestige, have a more compelling effect than their appearance in person would have. In one important way, however, mass media and face-to-face contacts are similar; they are both powerful weapons for molding, perpetuating and re-orienting personal identifications as well as other attitudes.

A Summary of Ego-Involvement

Ego-involvement is not a concept to designate a phenomenon obtained only from "trained observers" in the laboratory of the psychologist. It is one of the most common features of human behavior, and reveals itself constantly in everyday human relationships.[3] As is well established by now, our reactions are functions of the organism *in a situation.* They are differential and selective, as determined by internal factors such as motivations or emotional states, by personal involvements, by other attitudes and the like, as well as by our perception or interpretation of the external situation. We do not react uniformly to the same remarks coming from different people. Our reactions are considerably, and at times totally, altered according to our established or expected relationship with the individual or group in question—that is, according to our *roles.* The group may consist of trusted friends or of proven enemies; of people like ourselves or of *outsiders* with varying degrees of emotional distance from us; we may perceive them as our equals, our superiors, our inferiors. They may be people with whom association as equals will not be tolerated by the members of our "set". They may be people whose presence is eagerly sought; the occasion may enhance our "personal worth" in the eyes of friend or foe. In all these situations (and the number could be multiplied indefinitely) our *ego* is actively involved in one way or another. When we are thus ego-involved our reactions are considerably modified positively or negatively. Diverse cases of these differential reactions due to personal involvement have been subjected to experimental investigation during the last decade. It has been shown quantitatively in several studies that performance in a task may be considerably altered, not only by the presence of other individuals, but also by awareness

---

[3]For a more extensive discussion, see "The Psychology of Ego-Involvements," by Muzafer Sherif and Hadley Cantril, Wiley, 1947.

of the level of the performance of others whose ability in our eyes is superior, equal or inferior to ours. In short, when the ego is involved in any situation, in any capacity, our reactions are not impartial. We become highly selective, accentuating certain aspects, glossing over other aspects to the point of recasting the whole situation to protect or enhance our ego.

The formidable word, "ego", is not a mystic, immutable entity. It is a genetic product, formed in the course of development of the individual, particularly in relation to his social setting. Neither is it a solitary structure. It consists of certain attitudes, related to what the individual comes to consider "I", "me", "mine", etc. We designate attitudes thus related as "ego-attitudes". The ego-attitudes are basically governed by the same principles that govern the formation and functioning of any attitude. They define our established relationships to other individuals. These may be interpersonal relationships such as kinship or friendship, or group relationships such as gang, club, church, state, nation, socio-economic class, international affiliations and the like. Ego-attitudes are situationally aroused when our established identifications are "tapped" in one way or another. The same joke about ourselves which may be taken in a good-natured way in our circle of friends may cause violent reactions in a situation in which we feel uneasy and compelled to protect our personal worth.

The major ego-attitudes and hence the ego are derived primarily from the values of the group or groups with which we identify ourselves. The very character of identification is built up on the basis of attitudes formed in relation to the person, group or institution. The continuing process of our personal identity consists mainly of the constellation of established attitudes in relation to groups and individuals. In accordance with these ego-attitudes we have loyalties, duties and responsibilities in relation to others. When these established ties are disrupted, feelings of insecurity and anxiety arise.

Mass Media and Social Change

With this brief characterization of our concepts, we turn to examples of the occurrence and significance of ego-involvement in connection with movies, radio and the press. However, we must mention first a feature of ego-psychology which is most relevant to the problem of mass media in general.

Once the ego is formed, there is a tendency to avoid being "left out" as a person in any situation of which we are a part. In a group of good friends whose opinions matter to us, we make a point of showing that we understand a joke, that we catch the drift of a subtle conversation *whether we actually do or not.* We laugh or smile amiably with the others, because it is frustrating to feel psychologically excluded. The Middletown lady tries to keep up with the latest books recommended by the "Book of the Month Club". She feels, consequently, that she has to be prepared to remark on the fine points of, say, *The Egg and I,* at the next meeting of her club. Likewise, the members of a select social group feel they are back numbers if they are not "au courant" on the latest Paris fashions.

With the staggering power of reaching millions of people at the same time, or within a short time, modern mass media create atmospheres which practically compel people to "fit in "—i.e. to become ego-involved. Or, to use a popular expression, they produce a "band-wagon" effect, which tends to embrace people in ever-enlarging proportions. Once people are ego-involved by this atmosphere or band-wagon effect, their attitudes are more easily molded or manipulated in a desired direction (e.g. favorable to casting a vote, making a contribution etc.) Many ads illustrate how people are induced to become personally involved in this way: "Get *your* copy today and become one of the great company of ———— readers"; "Get in the swim with a ———— bathing suit." The radio, movies and newspapers have become powerful agents for creating band-wagon effects which are potent in enlisting the personal involvements which lead to desired behavior.

Recently Merton gave a detailed analysis of a striking case of ego-involvement achieved by means of the radio. Many of us still remember the Kate Smith "marathon" war bond drives. In Merton's words: "September 21, 1943, was War Bond Day for the Columbia Broadcasting System. During a span of eighteen hours—from eight o'clock that morning until two the next morning—a radio star named Kate Smith spoke for a minute or two at repeated intervals. Stardom implies a mammoth audience: it was estimated that in 1943 some 23,000,000 Americans listened to Smith's daytime programs in a week and some 21,0000,000 to her weekly evening program."[4]

The result was that she got thirty-nine million dollars worth of bond pledges in the course of that one day. Among the appeals she used in her marathon drive the most effective were those which sought to get her listeners personally involved. Content analysis presented by Merton shows that "sacrifice

[4]Merton, Robert K., "Mass Persuasion—the Social Psychology of a War Bond Drive." Harper, 1946. (P. 2.)

themes" (arousing people to do their share) and "participation themes" (appealing for direct personal involvement) constituted about 70% of the material presented. A concrete illustration is as follows:

> "Could you say to Mrs. Viola Buckley—*Mrs. Viola Buckley whose son Donald was killed in action*—that you are doing everything you can to shorten the war—that you are backing up her son to the limit of your abilities?"

Such appeals creating group atmospheres, *against the excited background of the war situation,* produced effective ego-involvement and action on the part of tens of thousands of people, as the huge sum pledged indicates. These ego-involvements on the part of listeners are typified by the following reactions of two contributors.

> "Well, Dad, we *did* something. I was part of the show."
> "We felt that others had been impressed and bought a bond. And the fact that *so many people felt the same way made me feel right—that I was in the right channel."*

Ego-involvements may be quite general, or they may become personalized and specific. When one enjoys a movie, a radio drama or a novel, one projects himself into the situation and lives it vicariously through a kind of identification. Thus one enjoys a travelogue of the South Pacific, a March of Time dramatization or a good short story. But the reader or listener is likely also to identify himself with a leading character in the plot and participate vicariously in the action by way of that particular role. Or again, an individual may become ego-involved with a particular newspaper or magazine columnist or radio commentator and depend unconsciously upon the views expressed for his own ideas and attitudes.

In the moving picture ego-involvements are at a premium. The visual and the auditory are synchronized in a most realistic way. Movies leave little to the imagination. They have a world of scope and dramatic effect as compared with the legitimate stage. The darkened movie theater facilitates this process of ego-involvement by eliminating distractions of the sort usually present when we read or listen to the radio. When we go to a movie we expect to be entertained; we have a passive rather than an active mental set, which also helps. Add to this the fact that practically all movie plots are built around "human interest" themes compared with only a fraction of radio, newspaper and even magazine content, and it becomes clear why movies afford maximum opportunity for identification.

However in the movies the personalized sort of ego-involvement is even more striking. An extensive survey reported in 1941 on the tendency of movie theater-goers to project themselves into situations shown on the screen, "to imagine themselves in the place of the star, or (perhaps unconsciously) to pretend they *are* the star." It was found that a star's popularity is greatest with his own age and sex group. Mickey Rooney was most popular with boys his own age; Judy Garland and Deanna Durbin with post-adolescent girls. Paul Muni, Lionel Barrymore and other mature actors were most favored by men over thirty-one; actresses like Joan Crawford, Claudette Colbert and Norma Shearer by mature women. Most of the female stars were more popular with women than with men, and vice versa for the male stars.[5]

This personal identification is especially intense in the case of youth. Apparently movie actors and actresses represent beauty, glamor, romance and fame —all of which are skilfully played up in other news media by the 400 correspondents assigned to Hollywood. In his study of Hollywood, Leo Rosten says:

> "Each day millions of men, women and children sit in the windowless temples of the screen and commune with their vicarious friends and lovers, to ride with Autry, love with Garbo, fight with Gable. These millions devour tons of strange magazines dedicated exclusively to Hollywood gossip and movie personalities. Each night they read the newspaper pages devoted to the chit-chat, the lingerie, and the petty history of the fabulous community which has captured their imagination."[6]

Another slant on this process of identification is given in the Payne Fund studies of the movies. Blumer discovered much of what he called "emotional possession" in children at the movies. The child often immerses himself in the picture to the extent that he loses ordinary control of feelings, thoughts and actions. The extensive autobiographies studied by Blumer revealed such emotional possession in the form of fright, sorrow, love and excitement.[7] These findings were confirmed by experimental studies of emotional reactions performed by Dysinger and Ruckmick.[8] Ordinarily this kind of emotional involvement is short-lived, but other investigators discovered that the sleep of some children was noticeably disturbed by certain movies.[9]

While the fact of ego-involvement in the movies is clearly established, it is harder to evaluate its effects on behavior. Summarizing the Payne Fund studies the chairman, W. W. Charters, concluded that the movies have "unusual power to impart information, to influence specific attitudes toward objects of social value, to affect emotions either in gross or in microscopic proportions,

[5]See Sherif, M. and Cantril, H. "Psychology of Ego-Involvements," 1947, p. 351.

[6]Rosten, Leo C., "Hollywood." Harcourt Brace, 1941, pp. 11-12.

[7]Blumer, H. "Movies and Conduct," Macmillan, 1933.

[8]Dysinger, W. S., and Ruckmick, C. A., "Emotional Responses of Children to the Motion Picture Situation," Macmillan, 1933.

[9]Renshaw, S., Miller, V. L., Marquis, D., "Children's Sleep," Macmillan, 1933.

to affect health in a minor degree through sleep disturbance, and to affect profoundly the patterns of conduct of children.[10]   However, as all the investigators found, it is very difficult to separate the effects of movies from those of other social influences, and to estimate properly the long-range effects.

Radio and Press Compared To Film

Radio listening does not provide as ideal a setting for ego-involvement as do the movies. It relies solely on the auditory sense and is subject to various interruptions. Human interest dramas, where a maximum of identification can occur, make up only a fraction of total radio presentation.

In an intensive study of radio listening habits, Eisenberg found that New York children ten to thirteen years old preferred radio programs to almost anything else but movies and funnies.[11]   They spent an average of six to seven hours a week listening, chiefly to dramas, comedies and variety programs. Between a third and a half reported sometimes lying awake thinking about the programs they had heard, or dreaming about them, which suggests considerable identification or "emotional possession". Identification is also common in adults. Herzog studied 100 women who listened to serial radio stories.[12]   The two commonest types of gratification they mentioned were emotional release and vicarious experience, both of which indicate ego-involvements.

The content of the press is far more varied than that of movies or even the radio. Conditions are less conducive to identification, which takes place mostly with respect to that part of the newspaper devoted to human interest stories, pictures, cartoons, comics and some of the features. It may, however, play a part when one reads signed columns, editorials and even straight news reports.[13]   Much of the magazine content and most books consist of fiction, roughly comparable to the plots of movies. Data show, in fact, that the movies have influenced our reading habits to a large extent. The publicizing of movies like *David Copperfield, Wuthering Heights* or *Great Expectations* caused a tremendous rise in demand for these classics at libraries and bookstores.

Probably the best study on ego-involvement in reading was done by Katharine N. Lind.[14]   Intensive case studies of children showed that a substantial

---

[10]Charters, W. W., "Motion Pictures and Youth," Macmillan, 1934.
[11]Eisenberg, A. L., "Children and Radio Programs," Columbia U. Press, 1936.
[12]Herzog, H., "On Borrowed Experience." Stud. Phil. Soc. Sci 9, No. 1, 1941.
[13]A landlady of one of the writers reported: "I read all the stories about accidents and robberies in the paper and imagine how awful it would be if it happened to me."
[14]Lind, K. N., "Social Psychology of Children's Reading," Am. J. Sociol., 41, pp. 454-469, 1936.

group read in order to escape into a dream world; identification was pronounced. A second group sought diversion and release from tension, evidencing some but not as much involvement as the first group. Even in a third category a certain amount of identification was found—among those who were seeking solutions to their problems and trying to discover the meaning of life. The fourth group read to obtain information related to their specialized interests. Lind concluded the major facts on attitudes occur where personal indentifications are made; she saw danger in the "escapist" type of reading.

Mass Media and Social Change

Looking broadly at the effects of the mass media of communication, we see that, along with other modern technological developments of which they are a part, they are profoundly altering our patterns of culture. Their consequences are international as well as national, in war and peace. Through their function of disseminating news they keep us in touch with our world. They provide possibilities for us to live far richer than our forbears.

But these ready-made facilities for vicarious living also embody elements of danger. Students of communications note that we are falling into habits of passive enjoyment which lead away from the world of reality. The ease with which all kinds of ego-involvement take place, particularly in the movies and radio, may cause confusion and militate against development of well-integrated personalities.

A major consequence of ego-involvement is the adoption of new forms and values. Without doubt, this is the most important single effect of our gigantic sysytem of mass communication. It is true that the movies, radio and press, in various degrees, mirror the times and stay within the bounds of sanctioned values. But they never mirror a culture as a whole; they do not depict it in a comprehensive, realistic way. For one thing, the attitudes, and personal involvements of publishers, producers and other owners of mass media provide norms which give the content a generally conservative flavor. Their efforts to reach the widest possible audiences reinforces this tendency to avoid the more vital and controversial facets of the culture. Narrowing down the selection still further, they emphasize, within the areas of content which seem desirable to them, the more striking, dramatic, and emotion-arousing aspects, linked with popular interests of the times. Hence the stress upon conflict, violence and war rather than peace and cooperation, or upon themes like the desirability of money, power, luxury, adventure, and glamorous romance.

Thus the mass media, by selecting and stressing certain themes at the expense of others, have the effect of creating and perpetuating ego-involvements which will not endanger the status quo. The values stressed are typically those which make no contribution to the processes of social change. While some of the entertainment provided is very good, much of it tends to be unoriginal and stereotyped—e.g. the "boy meets girl" motif found in most movies. There are notable exceptions, of course; one thinks of the "Life of Louis Pasteur", the movies of Chaplin, or the forthcoming production of "Gentlemen's Agreement" —if the latter appears without its teeth being drawn! Social psychologists and many students of communications agree however, that the mass media can inform and entertain us, and at the same time challenge us to move on toward the new goals demanded by our changing world.

Some Remarks on the Role of Mass Media in So-called Tolerance Propaganda [1]

Paul F. Lazarsfeld

From time to time the question comes up whether friendly relations between racial groups can be promoted by propaganda in the media of mass communication like radio and newspapers. Many "tolerance" organizations spend considerable sums for such purposes. The main incentive for tolerance propaganda through mass media is probably the "success" of large-scale advertising. If we can sell soap this way, why shouldn't we also be able to sell good interracial relations?

There is little direct evidence which permits us to appraise the success or failure of such activities, but there is enough inferential material available to offer a basis for a brief discussion of the problems involved. One procedure is to start with a statistical model.

Let us assume that a representative sample of people in a community were interviewed as to their attitude toward a racial minority group. A few years later the same study was repeated. Comparing the average score obtained in the two samplings, we find an improvement in racial attitudes which we will call "greater tolerance." The higher tolerance score might be explained in three ways:

(a) Many persons did not change at all but a few showed a marked increase in tolerance, so that the slight average rise in score was due to the considerable change among a minority. (b) All the participants' scores showed a greater amount of tolerance. (c) Only a small percentage of those who were interviewed the first time changed their scores, but some people in the first study had died or migrated and new respondents had to be substituted employing, of course, proper sampling procedures. The data indicated that these new people were the ones who contributed the high tolerance scores, and therefore accounted for the higher average.

---

[1] This is publication #A-85 of the Bureau of Applied Social Research, Columbia University.

There are, of course, other possible combinations. But the above three types of increased tolerance should be logically differentiated in discussing the effect of mass media upon social groups. If we focus our attention on the presumable experiences of the individual respondents, the preceding distinction may be stated as follows:

(a) There are *conversions* where people change their attitudes towards minorities strongly and rather suddenly. (b) There are *slow acquisitions* of new attitudes where people change their opinions in small increments over a considerable period of time. (c) There are *substantial changes*. This term we will leave undiscussed at the moment, but will return to it presently with a number of examples.

What is the role that mass propaganda by radio and other media may play in the three main types of changes? We will take up each type in the order mentioned.

A. Evasion of Propaganda

We venture the opinion that conversions are rarely if ever brought about in a person just because he listens to a radio program or reads a pamphlet. This is a common sense experience and a generally accepted result of psychological research which has shown that tendencies towards discrimination against other racial groups are deeply imbedded in people's personality development. As a result, most people have a strong tendency to keep their discriminatory attitude structure intact. If they are faced with broad general tolerance propaganda, they try to evade its effect by a variety of psychological devices. A good illustration of this resistance to propaganda comes from a concrete study.

A Jewish defense agency developed a series of cartoons around the character of a "Mr. Biggott." The purpose of these cartoons was to caricature the intolerance exhibited by Mr. Biggott in a variety of situations. For instance, he was shown refusing to employ an American Indian because he did not like "foreigners and immigrants." In another cartoon, he was pictured standing in a cemetery in which soldiers of the recent war had been buried; in the caption he expressed his indignation that Italian and Jewish and good Anglo-Saxon soldiers were buried without proper segregation. Another cartoon showed him on his sickbed, refusing a blood transfusion from anyone but a 6th generation American.

A number of people to whom the cartoons had been shown were interviewed to learn how the general reader would respond. Many people had no difficulty understanding the meaning and intent of the cartoons. But a large number of respondents who, we knew from other sources, were intolerant, misinterpreted the cartoon series and so avoided applying its message to themselves. For example, a man with strong isolationist tendencies said that the cemetery scene showed that Mr. Biggott was indignant that so many people had been killed in the war. An anti-Semitic worker interpreted the sickbed scene as demonstrating how rotten the capitalists are: they need special blood for a transfusion. Another respondent considered this cartoon a caricature of upstarts: he himself was a 10th generation American while the fellow in the cartoon who was making the fuss was only a 6th generation American.[2]

But this mechanism of misinterpretation is still mild compared to what we call the "boomerang effect." Often people turn tolerance propaganda upside down to protect their own prejudices. When an anti-Semitic respondent was asked who he thought created the Mr. Biggott cartoons, he had a simple answer: some organization that wanted to show that a lot of people dislike Jews so that the rest of the public would feel freer to express their own hostility toward the Jews.

There are quite a number of other unconscious devices by which people are able to deflect tolerance arguments and thus keep intact their habitual ways of looking at minority groups. One of these is selective memory. If one were to ask some people that he knows to read some short stories which try to show that all nationality groups have good and bad sides and then have these people summarize what they have read, he would find that they have a very selective memory; they remember those elements in the story which correspond to their own preconceived opinions about the nationality groups discussed in the text.

In addition to these devices of evasion, there is also the process which may be called the "self-selection" of audiences. Most people read and listen only to those materials with which they are likely to agree. Several years ago there was a series of radio programs called "Americans All, Immigrants All." Each program discussed the contributions of a specific nationality group to American progress. Programs lauding the Italians had an audience made up largely of Italians; when the programs dealt with the contributions of Irish immigrants, the Irish were more likely to listen.

---

[2]A series of such studies was started at Columbia University's Bureau of Applied Social Research and were then continued on a large scale by the research department of the American Jewish Committee. A survey of the procedures is given in Jahoda, Marie and Cooper, Eunice, "Evasion of Propaganda: How Prejudiced People Respond to Anti-Prejudice Propaganda", *Journal of Psychology*, 1947, 23, 15-25.

B. The Acquisition of New Social Habits

A Southerner moving to the North, or a Fascist moving to a democratic country will often slowly and without any discernible turning point take on the attitudes and thought habits of his new environment. Social psychologists have studied this phenomenon of social learning in detail.[3] There seems to be agreement that "rewards" play a great role in this kind of change. If the old attitudes are likely to lead to conflict in the new environment, or if acceptance by the people who 'count' and other advantages, depend upon accepting the new folkways; then the newcomer will, after a while, act like the Romans. He doesn't experience his change as deception even though he had backed his old beliefs by reference to facts, the truth of which he had not tested. Now, he accepts, with little more evidence, other facts and uses them to fortify his new beliefs.

Such general environmental changes are subject to very little social manipulation. We cannot move all Southern Whites to the North in order to improve their attitudes towards Negroes. But there are two more manageable versions of this process which deserve special attention in the present context. One is organized social experiences and the other is organized personal influences.

(a) To exemplify organized social experiences, we draw upon a study which Robert K. Merton is conducting for the Lavanburg Foundation. His problem is to find out how living in various housing projects affects people. So far two communities have been studied in great detail: one with a population which is half Negro and half white, and another where different religious groups live together. Permission was obtained to quote the following sample of unpublished results:

> From three-quarters to nine-tenths of a cross-section of the American public has expressed itself as favoring residential segregation of Negroes. The great majority of whites expressing this view in the North have not, of course, lived in the same neighborhoods with Negroes. In the absence of direct experience, they could only give voice to a deep-seated prejudice. That a considerable proportion of these would have different opinions is indicated by the Lavanburg Foundation study of Hilltown, an interracial housing community in Pittsburgh. Before moving into this project, only 4% of the whites expected race relations to turn out well, whereas 21% were convinced that it would involve nothing but conflict. Most of the remainder had their doubts. After a few years, fully 21% found that race relations had turned out better than they had anticipated. Only 6% felt that it was worse than their expectations. More importantly, 3 of every 4 who had expected serious racial conflict found that their fears were unfounded. Direct experience

[3]"The Acquisition of New Social Habits," by John Dollard in *Science of Man in the World Crisis*. Edited by Ralph Linton, New York: Columbia University Press, 1945. "The Learning Process in Situations," Chapter 4, p. 155 in Murphy & Newcomb. *Experimental Social Psychology*. New York: Harper Brothers, 1937.

had shown what general admonitions for tolerance would probably not have shown: that interracial fears and hostilities were exaggerated and distorted beyond all resemblance to the reality.

But single institutions, such as community housing, have only a limited effectiveness in producing tolerance. Only when it is further supported by other institutions does it achieve its full potential for tolerance. Thus, among the white men and women in this community who had worked on the same job with Negroes, there was a greater willingness to admit Negroes to co-residence in housing projects. Fully 40% of those who had worked with Negroes were willing to live in the same community with them as contrasted with 24% who had not had this common work experience.

The drive for tolerance and civil rights is more effective when it proceeds on several institutional fronts at once. Thus, a housing community which has achieved peaceable interracial relations cannot long maintain itself if the larger community of which it is a part exhibits race hostilities. Two of every three whites in this community found themselves exposed to unflattering comments by friends residing elsewhere. And this invidious criticism corroded their willingness to remain in the community: fully 31% of this group preferred their previous place of residence in contrast to a scanty 13% of whites whose friends commented favorably on the community. The tolerant individual requires interlocking institutional support if his tolerance is not to suffer attrition. Once a favorable climate of tolerance has been established in a community, individuals living in that climate find their tolerance-quotient raised. That this holds for interreligious attitudes can be seen from another Lavanburg Foundation study of Craftown, a workers' housing community in New Jersey. The longer residents have lived in Craftown, the more likely they are to exhibit tolerance toward other religious groups than their own. Moreover, the fact that there is no spatial segregation of religious groups promotes personal ties between them. In the areas of Craftown which happen to be peopled by co-religionists, one's friends are primarily of the same religion. But in areas comprised of people of several religions, Protestants and Catholics alike find friends among other groups as well as their own. All this is no automatic process making for tolerance, but it does reveal that with appropriate institutional conditions, mutual toleration can flourish.

This is just one example of a general observation. When people of different groups can live together under planned and organized conditions, the result is usually a decrease of antagonism. But the experience must be long-lasting and it must be well organized, not an occasional slumming trip to see "how the other half lives." There must also be adequate provisions for ironing out occasional frictions, for discussing difficulties when they come up, etc.

Radio and other mass media can play a useful role in such developments. They can assist those agencies which make a systematic effort to influence people's attitudes by organized social experiences. Institutions are more influential than mass media, but mass media can considerably strengthen the effectiveness of institutions. We know, for example, that school teachers can decrease discrimination among their pupils. Over a period of years, they can slowly acquaint them with biological facts about races; they can set up groups in which children of different creeds or nationalities work together; they can casually counteract prejudices which were inculcated in careless homes. No series of radio programs can do as much. But a local radio station can give prizes to the most successful teachers in town, or it can single out for special commendation the schools which have the best tolerance programs. Conversely, bad practices can be exposed.

Such considerations would lead to the expectation that mass media will be most effective if they are used in very specific situations. A tolerance agency might do well to keep informed about where and when racial tensions arise. A bi-racial housing project in one locality might be opposed by real estate interests. In another community, a flagrant case of discrimination in employment might flare up. That would be the opportune time for the agency to use its funds for broadcasting, newspaper ads and so on. This would be a more difficult administrative task than obtaining a sustaining program on a network but it would probably be more effective.

(b) American political parties have since their inception relied on what are called "machines." These are the networks of personal influences which keep the loyalties of the voters alive and get them to the polls on election day. Systematic research has shown that such organized personal influences are indeed an important way to affect people's attitudes.

A recent study of political opinion and behavior found that in comparison with the formal media of communication, personal relationships are potentially more influential for two reasons: their coverage is greater and they have certain psychological advantages over the formal media.[4]

Some of the specific reasons which seem to make face-to-face contacts especially advantageous as a propaganda device are the following:

Personal contacts reach the undecided. The data indicates that people who have not yet made up their minds on an issue are more likely to listen to other people and are less likely to expose themselves to formal media of communication.

Personal influences are more pervasive and less self-selective than the formal media. People with opinions are likely to choose on the radio and in printed media the stories with which they agree. It is harder to limit personal conversations to those people with whom one agrees. In other words, chance exposure to an opposite point of view is more likely to happen in personal contact than with formal media. (Most people live in groups where the majority agrees with them, so the difference mentioned here is only a relative one. But we cannot enter into these details.)

In face-to-face contact, if the propagandist meets resistance, he can be flexible in his argumentation. He can choose the occasion at which to speak to the other fellow; he can adapt his story to what he presumes to be the other's interests and his ability to understand. Radio programs, on the other hand, or magazine stories have to be addressed to an "average" audience with "average" reactions which very often might fail to materialize.

---

[4]Lazarsfeld, Paul F., Berelson, B., and Gaudet, H. *The People's Choice,* Chapter 16, passim. New York: Duell, Sloan & Pearce, 1944.

There are some indications that people are more distrustful of formal media than of personal influences. This question of distrust, however, has not been investigated enough.

Finally, the rewards and punishments are more directly experienced in personal contacts. If one does not accept what the neighbor says, he can be "punished" immediately for being unimpressed or unyielding; the neighbor can look angry or sad, he can leave the room and make his fellow feel isolated. The speaker on the radio or the writer of a pamphlet can only intimate or desribe future deprivation; the living person can create them at once.

The conclusion of this study is particularly applicable to tolerance organizations concerned about the use of mass media of communications:

> In the last analysis, more than anything else people can move other people. From an ethical point of view this is a hopeful aspect in the serious social problem of propaganda. The side which has the more enthusiastic supporters and which can mobilize grassroot support in an expert way has great chances of success.

In the field of group relations, organized personal influences or "machines" have been utilized in a variety of ways: discussion leaders, action groups, back-of-the-yard movements have been set in operation. The experience has always been that such devices are successful while they are in operation, but that they are very difficult to maintain. If they are organized by volunteers, they tend to be transitory. On the other hand, if they are operated by paid personnel, they are extremely expensive. It is at this point that the mass media come in. They can make the work of the volunteer easier and thus keep him on the job longer, and they can make the work of paid personnal more efficient and thus make funds last longer. There are many ways in which mass media can be tied in with the techniques of organized personal influence.

It is easier, for example, to develop face-to-face contacts during a week following a widely publicized speech on the radio. A local leader might not be an inspiring speaker himself, but he might be effective as a discussion leader after a group has listened to a central radio program. The Canadian Broadcasting Company, for instance, uses an excellent system of listener groups in which discussion leaders reenforce the effect of programs directed to farmers. If money is spent on newspaper promotion, it should be in cities where there are active citizens' groups which can make maximum use of the material. And conversely, if new groups are to be created in a city, the support of local newspapers and radio stations should be enlisted at the same time.[5]

As far as the slow reconstruction of attitudes goes, mass media can be helpful in two subsidiary ways. They can back up pertinent institutions and they can facilitate the work of organized personal influences.

---

[5]Hill, Frank E. & Williams, W. E. *Radio's Listening Groups.* New York: Columbia University Press, 1941.

Lazarsfeld, Paul F. "Audience Building in Education Broadcasting," *Journal of Educational Sociology,* Vol. XIV, May 1941.

C. Substitutional Changes

Suppose Mr. Smith is a sheriff and he definitely has an anti-Negro prejudice. How could this situation be changed? We might try to influence Mr. Smith's attitudes toward Negroes; or we might try to get a sheriff in at the next election who has an attitude more to our liking. If the latter turn of affairs takes place in many counties, then we will one day find that the attitude of sheriffs toward Negroes has improved. This might come about without any individual person having changed his attitude.

The peculiar characteristics of this type of change are often overlooked. Sociologists make a distinction between a person and the role he plays. We are often most concerned with changes of attitudes attached to certain positions rather than with those which are part of the individuals who temporarily hold these positions.

This phenomenon is not restricted to occupational or otherwise specified positions. It can also come about by a rather intricate play between generations. An immigrant Irish Catholic might have rather outspoken anti-Semitic tendencies. After coming to this country he hears a good deal about the principles of American democracy, but this might not affect his own feelings which have developed in early childhood and adolescence as a result of strong environmental influences. Still the egalitarian phraseology which this immigrant hears constantly keeps him from exercising too strong an influence on his children in racial matters. The children in turn, as they grow up, are freer to make their own choices. They are subject to a greater range of influences than if they had grown up in a more tightly knit environment. Consequently, some of them might be much less anti-Semitic than their father. When they have finally matured and substituted for their father as respondents in a public opinion sample, they contribute to an improved average attitude score.

This is not the place to analyze in detail this process of substitutional changes which offer some puzzling difficulties. Changes in sex mores are especially useful in exemplifying the problem. The average individual probably becomes more conservative in sex matters as he grows older. Still over the last decades, the sex mores of subsequent generations has become freer. The main mechanism which one has to look for in this process is the discontinuous changes of institutions. Due to chance or to some historical event, or to the successful insistence of a single individual, a law might be enacted or a new type of school created which, in turn, over a long period of time, would change the conditions under which people grow up and acquire their thought habits.

It is true that such institutions couldn't persist if they were actively opposed by a large part of the community. But between active support and 'active opposition by the majority, there is a broad area of indifference. A large number of people might not care what race attitudes the sheriff has. If the new sheriff does just as good a job as the previous one and is also fairer to Negroes, after some time the majority will feel that his way of handling Negro matters is the reasonable and "natural" one.

These substitutional changes in attitudes are probably the ones on which the "gradualists" pin their hopes for social progress. At their best, they take a long time, probably several generations. The role of mass media in this process is as complex as the process itself. A basic prerequisite is that the younger people have more options from which to choose. If the mass media continuously put before the public the ideas and examples of racial and religious tolerance, then the chances are better that some of the "newcomers" will take up a liberal point of view.

It is probably out of vague considerations of this kind that some organizations invest so heavily in a broad and diffuse front of tolerance propaganda through mass media. It has been said in jest that every Jewish defense agency hopes that one day the pretty secretary in a movie will be called Miss Horowitz and not Miss Kelly. As a result, they hope many a young non-Jewish boy will consider it more conceivable to marry a Jewish girl. There is, however, an intrinsic difficulty in this possible value of mass media for facilitating substitutional change. While they might lead to some young people developing less prejudice, they might, at the same time, reenforce and bring to the fore the intolerance of those who have already structured their discriminatory attitudes. Unfortunately, such boomerang effects will come about more quickly and perhaps in much more drastic form than will long range substitutional changes. Which of these two effects of tolerance propaganda in mass media is stronger in the long run will probably depend upon the historical situation.

The preceding remarks are intended merely to point up some of the problems involved in our topic and to indicate where sound investigations are needed. The general theory of mass propaganda is still very immature. Still one should not forget that some successful efforts have been made to pretest specific propaganda devices. The work that has been done by experimental psychologists and techniques like the Program Analyzer test (which is being reported on in another paper in this issue) should certainly be brought to the attention of those who are responsible for propaganda campaigns in tolerance organizations.

The Movies: Stereotypes or Realities?

RALPH H. GUNDLACH

In June 1947 a news report expressed the concern of our State Department over the ideas which the peoples of the world have about the United States and its citizens. The State Department wanted to depict a "true picture" abroad of American life and ways in order to combat the "distorted" view circulated by foreigners. The State Department was reported as unhappy about the Hollywod movies on the grounds that these pictures of America, "purveyed abroad for profit", do not differ very much from the ugly portrait painted by our foreign detractors. The story goes on to give as an example, the conception in foreign minds of United States women as being pin-up girls, pampered parasites and divorce chasers, or else as Tobacco Road peons. The State Department, in this interview, did not extend its concern to the effects of these movies upon the average American's conception of our way of life; which, however, is our problem.

A Department of State is an unusual quarter to raise the questions about whether the movies are pure entertainment, unmixed with political and economic overtones; and whether the movies, as a business, shape the product of its artists somewhat to its standards, and indirectly pattern the thinking and style of action of a large part of its audience.

There are certain fundamental ideas in social psychology which serve as a basis for considering these problems of the relations between business, art, entertainment, propaganda, and society. Four of these notions may be briefly reviewed, before discussing movies in our culture.

Social Norms and Perception of Events

The most general notion is concerned with how different peoples, such as the "foreigners" the State Department worries about, and we ourselves, learn to view and interpret the events of the world.

Every society in the world has developed an over-simplified account of the world and how it works, and a set of manners or morals to regulate the ways of persons in each group or class, how they should act with regard to each other.

The society hits upon some simple account because things are so very complex and human capacity to see and understand is so limited. For instance, testimony from witnesses at any traffic accident is conflicting; and differs from what really happened. People give conflicting evidence about even the simplest situations, about events which may not involve any wishful thinking or emotional bias, nor any deliberate attempt to convince or distort.

Nevertheless, everyone in every society wants to know how things work, wants a comforting explanation of why things are so; and wants to be able to find his way around his home, his community, and his world with assurance, security, and ease. There are few events we cannot name, and having named, assign them to some convenient pigeon hole. We know how to deal with objects of THAT category. Thus, with the help of ancestors, through folklore and the establishment of customs and conventions,—and in some societies, in part with the utilization of the marvelous tool of scientific method—every group has built up its own limited consistent picture-in-their-heads of how the world ticks. Some work spells on idols; some tell their wishes to snakes who are the messengers of the gods; some drive out devils; some administer sulpha; some eat meat; and some won't look at their mothers-in-law.

The children in each culture, and in each class in the culture, learn from their parents and associates, and soon accept unconsciously, uncritically, as "natural", their ways of looking at and dealing with events and social relations, based upon some basic and fundamental assumptions about the world and how to manage it.

The culturally accepted folkways, and attitude systems serve not only to provide a frame to classify the observed events of the world; they also serve to define the values for the members of the group; and they serve to regulate the social relations between members of different ages, sexes, and classes. The "way of life" of the French peasant, the Soviet collective farmer, the Chinese war lord, or the dime store sales girl, is not something objective in the environment. In each case it is a readiness to interpret and to act, a method of explanation that has been built up in each of them by their cultural traditions.

Pictures of Groups Instead of Individuals

A major feature of these value-attitude systems is that they help interpret the relations of persons in one class or group to those of other groups. Each of us belongs to many groups; our family, our block, our school group; our age and sex groups; our occupational, racial, regional, national groups. We know how to treat members of other groups; the traffic violator knows what to expect from the police judge; the hungry husband knows where and when to expect dinner; the department stores know how to extend credit to customers.

Because of our limited abilities, we tend to think of all the members of any group in simple, generalized terms. Members of the family and friends, members of the major groups with which we identify ourselves, we treat as individuals, with unique, personal, and important charms and characteristics. Members of any "out-group", however, tend to be treated as all alike, all having the characteristics attributed to this "typical" member. Studies of "social distance" and of racial and nationality stereotypes show that many Americans have well-defined and articulated notions about the personality characteristics of members of racial and occupational groups, whether Irish, Turks, Jews, English, Negroes, Germans, or white Americans.

Self-Reinforcement of Generalizations

Although generalizations about classes of people may have a major function as convenient, simple symbols, as easy and helpful ways of adjusting social groups to each other, they also can lead to much harm, and to patterns of thinking which get farther and farther from reality; and hence become non-adjustive. An effete British author made the classic remark that nature imitated art. It is certainly true that many stereotypes in our thinking take precedence over reality. Extensive studies of the development of racial prejudices in white children toward their Negro associates have shown that the determining factor was NOT the actual experience of the children.[1] The white child's attitudes were shaped and determined by the attitudes expressed by his parents and other important elders. He absorbed the parental (cultural) value-attitude system, and with that standard, now interpreted his experiences with Negroes: they were either examples of the stereotypes, or odd exceptions to be dismissed. This means that we do not necessarily "learn by experience." We often cherish our prejudices.

Similar evidence has been reported in the studies of the effects of the depression upon people's religious beliefs, and their conservatism or radicalism.[2] People with strong religious beliefs before the depression found their experiences with unemployment and poverty strengthened their faith. People who were irreligious, on the other hand, found the same pattern of experiences strongly reinforced their skeptical disbelief. Nor did hard times convert workers and unemployed to radicalism or revolutionary beliefs. The indoctrination with "The American Way" was so firm, so extensive, so ingrained with all their

---

[1]Horowitz, E. L. "The development of attitude toward the Negro." *Archives of Psychology*, XXVIII, No. 194, 1936. See also Eugene Hartley, *Problems in Prejudice*, King's Crown Press, N. Y. 1946.

[2]Eisenberg, P. & Lazarsfeld, P. F., "The psychological effects of unemployment." *Psychological Bulletin*, 1938, 35, 358-390.

emotional habits and unquestioned attitudes, and with their unconscious reactions as to what was good and what was "natural", that they never stopped to question. They never got to a position where they could see the foundation of the assumptions with which they were complacently or neurotically rationalizing the events around them.

The Norm and Conformity

The final concept from social psychology has to do with the functions of stereotyped thinking in times of crisis and social change. In a changing world, the conventional and established social norms become instruments to maintain or re-establish the old social order. They become agencies for imposing social conformity and resisting the drive for improvement of life for the more handicapped classes. The stereotypes float farther away from reality, and become visionary dreams of what the "social leaders" want life to be like. But the account is hollow and empty, formulated on a verbal, sentimental level, above the planes of reality.

In an age of standardized housing, of mass, belt-line production, of department and chain store distribution, frequently we are asked to visualize ourselves as rugged individualists, indulging in gallant knight-like romances, and achieving rich success which we will live to enjoy in a little gray home in the west. The value-patterns become "what ought to be". They approach the level of mythology. Toward rivals we wish to keep as inferiors, the stereotypes may become bigoted prejudices which are imposed as widely as possible, and with intolerance, or even explosive violence against transgressors. These are the patterns which serve to enforce a subordinate role on minority groups, which are used to justify, for instance, putting and keeping Negroes in an inferior place.

In the turmoil of our changing world, in the disruptions, uncertainties and shifts of world shaking crises, there are great battles being waged whose outcome will shape our future. There is not only the competition and rivalry among the top group for power; there is also a great cleavage in society with regard to the major direction our world shall take as it reshapes itself; a conflict between the scattered, disorganized forces of common peoples that would bend the future of the world toward greater democracy; and the tightly knit forces of world conservatism, who see democracy as a threat to their power and way of life.

The Moral Decision of the Artist

With these concepts in mind about society, and the function of social values and stereotypes, one can more clearly see the role of artists and writers.

It is the artist whose insights and vivid images do so much to focus our thought about our world, whose pictures and phrases integrate our feelings and mold our understanding. They provide us with communicable experiences which we may share.

The artist must choose sides. He has a position, whether unconsciously assumed, or deliberately selected. As the State Department pointed out, there can be no story, no moving picture, which is "pure entertainment." There is always the selection and presentation of some material, and with some goal, some value-system, in mind. The story reflects or comments upon some phase of our lives and times. The work of the artist can (a) be realistic and adjustive; it can appraise and evaluate a situation, pose a problem, aid in our understanding and capacity to deal with the world. Or the artistic product may (b) take the direction of romantic escape, wishful thinking, and a paralysis of understanding or action. The artist can use stereotypes in place of reality.

As I see it, most of the better artists and writers work with the richness of reality; they express something of general significance, in terms of a particular case. Their interest and intent is clearly expressed in such a publication as the *Proceedings of the Writers Congress, 1943.*[3]

There is major pressure, however, to write in stereotyped terms. Pressure from the business demands of the industry, and from the profitableness of conformity with conservative mythology. From the point of view of the writer, clichés are convenient and compact; they are easily understood by the largest audience; they conform to the standard social pattern of the dominant group which makes them acceptable and "non-controversial", even if empty. From the point of view of the industry, cliché writing is acceptable because the operators are not in business for their health, nor even to spread democratic notions throughout the world. Movies have an attendance of 80 or 90 million customers a week, and the industry would like to raise it if possible.

Business men speak of the radio, newspapers and journals as media of advertising. These outlets are used not simply to sell specific advertised goods; they are also media for expressing a particular point of view. Although moving pictures do not sell any special product, they are a mass medium of communication, and can be used to extol a fictionalized, unreal mythology about American life. They can sell good will for the Status Quo.

There are several bits of data which serve to analyse the character of most of our moving picture art. One source is the bi-weekly report of 13 Hollywood Women's organizations which review current moving pictures for their ex-

---

[3]*Proceedings Writers Congress,* University of California Press, 1944.

tensive membership. Here are some quotations from their comments on 100 pictures selected over the period from October 1946 to April 1947 which reveal a consistently evaluative and probably unconscious point of view of these major leaders in the community, as well as the quality of the pictures produced:

"The usual objectionable liquor situation is injected." "The brash and aggressive hardened criminal." "It proves its lesson in sin." "She is charming as the balancing force of good." "However, no sympathy is aroused for any of the (evil) characters." "A fine example of family devotion and solidarity." "Shows irreverance for the cloth." "The problem of divorce is lightly dealt with." "The bad policy of ridiculing a police officer." "The theme idea of a hereditary desire to kill (which the review did not hold objectionable) makes it unsuitable for children."

Of the 93 identifiable male leads in these 100 pictures, over half were "gentlemen", wealthy business men—ranchers, oil well owners—or successful professional men. A dozen were band leaders or artists. There were 17 gangsters, crooks, racketeers and crooked politicians. Eleven were soldiers or veterans. Two were workers: a fisherman and a coal miner.

Of the 53 female leads that were other than decorative bait, half were rich, or heiresses, or were posing as such and hoping to dupe some wealthy man into marriage before the deception was found out. Seventeen more were actresses, singers or models. The remaining 10 included 2 college girls, 2 gifted neurotics, divorcees, a secretary, a "moll", a waitress, and an unmarried mother.

Eighteen other leads included angels, devils and spirits, fawns, rabbits and horses, children, comic strip figures, and the atom bomb.

A rough classification of these 100 pictures showed that about a third of them were concerned with sex triangles in marriage and divorce, 7 show quick ways to wealth and sex, 7 were romantic and adventurous westerns, 9 were musicals, 16 were crime and mystery thrillers, a few were fantasies, 4 took up the manners and customs of romance in other times, 10 dealt with problems of character and personality, and about 12 might be classed as dealing with social questions. Of these last, 2 took up seriously the problems of returning service men and their adjustments to the civilian community. "The Stranger" presents the problem to a peaceful world of an escaped Nazi attempting to establish himself in a democratic society. "Beginning of the End" dramatizes the problems of living with the atomic bomb. These are important, significant dramas.

A recent study of the treatment of characters in popular fiction shows a trend very like the pattern in motion pictures.[4] The authors report that "Ameri-

---

[4]Berelson, B. & Salter, P. J., Majority and minority Americans: an analysis of magazine fiction. *Public Opinion Quarterly*, 1946, Summer, 168-190.

cans" make up 90% of the characters in popular fiction, although they constitute only about 60% of the actual group. These fictional Americans are usually pictured as possessing desirable personalities, having high incomes, in high social positions, and they make love to and marry other Americans. The non Anglo-Saxon minorities, on the other hand, are usually in minor roles, come from low occupational and income groups, have as jobs, serving or working for the Americans, and are of inadequate character—such as the amusingly ignorant Negro, the gangster Italian, the sly and shrewd Jew, the backward Pole. The authors conclude that the reading public is constantly exposed to prejudices and the stereotypes attached to minority groups; but that he is never exposed to any serious and direct presentation of these problems. The stereotypical thinker can find continual support for his conventional prejudices, confirmation for his animosities toward other minority groups.

To the same effect, an analysis of 100 motion pictures involving Negro themes or Negro characters, made by the Bureau of Applied Social Research, reports that in 75% of the cases the Negro is presented in stereotyped and disparaging ways, and is presented in a favorable way in 12% of the characters.[5]

What may we conclude?

As a consequence of the variety of pressures, some of which have been mentioned, of the pictures which get produced a substantial proportion tend to provide an escape from the frustrations of living through wishful thinking and conventionalized phantasy. Three major themes seem to predominate in this romanticising of life. One gives an idealized picture of what the world and society would be like if our stereotypes were true: virtue is rewarded, poor men become rich, the hum drum becomes exciting, and vice never pays. Another theme provides an opportunity to get our pleasures vicariously, through identification with the heroes and heroines. Vicariously we rise to wealth, success and romantic bliss, in the arms of our favorite, crooning, movie star. The third theme provides a special opportunity to indulge in aggressive, hostile feelings, to vent suppressed emotions from thwarting, in the sadistic crime mysteries and the adventure thrillers.

On the other hand, there is a small but growing body of pictures that are realistic and objective, that take a human, general problem and make it clear and vivid, and provide the man in the audience with new insights into himself, his social relationships, his society, or his future. It is more difficult; there are odds to overcome that are beyond the ordinary problems of creative work; but the product can be so much richer.

---

[5] The Writers' War Board. How writers perpetuate stereotypes. 1945. (Pamphlet).

Analyzing the Content of Mass Media[1]

S. S. SARGENT AND GERHART SAENGER

For many years students of public opinion have sought valid ways of estimating the influence of mass media of communication. Just after the first World War interest focussed on propaganda and most of the effort went into "propaganda analysis". 1937 saw the founding of the Institute for Propaganda Analysis which published monthly analyses of campaigns and popularized the "seven devices of the propagandist".[2] Actually these devices made more impression on amateurs than on professionals. Furthermore, propaganda analysis involved the very real difficulty of differentiating propaganda on the one hand from news, education, entertainment and scientific findings on the other.

Shortly before 1940 specialists in public opinion began turning toward "communications analysis" as a broader and more satisfactory approach. Stimulated by a need for the study of wartime communications, Lasswell, Kris and Speier, Bruner and others increased their efforts to find valid criteria and procedures for evaluating the products of press, movie, radio and other mass media.

One question now of interest to social scientists is this: how well do the experts agree on procedures to be used in analyzing communications? What steps still need to be taken before we have a systematic, comprehensive and valid schema?

It is well accepted that a distinction should be made between *intent, content,* and *effect* or *response* analysis. The first is almost impossible to perform, as the motives of originators are obscure or unknown. Response analysis is costly and time-consuming but very important both for practical reasons and for the light it throws on content analysis.[3] The content of communications, however, is available for detailed study and, if properly done, throws some light on the intent of originators and forecasts the responses of recipients.

---

[1]This paper is a report on part of the findings of a SPSSI Committee on "Content and Symbol Analysis"; members and consultants of the committee included the writers and B. Berelson, E. Kris, M. Stewart, and R. K. White. Only the writers, however, are responsible for the present report.

[2]See bulletins of the Institute for Propaganda Analysis, 1937-1942. The best example of use of the seven devices is "The Fine Art of Propaganda" A. M. and E. B. Lee, Harcourt Brace, 1939. (A study of Father Coughlin's Speeches.)

[3]R. K. Merton's recent "Mass Persuasion", a study of Kate Smith's 1943 bond-selling marathon, is a notable example of response analysis.

Some Systems of Classification

What, then, are the accepted procedures in content analysis? Lazarsfeld and Merton summarize them as follows.[4]

1. Symbol-counts. Identifying and counting specified key-symbols in communications.
2. One-dimensional classification of symbols. Classifying according to whether symbols are employed in positive (favorable) or negative (unfavorable) contexts.
3. Item-analysis. Classifying sections or segments of the material according to attention-value.
4. Thematic-analysis. Classifying in terms of the supposed cumulative significance of a series of items.
5. Structural analysis. Classifying according to interrelations of themes (e.g. complementary, integrated, interfering).
6. Campaign analysis. Dealing with the interrelations among a series of documents, all of which are designed for a general over-all purpose.

Harold Lasswell has gone farthest in systematizing content analysis. Summing up his views in a recent publication, he states[5]

"An adequate content analysis results in a condensed description of (1) the frequency with which selected symbols have been mentioned, (2) the number of times that the mentioned symbols have been presented favorably, neutrally, or unfavorably, and (3) the number of times the presentations have been made with given degrees of intensity (intensity being measured in terms of prominence—position and emphasis—and dynamic symbol style)."

While these two summaries are representative of the views of communications experts, not all analysts follow the procedures suggested. Some stress quantitative treatments; others favor qualitative descriptions. Some use small units as their base, while others prefer whole paragraphs and themes. They differ as to determination of prominence or intensity, whether or not to bring in values, goals, devices, mechanisms, and so on. More important still, analysts fail to agree upon the frames of reference used to determine the procedures, or, worst of all, fail to recognize that such frames are involved.

It is, of course, extremely difficult (and may turn out to be impossible) to set up a systematic and comprehensive schema for content analysis. The approach and criteria used will differ according to the medium and topic—for a news column, an editorial, a short story, a novel, a movie drama, a "funnies"

---

[4]Lazarsfeld, P. F. and Merton, R. K., "Studies in Radio and Film Propaganda", Trans. N. Y. Acade. Sci., 1943, vol. 6, #2, pp. 64-65. (Descriptive material in the summary has been somewhat shortened.)

[5]Lasswell, H. D., "Describing the Contents of Communications", in "Propaganda, Communication and Public Opinion", by Smith, B. L. et al., Princeton, 1946.

strip, or a radio serial. Furthermore, the analyst's aims and hypotheses influence his procedures. For example, Berelson and Salter became interested in short-story treatment of people in terms of racial, religious and national background.[6] Hence they studied the characters' roles, status position, ethnic origin, personality traits and goals. If the investigators' interests had been different, they might have analyzed speech, dress, age, humor, sexual references, dramatic suspense or other characteristics found in the stories.

The ultimate aim of content analysis is to give information about the probable reactions of recipients, so its validation is to be found in studies of responses. Ideally, a response analysis should be made for all material which seems significant. This, of course, is impossible. So we do the simpler job of content analysis, always guided by knowledge and assumptions about effects on audiences. When we speak of a presentation as prominent, when we identify a stereotype, a device or a defense mechanism, we are assuming—possibly with and possibly without justification—certain kinds of behavior on the part of recipients.

Suggested Frames of Reference

The writers maintain that the various content analysis procedures used and suggested do not all belong, psychologically speaking, on the same level. They have differing frames of reference or parameters, which must be taken into account if the procedures are to yield valid results.

Tentatively we suggest three levels, and will describe and illustrate each. These levels are: 1) analysis which stays close to the communicated materials per se, 2) analysis which is related to certain objectively determinable facts or events, 3) analysis which depends upon knowledge of cultural factors and the responses of various kinds of audiences. Let us examine each of these in more detail.

1. Analysis which sticks to the communicated content is, generally speaking, relatively simple to perform and most susceptible to quantitative treatment. One procedure is to count the symbols referring to objects, events, persons or ideas. Units may range from words to sentences, themes or topics, depending on the complexity of the symbol and the purpose of the analyst. Typical symbols used include the names of important public figures, business, labor and other groups, or whole ideologies such as communism or fascism. Among

---

[6]Berelson, B. and Salter, P. J., Majority and Minority Americans: an Analysis of Magazine Fiction. *Pub. Opin. Quart.*, Summer, 1946.

others, Kris and Speier have used such symbol counts to determine the pre-occupation of Nazi propaganda with specific targets at various stages of the Second World War.[7]

Another procedure at this level is Lasswell's "purport analysis", i.e. classification of statements into "identifications", "demands", and "acceptances".[8] Berelson and Salter also stay close to the communicated content when they classify the goals of short-story characters into "heart" goals and "head" goals. Heart goals are exemplified by romantic love, marriage, idealism, affection, patriotism, etc. and head goals by solving a problem, self-advancement, money, security and power.[9]

Prominence can be measured by studying the content with reference to the position of an item in its total context, the amount of space or time devoted to it, the use of headlines, color, boldface type, sound effects, etc. Closely related is selectivity, by which we compare the relative amounts of space devoted to persons, groups, events and issues in different media of communication. Such studies, for instance, have sought to compare the relative emphasis on sex in American and foreign movies. This kind of analysis was admitted in a court action before the Federal Communications Commission in which Milton Stewart undertook to prove that a certain radio station violated the radio code by not giving enough time to labor.

Impartiality may be measured by studying the extent to which both sides of a controversial issue are presented in the content. Recent studies of this sort indicate a notable lack of impartiality on the part of our newspapers during election campaigns. Adoption of this type of analysis has been proposed to UNESCO in order to establish standards for freedom of the press in various countries.

Certain other procedures might also be included at this first level; for example, whether the content is predominantly cast in rational or emotional form, whether it consists mostly of facts and figures or of dogmatic and un-supported statements, and the like.

2. The first level of analysis involves little or no reference to external objects, situations or events. At the second level, however, we become specifically concerned with relations to the world outside.

---

[7]Kris, E. and Speier, H., German Radio Propaganda, Oxford, 1944.
[8]Lasswell, op. cit., pp. 84-86.
[9]Berelson and Salter, op. cit. The study showed that the "American" and "Anglo-Saxon" characters were depicted as striving for the socially more approved "heart" goals; minority group members were relatively more interested in the less approved "head" goals.

For example, we may analyze the content in terms of the accuracy with which persons and situations are described. Often accuracy is most difficult to determine, but it can be indicated only by some kind of independent criteria. Somewhat easier to perform are studies of distortion and omission, as when a newspaper reports the remarks of one man in a radio debate and omits those of his opponent. This technique can also bring to light various subtle kinds of distortion, such as the occurrence in the movies of a number of upper class and wealthy characters quite out of proportion with their existence in real life.

Often changes in content can be related to changes in the national or world situation. Kris and Speier showed that German propaganda during periods of defeat used chiefly the symbol "Germany" whereas during the period of victory the terms "party" or "national socialism" were emphasized.[10]

3. The third level of analysis depends definitely upon knowledge of the culture and of the presumptive audience.

Lasswell's "presentation analysis"—his classification of items into "indulgent" and "deprivational" is in this category. Knowing the culture and the reactions of expected recipients is a prerequisite for accurate labeling as indulgent or deprivational. Often, of course, such knowledge is common and obvious. But, as Lasswell adds, "for many investigations it is important to have rather special information about predispositions of the audience. Only a careful psychological investigation, for instance, can justify us in considering certain 'upper class' intonations of voice in a radio program as deprivational of an audience composed, for example, of middlewestern farmers."[11]

Again, knowledge of the culture of the recipients is necessary for identifying and evaluating stereotypes properly. An analyst cannot even pick out stereotypes unless he knows cultural and sub-cultural patterns. "City-bred", "college educated", "well-to-do" may have negative connotations in our nation at large, and particularly among rural and small-town residents, yet the stereotype might have an opposite flavor for urban professional people.

The cultural and respondent frame of reference is important also in connection with identification of the originator of communicated content,—the writer, publisher, radio commentator or movie producer. To analyze these factors properly, the analyst must know which persons, group and media have prestige and authority for which groups of recipients. A Chicago Tribune editorial or a message from Col. McCormick will be evaluated differently by a

---

[10]Kris and Speier, op. cit.
[11]Lasswell, op. cit., p. 92.

content analyst depending on whether its audience is a group of Chicago intellectuals or the Rotary Club of Peoria or Indianapolis.

Obviously, in similar vein, characterizations of content in terms of "devices" or "mechanisms" cannot safely be made unless the analyst knows how the recipients will probably react. One can identify a "plain folks" or a "bandwagon" device on the basis of content alone, but such a characterization is meaningless unless the analyst has some assurance the device will produce certain responses in the audience. Similarly, it is rather academic to read all sorts of "mechanisms" into content—e.g. identification, displacement, compensation etc.—without knowledge of the personalities of the recipients. When an analyst knows his culture and his audience, however, he can make a meaningful interpretation which is significant because it forecasts the reactions of the audience. A person unfamiliar with German culture and with the Nazi "Weltanschauung" would do a miserable job analyzing one of Hitler's speeches; he would miss significant aspects all the way from its general tone down to stereotypes like "Blut" and "Boden."

Effective content analysis cannot be done by studying communicated material per se, however quantitative and refined the methods may be. Many of the analyst's criteria and procedures are based upon knowledge about outside events and conditions, and about expected audience responses. We must first recognize that these frames of reference exist. Then, by increasing our information and understanding in these areas we shall improve our analyses of content, and thereby our comprehension of the effects of mass media.

Pre-Testing a Motion Picture: A Case History

BERNARD D. CIRLIN AND JACK N. PETERMAN

Time was when the motion picture industry used only the sneak-preview to test their completed or almost-completed films. During the past several years, however, the industry has increasingly turned to more definitive and scientifically accurate measures of audience reaction. One such program of measurement, using the Cirlin Reactograph, is currently being applied by the present authors to the films produced by one of the five major studios. The following is a brief description of how the technique was actually used in the case of a specific film.

The film in question was a very high budget production based on a recent best-seller novel. All shooting had been completed on the film and a two hour and forty-seven-minute rough-edited print had been assembled. During preliminary conferences with the producer, director, and editor, special problems with regard to the picture's final form were discussed. With these, as well as the editing problems common to most films as a guide, the actual program of pretesting audience reaction was begun.

As a first step, the editing script was carefully analyzed for content and continuity. Each sequence, scene, and situation was delimited and timed in minutes and seconds from the moment the picture started.

A stratified cross-section of two hundred people were then invited to a showing of the rough-edited version of the film. These people were carefully selected to match the known distribution of the movie going public with regard to age, sex, education, economic level, and frequency of movie attendance. Each person in the audience was given a pair of small buttons. One button was red, the other green. They were instructed to hold the red button in the right hand and the green button in the left. When they saw or heard anything on the screen which they approved of, or liked, they pressed the green button in the left hand; when they saw or heard anything they disliked they pressed the red button. Neutrality was indicated by pressing neither button. The opinions thus expressed were electrically recorded on the moving tape in the Reactograph.

The Reactograph itself (an outgrowth of the Lazarsfeld-Stanton Program Analyzer first developed at the Bureau for Applied Social Research at Columbia University) is basically a polygraph which automatically records, for each individual, a continuous, solid line if that individual is pressing the green button to indicate "like", a dotted line for "dislike", and no line at all if neither button is pressed.

Before the running of the feature film the audience was shown an eight-minute short. This gave them an opportunity to become accustomed to expressing their "likes" and "dislikes" via the buttons. It also gave the operators an additional chance to check on the operation of the equipment and to see whether the audience was following instructions on the use of the buttons. (Previous tests with the Reactograph in both the fields of radio and motion pictures have shown that only one subject in two hundred ever confuses the two buttons.)

The feature film was then shown and the audience judged the film—uninterruptedly from beginning to end. Upon completion of the showing the audience were interviewed as a group by a trained psychologist and comments were obtained as to the "why" of their attitudes to specific portions and aspects of the film.

After the test session, the electrically recorded opinions of the entire audience were collated into an "Audience Reactograph Chart" and an analytical report drawn up based upon the chart and interviews. (Incidentally, a split-half comparison of the audience's reactions to this film showed a similarity which almost amounted to exact identity.)

The main purpose of the Reactograph Chart and report is as an aid in cutting and editing. Since the chart accurately portrays the audiences' reactions for every second of the film, it is possible to spot not only scenes and sequences, but even specific words or phrases. It shows:

> Reactions to the name of the film.
> Parts of the film most liked.
> Actors or characterizations that were especially liked or disliked.
> Parts most disliked.
> Situations that antagonize a segment of the audience.
> The characteristics of any particular segment of the audience which either liked or disliked a specific portion of the film.
> Where the audience tired of a scene which they originally liked very much, and scenes and sequences that were considered too long.
> How well the audience received emotional sequences.
> Sequences that built up audience acceptance gradually.
> Closing scenes that were especially well liked or disliked.

In the case of the particular film under consideration, it was found that the title of the film, previously well publicized by the fact that it was a best seller, brought a high degree of expectancy from the audience. Several portions of the film which presented natural cataclysms in a highly dramatic fashion elicited a high degree of approval. However, one of these was evidently too prolonged since a large proportion of those who had indicated marked approval of this sequence turned against it before it was over. In the post-test interview they underscored their feelings that there was "too much of it."

Certain religious aspects of the story received considerable emphasis in the film. The audiences' reactions showed that these parts of the film might advisably be reduced in importance.

About half-way through the film there is a prolonged and emotionally charged presentation of a death bed scene. In this scene the author crystallizes the underlying philosophy and moral of the entire story. The special appeal of the film and this scene in particular was directed to the women in the audience. Understandably, the producer was anxious to know how well and by whom this scene was accepted. Analysis of the chart and the interview comments showed that despite its length the scene was very much liked and especially so by the women.

Finally, the analysis of responses indicated that one leading actor in the film did not fulfill the expectations of the audience. Subsequent re-editing of the film was made to strengthen the character he portrayed.

Perhaps the best resume of the role which the Reactograph testing played in production of this film is contained in a memo which the producer wrote:

"The Cirlin Reactograph Report, or rather, reports and charts . . . , gave me in advance some reactions which were astonishing to me but later completely substantiated. . . .

"The completed picture as released will have been altered and or corrected to agree with those indicated reactions. . . .

"An important asset of your system is the timing factor of your chart which permits the instant and accurate identification of the exact second of time, hence the exact words of a speech or the exact instant of pictorial action, when a favorable or unfavorable audience reaction occurs.

"I find interesting and valuable the fact that your chart can reveal personal distaste for subject matter beside and beyond the same group's appreciation of the emotional content of that particular scene, dialogue or situation.

"Your chart and reports are of practical and important help to me in isolating those particular moments of my picture that I have since made every effort to eliminate or revise or correct. No less important to me is the emphasis your reports gave to the favorable response, in some instances completely contradicting my previous opinion of certain scenes and climaxes."

Radio Audience Measurement: and Its Limitations

W. S. ROBINSON

In the United States the function of radio broadcasting is commercial and competitive. The essential function of a radio program is to influence the purchase of individual members of a public by subjecting them to a stimulus known as the sponsor's "commercial." For the sponsor, the commercial *is* the program, and what the audience regards as the program is merely the chocolate coating to the pill.

The purpose of audience measurement is to supply information whereby the sponsor can become more efficient in his business of influencing purchases, or the broadcaster can become more efficient in his business of selling time to the sponsor.

At present nearly all radio audience measurement is carried on by a single concern, that of C. E. Hooper and Associates, which has been in continuous operation since 1938. While Archibald Crossley really initiated radio audience measurement (in 1929) his organization was the first to die. A more important competitor of Hooper until early 1947 was the C. A. B. (Cooperative Analysis of Broadcasting), a joint venture of the Association of National Advertisers and the American Association of Advertising Agencies, which sold its services to buyers of radio time on a non-profit basis. Hooper's only important competitor of today is the A. C. Nielsen Company, whose ratings are based on data supplied by a mechanical recorder connected to the set, and whose coverage is severely restricted by the number of recorders available.

"Hooperatings" on sustaining, government, and sponsored network programs, and on individual radio station audiences as well, are published regularly, the more important ones bi-weekly, and are sold to seller and buyer of radio time alike. A distinctive feature of the Hooper technique is that the information from which ratings are made is collected by the "coincidental" method, the interviews by which the audience of a program is measured being made while the program is on the air. Interviews are made by telephone, each interviewer calling telephone numbers at random and at a constant rate from the beginning of the program to the end.

Alternative to the coincidental method are methods based upon recall, which ask a respondent to list the programs he heard during a given time-span, or ask him to pick from a printed list of programs available those to which he actually listened. While recall methods are used today for some purposes, they ceased to be used for general ratings when the C. A. B. adopted the Hooper coincidental technique.

A second and still-live alternative to the coincidental method is Nielsen's use of the mechanical recorder, which gives a continuous record showing when the set is in operation and the station to which it is tuned. An incidental advantage in using a recorder is the possibility of collecting fairly extensive background information about the listening family, and of relating this to listening behavior. An obvious disadvantage is that the tape merely records set operation, and not the number of listeners present, or even whether there is a listener present.

The significance of audience measurement to the radio industry, its influence upon the form, content, and scheduling of programs can be evaluated only by comparing the services which current audience measurement provides with the uses which the sponsor would like of audience data.

The sponsor assumes, to put the matter in gross terms, that there exists in at least some members of the audience a latent and more-or-less complex stimulus-response pattern, to which the commercial announcement is the stimulus, and the purchase the sponsor wants to induce is the response. The effectiveness of the sponsor's program in selling his product is assumed to depend upon the

(1) *Coverage* of the program, measured by the number of persons it is capable of reaching;

(2) *Attention-value* of the program, measured by the number of persons who actually listen to it; and the

(3) *Effectiveness* of the stimulus, measured by the number of persons the commercials cause to respond in the desired way.

The effectiveness of the stimulus in turn depends upon the natures of
   (a) Stimulus,
   (b) Subject, and
   (c) Response desired.

To use radio advertising intelligently, the sponsor needs data which will enable him to answer certain questions from each of these fields.

I. Coverage

The multitude of specific causes which determine how many people will listen to a radio program are divided by a long-standing convention into two classes, generally referred to as the two "variables" which influence the size of an audience. These are the "coverage" of the program, and the "attention-value" (or "recruiting ability") of the program.

Attention-value has to do with the program itself and things which are inseparable from it—its content, the talent employed, time of day when presented, day of week when presented, size of the audience got at the same time by competing programs and stations, size of the audience "given" it by the immediately preceding program.

Coverage has to do not with the program itself, but with the facilities over which the program is presented. A sponsor buys coverage by the station. When he adds more stations, he increases the coverage of his program. He increases the size of his audience too, not because the program is better, but because it is capable of reaching more people.

Listeners exhibit preferences for stations and networks as well as for specific programs, and if one station has more habitual listeners than another, it can obviously introduce a program to more people than the other. The problem of coverage is involved in the selection of the network or station which will give the largest number of potential listeners of the kind he wants, i.e. the network or station which has the greatest "following."

The Audience-Unit

The coverage of a network or a station may be measured in individuals or in families (or homes.) Most products consumed by individuals, however, are bought by a representative, e.g. the housewife, and therefore the audience usually needs to be measured in terms of families, i.e. housewives.

Obviously, the coincidental method here has an advantage over the mechanical recorder. The coincidental telephone interview includes a question asking how many men, women, and children were listening to the program when the telephone rang. While the basic unit in reports based on coincidental interviews is the home, the reports also state the number of men, women, and children per listening home. On the other hand, the recorder does not record who is listening, and it therefore leaves the unit of listening undefined. The unit, in fact, is a shifting one, since in the daytime only the housewife is normally present, while in the evening the listening unit is more likely to be the family, or at least its nucleus.

The Measurement of Coverage

The effectiveness of a radio station in reaching a specified audience during a given interval of time, depends not only upon the number of persons who listen to the station, but also upon how long they listen. For this reason, the fundamental measure of a station's coverage in a competitive situation is the percentage which it obtains of the audience's total listening time, its "share of time" percentage, rather than the percentage which it obtains of the total number of persons listening, its "share of audience" percentage.

The Hooper coverage ratings for stations in 32 cities are stated by Hooper to be the percentages of the average weekly audience obtained by these stations, that is, the share of audience percentages. It does not seem to be generally recognized, however, that for the coincidental method a share-of-audience rating is at the same time a share-of-time rating.

The Hooper percentages are determined on the basis of telephone calls, and for any one call the report that the radio was tuned to a given station means that one *family* out of the total number called was listening to that station. The percentage of calls in which the radio was tuned to that station is its share-of-audience percentage. It is a share-of-audience percentage because the unit in terms of which it is stated is an audience-unit, a family, each call representing one family, and the total number of calls representing the total number of families or the audience.

The same call, however, is just as validly described with time as the unit rather than the family. Calls made at a constant rate represent very brief sample intervals from the total listening *time* of the audience. Each call is therefore one unit of time from the total sample of unit listening times. The percentage of calls in which the radio was tuned to a given station is thus the percentage of the total number of listening-time units for which the radio was tuned to that station, i.e. the percentage of the total listening time obtained by the station. Because the calls are made at a consant rate, they are representative not only of the families who answer but also of the times at which they are made.

Coverage ratings based on actual listening behavior, however, are by no means extensive enough for either sponsor or broadcaster. The Hooper percentages are limited to stations in a selected list of large cities, and Nielsen ratings are even more severely restricted. The networks have therefore devised a number of indirect indexes of coverage [for use in the highly competitive business of selling time.] These indexes are based on large samples. The data are collected by a combination of methods in which the voluntary return of postcard questionnaires predominates.

Two such indirect indexes are in common use. One is the so-called "most-listening" percentage, the percentage of the total radio families within an area who report that they listen "most" to the given station. The other is the percentage of the total radio families who report that they listen "regularly" to the given station. While these indexes provide some grounds for making network coverage comparisons, they provide at least an equal amount of confusion, because they present strikingly different pictures of competitive network coverages. However, a recent study[1] indicates that the most-listening percentage bears a consistent and effectively linear relation to the percentage of the total listening time obtained by a station, regardless of whether that percentage is determined by the C. A. B. or by Hooper. While the empirical data supporting this conclusion refer only to stations in the 32 cities for which Hooper share-of-audience (share-of-time) percentages are available, a mathematical rationale is provided which makes plausible the extension of the findings to areas and stations for which share-of-time percentages are not available.

An inherent weakness of the coincidental method is its inability to supply ratings for sub-populations. It is obviously impossible in a telephone interview to obtain reliable information as to income, occupational status, or education, and telephone interviews are normally limited to large cities for practical reasons. Hooper does supply ratings broken down by sex, which is probably the most important of the background characteristics. He also provides separate ratings for children and adults. The meaning of this rudimentary partition of the population by age however, is somewhat obscure, because the respondent himself sets the point of division between childhood and adulthood. The respondent is simply asked to state "how many men, how many women and how many children, including yourself, were listening to the radio when the telephone rang."[2] With these two exceptions, the coincidental method supplies no subpopulation coverage ratings.

The mechanical recorder is in a better position here, at least potentially, because contacts with the respondent necessitated by the installation and serv-

[1]Ken Greene and W. S. Robinson, "The Relation between the Percentage of 'Most' Listeners to a Radio Station and the Percentage of the Total Listening Time Obtained by It," *The Journal of Psychology*, 1947, *23*, 255-281.
[2]Matthre N. Chappell and C. E. Hooper, Radio Audience Measurement, Stephen Daye, New York, 1944.

icing of the recorder permit the collection of reliable and fairly extensive background information. Nielsen, for example, supplies ratings for three sub-populations by income, five by size of locality, and two by telephone possession. At present, the utility of his ratings is limited because of the small size of the sample.

Certainly adequate ratings for even the more important sub-populations in the radio public are not yet available. Indeed, lack of sub-population ratings in the past has had an important influence upon the form, content, and general tone of present day broadcasting. Without sub-population ratings, radio attracts only sponsors selling products of mass appeal, and the common denominator to the interests of the total radio audience must of necessity be common. Potential sponsors interested only in specific sub-populations, even though these may numerically be very large, have naturally selected communication channels for which sub-population data are available. Availability of sub-population ratings would lead to the use of radio by sponsors aiming at sub-populations with better defined and more varied interests than those which constitute the common denominator for the total radio audience. So long as it remains a tool for selling, radio broadcasting can achieve diversity and vigor only when it serves, selectively, the interests of the diverse sub-populations among the radio audience.

2. Attention-Value

The total potential influence of a program is measured in terms of coverage, the total audience reached. But the size of the audience is a function not only of the facilities which carry the program, but also of the program itself, i.e. of its attention-value. There is an important difference between measurements of coverage and measurements of attention-value. The purpose of a measure of coverage is absolute, while the purpose of a measure of attention-value is comparative; it is used to compare the attention-values of different programs at one time, or of the same program at different times.

It was for the purpose of comparing attention-values for different programs that Hooper developed his 32-city "network program ratings." In a measure of attention-value alone in terms of listenership, the influence of coverage on listenership has to be excluded. To equate coverage differences between network programs, Hooper makes measurements only in places where all networks are heard equally well during both the daytime and the evening, viz. the 32 cities. Presumably, then, audience differences represent differences between the attention-values of different programs apart from coverage differences.

The assumption that the 32 cities are "areas of equal opportunity," for example, however, has met some criticism. Certainly the assumption has to be demonstrated, as Hooper himself realizes. The demonstration itself would be no mean feat. It would require the selection of 32 large truly representative samples. Moreover, it would require a genuinely good method for assessing the "opportunity" which the respondent has to listen to the stations of different networks, a method which gave due importance to the type and condition of the respondent's receiving set.

Moreover, while program comparisons based on network program ratings assertedly do not reflect coverage differences, in actuality they do, though to what extent no one knows. The important comparisons involving network program ratings are inter-network comparisons, which means that the ratings compared are for programs carried by different groups of stations. Now the coverage which the sponsor buys by the station involves by Hooper's own definition[3] not only quantitative components such as signal strength, but also listening habits and preferences associated with specific stations and networks. I have been unable to find in any description of network program ratings a statement that the 32 cities are areas of equal opportunity in terms of audience listening habits, and they undoubtedly are not.

Even a network program rating, therefore, reflects coverage as well as attention-value. This offers no dificulty when ratings for two programs carried by the same network are compared, for the constant bias due to inclusion of the human component of coverage would not appear in the difference between the ratings. But in the more important inter-network comparisons, the bias due to coverage differences does not vanish. The conclusion, therefore, is that the influence of coverage on size of audience has not been removed from network program ratings, but that at best only part of it has, and that inter-network comparisons reflect differences in coverage as well as attention—or recruiting-value.

How important the coverage-difference bias is in network program ratings it is impossible to say. Theoretically, at least, it would be possible to find out, but I do not know of any attempt to do so.

Comparison Between the Same Program at Different Times

While the coverage-bias makes ambiguous the sponsor's estimate of the attention-value of his own program in comparison with others, as long as the

---

[3] o.b.c.t., p. 21-23.

bias is constant it will not affect the comparison of network program ratings for his own program at two different times. Such comparisons tell him how the attention-value of his program changes over a period of time, and he would like to use this information to learn how to increase the attention-value of the program by observing what happens to the rating following changes in the program. In fact, Hooperatings are widely so used, especially in the retrospective evaluation of the "quality" of the presentation.

Undoubtedly one could determine the effect on its attention-value of a major change in a program, e.g. in its "big-name" talent, by comparing its rating for sufficiently long periods before and after the change. But sponsors are concerned mainly with short-term changes and their evaluation, and the tendency is to regard a jump in the bi-weekly Hooperating as evidence that "in our last two shows we were on the right track." Short-term comparisons of the same program's rating at different times, however, involves a certain amount of interpretative ambiguity due to ignorance as to how an audience is recruited.

It is commonly assumed that when the Hooperating goes up it goes up because of an increase in the attention-value of the program, and Hooper supplies a graph so that his client can determine whether the change is statistically significant. However, a program is different from week to week, and there is, or ought to be, some uncertainty as to which programs a Hooperating increase should be attributed. This is not the minor uncertainty caused by the fact that Hooperatings appear bi-weekly and programs weekly, but rather the uncertainty caused by ignorance as to the lag between a change in the program's attention-value and the resulting change in its rating, and this in turn is the effect of ignorance as to how the audience of a program is recruited.

The bulk of Hooper's data collecting is by telephone. It is both cheap, and easy to supervise and carry out. On the other hand, the range of problems that it can handle is restricted by what can be learned in a telephone interview. In fact, Hooper's wholehearted specialization in telephone interviewing seriously detracts from the utility of his unique coincidental data.

How, and when, does a better program acquire a bigger audience? No one knows. If a given week's program is suddenly much better than it habitually has been, how long does it take for the effect to show in the size of the audience? It is possible that part of the effect is immediate, as it would be, for example, were a listener to call the members of his family to hear. Word of mouth recommendation undoubtedly plays a part in recruiting new listeners also, and in this case the effect on audience size would be delayed. But how long delayed? Probably the maximum effect of a good week's show on the audience would appear the next week, but likewise there would be some recommendations that would not bear fruit until the week following. But how many? There are a number of ways in which new listeners might be recruited, and the lags to be expected before their effects on audience size should appear are different. Consequently the interpretation of a Hooperating change becomes a guessing game, and unnecessarily so.

This is merely an instance of the fundamental weakness of today's audience research: failure to study the listener except in terms of his numbers. It has long been realized in psychological research that in social situations measurement of itself rarely produces knowledge, either useful or theoretical. It is in the combination of statistical and motivational research that most meaningful socio-psychological knowledge is made. Even the anlysis of "reasons for" and the asking of "why?" can be codified and objectified, and, moreover, is usually a prerequisite for making sense of measurements and statistical regularities based upon them.

The Significance of Audience Measurement in Motion Pictures

LUELYNE DOSCHER

In the field of audience study social scientists have developed highly specialized and elaborate techniques of measurement, but there has been a far slower growth of awareness of the underlying assumptions and the necessary implications of the techniques. The methods of estimating the size and make-up of press, magazine, radio, and now motion picture audiences have become ever more "exact." And there is wide-spread reliance on such techniques for direction in planning the content of these media. The currently increasing use of audience measurement in motion picture production makes it important to re-examine both the use to which these refined techniques are put, and the assumptions about audiences which underlie them.

The Motion Picture Industry as the Client

Audience measurement has been used in most media as an estimator of sales—both actual sale and potential sale. The number of people who recognize a brand name, or those who remember the products advertised on radio programs during the day, or the number of people who look at page three of a newspaper, or the size of the listening audience for Bob Hope have been the legitimate objects of audience measurement. The maximum service the techniques could provide was to locate the maximum audience. In this same light, the motion picture industry, for the most part, enthusiastically accepts audience estimation as a means of predicting and increasing box-office returns. The interest is in how many people will go to see the particular "product". Should a situation arise in which not enough people know about the picture in advance of its release, or a star is liked by only a critically low percentage of the population, the picture waits for a more opportune moments for release, to be determined by further measurement. Audience measurement acts in this way as a sort of insurance against box-office failure.

In general, these techniques appear to be employed to measure "what the public likes," so that the motion picture industry may provide it, at the time when the public "likes" it. The investigators examine the audience and determine[1]

---

[1] The exactness of the determination does not immediately concern us. One technique of obtaining these percentages is described in this issue. Audience Research, Inc. uses a technique which algebraically sums the percentages of the audience registering like (as positive) and dislike (as negative) to the stimulus.

that a certain percentage of the audience "likes" or "dislikes" the projected picture. Presumably then, the industry may infer that the general population will go (or not go) to see it.

A possible consequence inherent in this approach is a reinforcement of the tendency toward standardization in the motion picture. If "what-is-liked" as shown by the scientific techniques, proves to be good box-office, there is a great impetus to present "what-is-liked" repeatedly. This repetition leads certainly to the exclusion of "what-is-disliked" and probably to the exclusion of "anything different." This limitation on what is available for public consumption 'reduces the choice between pictures. The choice of what is "liked" becomes a decision between two equal bales of hay, and whatever the validity of the original measure of what is "liked", subsequent measures reflect less and less choice. The repetition of the formula discovered by audience measurement may thus be unintentionally reinforced by further audience measurement, since the 'formula picture will presumably continue to be "liked" on the same basis as it was initially until the social atmosphere changes so radically as to create new demands on the part of the audience.

The break in this circle of reinforced formula cannot at present come from the audience estimators, for it involves activity which is outside their prescribed range. No clues to whether the audience *would like something else* even better are provided by the present audience measurement techniques, nor are they looked for from this quarter by the industry. As Gundlach points out in another context in this issue, there is no concern with whether the audience *could use something else* better. The present orientation of the industry causes the audience estimators to assume the role of offering a scientific "yes" or "no" as a supplement to the producer's convictions on what the members of the audience will like. The technicians are not expected to explore further fields which the audience *might* appreciate, or find use for.

The tacit acceptance of this role by some of the audience technicians is exemplified by the remark of one of the Audience Research, Inc. executives, quoted in *Time,* July 22, 1946, to the effect that "We deal with people and money; we're not interested in morals and that stuff." Contrasting views on the role of the audience investigator in motion pictures have not yet been made articulate by the technicians.

The Service as Research

What new things, we might ask, disregarding the use made of these facts by the motion picture industry client, do the audience estimators find out? Are they building a body of useful knowledge in addition to serving the specific needs of their clients? One approach to these questions is the examination of the recorded data gathered by the technicians. These consist, for the most part, of the reports presented to the clients, some of which are released to the general press. These present the definitive answers demanded by the producers to such questions as, "Shall I cast John Jones in this film—yes, or no?" And although the researchers are clearly aware of the fine distinction between the facts which they gather showing that "a majority of the potential audience likes this star," and the statement that "*The audience* likes this star very much," (omitting the qualifying statement, 'on the average') the requirement of an unequivocal answer makes it more convenient to use a single statistic, or its equivalent 'yes' or 'no' to describe the complex audience. The audience is reduced, in its multiple relations with the total film, to a single statistic. Or, not even the statistic is presented, but only its roughly equivalent qualitative 'yes' or 'no' statement. This leaves the client with the impression that the audience has been completely described, and gives no 'voice' to the diverse persons who constitute the audience.

Another aspect of the tendency to oversimplify the complex entity which is the audience is the convention of reporting the reaction of a larger or smaller part of the audience as though it were a larger or smaller reaction on the part of all in the audience, without explicit recognition of the assumptions underlying this.[2] A continuous chart is made by the measurement technicians of each audience-film test, to report on the indicated like or dislike of an audience throughout the film. The chart is made as a summary of the percentage of the audience registering like or dislike (in the method outlined elsewhere in this issue) or some combination of 5 'degrees' of like-dislike (in the audience research, Inc. Technique) as recorded electrically at successive points in the film. Each point on these charts represents a proportion of the audience. The impression conveyed by the chart, to the layman, is one of a *changing degree of liking* characterizing each individual in the audience, rather than only a *changing percent of the audience* reporting like (dislike). At best, this could be considered only an index of the *mean* degree of liking.

The uncertain assumptions of this interpretation of the continuous chart may also be explicitly disregarded by investigators themselves, in the flush of enthusiasm over results, as is indicated by some of the comments included in

---

[2] If degrees of liking are distributable, then the percent of the audience 'liking' satisfies the statistical requirement as an index of mean degree of liking when, at the points in the film being compared only if 1) the distributions at each point are identical (in shape, variance, etc.) except for their means, and 2) there is for each individual a 'threshold' at which he will indicate like (dislike) and which remains constant for him at each point in the film.

the report on the film, *Valley Town,* by Sturmthal and Curtis.[3]   In this report, they have made such statements as: "Some exceptional parts *more disliked* by females. . .", and "The higher-educated *dislike more strongly* the unemployed family. . . ," and "They do not begin to express *stronger liking* until after the first four sequences."[4]   These comments tend to solidify the impression that the continuous chart is incontestably a record of the *degree of liking* of all in the audience.   What the investigators did have a record of was: "Some exceptional parts 'disliked' by more females. . .", etc.

This rather minor point has significance in relation to its two important consequences.   In the first place, these data are prepared for use by people in the motion picture industry who are for the most part completely unaware of the fabric of meaning, and the qualifications attached to any statisitc.   They do not think of statistics as representing distributions; they are unaware of the actual or hyypothetical correlations of one set of statistics with another; they are unaware that statistics represent probabilities rather than certainties, in prediction.   These important shades of meaning which do tend to reflect the varied character of the audience are not grasped by the industry users of the data—the single statistic *is* the audience to them.   Secondly, and more significantly for psychologists, the investigator may become absorbed in the refinement of his statistic, and so neglect to question its adequacy for a total description of his audience in the communication situation.[5]   The fact that a distribution of reaction levels

---

[3]Sturmthal, A. and Curtis, A.   "Program Analyzer Tests of Two Educational Films," in *Radio Research,* 1942-1943, Paul F. Lazarsfeld, editor; Duell, Sloan and Pearce, New York, 1944.

[4]Emphasis supplied.

[5]Audience Research, Inc. provides six audience-summary services in addition to a "Preview Profile," which is made under conditions roughly similar to those described elsewhere in this issue for the Audience-Reaction studies.   These services are:
Pre-production testing
    1.   Title
    2.   Story (theme)
    3.   Cast
Miscellaneous
    4.   Audience-Penetration
    5.   Want-to-see
    6.   Continuing audit of marquee values.
The "pre-production" items are tested against standards whose qualities have been established by the ARI. The percentage of respondents responding positively to each is an index of how the audience-as-a-whole will greet the item.   Post-production release of a picture waits until the *audience penetration* (knowledge by the population of the picture, its theme, title, characters) reaches a critical percent—if x% of the population knows about it, it is 'safe' to release.   *Want-to-see* is a measure of the prospective appeal of a film in terms of the percent of the population who will want to see it, estimated from a combination of the percents approving the title, story and cast.   The *audit* assesses the sales value of actors, in terms of the percentage of a cross-sectional sample of the population, which prefers them.

and types underlies the unifying statistic is lost on the industry user of the data, and is sometimes neglected by the researcher.

The relevant behavior of the audience members, when they are not in the theater, in relation to their motion picture experience, is still further distant from the area investigated with present audience measurement techniques. The methods indicate nothing about how the people of the audience utilize their motion picture experience outside the theater. Some of the audience activities and feelings about films are tapped before they reach the theater, and "Preview Profiles" and "Audience-Reaction" studies make a fair start at studying some of the things which the audience does and feels inside the theater. But the behavior of the audience inside the theater is only a small portion of the total of "what the movie *means* to the audience." What it *means* includes especially such things as how strongly the people in the audience consider the film's content as real experience, and to be relevant to their daily lives. It includes how seriously the individuals in the audience take the film as offering a solution to present personal problems, or potential personal troubles. The meaning of the film is incomplete without a knowledge of how much the routine lives of the audience members are affected by the film, and in what way. And basically, the significance of the film includes the extent to which the basic orientations of the members of the audience, or their life spaces, are restructured by the films. These problems have received only very sketchy answers, and the measurement of the audience within the theater alone is not in itself adequate to their solution.

Projected Service to the Public

To deal with the significant problems comprehended under the question, "What happens to the members of the audience when they see a film?" audience study, as it exists today, needs to be enlarged, by the addition of other significant techniques. This enlarged study could profitably include more extensive content analysis. It should utilize the diagnosis of the needs of the individual in our society; and essential to it is the study of the dynamics of the audience situation.[6] This merged approach ought to afford constructive information for those seriously concerned with motion pictures (especially writers and directors) as to the areas in which the felt needs of the population lie and some of the acceptable means for satisfying those needs.

------

[6]George H. Mead, *Mind, Self and Society;* University of Chicago Press, Chicago, 1934, has given a person to person model of the dynamics of the communication situation. This formulation needs concretization and expansion by research in the actual audience-to-mass-medium behavior situation. The lack of such concrete information led Mead to the rather inadequate discussion of the motion picture situation as reverie in his "The Nature of Aesthetic Experience," International Journal of Ethics, 1926, 36:382-393.

The distinctive contribution, for instance, of personal dynamics (the needs, motivations, group identifications, etc. of the person in his life space) to this merged approach would be a delineation of the experienced needs and frustrations, and the sources of satisfactions which are present both in general behavior and in special forms in the motion picture situation.

The potential meaningfulness for the audience of what the writers and directors put into the film becomes realized only in the utilization of what knowledge we may glean of audience dynamics. This means that we must know the nature of the interaction of the audience with the content symbols of the film, in a variety of contexts. The anaylsis of the motion picture experience must include the study of the course of restructuring of approaches to life's problems by the individuals in the audience, both apart from and as a result of the movie experience. The analysis of the film experience means there must be extensive investigation of the degree of universality of meaning of the content symbols. The mere break-down of a film's content into so-and-so-many items which appear significant to the investigator on the basis of more or less well-formulated hypotheses; (e.g. two mothers, or five "indulgent" situations) allows us to predict audience behavior only insofar as the a priori assumptions of the investigator happen to coincide with what the items in the content do mean to the audience. The role of content analysis will be of increased significance when the psychological distinctness of these content items, as differentially meaningful for the audience, has been validated by consulting the audience, and when the extent to which their meaning is universal is discovered by observing the actions of the *audience* members in relation to them. We will then still need to know what relation these content items may be made to bear to the audience's approaches to life problems, and the role which they can play in the re-constructing of the chaotic or inefficient areas in the audience member's world.

In summary, this merged approach could be an instrument for uncovering the areas in which the people composing the audience require information, and seek satisfactions, and it might provide clues to how most effectively to utilize the medium of film to provide this service to the audience.

The fulfillment of this social role envisioned for motion pictures, partly through the medium of audience study, is dependent on the philosophy of the purpose of the mass media. It would be unrealistic to ignore the present divergence of motivation on the part of the motion picture industry and the enthusiastic researcher. For this reason, it must be stated that the promise contained in extended audience study is no guarantee that it will be utilized to the full extent of its potentialities in the near future. With the techniques which motion picture audience study has inherited from market research, it has also inherited the attitude that the object of research is a "product." This raises a question which is perhaps focal to the problem of the function of audience measurement, which may be phrased as, "Are motion pictures products in the same sense as breakfast foods and toothpaste?" It may be that the "product" made in Hollywood is unique in its social function, and that, therefore, the function of measurement in the mass media is similarly unique.

Summary

FRANKLIN FEARING

It is understandable how even the most shock-proof social scientist may be startled out of his professional calm by the almost catastrophic results of the famous *invasion from Mars* broadcast as analyzed by Hadley Cantril. Equally startling, although less asocial in its implications, is the fact that thirty nine million dollars worth of War Bonds were sold as the result of a series of two-minute broadcasts by a *single person* on September 21, 1943, as described in Robert K. Merton's *Mass Persuasion*. The professional social scientist and the layman may well look at each other in wild surmise. What do these events signify? How are these results achieved?

At first glance it may not be easy to understand how radio programs such as these, or motion pictures, are *communications*. Who is communicating? What is communicated? These are basically important questions, of course. But they do not completely cover the complex psycho-social problems of films and radio. There are at least three characteristics of the communicative situation created by the mass media which make is unique. The first is the *size, diversity and psychological complexity of the audience*. The second is the *dynamic, creative and selective character of the audience reaction*. The third is the *uniquely evocative character of the stimulus values* residing in the swiftly changing audio-visual-verbal patterns of which these media are composed. These are not independent phenomena, but highly inter-dependent dimensions of a single complex social situation. These constitute the frame within which the social meaning and the research problems of the mass media of communication will be found to lie.

It may be questioned if in terms of psychological methodology or theory we are yet fully prepared, scientifically speaking, to cope with a situation which has developed with such suddenness and possesses such complexities. The very massiveness and dramatic nature of the social impact of these media of communication, their vast potentialities in a democratic society, and the urgency of the problems which they present has tended to engender attitudes of suspicion, even hostility, on the part of many people. This negativism has expressed itself in a variety of ways ranging from attitudes of devaluative condescension toward the mass media, so characteristic of certain intellectuals, to forthright patterns of institutionalized restriction.

The early research in the field of the mass media, especially films, reflected the general negativism. The famous Payne Fund studies of the effects of motion pictures, although they broke ground methodologically speaking, seemed mainly concerned with discovering how *harmful* the movies were, rather than exploring their possibilities in a democratic society.

Accelerated, no doubt, by the educational uses to which films and radio were put by the armed services in World War II, a more positive type of research and thinking has developed. The Army and Navy, undeterred by nervousness about "propaganda", or the pressures of special interest groups, frankly recognized that films and radio programs could shape human attitudes, that they were proper media for expressing ideas and values.

The present collection of papers presents only a small sample of the types of approach to a very large field. It indicates how a group of persons professionally concerned are currently identifying some of the problems, and developing methods for their solution.

Dr. Lazarsfeld shows that although the planned use of the mass media to reduce prejudice toward ethnic minorities may boomerang, when used in conjunction with other agencies and particularly when joined to the techniques of personal face-to-face persuasion, they may be very effective.

The problem of stereotyping has persistently haunted both radio and films. "Uncle Tom" stands for the Negro, the blood-thirsty, irresponsible "zoot-suiter" stands for the Mexican, and the wily Oriental lisping in pidgin-English represents the Chinese or Japanese. Dr. Gundlach points out that these and similar "pictures in our minds" do not represent reality, and their use in films and radio prevent these media from achieving their full stature.

Another problem for the social psychologist concerned with the mass media is content analysis. Drs. Sargent and Saenger review the various methods used in this important field. They make the significant point that the "content" of a film or radio program must be something which has meaning for the recipient. To understand content *as communicated* it is necessary to know the social and cultural backgrounds of the recipient.

In the paper of Drs. Sherif and Sargent the concept of ego-involvement is presented as the basis of meaningfulness of the mass media for the individuals in the audience. They make the point that all mass media, especially motion pictures, afford extremely favorable situations in which individuals find satisfaction for their ego-needs.

The techniques of analysis of audience reaction to films and radio have received more attention than any other aspect of the mass media of communication. This is due, in part at least, to the fact that the production of motion pictures and radio programs is a business enterprise. The operators of these enterprises, naturally, wish to know to what extent the product meets with the approval of the customers. The question of what the public "wants" or what the public "likes" is crucial both from the point of view of the *entrepreneur* and those concerned with the social utilization and meaning of films and radio. The interests of these two groups are not necessarily in conflict, but in the field of audience analysis the differences in emphasis become evident. The papers of Messrs. Cirlin and Peterman, Luelyne Doscher and Dr. Robinson cover certain phases of this many-sided problem.

The reader of these papers becomes aware of the special character of the problems presented by the mass media. It is possible that a radio program listened to by 20 million persons or a motion picture seen by 50 million may have effects as explosive as those of an atom bomb. A new order of social phenomena, requiring new methods of analysis may have appeared. This is the challenge of the mass media to the social scientists.

America, Mass Society and Mass Media
Journal of Social Issues, vol.16 no.3, 1960.

Reprinted by permission of the Society for the Psychological Study of Social Issues.

The JOURNAL *of* SOCIAL ISSUES

Volume XVI   Number 3

1960

America, Mass Society and Mass Media

Issue Editor: Warren G. Bennis

America, Mass Society and Mass Media[1]

Raymond A. Bauer and Alice H. Bauer

I. What Model of Study Can Be Used

There seems to be little doubt that there is some determinate relationship between a society and its system of communications. Certain gross relationships seemed obvious. It is certainly more than an accident that the society most developed technologically should also be the society in which mass communications are also most developed. The history of the growth of the American system of communications can be written largely in technological and economic terms. The extensive development of the mass media for transmission of information and entertainment depended on a high level of technological advance and a great deal of wealth and social leisure. It is equally certain that there is also a determinate relationship in the other direction, that a society as complex and extensive as ours requires a flow of information and ideas that could not be handled by more primitive means. It has also been suggested—although this is a moot point—that our civilization generates a demand (apart from and beyond opportunity) for the vast amount of diversion and entertainment that is produced by our press, radio, movies, and television.

There is a considerable body of speculation and generalization concerning the relationship of the mass media of communication to American society. While there is a wide variety of assertions—optimistic and pessimistic, specific and general, informed and uninformed, sophisticated and naive—on this topic, there is only one position of prominence which approximates a coherent "theoretical" statement, the so-called theory of mass society and mass culture. We use the word "theoretical" in quota-

---

[1] In the several years since this essay was written in 1956–1957 (as part of a larger study of American society being conducted by Professor Walt W. Rostow in the Center for International Studies, M.I.T.) a good deal of material has continued to appear on this topic. In our judgment the newer material (essays and empirical data) would not cause us to change the positions we took at the earlier period. There is, of course, a temptation to cite such newer data when it seems to favor one's foresight. However, rather than succumb to such a temptation we have limited ourselves in mid–1960 only to such editorial revisions as seemed needed for additional clarity. The arguments (and the sources) stand as of mid–1957.

tion marks because we agree with Bell[2] that the statements of the proponents do not in fact constitute a set of interrelated propositions of sufficient coherence to justify the label of a theory. Nevertheless the "theory of mass society" must, by virtue of its provocativeness, the articulateness of its supporters, and its prevalence among intellectuals, be taken as the point of departure in a discussion of the role of the mass media in America.

The essentials of the theory are rather familiar.[3] Bell summarizes them briefly:

> The conception of "mass society" can be summarized as follows: The revolutions in transport and communications have brought men into closer contact with each other and bound them in new ways; the division of labor has made them more interdependent; tremors in one part of the society effect all others. Despite this greater interdependence, however, individuals have grown more estranged from one another. The old primary group ties of family and local community have been shattered; ancient parochial faiths are questioned; few unifying values have taken their place. Most important, the critical standards of an educated elite no longer shape opinion or taste. As a result, mores and morals are in constant flux, relations between individuals are tangential or compartmentalized rather than organic. At the same time greater mobility, spatial and social, intensifies concern over status. Instead of a fixed or known status symbolized by dress or title, each person assumes a multiplicity of roles and constantly has to prove himself in a succession of new situations. Because of all this, the individual loses a coherent sense of self. His anxieties increase. There ensues a search for new faiths. The stage is thus set for the charismatic leader, the secular messiah, who, by bestowing upon each person the semblance of necessary grace and fullness of personality, supplies a substitute for the older unifying belief that the mass society has destroyed.[4]

The key event in the evolution of the mass society (not always explicitly acknowledged) was the development of printing. Once it was possible to disseminate printed material to large numbers of persons at low cost, a number of things began to happen. The intellectual and artistic level of printed material, it is argued, was watered down to suit the popular taste. With successive technological advances—movies, radio, television—the economics of mass communications demanded that a suc-

---

[2] Daniel Bell, "The Theory of Mass Society," *Commentary,* July, 1956, 75–83.

[3] A representative statement of this view may be found in C. Wright Mills, *The Power Elite,* New York, Oxford University Press, 1956, Chapter 13, "The Mass Society." Bernard Rosenberg and David Manning White, editors, *Mass Culture,* Glencoe, Ill. The Free Press, 1957, contains a good sample of representative essays by proponents of the notion of the mass society and mass culture. This volume contains also a number of well presented dissents.

[4] Bell, *op. cit.,* p. 75.

cessively broader audience be reached and hence that the level of performance be more and more accommodated to the least common denominator of taste. On the one hand, the public (the alternate term is "masses") became the patron of the arts. On the other hand, the broad mass of people also became the victims of mass communications. Being "atomized" by industrial society they developed an insatiable appetite for narcotizing diversion, a circumstance which makes them susceptible to the machinations of the few who control the media of communications. One result of this process, it is alleged, is that the groundwork is laid for totalitarianism. Another result is the progressive deterioration of the arts and of cultural taste. The general argument is bolstered by a number of subsidiary propositions. The mass media, by portraying debauchery and violence, stimulate the same sort of behavior in the masses. The mass media became a substitute for "real" experience, etc.

Many of these features of mass communications are blamed by some critics on specific groups or individuals who are regarded as being in a position to correct the abuses and improve the quality of information and entertainment (more properly, to replace entertainment by art since in these discussions the two are often placed in opposition to each other). However, the pure version of the "theory of mass society" treats the possibility of such reform as an illusion:

> There are theoretical reasons why Mass Culture is not and can never be any good . . . The mass man is a solitary atom, uniform with and undifferentiated from thousands and millions of other atoms who go to make up "the lonely crowd," as David Riesman well calls American society.... My own feeling is that, as in the case of the alleged responsibility of the German (or Russian) people for the horrors of Nazism (or Soviet Communism), it is unjust to blame social groups for this result. Human beings have been caught up in the inexorable workings of a mechanism that forces them . . . into its own pattern. I see Mass Culture as a reciprocating engine, and who is to say, once it has been set in motion, whether the stroke or the counterstroke is "responsible" for its continued action?[5]

A number of writers accept a large portion of the "theory of mass society" but view the role of the mass media more optimistically. Authors such as Lyman Bryson and others see the mass media as binding the industrial society together, as serving as a latter-day town meeting, folk ceremony, town crier, etc.[6] This is to say they agree with much of what

[5] Dwight Macdonald, "A Theory of Mass Culture" in Rosenberg and White, editors op. cit. These quotations are taken from pp. 69–72. Although they do not occur in sequence in the text they form the essence of Macdonald's argument.

[6] Lyman Bryson, editor, The Communication of Ideas; a Series of Addresses, New York: Institute for Religious and Social Studies, distributed by Harper & Bros. 1948.

the critics of mass society have to say, but are less pessimistic about the side effects of mass communications and more optimistic in general about the fate of our society. For the most part, the position of the defenders of mass communications is less well developed, does not cut so deep, nor does it pose so many meaningful problems. It is not out of disrespect for the proponents of the more optimistic view that we have decided to focus our attention on the critics; it is rather that the critics constitute more of a challenge by virtue of their numbers, the plausibility of many of their dire predictions, and the elaborate machinery of scholarship they have mobilized.

The over-all approach we would like to adopt is that of a parallel comparison of the "pure" form of the theory of mass society as it applies to the role of mass communications with the findings and the theoretical models of empirical researchers of mass communications. In doing this, we will have, of course, to indulge in certain exaggerations. The distinction between the "theorists" and the "researchers" is difficult to maintain empirically, since there is at many points a considerable overlap of personnel. Furthermore, not all the "theorists of the mass society" agree at all points with the more extended version of that position. Nevertheless, the attempt seems worth the effort. Where there is an appropriate body of data, we will ask whether or not it squares with the theory of mass society. Where there are no direct data, we will compare the assumptions of the researchers with the assumptions of the "critics of mass society." It does not follow inevitably, of course, that the assumptions of the researchers are necessarily more correct than the assumptions of the commentators. However, the assumptions of the researchers are more likely to be conditioned by their direct contact with empirical data. For this reason it seems worthwhile to proceed on an assumption of our own, that the assumptions of the researcher are likely to be closer to "reality."

The reader may perhaps be alert to the oft-made assertion that the researchers were hired to prove to advertisers that the mass media could influence buying habits.[7] This could lead one to anticipate that the researchers are therefore prejudiced in favor of the mass media. Though honest men, they may in fact be so prejudiced. If they are, then our general observation that it was precisely the attempts to "prove" (or, more neutrally, assess) the effects of the mass media which led to a realization of their limitations, is all the more remarkable.

II. The Communication Model's Assumptions[8]

The Myth of the Omnipotent Media

Prior to World War II a substantial portion of the literate Americans seemed morbidly preoccupied with the power of the mass media. Ex-

[7] cf. David Riesman, "Listening to Popular Music," in Rosenberg and White, editors, op. cit., 408–409.

[8] The same line of argument as we employ in this section will be found in

posés were written of the "lords of the press," of the domination of the mass media by "special interests," and of the low, conniving, sinister, and —of course—spectacularly successful tactics of such "propagandists" as George Creel, Ivy Lee, and Edward L. Bernays. Undergraduates were offered courses in "public opinion and propaganda" in which a good portion of the course time was devoted to training them in the analysis and detection of distortion in the press and radio. The Institute for Propaganda Analysis was formed. Adult education sessions were held. The U.S. Senate conducted an investigation of "munitions industry propaganda" upon our entrance into World War I. Readers, writers, researchers, social critics, almost everyone who viewed the mass media, whether from inside or out, shared the common tacit impression of their omnipotence. The predominant view was that there was almost a one-to-one relationship between the content of the media and their impact on the public. A recent critic of the mass media says: "The opinion-maker's belief in the media as mass persuaders almost amounts to magic. . ."[9] This belief in the magic of the media was not in the past confined to the opinion maker, but shared with him by the researcher and the critic.

Katz and Lazarsfeld point out that the mass media were regarded historically either with optimism as being potentially the functional equivalent of the "town meeting" in the new urban society, or pessimistically "as agents of evil aiming at the total destruction of democratic society"— this latter view corresponding to that of the present-day critics of the mass media. Both parties, however, shared the same implied premises:

> From one point of view, these two conceptions of the function of the mass media appear widely opposed. From another viewpoint, however, it can be shown that they are not far apart at all. That is to say, those who saw the emergence of the mass media as a new dawn for democracy and those who saw the media as instruments of evil design had very much the same picture of the *process* of mass communications in their minds. Their image, first of all, was of an atomistic mass of millions of readers, listeners and movie goers prepared to receive the Message; and secondly, they pictured every Message as a direct and powerful stimulus to action which would elicit immediate response. In short, the media of communication were looked upon as a new kind of unifying force — a simple kind of nervous system — reaching out · to every eye and ear, in a society characterized by an amorphous social organization and a paucity of interpersonal relations.[10]

Elihu Katz and Paul Larzasfeld, *Personal Influence*, Glencoe, Illinois: The Free Press, 1955. These authors assemble a good deal of research evidence in support of the researcher's model of communication. While our presentation agrees with theirs, our own view of the researcher's model evolved independently, although largely out of the same evidence.

[9] Mills, *op. cit.*, p. 315.

[10] Katz and Lazarsfeld, *op. cit.*, p. 16.

It is ironic, or perhaps inevitable, that this view is retained in substantial fashion by only the critics of the mass media. We say that it is perhaps inevitable that this group retains this image because without this image they could not maintain their present level of alarm over the impact of the mass media. It would still be possible to be critical, but not with the same degree of intensity, and with the same degree of assurance that the content of the media could be equated with their effect on the populace.

There were many sources, some negative and some positive, of this earlier exaggerated view of the power of the mass media. One of them was the bragging of World War I propagandists, such as George Creel. Their boasting, and the horrified reactions of the exposers of wartime propaganda reenforced each other. Secondly, a relatively few newspapers and then radio chains began to dominate the mass media. The absolute number of daily newspapers began to shrink after the first decade of the century, even though the population was growing rapidly. As far as the remaining newspapers were concerned, their independence was prejudiced by the growth of newspaper chains, and the wire services. In the thirties, radio, the new medium, appeared to be becoming even more "monopolistic" than the press. To these actual developments we must add a third factor, the attitude of Marxists toward capitalist society. Even if there had been no changes in the structure of the American mass media, or the experience of World War I propaganda, it is likely that many American intellectuals of the thirties would have been concerned with the fact that the mass media were owned by capitalists and largely financed by the advertising of other capitalists.

To the above factors must be added a fourth negative one. Most communications research prior to World War II was concerned with the structure of the media, with their content, and with the nature of their audience or readership. The study of effects was much more poorly developed. It is highly improbable that any one of these researchers in response to a direct question, would have said that there was a direct linear relationship between the content of the communications he was studying and the effect of this content on the audiences he studied. Yet, either this assumption was built into his work, or he had to question it directly by studying effects rather than taking them for granted. Needless to say, effects were studied and the more they were studied, the more vulnerable became the notion of the omnipotence of the mass media. Effect studies date back well into the early twenties. However, it was not until approximately the beginning of World War II that their full impact was felt and the researchers' model of the role of the mass media began to diverge explicitly from that which is still held by many commentators on mass communications.

We will dwell at some length on the developments in communications research which challenged the notion of the omnipotence of the mass media. For this reason we shall pause briefly to note a convergent trend arising out of the practical experience of the "operators," the opinion makers. This development is recorded by Kris and Leites in their essay on "Trends in Twentieth Century Propaganda."[11] The authors note that there was a great disparity between the propaganda of World War I and that of World War II. There were three areas of difference: World War II propaganda was less emotional; it was less moralistic; "propaganda during the second World War tended to put a moderate ceiling on grosser divergences from presently or subsequently ascertainable facts, divergences that were more frequent in propaganda during the first World War."[12] In other words, despite the greater development of the mass media in the latter period, they were employed with a more modest conception of their powers.

Kris and Leites place two interesting qualifications on their generalizations. The trend they note became more marked as World War II progressed. Second, it is more true of the propaganda of the Western democratic countries (which, by the way, were the areas in which communications research predominated) than of the propaganda of Germany and Russia.

They attribute this trend, at least in part, to the development of resistance to propaganda among the Western peoples during the period between the wars. There seems to be little doubt that there is a large measure of truth in this point. It is scarcely probable that both the communicators and their audience were not affected by the spate of propaganda exposés in the period preceding World War II, and that the communicators as a consequence were more alert to creating conditions of confidence. To the extent that this factor carried weight, it is possible that the "myth of omnipotence" was *more* accurate in the prewar period. It is our suspicion, however, that it was extremely inaccurate even then. But, whatever weight we give to the argument of Kris and Leites as to cause of this shift, the fact remains that World War II propagandists became progressively more conservative in their estimate of what could be accomplished by the skillful manipulation of words.

Dissolution of the Myth

In the Foreword to Katz and Lazarsfeld's *Personal Influence,* written in 1955, Elmo Roper comments:[13]

---

[11] Ernst Kris and Nathan Leites, "Trends in Twentieth Century Propaganda," reprinted in Wilbur Schramm, editor, *The Process and Effects of Mass Communication,* Urbana: University of Illinois Press, 1955, 489–500.

[12] *Ibid.,* p. 491.

[13] Elmo Roper in the Foreword to Katz and Lazarsfeld, *op. cit.,* p. xv.

> As the result of my own research into public attitudes I have come to the tentative conclusion that ideas often penetrate the public as a whole slowly and — even more important — very often by interaction of neighbor on neighbor without any apparent influence of the mass media.

Perhaps some statement of this sort might be found among the public utterances of opinion pollers of the prewar era. However, Roper's phraseology implies what our own judgment suggests, that it is highly unlikely that any one would even have asked himself the relevant question. In this question we would like to trace the sequence of events that led to the dissolution of the myth of the omnipotence of the mass media in the minds of the researchers.

During the thirties, concern over control of the press by representatives of limited interest groups was naturally most actively focused on the field of politics. In an era when Franklin D. Roosevelt enjoyed overwhelming popular support, the press was overwhelmingly opposed to him. Recalling as best we can the feel of the mid-thirties, we have the impression that Roosevelt's victory was regarded as a personal triumph. Politically it seemed to be a fluke. While this might have led to doubts about the role of the press, there was in fact, no strong initial tendency to question the power of the press, Rather the lesson that was learned from the 1936 election was that the press did not represent majority opinion; and therefore, one had all the more reason to fear its power.

The turning point in the communications researcher's view of the model of mass communications came during the 1940 electoral campaign. True, Roosevelt won again in the face of a hostile press. But more pertinently, Lazarsfeld *et al.* did a study of voting behavior in Erie County, Pennsylvania.[14] This study was designed to test the influence of the mass media on voting in a presidential election. The results of this portion of the investigation were essentially negative. There was little evidence of people changing their political stand as a result of the influence of the mass media. As we have indicated above, negative results from effect studies had earlier precedents. The status of the Erie county study as a turning point, therefore, must be attributable to several novel factors:

(1). Since this was a large-scale, very carefully conducted survey employing the panel technique of following the opinions and behavior of a sample of people over several months, the Erie County findings were perhaps the most convincingly negative to that time.

(2). The gathering of additional data permitted a provisional exploration of an alternative model, that of the "two-step flow of communications." This two-step model was suggested by the fact that the

---

[14] Reported in the now famous, Paul Lazarsfeld, Bernard Berelson, and Hazel Gaudet, *The People's Choice*, (2nd ed.), New York: Columbia University Press, 1940.

persons who actually changed their voting intentions, had done so as a result of personal contact rather than under the influence of the press or radio.

(3). The notion of the "two-step flow" was not permitted to die. The continuing research interests of Paul Lazarsfeld and his colleagues and the existence of the Bureau of Applied Social Research at Columbia University, resulted in an active exploration of this new model in a series of studies aimed at locating "opinion leaders" and patterns and processes of personal influence.

(4). As so often happens, "the times were ripe," and other studies produced convergent results.

This was most marked with respect to wartime informational programs. The World War I propagandist was free to ply his trade unhampered by any feedback from his audience. But, between the wars, the technique of survey research had been developed, as had social psychological methods of experimental evaluation of the impact of communications.

Some of the survey assessments of the success of public information campaigns produced dismally discouraging findings. The following example is merely illustrative:

> . . . a survey was conducted early in the war to determine why people bought war bonds. Most of them (65 per cent in April, 1943) said it was to finance the war; at this time 14 per cent said it was to help inflation. A tremendous advertising campaign was conducted in the next few years, with the prevention of inflation an important theme. In June, 1945, 68 per cent of the people thought bonds should be bought to help finance the war and 14 per cent thought they should be bought to help prevent inflation.[15]

The Research Branch, I & E Division of the War Department, conducted careful experimentation on the effects of mass communications.[16] Other experimental studies in the past had been premised upon the differential effect of various types of communications and media. But these experiments, being larger in scale than any previous research program of like nature, and coming at a time when field research was producing such marked negative findings, drove one more wedge into the image of an omnipotent mass communications system by showing that communications are highly differential in their impact. To cite as an example, one of the most famous of these experiments, whether a one-sided or two-sided presentation of an argument was more effective, depended on the initial attitude of the audience.[17]

---

[15] Mason Haire, *Psychology in Management*, New York, McGraw-Hill, 1956.

[16] Reported in Carl I. Hovland, Arthur A. Lumsdaine, and Fred D. Sheffield, *Experiments in Mass Communications*. Princeton, Princeton University Press, 1949.

[17] *Ibid.*, Chapter 8.

Even though experimental studies demonstrated the variability of response to communications, such studies were by no means as persuasive as were additional field studies which continued to demonstrate the limited effectiveness of mass communications under many conditions. Whereas social scientists of the prewar period wrote exposés of "principles of propaganda," those of the postwar period wrote articles such as "Some Reasons Why Information Campaigns Fail."[18]

One of the most conspicuous failures of an information campaign was the attempt in 1947–1948 to bring information about the United Nations to the people of Cincinnati.[19] In an effort to stimulate interest in and convey information about the United Nations, two organizations literally bombarded the city of Cincinnati with an informational campaign over a period of six months. Radio stations scheduled 150 spot broadcasts a week. The newspapers played up United Nations news over the six months' period. This use of the mass media was supplemented by less formal means. Hundreds of movies were shown. "In all, 59,588 pieces of literature were distributed and 2,800 clubs were reached by speakers supplied by a speakers' bureau." "The objective was to reach in one way or another every adult among 1,155,703 residents in Cincinnati's retail trading zone."[20]

The National Opinion Research Center conducted a survey of the local opinions and attitudes toward the United Nations at the beginning and at the end of this six-months' period. As far as increasing knowledge of the United Nations was concerned, the campaign was a failure: ". . . the before and after scores remained remarkably constant; for example, in September, 34 per cent said they had heard of the United Nations' veto power and 7 per cent could explain how it worked; in March these figures were almost unchanged — 37 per cent and 7 per cent."[21] This was approximately the picture on all items. While a few improved over the six months' period, others became worse, and still others were unchanged.

The major explanation of the failure of the informational campaign lay in the fact that the people who were initially best informed and least in need of information were precisely those who were most likely to be exposed to the communications. The less well informed peo-

[18] Herbert H. Hyman and Paul B. Sheatsley, "Some Reasons Why Information Campaigns Fail," reprinted in Guy E. Swanson, Theodore M. Newcomb and Eugene L. Hartley, editors, *Readings in Social Psychology*, 2nd ed., New York: Henry Holt and Co., 1952, 86–95.

[19] Reported in Shirley A. Star and Helen MacGill Hughes, "Report on an Educational Campaign: The Cincinnati Plan for the United Nations," *American Journal of Sociology*, January, 1950–'55, 389–400.

[20] *Ibid.*, p. 390.

[21] *Ibid.*, p. 392.

ple, who in fact indicated their own need and desire for information, simply were not reached; their interest was not sufficient to cause them to attend the communications.

We have, of course, no intention of maintaining that the mass media have *no effect*. We do believe, however, that the accumulated evidence of communications research challenges sharply three premises that underlie, either implicitly or explicitly, the model of communications still held by the "critics of mass society" and which have been abandoned by the researchers: (1) that informal communications play a minor role, if any, in modern society; (2) that the audience of mass communication is a "mass" in the sense of being socially "atomized;" (3) that content and effect may be equated.

The Role of Informal Communication

Certainly no single individual has ever said that there were *no* informal communications in an industrial society. Yet, inevitably, in studying the differences between communications in a modern industrial society and a folk society, one tended to emphasize the relative unimportance of informal communications in a society dominated by the mass media. The obvious thing to study was the distinctive, new phenomenon of a system of mass communications. The tacit assumption of both social theorists (whether optimistic or pessimistic in their approach to the media), and of communications reseachers up to World War II, was that informal communications played no crucial role in a "mass society." ciety."

Probably the main support for this assumption was, as suggested above, the amount of attention devoted to such significant social events as the development of the press, the growth of the movie industry, and the emergence of radio broadcasting. Additional support was found in the belief that primary groups had little role in a modern industrial society. As Shils points out in his review of the study of the primary group,[22] American sociologists of two or three decades ago tended to regard primary groups as an anachronism.[23] European social theorists (among them, Marx), whether pessimistically or optimistically, looked forward to the "new society" in which informal primary groups would disappear. Marxist utopianism, it will be remembered, eulogized rather than deprecated the dissolution of such primary groups as the family. While the present day "theorists of mass society" deprecate rather than

---

[22] Edward A. Shils, "The Study of the Primary Group" in Daniel Lerner and Harold D. Laswell, editors, *The Policy Sciences; Recent Developments in Scope and Method,* Stanford: Stanford University Press, 1951, 44–69.

[23] It is true, as Shils notes, that members of the Chicago School of Sociology (Thrasher, for example) did studies of primary groups, but these groups were not regarded as an integral part of the evolving society.

eulogize, they follow in the tradition of assuming that primary groups dissolve under the impact of industrialization.

As so often in this essay, we are confronted with covergent phenomena when we analyze the transmutation of the social scientist's model of mass communications. The importance of the primary group in American society began to assert itself in various areas of inquiry sometime around the mid-thirties. In the field of practical endeavors this rediscovery of the primary group was most dramatic in industrial sociology and psychology. Since the classic studies of Mayo, Roethlesberger, and others at the Harvard Business School, the field of industrial relations and business administration has been dominated by a concern over informal human relations in industry. Simultaneously social science researchers such as Lewin and Moreno turned their efforts to studying small groups. The reasons for the increased interest of social scientists in the study of small groups and interpersonal relations are, of course, complex. But the fact remains that, in this alleged mass society of atomized individuals, the most active area of research in American sociology and psychology has been precisely that sphere of human behavior which was supposed to disappear, or at least to atrophy radically.

In the field of communications research it was the aforementioned Erie County Study which marked the turning point in the attention which researchers devoted to informal communications. Under the stimulus of the "two-step" model of communications, researchers from the Bureau of Applied Social Research began the search for "opinion leaders" who mediated between the media and the broad mass of the population. Successive studies indicated that the original two-step model was somewhat overly simple.[24] "Opinion leaders" were not a single type of person. They varied with the subject matter under consideration. They exercized their influence in varying fashion. The flow of influence was not always "downwards," but sometimes "upwards" and "sidewards." The network of communications is a socially structured one depending upon established patterns of social relations.

Since the Bureau of Applied Social Research has spearheaded this work on informal communications, one of its most recent products may be taken as an example of the new focus of interest in research. Menzel and Katz report a study of the spread of the use of a new drug in the medical community.[25] In this study, the established pattern of interrela-

---

[24] Since the following passage was written, an article by Elihu Katz has been brought to our attention in which he makes virtually every one of the points contained in the next several pages. Elihu Katz, "The Two-Step Flow of Communication: An Up-to-Date Report on an Hypothesis," *Public Opinion Quarterly*, Spring, 1957, *21*, 61–78.

[25] Herbert Menzel and Elihu Katz, "Social Relations and Innovation in the Medical Professsion: the Epidemology of a New Drug," *Public Opinion Quarterly*, Winter 1955–1956, *19*, 337–352.

tions of the doctors in the community, both socially and professionally, is taken as the matrix within which the pattern of interpersonal influence takes place. The point of entry of information about the new drug into a New England medical community was studied, together with the time of adoption of the drug (measured by the date at which it was first prescribed), and the patterns and mechanisms of influence. The pattern of findings is too complicated to permit summarization. However, we may quote the authors' concluding remarks about the basic communications model:

> . . . we have found it necessary to propose amendments for the model of the two-step flow of communications: by considering the possibility of multi-step rather than two-step flow; by noting that sources other than printed publications may be the channels to the outside world maintained by the opinion leaders; by noting that the model may not apply to channels of low prestige and usually easy accessibility; and by differentiating various kinds of leadership, especially by emphasizing the differential roles of the innovator or pioneer on the one hand and the opinion leader or arbiter on the other.[26]

Obviously the subject matter of this study, the adoption of a drug in the medical community of a specific city, is not one which is ordinarily handled by the mass media, and it is equally clear that a group of doctors is not a representative segment of the population. What is relevant about this study, however, is that attempts to trace patterns of informal communications associated with topics dealt with in mass communications led to the use of a sociometric design rather than to a traditional sample survey.

The use of the sample survey, which has virtually dominated communications research in recent decades, accepted implicitly the notion of the "atomized" individual. A sample of individuals is selected out of a population which may or may not be characterized by structured interpersonal relationships. (We are arguing, of course, that such structured relationships invariably exist in the population from which the sample is drawn.) The nature of the data inclines one to accept the individuals in the sample *as individuals,* or at best to look at them as representative of certain categories in the population; i.e., the young *v.s.* the old, the poor *v.s.* the rich, etc. Any attempt to reconstruct the *structure* of interrelationships from which the sample was drawn may not be impossible, but is in the nature of things a *tour de force.* Any attempt to trace the actual flow of communications is even more difficult.[27] Hence, an ef-

---

[26] *Ibid,* p. 352.

[27] Whether or not it is necessary to say so, we would like to be explicit in stating that the above comment is not intended as a serious criticism of sample surveys *per se,* nor as a forecast that they will decline in use. At the present stage of the study of *informal* communications, however, there are advantages to working with a total, though small and specialized group.

fort to trace out the network of communications and influence, as Menzel and Katz did, demanded the identification and study of the whole of some subsystem within the over-all societal communications network.

Interest in informal communications has by no means been confined to scholars working at the Bureau of Applied Social Research. It is exemplified in the work of the Program on International Communications at M.I.T., and in the entire area of recent attitude and opinion research. A perusal of the pages of the *Public Opinion Quarterly* will quickly establish the fact that this is the burgeoning area of investigation. Just as sociologists and psychologists have turned to the study of small groups, so are communications researchers tending progressively to concentrate on micro-systems rather than macro-systems such as the entire American society.

The fact that so much of communications research is currently focused on informal communications does not, of course, prove the importance of this type of communications in American society any more than the absence of such research proved the lack of importance in the prewar period. There are many reasons why scholars concentrate their efforts on certain types of problems. However, interest in this area arose out of a growing sense of the limitations of the mass media. Furthermore, the researchers have presented sufficient evidence for their position that they have been able to get financial support from advertisers, manufacturers, and, most amusing, from the publishers of such mass media as Time, Inc., and Macfadden Publications, Inc. Whether the researchers be right or wrong, their *assumptions* about the role of informal communications in American society square poorly, if at all, with the notion of "the mass society."

In closing this discussion of research on informal communications, we would like to comment on an interstitial area in which there has been relatively little work done, but which is pertinent to the model of the "mass society." It is one of the postulates of the "theory of mass society" that among the primary groups which are dissolving under the impact of social change is the neighborhood community. Morris Janowitz, in his study of the community press in the Chicago metropolitan area[28] builds the thesis that local newspapers are serving to give cohesion to the neighborhood communities in metropolitan areas.

Certainly neither Janowitz nor the present writers would contend that a Chicago neighborhood held together by a weekly newspaper was not qualitatively different than a seventeenth century European village. However, his work contributes to the evolving realizations that the distinction between folk and urban society can be and has been largely overdrawn.

---

[28] Morris Janowitz, *The Community Press in an Urban Setting*, Glencoe, Illinois, The Free Press, 1952, *passim*.

While we do not share the belief of the "theorists of mass society" that totalitarianism is the logical extension of industrial society, it is worth noting that informal relationships continue to play a crucial role in even so brutally a total society as Stalin's Russia, and furthermore that the very nature of totalitarianism serves to solidify some and create other primary groupings.[29] Certainly it was Stalin's intent to create a social order which closely approximated the bugaboo of the mass society. The divergence between the reality of the Soviet system and Orwell's *1984* is a good measure of the irreducible, minimal role which primary groups and informal processes play in any society.

This section on the study of informal communications must close on an ironic note. We have at various points talked about the convergence of different areas of investigation. Now we must note one conspicuous failure to converge. For years, rural sociologists (significantly for this point, a group low in the prestige hierarchy of sociology) have been working on the pattern of interpersonal communications and influence in connection with the introduction of innovation into farm communities.[30] The systematic problem is identical with that which concerns the student of informal communications, yet the work of the rural sociologists has had virtually no impact on the main body of communications research.

The Mass Audience as a "Mass"

We have already pointed to the fact that communications researchers have become preoccupied with the role of informal communications in modern society. The issue to be discussed here is a related but distinct one, namely, the influence of social factors on the individual in his relation to the mass media. Whereas previously we were concerned with the way in which informal communications *via* established social relationships supplemented more formal communications, we are now concerned with the way in which use of and reaction to mass communications is affected by social relationships. We take as our point of departure the contention of the theorists of "mass society" that such societies are characterized by an "atomization" of interpersonal relationships.

Communications in a folk society take place in a social context. The primitive child hears a folk tale sitting around the fire in the company of his family and peers. Modern man, on the other hand, reads the newspaper in lonely solitude on the crowded subway. His wife listens to the soap opera in isolation, etc.

---

[29] Cf. Raymond A. Bauer, Alex Inkeles, and Clyde Kluckhohn, *How the Soviet System Works*, Cambridge, Harvard University Press, 1957, *passim*.

[30] For an example of the former, cf. "Sociological Research on the Diffusion and Adoption of New Farm Practices: A Review of Previous Research and a Statement of Hypotheses and Needed Research," Lexington, Ky.: University of Kentucky, 1952 (pamphlet).

Critics such as Herbert Blumer have argued that the word "mass" has two meanings in the term mass communications. Not only are these communications directed at large numbers of people, but this "mass of people" is also a mass in the sense of being socially disorganized. As a matter of fact, it is argued that modern man turns to the mass media precisely because he is alone, lonesome, hollow, atomized. The mass media are the twentieth century opiate of the masses. They are alleged to be the substitute for healthy, rewarding interpersonal relations.

There is unquestionably a good deal of truth in Merton's observation that the manner of many radio and TV personalities is deliberately designed to create a *"pseudo-gemeinschaft,"* a feeling of togetherness (begging the question of its complete desirability) more characteristic of a folk society. However, there is a certain *prima facie* naivité to the view that the target of mass communications is "atomized." Certainly the amount of discussion generated by telecasts of the World Series, by news of the latest rape or murder, or by last night's quiz show, cannot have escaped the attention of the critics. While it may be argued that these communications follow after "atomized" exposure to communications, reference group theory tells us that it is virtually certain that these anticipated audiences influence the individual at the time of exposure, and that while he is physically alone he is psychologically in the company of others.

The notion of "mass" as applied to mass communications, as Freidson has pointed out, stands in opposition to a good deal of data. Moviegoing, once selected by Blumer as an example of isolated, individualized communications behavior, is very much a social phenomenon. The decision to attend movies is socially determined; they are attended in the company of others; and they are discussed afterwards.[31] Riley and Riley[32] have shown that children's selection and reaction to TV programs is a function of their relations to their peer groups and their families. Rossi and Bauer, and Bauer and Gleicher,[33] found that communications behavior in the Soviet Union was a function of the individual's involvement in the Soviet system. Eisenstadt has similar findings among Israeli immigrants.[34] Addiction to popular singers or movie stars generates face-

---

[31] Eliot Freidson, "Communications Research and the Concept of the Mass," *American Sociological Review,* June, 1953, *18,* 313–317.

[32] Matilda Riley and John W. Riley, Jr., "A Sociological Approach to Communications Research," *Public Opinion Quarterly,* Fall, 1951, *15,* 445–460.

[33] Peter H. Rossi and Raymond A. Bauer, "Some Patterns of Soviet Communications Behavior," *Public Opinion Quarterly,* Winter, 1952–53, *16,* 663–666. Raymond A. Bauer and David B. Gleicher, "Word-of-Mouth Communication in the Soviet Union," *Public Opinion Quarterly,* Fall, 1953, *17,* 308–309.

[34] S. N. Eisenstadt, "Conditions of Communicative Receptivity," *Public Opinion Quarterly,* Fall, 1953, *17,* 363–374.

to-face fan clubs among adolescents (and adults). Newspapers are read for the raw material with which to impress one's fellows.

There are dissenters of the interpretation we put on these data, however. Maccoby, for example, found that television brings the family closer together, but that the resultant social life is "parallel" rather than interactive.[35] We cannot quarrel with these investigators' interpretations of their own data. They do, however, find that radio listening and TV viewing take place in a social context.

It would be senseless to maintain for a moment that there are not fundamental qualitative differences between communications behavior in a society dominated by mass media and in a traditional folk society. We would only maintain, along with Freidson, that:

> On the basis of this material and on the experience and behavior of members of the audience, it is possible to conclude that the audience, from the point of view of its members, at least, is *not* anonymous, heterogeneous, unorganized and spatially separated. The individual member of the audience frequently does not manifest the selective activity characteristic of the mass, and when such selection has been observed to occur, it appeared to rise out of the stimulation of organized social processes rather than merely the individual's personal interests. Given this, it is possible to conclude that the concept of the mass is not accurately applicable to the audience.[36]

While Friedson's conclusion may be accepted as a convervative reflection of extant research findings, the following passage by Katz and Lazarsfeld suggests what future research may uncover:

> We have learned over the last decade that there is good reason to suspect — although there is really no empirical evidence available — that some of the most effective radio broadcasts involve the presence of planned listening groups rather than isolated individuals. Father Coughlin's radio success, for example, appears to have been built on group listening. And we know from a recent study of communications in Soviet Russia that the channels of communication there depend heavily on in-person presentations to organized groups and that mass communications are superimposed upon this interpersonal framework. A related point — that individuals will reject a communication which seeks to separate them from their group — is a central finding of Shils and Janowitz (1948) in their study of allied propaganda to German troops during World War II.[37]

In summary, the researchers, in addition to being impressed with the role of informal communications in American society, are also im-

---

[35] E. E. Maccoby, "Television: Its Impact on School Children," *Public Opinion Quarterly*, Fall, 1951, *15*, 424–429.

[36] Freidson, *op. cit.*, p. 316.

[37] Katz and Lazarsfeld, *op. cit.*, p. 28.

pressed with the role of interpersonal relationships in affecting the way one responds to mass communications. The communications model of the researchers diverges from that of the critics of mass society in these respects, as well as in the degree of power of the mass media, and in the inferences which may be made as to the relationship of content to effect.

The Equation of Content and Effect

The last of these premises, that content and effect may be equated, may well be denied by the critics of mass society. Yet we believe it is implicit in their position. The mainstays of their case are content analysis, argument, and illustrative anecdote. The arguments are invariably persuasive and sophisticated,[38] and since there is little doubt that the mass media play a varied role, there can be equally little doubt that their arguments offer an accurate description of the processes at work in *some* segment of the population. But, it is precisely this diversity of effect that makes illustrative anecdotes and content analysis devices of limited validity for assessing effect. (We have *no* criticism of many other uses of content analysis.) There can be little doubt that, in a population of more than 150 million persons, TV has precipitated acts of violence in some portions of the populace—just as did the advent of the lollypop and the ice cream cone. However, as much as one may deprecate vulgar quantification, the relevant questions are quantitative ones, and we shall have more to say about the quantitative evidence later.

More to the point is the use of content analysis. We are told that there were X number of murders, and Y acts of violence shown on TV in a given period of time; or that heroes and heroines are depicted in such-and-such a fashion in a given sample of movies or magazine articles. Such findings serve well to alert us to the low artistic state of the media, and they may give us a good deal of insight into our culture and values. But it is precarious indeed to infer from this content its impact on its audience. Lest we seem to cavil unduly we prefer to quote the distinguished sociologist Robert Merton in his introduction to Dallas Smythe's content analysis of New York television. Smythe had found that nearly 3,000 acts of violence had been portrayed on New York television programs during the course of a week. Merton comments:

> Nothing in these figures can tell us about the psychological and social effects upon television audiences of these numerous episodes of violence, nor does Mr. Smythe move beyond his evidence to guess at the effects. It cannot simply be taken for granted that violence on the scene is emotionally damaging to the spectator. When violence becomes conventionalized, for example, as in the well-grooved patterns of the Western movie,

---

[38] Cf. as an extreme example, Frederick Wertham's work on children and comics, *Seduction of the Innocent,* New York: Rinehart & Company, 1954.

it may not cause the least distress or damage to children who know that the noble hero will irresistably triumph over the blackhearted villians but that, for this to happen in proper style, the good men and bad men must first work their way through a sequence of ambushes, fist fights, and gun play in which injuries and even occasional death become more symbolic than real.[39]

In general our contention that content and effect of communications cannot be equated rests on the evidence presented throughout this essay as to the variability of response to communications. We pause here only to record our reservations; and also to draw forcibly the distinction between imputation of effect, and the moral and aesthetic issues on which content analysis may be extremely pertinent. That is to say, the statement of Merton, with which we concur, that violence on the TV screen cannot be assumed to be emotionally damaging to the spectator, is neutral with respect to the quality of TV programming itself. The critics of the mass media would be on far firmer ground if they were to keep these two issues separate.

III. Research Evidence On The Impact Of The Mass Media

In the preceding chapter we were concerned mainly with the comparison of the contrasting assumptions about the communications process in American society. We indicated merely that the model held by the theorists of mass society and the model held by the empirical researchers did not fit well with each other. There is no necessary reason to believe that the assumptions held by researchers are correct. In this section we will extend our concern beyond the communications model of mass society. We will deal with certain specific effects postulated by the theory of mass society, but we will also try to make a more general assessment of the status of our knowledge on the effects of mass media.

The mass media have been alleged, among other things, to: (1) change specific attitudes, (2) re-enforce existing attitudes, (3) offer diversion and recreation, (4) enhance aesthetic experience and level of culture or (5) lower aesthetic tastes, (6) stimulate specific behaviors or (7) furnish vicarious experience and presumably thereby inhibit overt behavior, (8) furnish knowledge, (9) divert time away from more desirable activities and/or (10) divert time away from less desirable activities, (11) divert money away from other activities (more or less desirable), (12) give status and prestige (both directly and vicariously), (13) destroy reputations, (14) etc. . . . It can readily be seen that as long as this list of imputed effects is, it does not by any means exhaust the major categories of effect that might be investigated. We

---

[39] From Robert K. Merton's Introduction to Dallas W. Smythe, *New York Televison: January 4–10, 1951–1952*. New York TV Monitoring Study No. 4, Urbana, Ill: N.A.E.B., 1952, v.

have not, for example, suggested the vital distinction between short-run and long-run effects nor the question of combinations of effects, such as changes of attitudes which are and which are not accompanied by changes of behavior, etc. While the number of sound, general statements which may be made is very limited, the number of fairly well-established, specific findings is large — so large in fact as to defy summary in an essay such as this. Accordingly, our treatment must be selective; and for this reason we refer the reader to several excellent, comprehensive summaries in which he may browse for his further enlightenment:

(1) Joseph T. Klapper, *The Effects of the Mass Media* (New York: Bureau of Applied Social Research, Columbia University, 1950). This volume is the most comprehensive, as well as an exceedingly competent, review of the data on the actual societal impact of the mass media. Klapper is working at present on a revision entitled *Effects of Mass Communication,* which will be published by The Free Press late in 1960.

(2) Carl I. Hovland, "Effects of the Mass Media of *Communication*," in Gardner Lindzey (ed.), *Handbook of Social Psychology* (Cambridge: Addison-Wesley, 1954), II, 1062–1103. Hovland concentrates more on experimental findings, in contrast to Klapper's greater emphasis on field data. We will have more to say about the merits and limitations of the two approaches in the text below.

(3) Leo Bogart. *The Age of Television* (New York: Frederick Ungar, 1956). This is the most comprehensive review of the research data available on any single mass medium. Bogart has assembled virtually every research study done up to the middle of 1956, and subjected the data to a very close and careful summary analysis.

A perusal of any substantial bibliography on communications will yield a considerable number of items with attractive but misleading titles. For example, a volume entitled *Television's Impact on American Culture*,[40] while a very good collection of essays on the status, background, and prospects for educational television, presents little or no *empirical* data on the impact of TV on American culture. Or, Fearing's *Social Impact of the Mass Media of Communication,* referred to above, is a sensitive and sensible presentation of a model for the study of the impact of the mass media, but presents no data on impact. Despite a plethora of intriguing titles, speculative generalization, and an excellent body of laboratory research, there is little empirical evidence of the effects of the mass media on American society as a whole.

Research Evidence
Experimental studies

In this and the following two sections, we will confine our attention to the nonrecreational and noncultural effects of mass communications.

---

[40] William Y. Elliott (ed.), *Television's Impact on American Culture* (East Lansing: Michigan State University Press, 1956).

Systematic experimental studies of communications and their effects have been carried on for well over two decades. Even though much of the evidence is complicated and some is contradictory, it is possible to say that a good deal has in fact been learned about the effects of communications under controlled conditions.[41] Some of the generalizations which may be made with more firm confidence are such as these: It is easier to transmit information than to change attitudes. Simpler material is more readily comprehended when presented orally, and more complex material when presented in written form. Two-sided arguments make the audience more resistant to counterpropaganda. People remember more of arguments which are congruent with their values. Whether or not the audience regards the communicator as trustworthy seems to have little influence on whether or not factual information will be remembered; however, if the communicator is not trusted, the audience is less likely to accept his point of view. Yet, over time, the source of the communication may be forgotten, and then the point of view of the mistrusted communicator will tend to be accepted.

Experiments with communications in small groups demonstrate that the *flow* of communications will be affected by the status of individuals within the group and by the over-all cohesiveness of the group.[42] As long as the group is bound together, communications will be directed at those persons who deviate from the group norm. But, this is not true in situations where the group may split up. Persons who have had their confidence shaken in their opinions will talk to other persons who agree with them and thus restore their previous level of confidence,[43] etc.

On other points there is confusion. One of the oldest questions to which research was addressed was of the relative effect of "emotional" and "rational" appeals. The evidence is ambiguous. Another question is: which is more effective, the first communication or the most recent one? Sometimes it is one, sometimes the other, depending on the circumstances. Personality, intelligence, and education affect *susceptibility* to communication, but the relationship is not simple. People of higher intelligence, for example, are more likely to comprehend a communication but are also more likely to be critical of it. It is conceivable that a message may be sufficiently difficult to comprehend so that *only* intelligent people will be influenced. If the intelligibility of the message is improved, less intelligent people may prove more susceptible to influence, etc.

---

[41] The most convenient summary of experimental findings will be found in Hovland, *Loc. cit.*

[42] A convenient summary of the small group data will be found in Harold H. Kelley and John W. Thibaut, "Experimental Studies of Group Problem Solving and Process," in Lindzey (ed.), *op. cit.*, 735–785.

[43] May Brodbeck, "The Role of Small Groups in Mediating the Effects of Propaganda," *Journal of Abnormal and Social Psychology, 52,* (March 1956), 166–170.

The number of such specific findings is so great that the reader is likely to assume that they are of great help in assessing the impact of the mass media on American society. Actually, their value is at present quite limited for this purpose. As Hovland points out at the end of his summary of the literature on effects of mass communications,[44] we are very much in need of "communications engineering." Communications research has done much to help us identify the relevant parameters of the problem, but the crucial job of giving values to these parameters is yet to be done.

The need for the "engineering" of present experimental findings of communications research can be demonstrated rather simply. The salient findings of all communications research is that virtually *every message has a differential impact*. Except under very special conditions which seldom if ever obtain in the real life situation, we can expect no message to be uniformly successful. Even a cry of "Fire" in a theatre is likely to fall on a few skeptical ears. There is one study in the experimental literature which produced virtually unanimous results. Annis and Meier[45] planted stories about an unknown Australian politician in a college newspaper. Some students saw only an issue of the newspaper which carried a favorable story; others saw only the unfavorable story. When the students were subsequently asked their opinions of the Australian politician the attitudes they reported were almost unanimously in line with what they had read. What is interesting about this study is that the experimenters were able to work with subjects who had no prior information about this politician, and the experimenters were able to maintain a complete monopoly over the new information available to the subjects. Klapper, in his summary of the literature on the effects of the mass media, states that the one condition most likely to produce effective communication is that in which a monopoly over information is maintained. Yet, this is precisely the condition that virtually never obtains in the "real life" situation. Even a communist totalitarian state cannot maintain a monopoly over communications, although this has at times been a keystone of Soviet communications policy.[46] In the absence of a monopoly of information a diversity of response is assured, and hence the assessment of impact becomes an "engineering" rather than a "theoretical" task.

We shall have occasion to point out several times in this essay that mass media of communications exercise a distinctive advantage in *inverse* proportion to the importance of the issue involved. A monopoly of in-

[44] Hovland, *op. cit.*, p. 1099.

[45] Albert D. Annis and Norman C. Meier, "The Induction of Opinion Through Suggestion by Means of 'Planted Content,'" *Journal of Social Psychology*, 1934, 5, 65–81.

[46] Cf. Bauer and Gleicher, *op. cit.*, pp. 297–298.

formation is possible in proportion to the newness of an issue and its lack of relationship to previously important issues. Thus, Hovland[47] attributes F. L. Mott's low correlation between newspaper editorial policy and popular voting in part to the fact that election issues are typically *major* issues on which the public is moderately well informed.

To say that our existing findings indicate that every communication must be assumed to have a differential effect is to praise, not to criticize, the state of communications research. As research has progressed, "deviant cases" are no longer regarded as "accidents" but as the subject of systematic investigation. We no longer ask "what type of message is most effective," but "what type of message is most effective with what sorts of people under what circumstances." Specification of the sources of differential effect of communications offers the possibility of much more precise prediction and analysis of the impact of the mass media.

Suppose we take as an example the previously mentioned famous experiment of Hovland, Lumsdaine, and Sheffield[48] on the relative merits of one-sided and two-sided arguments. Suppose further that we were trying to decide on how best to promote the sale of seat belts for automobile safety. We have to decide whether or not to acknowledge in our messages the fact that there have been a few freak accidents associated with safety belts. The Hovland experiment suggests that we should first find out (1) how many and what sorts of persons know about these freak accidents; (2) how many people are initially favorable to our case, and how many are opposed. Having found out the relative distribution of favorably and unfavorably disposed persons, we should then (3) take a close look at the educational level of each. In a complicated case, we might have to (4) determine the cut-off point at which increased education makes a two-sided argument more effective. We may come out with a fairly firm conclusion that a one-sided communication will sell more seat belts, taking everything into consideration; e.g., the major potential market lies with less educated people who favor "safety" in general, but need to have their awareness of the issue sharpened. But then, suppose we find out that a newspaper campaign is going to be waged against the use of seat belts. We hustle back to the drawing boards to feed into our computations the extent to which a two-sided communication will be more effective against counterpropaganda (a factor which probably would have to be derived empirically in each instance). The experimental studies have taught us what questions to ask, but they have not given us all the requisite answers.

The job of the "science of communications" is to identify the crucial variables in the communications process and determine the pattern of interaction of each on the others. The distribution of these variables in

[47] Hovland, *op. cit.*, p. 1064.

[48] Hovland, Lumsdaine, and Sheffield, *op. cit.*, Chapter 8.

any given population is a separate problem. To date, we think it may be said with safety that in most instances the differential impact of communications is to be explained in terms of differential characteristics of the various segments of the target population; but in most instances we do not know the distribution of the relevant characteristics in the American population with sufficient precision to put these generalizations to their full potential use.

This is not to say that we are totally without knowledge of the relevant characteristics of the American population. For example, we often know or can readily determine the distribution of existing attitudes with adequate precision. In addition to a certain amount of systematic data gathered by social scientists, many communications practitioners have a sensitive, intuitive knowledge of the American public which serves as a good first approximation of the sort of more systematic information which we would desire optimally.

There may be occasional limiting conditions under which mass communications may produce a unanimous effect. There are also times in which the "deviant cases" may be so few as not to be of practical importance. The more important the issue, however, the less likely is the effect to approach unanimity, because of the public's stronger interest in and knowledge of the problem. Therefore, the present status of communications research indicates that any study of the impact of the mass media must be one of the *demography of effect* — the relative distribution of effects throughout the population. The major job of charting the appropriate population parameters remains to be done.

Who Listens

A distinctive characteristic of mass communications is the latitude of attention given to the potential listener, viewer, or reader. Mass communications are broadcast. This means simultaneously that the intended audience cannot be forced to attend, and the unintended audience cannot be excluded. Let us concentrate for the time being on only the first part of this statement.

One of the indisputable findings of communications studies is that people tend overwhelmingly to attend to those communications which coincide with their own predispositions. One of the present writers, for example, was interested in the effect which various versions of a controversial event might have on the views of people some two years later.[49] Initially, a high degree of correspondence was found between their views of the event and the reported sources of information on what had happened. It appeared that newspapers did indeed influence people's

---

[49] John C. Eberhart and Raymond A. Bauer, "An Analysis of the Influences on Recall of a Controversial Event: The Chicago *Tribune* and the Republic Steel Strike," *Journal of Social Psychology, S.P.S.S.I. Bulletin,* 1941, *14,* 211–228.

beliefs about what went on in the world. However, we then gave our subjects attitude tests on the issue involved (labor relations). We found, as had others, that people read newspapers that agreed with their own position. We were left completely at sea as to the direction of causation: did they select newspapers that suited their attitudes, did the newspapers shape their attitudes, or both, or in what combination? This finding is typical of a great deal of communications research.

The problem of attention is crucial to the assessment of the effects of the mass media. For example, Lipset *et al.*[50] report that attitude changes can be effected quite readily in a laboratory situation, but that precisely those people whose attitudes can most easily be changed are the type of people who are least likely to listen to the sort of educational program which had been the subject of the experiment. Such behavior is predictable from experimental findings, field research, and common sense. Persons least informed on a given topic are most susceptible to change by new information. They are also likely to be least interested by far in the subject. (This is why they are least informed.) Hence they are also least likely to expose themselves to messages on the topic. The practical importance of this "vicious circle" have already been indicated by the Cincinnati study reported earlier in this essay. It seemed to account for the fact that a full six months of intensive "educating" produced no results.

This tendency for people to expose themselves to communications which reinforce their own beliefs appears, at first glance, to be a vicious, unbreakable circle. Even when one exposes himself to the views of the other side, the function of this exposure may be to strengthen his original predispositions. Thus, the Republican TV viewer watching the Democratic National Convention comes away heightened in his anti-Democratic fervor more often than he comes away shaken in his Republican allegiance. Experimental studies of anti-prejudice communications have shown a discouraging "boomerang" effect.[51] Prejudiced subjects tend to reinterpret even the most implausible stimuli in such a way as to reinforce their prejudices. This pattern of events had led some writers to suggest that the major function of the mass media is to stabilize the existing belief system of the population. Indeed, one is sometimes led to wonder how opinions *ever* change. However, this disposition of the individual to listen to and read what he wants to hear and see is analogous to, and has the same essential weakness as, the disposition of a totalitarian regime to maintain a monopoly of information. No such monopoly,

[50] Seymour M. Lipset, et al., "The Psychology of Voting: An Analysis of Political Behavior," in Lindzey (ed.), *op. cit.*, pp. 1124–1176.

[51] Patricia L. Kendall and Katherine M. Wolf, "The Analysis of Deviant Cases in Communications Research," in Paul F. Lazarsfeld and Frank N. Stanton (eds.), *Communications Research: 1948–49* (New York: Harper and Brothers, 1949), 152–179.

whether from the point of the receiver or the communicators, is possible.

Even though a given individual may seek out only reinforcing information, the nature of communications is such that he will inevitably be exposed to contrary information. Every skillful communicator capitalizes on this circumstance. The devices which have been employed have furnished much grist for the mill of the *New Yorker's* feature, "Letters we never finished reading," but it also happens more naturally. Business leaders interviewed in connection with the Foreign Trade Study of the Center for International Studies at M.I.T.[52] reported that they learn about foreign trade policy not from their *preferred* sources of information on this topic, but from their habitual sources of general news. Few adults would bother to watch a TV show directly concerned with teaching racial tolerance. But a Negro character portrayed sympathetically in the body of a regular TV drama will convey the same message. The problem of accidental exposure is the stock in trade of the professional communicator,[53] even though it has had little research deliberately addressed to it. It suggests again why the effects of the mass media may be minuscule in the short run, but greater in the long run.

The phenomenon of self-selection in communications exposure is also the explanation for our ignoring a considerable body of correlational studies from which effects of mass media have on occasion been inferred. In the early thirties, some (though not all) studies found a correlation between children's movie attendance and undesirable personal and social characteristics. It is doubtful — in view of the generally increased sophistication of communications research — that the same scholars would at the present time draw the conclusion that these traits were "caused" by attendance at movies. Correlations between undesirable behavior and/or personal traits and communications exposure are still cited as evidence of the effects of communications. However, this is done increasingly less often by persons trained in research.

It may be argued that the problem we are talking about is a general one of scientific inference, that one can never assume direction of causation from correlations in the absence of other evidence, but that on practical grounds one often has good reason to assume at least *some* effect in a given direction. In most instances we do in fact find upon more extensive investigation that correlated variables "interact," i.e., that there is "causation" in both directions. However, with respect to "effects" and

---

[52] These data have since been published in Raymond A. Bauer and Ithiel de Sola Pool, *American Businessmen and International Trade: Code Book and Data From a Study on Attitudes and Communications* (Glencoe, Ill., The Free Press, 1960).

[53] e.g., Perhaps the most flagrant case is the use of seductive covers on paperback books. The intention presumably is to get the reader to expose himself to the contents of the book on false pretenses.

communications exposure, the case seems to be somewhat different. Up to this point, there is a vast amount of data indicating that personal characteristics influence communications exposure, but little if any firm data indicating that *mass communications, under field conditions,* influence personal characteristics.[54] Considering the state of our present knowledge, the reasonable conclusion to reach in any given instance (in the absence of specific information to the contrary) is that any correlation between communications behavior and the personal characteristics of the people involved is a result of *selective exposure,* rather than evidence for the effects of communications.

Successful Mass Communications

Despite our apparent agnosticism, neither we nor anyone else believes that the mass media have no effect. Even if we grant the probability that the effects may be mainly long-run effects, the fact remains that the mass media have on occasion produced dramatic short-run results. Orson Wells' broadcast, "The War of the Worlds," sent thousands of panic-stricken citizens fleeing from their homes. Kate Smith's war bond drive sold millions of dollars of bonds. The TV program, "The $64,000 Question," brought about a shortage of Revlon products on drug store counters, etc.

Actually the number of such dramatic events is rather small (though they have been thoroughly memorialized in the literature), and their implication has, by and large, been missed. Even in the minds of many professional psychologists there lurks the notion that actions are more "real" than attitudes, and therefore a change in behavior is more difficult to accomplish than is a change of attitude. The opposite is true. One of the generalizations from experimental studies is that "facts" are accepted more readily than "opinions." Looking over a range of the situations in which mass media have been conspicuously effective it appears that they have been effective to the extent that they have capitalized on extant attitudes and, explicitly or implicitly, have fed in "facts" which have suggested an easily available course of action which served those attitudes or values.

This general point, as may be expected, has not gone unnoticed by other writers. Perhaps the most pertinent commentary has been made by Gerhardt Wiebe, who at the time of writing was director of research for C.B.S.[55] Wiebe addressed himself to the question of the comparative success of the mass media in merchandising commodities and in selling good citizenship. Advertising, he argues, succeeds because (and when)

---

[54] Again, we are not saying that this does not happen. We assume that it does. We are talking only about the relative paucity of firm data indicating just when and how it happens.

[55] Gerhardt Wiebe, "Merchandising Commodities and Citizenship on Television," *Public Opinion Quarterly,* Winter 1951–52, *15,* 679–691.

it suggests direct feasible action based on salient motives. When the announcer suggests, "You can save your wife from dish-pan hands if you will step into your local dealer's and buy her an Automatic Dish Washer," there are no changes of attitudes (except possibly toward money) involved. A whole range of established attitudes can be mobilized in support of this action: love of one's wife, love of gadgets, desire to prove one's adequacy as a provider, the husband's own abhorence of washing dishes, etc. The appropriate social machinery is readily available — on your own street corner. Let the same sponsor present a program on juvenile delinquency and the picture is much different: 1) He has to impress his audience with the importance of the problem — probably not too difficult. 2) He asks them to invent and create the appropriate social mechanisms, which is virtually impossible. In sum, noticeable results from mass communications have been conspicuous in inverse relationship to the amount of attitude change and social innovation involved. Short-run evidence of *attitude* change under field conditions is rare.

One of the major implications of the relatively greater success of the mass media in producing changes of behavior (as contrasted to changes of attitude) has gone unmentioned by the students of mass communications. A considerable body of common sense observation, clinical data, and, more recently, experimental findings indicates that in many instances attitude change follows after behavioral change. Such common phrases as "rationalization," "sour grapes," etc., are adequate labels for the process at work.

A hypothetical example might be the following: A few years ago the Ford Motor Company featured "safety" in its automobile promotion. At this time a given man buys a Ford for a combination of reasons that are irrelevant to the issue of safety. He may, in fact, have heard that Ford dealers were giving bigger trade-ins because they were unable to sell cars as a result of the manufacturer's heavy reliance on the promotional issue of "safety." Once he has bought a Ford, primarily, let us say, because it is cheap, one of his buddies chides him: "You didn't fall for all that bull about safety, did you?" If he replies defensively, as he probably will, there is a good chance that he will end up as an articulate, convinced champion of safety devices in automobile design.

Research under the direction of Leon Festinger has shown that precisely this sort of attitude change follows after a commitment to action.[56] Confirmed cigarette smokers are more likely to deny that any relationship has been established between cigarette smoking and lung cancer. Recent car buyers read advertisements which confirm them in the wisdom of their decisions, etc. Kelman, working independently of Fes-

[56] Cf. Leon Festinger, *A Theory of Cognitive Dissonance* (Evanston, Ill: Row, Peterson, 1957).

tinger, has affected children's attitude toward comic books by "bribing" them to make statements in favor of one or another type of comic. Kelman's findings make it possible to specify conditions under which a private change of opinion will and will not accompany the coerced change of public position.[57]

Our suspicion is that one of the major ways in which mass media influence public attitudes is via the second-order effect of having first elicited behavior based on existing attitudes. Public attitudes, according to this model, change by a process of drift: behavior is elicited which places some (but not much) strain on existing attitudes; attitudes are accommodated to the behavior; a new bit of behavior produces another small accommodation; etc. If this suspicion is correct, then it makes sense that the media may have considerable long-range effects which would not be detected by the customary sort of investigation.

In summary, the following can be said about the nonrecreational, noncultural effects of the mass media:

1. Technically, there is little difficulty in conveying factual information. This is the simplest of effects to achieve and is conditioned only by two provisos:

a) The audience's attention must be attracted — a major problem.

b) The subject matter is not so challenging as to be perceived in a distorted fashion by any large segment of the audience — an infrequent problem, but one which may occasionally assume major importance.

2. Where appropriate attitudes and motives exist, it is not ordinarily too difficult to influence behavior, providing the message is in the form of "information" relevant to these attitudes and motives. The provisions which hold for the transmission of information hold, naturally, for the influencing of behavior; i.e., there must be attention given to the communication, and the information must be perceived without appreciable distortion.

3. Attitudes are more difficult to influence. It is true that in many instances it is difficult to draw the line between a change of behavior and a change of attitude. Despite this difficulty, we may still say that evidence for short-run attitude changes via the mass media is sparse. Changes of fundamental values and attitudes, insofar as they are conditioned by the mass media, take place gradually, and may be a result of changes of behavior. Or, they may be the result of changing conditions in the "real world" which are communicated via the mass media as "information." Thus, apropos this final point, if Americans have become more internationalist in the postwar world, this may be viewed more as a function of an actual change in the world situation than of the effects of the mass media, even though the latter did play a role in the

[57] Herbert Kelman, "Attitude Change as a Function of Response Restriction," *Human Relations*, August 1953, *6*, 185–214.

interpretation of these events. Since the development of internationalist attitudes may be regarded as a long-range effect, we might take an example of the Japanese attack on Pearl Harbor as an instance of short-range effect. Certainly this attack influenced American attitudes toward Japan, but the role of the newspapers in this instance was one of transmitting the fact of the attack. We find it difficult to conclude that it is meaningful in such instances to speak of "the impact of the mass media," except in the technical sense of distributing information widely and rapidly.

A final note on the mass media as disseminators of information: Some case studies have indicated that there are variations in the circumstances under which the mass media play a dominant role in the diffusion of news.[58] News of Roosevelt's death seems to have spread predominantly by interpersonal communications (though certainly conveyed initially via the mass media). However, news of Senator Taft's death and news concerning a local event studied by Leo Bogart was received by most persons directly via the mass media. While the reasons for these differences are by no means firmly established, Larsen and Hill offer the very plausible suggestion that the relative role of the mass media and of interpersonal communication in the diffusion of news is a function of two factors: the time of day in which the event occurs, and the interest value of the event.

The question of the time of day at which a news event is released is, of itself, of interest since it raises the possibility that news released at different times may flow over different channels. However, of more central importance for understanding the role of the mass media *vis-à-vis* informal communications is the inherent interest of the event. Informal, interpersonal communications have to be largely "self-starting," i.e., there has to be a reasonably strong motive for information being passed on. On the other hand, acquisition of information from the mass media may, in some instances, be largely "accidental." That is to say, a given individual may be exposed to incidental information while attending to the mass media for other reasons. The same process may happen also in interpersonal communications, but one is not likely to pass such information on. Informal interpersonal communications can reach a large number of people only if the information is passed on, and this will happen only if there is widespread interest in the event *and* in its transmission.

Unquestionably the mass media play a primary role in the dissemination of news in our society. The mass media must certainly ac-

---

[58] Cf. Otto N. Larsen and Richard J. Hill, "Mass Media and Interpersonal Communication in the Diffusion of a News Event," *The American Sociological Review,* August 1954, *19, 426–33,* and Leo Bogart, "The Spread of News on a Local Event: A Case History," *Public Opinion Quarterly,* Winter, 1950–51, *14,* 769–772.

count for the major portion of the total flow of information in our society. We only intend to say, however, that the distinctive impact of
the mass media *per se* may well be inverse to the importance to the community of the information being transmitted.[59]

The Effects of TV

In the preceding pages we have discussed the short-range effects of
mass communications, even though asserting from time to time that their
major effects were probably long-run. Communications effects are most
reliably studied in the laboratory over a short period of time; but the
most relevant effects are those which take place in society over a long
period of time. Almost all socially important assertions about the effects
of mass media refer to their long-range impact. Yet long-range effects
are virtually impossible to study systematically, since each of the criteria
by which we might judge the effects of the mass media is affected by a
wide range of additional phenomena. Furthermore, assessment of the
effects of the mass media is hampered by the fact that we have little in
the way of comparable measures of the state of affairs before the introduction of the mass media.

For the latter reason there are some unique advantages in taking a
separate look at the newest of the media, TV. Television came onto the
American scene when research procedures were well developed. It is currently the medium which attracts the most critical attention. Finally, the
available research literature has been conveniently, thoroughly, and intelligently summarized in two sources: Thomas Coffin, Manager of Research for N.B.C., has produced a short summary of research findings
up to the middle of 1955.[60] Leo Bogart has presented an exhaustive
review of findings up to the middle of 1956 in his book, *The Age of
Television*.[61] While both writers are associated with "the industry" —
Coffin with N.B.C. and Bogart with the advertising agency of McCann
Erickson — neither author can be accused of trying to whitewash "the
medium." The reader can satisfy himself readily on this point by reference to the two works.

TV has had a sudden and drastic impact on the American consumption of time and money. The number of television sets owned by Americans jumped from 10,000 in 1946 to 3,000,000 in 1950, and then to
more than 35,000,000 in 1956. The expenditure of money on electricity
for the operation of TV sets alone is estimated at $½ billion *per annum*.[62]

---

[59] For somewhat different reasons, word-of-mouth plays a special role in transmission of *important* information in a totalitarian society. Cf. Bauer and Gleicher,
op. cit., pp. 297–310.

[60] Thomas E. Coffin, "Television's Impact on Society," *"The American
Psychologist*, 1955, *10*, 630–641.

[61] Leo Bogart, *The Age of Television* (New York: Frederick Ungar, 1956).

[62] Estimate presented by Professor Sidney Alexander to an MIT Seminar,
1957.

Consumption of time is equally impressive. It is generally estimated that each of the more than 35,000,000 sets is turned on on an average of more than 5 hours a day.

The evidence is, in general, that viewing time does not decrease after the set has been in the house a number of years. It is rather difficult, however, to assess the meaning of this evidence at the present time. Program offerings, particularly during the daytime hours, have increased in recent years and this factor may have offset a "natural tendency" toward less viewing after "the novelty has worn off." Furthermore, recent research indicates that during daytime hours a large proportion of housewives may leave the set turned on even though they are not in the same room with it. In some instances the set is obviously on for the benefit of children in the family. However, many wives seem to leave the set turned on at times when no one is viewing it. Furthermore, there is an increasing tendency for viewers to do other things (eat, iron, mend, etc.) while watching TV. This was true of between 20 per cent and 34 per cent of women viewers studied in Columbus, Ohio, in 1955.[63] All in all, the amount of time spent viewing television remains roughly constant during the first four or five years the set is in the house. However, as some of the above considerations indicate, it is not possible to say at the present whether or not TV maintains its "psychological pull" and commands as much effective attention. We know of no universally agreed upon criterion by which to judge an apparently developing tendency for viewers to do other things simultaneously while viewing TV. The reader will have to pass his own judgment on the implications and desirability of this trend. Our own cynical prediction is that it will be regarded as "a good thing" by those generally well disposed toward TV, and as "a bad thing" by those ill disposed.

Where does the time come from? Mainly from radio listening. Between 1948 and 1955 the average hours of radio listening in homes possessing a radio dropped from 4.4 down to 2.4. In homes with TV sets, radio listening was even lower (1.9 hours).[64] The challenge of TV has forced radio into a new role. On the one hand, disc jockey shows have increased. But to offset this, there has also been a trend toward more extensive news coverage, and service of such specialized groups as night time workers, automobile commuters, foreign language groups, professional and hobby groups, etc. In brief, radio has become, in general, less of a "mass" medium.

The best trend studies of the effects of TV are those conducted by the firm of Cunningham and Walsh in "Videotown" (New Brunswick, N.J.). The Videotown studies (as did other data) showed that TV had

---

[63] Study conducted by Joseph M. Ripley, reported in Bogart: *The Age of Television, op. cit.,* 103–104.

[64] Cf. Bogart, *The Age of Television, op. cit.,* p. 107 (Nielsen ratings).

a drastic early effect on movie-going. However, since 1953, each yearly study has shown an increase in movie-going. In 1955, there was a two-thirds increase over the proportion of persons who in 1954 had reported going to the movies on an average weekday evening. This return to the movies has occurred without any decrease in TV viewing.[65] As a matter of fact, the "Videotown" studies indicate that the diversion of time away from other leisure activities is characteristic of only the early years of TV. Viewers in New Brunswick appear to have resumed most of their other leisure activities without decreases in TV viewing, suggesting either more careful budgeting of their time, and/or a simultaneous participation in several activities, such as is reported above.

Attendance at some sports events has been decreased by televising. Attendance and participation in minor sports, e.g., basketball and bowling, may be stimulated. In general, TV seems to compete more with spectator activities, and relatively little with active participation.[66]

TV interferes with reading. This is demonstrated in a wide variety of studies. Magazine reading is affected most, book reading next most, with newspaper reading very little affected. However, during the TV era, there has also been a widespread increase in the publishing of paperback books. Clearly the picture is complicated. The full range of data leaves little doubt but that TV viewing initially displaces a good deal of magazine and book reading. The "amount" of reading which is affected varies, and some of the criteria used in various studies are noncomparable; however, a drop of 20 per cent in the total volume read, or amount of time devoted to reading, is a fairly representative figure.

While the data are not conclusive, Bogart's analysis suggests that it is mainly recreational reading of a lower cultural level which is replaced by TV.

Obviously, TV has not been the only factor influencing magazine circulation in the postwar period. Nevertheless, the following comments of Bogart are relevant:

> High-brow magazines more than doubled their circulation since the war. In fact, the higher the educational level, the greater the growth. The great mass of general circulation of middle-brow magazines grew by about half. Magazines appealing to the *least* educated element stayed at about the same circulation level. Non-ABC magazines, many of which are at the lower levels of taste, dropped a fourth of their circulation, and comic books are struggling to hold their own. At least a partial explanation for this development is that television presents a greater distraction for the person of average or below-average education than for the better-schooled, who are also less apt to be repelled by the printed word.[67]

[65] *Ibid.*, p. 160, based on Cunningham and Walsh "Videotown" studies.

[66] Coffin, *op. cit.*, p. 635, based mainly on the work of Riley, Cantwell, and Ruttinger.

[67] Bogart, *The Age of Television, op. cit.*, 140.

In a similar vein, the gross income of rental libraries has dropped drastically, while the publication of *non*-fictional book titles has grown at twice the rate of growth of fiction.

Even if we discount a variety of findings which suggest that TV viewers resume of their reading after a few years,[68] we must take very seriously the possibility that TV has effected no substantial reduction in *serious* reading. Serious reading has, in fact, increased during the TV era. It might have increased even more in the absence of TV. But, on the other hand, there are a considerable number of instances of librarians who report that TV has stimulated book-reading. Studies of library usage indicate that book-borrowing is adversely affected mainly in the first year of TV viewing. All in all, television may be competitive primarily with recreational reading which is as low in its cultural level as comparable TV fare. The available data does not permit a clear-cut answer.[69]

What about television and children?[70] Many studies have been made of the number of hours spent viewing. While they are not en-

---

[68] "In their continuing studies of 'Videotown,'" Cunningham and Walsh's researchers reported a 53% drop in the number of adults reading a magazine during their first year with television. However, in 1953 magazine reading was 5% higher than in television's first year, and it jumped by another 70% in 1954." (*ibid.*, pp. 136–137.) These figures would indicate a strong *increase* in reading by the end of 1954. Conservatively, however, we would prefer to interpret them as indicating that the original loss had been offset.

[69] By this point the reader may be a trifle curious as to why some of these questions can not be answered more definitively. Part of the problem lies in the noncomparability of many findings. Further, many studies done with small and poorly selected samples produce contradictory results. Even under the best of circumstances there are difficulties in the interpretation to be put on perfectly good data. Consider the following complications: contrary to popular stereotype, it was generally the better educated people who bought TV first—because they could afford it; better educated people also read more, but because of their other values they are less likely to be "TV addicts." Additionally, cutting across all these considerations, most people who are highly exposed to one mass medium tend to be highly exposed to all others. Even if all such factors are held constant, the habits of people who have recently bought a TV set can be compared to the habits of TV habitues only with the greatest of caution. If the old timers view as many programs as the newcomers, this may reflect only the fact that the newcomers were opposed to TV in the first place and still have not become completely converted.

Many studies (particularly trend studies such as "Videotown") take care of such problems. In other instances, a careful analyst such as Coffin or Bogart can compensate for the difficulties by the use of the wide range of studies. In any event, generalizations are less easy to arrive at than one might hope.

[70] While here, as elsewhere in this essay, we have resisted the temptation to update our position, the reader should be appraised of two recent publications on this subject. 1) Lotte Bailyn, "Mass Media and Children: A Study of Exposure Habits and Cognitive Effects," *Psychological Monographs, General and Applied*, 1959, *73*, No. 2. 2) Hilde T. Himmelweit, A. N. Oppenheim, Pamela Vance, *Television and the Child*, Oxford: Oxford University Press, 1958.

tirely in agreement as to precise number of hours spent viewing, all indicate that the average school child spends from two to four hours a day looking at TV. (Parents, incidentally, do not seem to "view this with alarm.") Most studies indicate that parents regard TV as all-in-all good — keeping children at home and out of trouble, "educating" them, reducing friction within the family, etc. The majority of parents do not think that their children spend too much time viewing TV.

A number of studies have been made of the relationship of TV viewing and children's school performance and/or intelligence. In general, no relationship has been found. A few studies have found a moderate negative relationship between length of time spent with TV and grade performance or I.Q.; or a positive relationship between parental control over TV viewing and performance criteria. Certainly there is no evidence that TV has had any marked deleterious effect on any appreciable group of children. Such minor relationships as have been found may be merely the reflection of the values of parents of higher socioeconomic status. Thus, higher-status parents would be more likely to supervise their children's viewing of TV, and would also be likely to have brighter and more highly motivated offspring.

What happens to the manners and the morals of the youth as a result of TV? It is argued on the one hand that children learn violence by viewing it on the TV screen. It might be equally argued (using a rationale that the critics invoke in other contexts) that aggression is reduced by the catharsis of vicarious experience. The evidence — or rather the assertions of many people blessed with firm opinions — is quite well summarized by Bogart.[71]

In commenting on the testimony which was given before the Kefauver hearings on juvenile delinquency and its relationship to TV, Bogart says:

> Virtually all of the expert testimony submitted to the subcommittee, on both sides of this controversial subject, was based on professional judgment rather than on actual research evidence.[72]

We have commented before that all available evidence shows that in the vast majority of instances, communications have a differential impact. Unquestionably there have been children in whom disturbance and violence were precipitated by viewing TV. Against this we have evidence from mental hospitals that indicate that TV can also be soothing and diverting to agitated patients. Presumably TV has both "good" and "bad" effects. The citation of individual examples or the offering of plausible arguments is irrelevant to the only question of importance: i.e., the relative distribution of "good" and "bad" effects. The fact is that there is no single piece of solid data which can be accepted as in-

---

[71] Bogart, *The Age of Television, op. cit.*, p. 258 ff.

[72] *Ibid.*, p. 269.

dicating that TV has either increased or decreased immorality or delinquency among the young *or* the old.[73]

On the other hand, TV advertising appears to be effective. While there are some difficulties in assessing the value of TV as a merchandising agency, it seems demonstrated and accepted that this medium is an economically efficient device for advertising and selling wares.

Almost all authorities agree that TV does and will play an important role in American politics. Unfortunately, Bogart's book was written before the 1956 presidential campaign. While no one presently questions the value of TV in political campaigning, it seems that the pre-1956 views had overestimated the importance of this new medium. However, it will continue in all probability to make the appearance and manner of candidates matters of increasing importance in successive elections. Probably it will also move political in-fighting off the convention floor and more truly into the smoke-filled rooms where the TV camera can not reach.

What firm data do we have concerning the impact of TV? The picture is pretty much like that for other media. We are certain that people spend time and money on TV. By and large it competes with other forms of both recreation and intellectual activity. On this point, however, the data is inconclusive since there is evidence that many of these activities are resumed as people learn to budget their time more carefully, or to combine their activities. In general, it should be remembered, TV competes with *comparable* activities. For example, it is more

---

[73] It is impossible not to digress briefly on the subject of juvenile delinquency. Central to the question of the impact of TV is the casual assumption that there has been an increase in juvenile crime. Anyone with a moderately good memory and even a slight sense of humor ought to have some skepticism about the assertion that the "young are going to hell in a handbasket." Despite the assertions of J. Edgar Hoover and other guardians of the hearth, it is highly probable that juvenile misbehavior has decreased throughout the country. (This is not to rule out specific increases in some localities.) For an appreciation of the irresponsible use of statistics which lies behind the common belief that juvenile and other crime has increased, we refer the reader to Daniel Bell's "What Crime Wave?" *Fortune,* January 1955, *51,* 96 ff. As for J. Edgar Hoover's recent reports of the yearly increases in juvenile crime, we would only call attention to the fact that these increases are based upon a reporting system which Mr. Hoover is seeking constantly to improve. The average person is not aware of the immense gaps there are in the machinery for reporting crime, especially juvenile crime, etc. Every success Mr. Hoover enjoys in improving the reporting system will produce an apparent increase in crime.

Since we expect that these statements of ours may be greeted with skepticism, we would like in this one instance to violate our sense of restraint on not updating our sources. On April 22, 1959, *The Christian Science Monitor* reported on a new crime reporting system installed by the Boston police department (p. 9). The reason given for this new development was as follows: "The F.B.I. . . . threatened to drop Boston from its uniform crime-reporting list, charging that the city's figures were 'understated and inaccurate.' "

likely to displace attendance at sports events than to displace participation in sports. There is quite strong evidence that TV viewing is (for broad groups of children taken as a whole) unrelated to school performance. There is *no* respectable evidence either pro or con for the relationship of TV to violence and juvenile delinquency. As concerns the general level of popular culture and taste, we shall point out below that the TV era has also been an era of spreading interest in "the higher arts." The most avid partisan of television will not credit this entirely to the new medium. However, we hope also to convince the more fearful critics that the worst they anticipate has not yet happened.

IV. Alleged Effects Of Mass Media

Deterioration of Values and Taste:[74]

IMPACT UPON POPULAR TASTE

Since the largest part of our radio, movies, magazines, and a considerable part of our books and newspapers are devoted to "entertainment," this clearly requires us to consider the impact of the mass media upon popular taste.

Were we to ask the average American with some pretension to literary or esthetic cultivation if mass communications have had any effect upon popular taste, he would doubtlessly answer with a resounding affirmative. And more, citing abundant instances, he would insist that esthetic and intellectual taste have been depraved by the flow of trivial formula products from printing presses, radio stations and movie studios. The columns of criticism abound with these complaints.

In one sense, this requires no further discussion. There can be no doubt that the women who are daily entranced for three or four hours by some 12 consecutive "soap operas," all cut to the same dismal pattern, exhibit an appalling lack of esthetic judgment. Nor is this impression altered by the contents of pulp and slick magazines, or by the depressing abundance of formula motion pictures replete with hero, heroine, and villain moving through a contrived atmosphere of sex, sin, and success.

Yet unless we locate these patterns in historical and sociological terms, we may find ourselves confusedly engaged in condemning without understanding, in criticism which is sound but largely irrelevant. What is the historical status of this notoriously low level of popular taste? Is it the poor remains of standards which were once significantly higher, a relatively new birth in the world of values, largely unrelated to the higher standards from which it has allegedly fallen, or a poor substitute blocking the way to the development of superior standards and the expression of high esthetic purpose?

If esthetic tastes are to be considered in their social setting, we must recognize that the effective audience for the arts has become historically transformed. Some centuries back, this audience was largely confined to a selected aristocratic elite. Relatively few were literate. And very few possessed the means to buy books, attend theatres, and travel to the urban centers of the arts. Not more than

---

[74] The problem of assessing the alleged deterioration of values and cultural taste has been dealt with by a number of authors in a vein similar to our own. Because of its excellence and compactness, we cite *in toto* the following passage from Paul Lazarsfeld and Robert K. Merton, "Mass Communication, Popular Taste, and Organized Social Action," in Bernard Rosenberg and David Manning White, editors, *Mass Culture,* Glencoe, Ill.: The Free Press, 1957, 466–468.

a slight fraction, possibly not more than 1 or 2 per cent, of the population composed the effective audience for the arts. These happy few cultivated their esthetic tastes, and their selective demand left its mark in the form of relatively high artistic standards.

With the widesweeping spread of popular education and with the emergence of the new technologies of mass communication, there developed as enormously enlarged market for the arts. Some forms of music, drama, and literature now reach virtually everyone in our society. This is why, of course, we speak of *mass* media and of *mass* art. And the great audiences for the mass media, although in the main literate, are not highly cultivated. About half the population, in fact, has halted their formal education upon leaving grammar school.

With the rise of popular education, there has occurred a seeming decline of popular taste. Large numbers of people have acquired what might be termed "formal literacy," that is to say, a capacity to read, to grasp crude and superficial meanings, and a correlative incapacity for full understanding of what they read. There has developed, in short, a marked gap between literacy and comprehension. People read more but understand less. More people read but proportionately fewer critically assimilate what they read.

Our formulation of the problem should now be plain. It is misleading to speak simply of the decline of esthetic tastes. Mass audiences probably include a larger number of persons with cultivated esthetic standards, but these are swallowed up by the large masses who constitute the new and untutored audience for the arts. Whereas yesterday the elite constituted virtually the whole of the audience, they are today a minute fraction of the whole. In consequence, the average level of esthetic standards and tastes of audiences has been depressed, although the tastes of some sectors of the population have undoubtedly been raised and the total number of people exposed to communication contents has been vastly increased.

But this analysis does not directly answer the question of the effects of the mass media upon public taste, a question which is as complex as it is unexplored. The answer can come only from disciplined research. One would want to know, for example, whether mass media have robbed the intellectual and artistic elite of the art forms which might otherwise have been accessible to them. And this involves inquiry into the pressure exerted by the mass audience upon creative individuals to cater to mass tastes. Literary hacks have existed in every age. But it would be important to learn if the electrification of the arts supplies power for a significantly greater proportion of dim literary lights. And, above all, it would be essential to determine if mass media and mass tastes are necessarily linked in a vicious circle of deteriorating standards or if appropriate action on the part of the directors of mass media could initiate a virtuous circle of cumulatively improving tastes among their audiences. More concretely, are the operators of commercialized mass media caught up in a situation in which they cannot, whatever their private preferences, radically raise the esthetic standards of their products?

In passsing, it should be noted that much remains to be learned concerning standards appropriate for mass art. It is possible that standards for art forms produced by a small band of creative talents for a small and selective audience are not applicable to art forms produced by a gigantic industry for the population at large. The beginnings of investigation on this problem are sufficiently suggestive to warrant further study.

Sporadic and consequently inconclusive experiments in the raising of standards have met with profound resistance from mass audiences. On occasion, radio stations and networks have attempted to supplant a soap opera with a program of art, music, or formula comedy skits with discussions of public issues. In general, the people supposed to benefit by this reformation of program have simply refused to be benefited. They cease listening. The audience dwindles. Researches have shown, for example, that, radio programs of art music tend to preserve rather than to create interest in such music and that newly emerging interests are typically superficial. Most listeners to these programs have previously acquired an interest in art music; the few whose interest is initiated by the programs are caught up by melodic compositions and come to think of art music exclusively in terms of Tchaikowsky or Rimski-Korsakov or Dvorak.

. . . At present we know conspicuously little about the methods of improving esthetic tastes and we know that some of the suggested methods are ineffectual. We have a rich knowledge of failure. Should this discussion be reopened in 1976, we may perhaps report with equal confidence our knowledge of positive achievements.

So far we have taken as our main point of departure the actual evidence of existing research and have asked ourselves what effects of the mass media may be inferred from the available evidence. Now we would like to reverse the procedure and take a more direct look at some of the additional effects which the mass media are alleged to have and ask what sort of data would be required to assess these effects. In general, it would be our contention that such evidence is absent or ambiguous.

The most important effect which has been attributed to the mass media is that they bring about the long-range deterioration of moral values and cultural taste. It is rather difficult to do anything other than grant full credence to this assertion without appearing to defend bad taste and juvenile delinquency. Let us therefore make explicit the issue as we see it: *Statements concerning deterioration of taste and values can have meaning only if they are statements of comparison and/or statements of trend.* The issue is not that the cultural level of the products of the mass media and the cultural taste of its patrons is low by some absolute standard. The issue is that the level of culture and taste is *lower* than it was in the past in our own society, or that it is *lower* than in some reasonably defined sample of societies not possessing mass communications. If this is not the position of the critics, then they are merely saying that the present level of the arts falls short of some ideal mark and with this, there can be no quarrel even though we might not all agree exactly on the ideal criteria.

The following is a reasonably representative statement of the effects of mass culture and mass communications in bringing about the deterioration of the arts.

The decline of the individual in the mechanized working processes of modern civilization brings about the emergence of mass culture, which replaces folk culture or "high" art. A product of popular culture has none of the features of genuine art, but in all its media popular culture proves to have its own genuine characteristics: standardization, stereotypy, conservatism, mendacity, manipulated consumer goods.[75]

---

[75] Leo Lowenthal, "Historical Perspectives of Popular Culture," reprinted in Rosenberg and White, editors, *op. cit.*, p. 55.

To cope with this position in all its ramifications is to find one's self in the same position as Brer Rabbit in his historic fight with the Tar Baby. It is virtually impossible to disengage one's self since each successive issue, when dealt with, presents one or more others. For this reason we shall make every effort not to become involved gratuitously in the many inviting elements of controversy which this position presents. Stripping the issue to its essentials, if the theorists of mass society are correct, some combination of the following three events should take place:

(1) The level of artistic production should deteriorate;

(2) The availability of high cultural products should lessen; and

(3) The general level of taste should deteriorate.

In checking these propositions, certain rules of the game must be observed.

1. The comparison must be made with some society that actually exists or existed, and not with an idealized mosaic made up of choice features of a wide range of societies. We have yet to see this rule adhered to.

2. Comparable products shall be compared. For example, if our society shall be compared with that of Elizabethan England, the products selected should not be American comic books and Shakespeare's poetry. We must insist on the inclusion of certain Elizabethan pamphlets with which one of us once spent a delightful spring in the Newbury Library in Chicago. Also, as David Manning White suggests, bear-baiting should be accorded its proper place in Elizabethan culture.[76] A reasonable sample of cultural products for each era must be included in the comparison.

3. The producer, the sponsor, and the consumer of artistic products shall not be confused with each other. This is a particularly important consideration in assessing the range of the populace for whom a given cultural product has meaning. Who attended Shakespeare's plays, and how many peasants in the vicinity of Salzburg listened to Mozart's music?

4. Comparable elements of the society shall be compared. The viewer of Howdy Doody should not be compared with the Roman noble enjoying the beauty of Virgil's poetry, but with the ordinary Roman enjoying the circus.

5. There must be some consensus on artistic canons to be invoked; or, at the very least, both parties must exercise self-discipline in employing the terms "genuine" and "spurious" as convenient devices for disposing of embarrassing data.

Obviously the rules of the game which we would introduce take all

---

[76] Cf. David Manning White, "Mass Culture in America; Another Point of View," in Rosenberg and White, editors, *op. cit.* p. 14.

the fun out of the enterprise since the types of data which would be required are unattainable for any society other than our own and are not always available for ours. We can obviously never hope to make a decent comparison of the cultural level of our society with a prototypic, median, modal, or average folk society, nor with the "high culture" of any previous Western society. Our best hope is to look for trends within our own society within our own time. Are things getting better or worse?

(a) *The level of artistic production:* This is a point on which one should probably best plead *nolo contendere.* Artistic creation is difficult for contemporaries to assess. Periods in which creativity flourish are only partially related to other aspects of the society. A particularly high state of the arts at a given time would be a dubious basis for predicting the future of the arts within a given culture (except that they might be expected to become decadent within the genre being practiced). On the other hand, particularly low periods are, by force of circumstance, usually followed by improvement.

Within Western society, the several national cultures have each had "high" and "low" points of artistic creativity. Scholars generally agree that the rise, if not the fall, of artistic creativity is related to other historical developments. However, there is no instance, to our knowledge, of any country which has experienced a marked period of economic growth without some accompanying marked artistic activity unless it be the U.S.S.R. Even Victorian England, deficient in so many areas of taste, was blessed with major poets and novelists. On the other hand, many of the major national cultures have had distinctive artistic strengths and weaknesses which have characterized them throughout historical periods of marked change. To cite England once more, the English have had a distinguished literature through many centuries while remaining relatively undistinguished in music and the graphic arts. Yet the England of today is many epochs removed from the England of Boewulf. Apart from the inherent difficulty of assessing contemporary artistic production, the establishment of causal connections between art and other aspects of society is itself a sticky business.

The critics of popular culture argue that potentially creative talent is bought off to produce inferior products. This argument has two prongs: (1) The artist's time is diverted. (2) His talent is perverted and he can no longer produce "high art." But, the opposition will answer, the mass media support a vastly larger number of artists than were able to live off their art in the past. These artists have the leisure in which to pursue their highest instincts. Furthermore, the best of them are able to experiment within their medium and do not pervert their talents. Such arguments can proceed in an endless circle of "yes, buts," but we know of no data which would provide a definitive answer to the question of whether or not mass communications have effected a lowering of the standard of artistic creativity in this country in the past few decades.

The most persuasive argument that is offered by the critics of the mass media is that of Clement Greenberg.[77] Greenberg contends that popular taste demands the production of "kitsch" — adulterated, pseudo-high culture products which are dangerously close to true art. Most of the theorists of mass society believe that this "kitsch" will strangle "true art." It is equally plausible, of course (and there is illustrative evidence for the *existence* of the process), that it may serve as a means of introducing the great masses of the public to "true art," and thereby produce unprecedented support for high culture. The defenders of the mass media would point, at this juncture of the argument, to the successful production on TV of Shakesperian and classical Greek plays, to the original works of Menotti, etc. Again, the key question is a quantitative one: which process is stronger? And again, these are precisely the data which are lacking.

(b) *The absolute availability of high cultural products:* The operational criterion of whether or not there has been a change in the availability of high cultural products to persons interested in them should be the following: Has a given person, living in a given city, equal access to the same quantity and quality of art as he would have had at any time in the past *in that same city?* On the average, the answer to this question must be "yes." It would be rather difficult to argue that the *absolute* availability of high cultural products had declined in American society during the past several decades. It might well be argued that their *relative availability* had declined because of the enormous growth of popular culture. It might be further argued that this relative growth of popular culture spelled the doom of high culture; that Gresham's law operates in the cultural as well as the monetary sphere. This argument demands that we look at what has happened to popular taste during this period.

(c) *Trends in popular taste:* Despite fears that mass communications would produce a marked lowering of popular taste, American society of the past decade or so has been experiencing what would be called a "cultural revival" if one were to look at the data with no preconceptions of the type of society we have. While some writers have bewailed the decline in artistic taste of the American public, one must also note that other writers of equal competence have rendered an opposite verdict. We might, for example, cite a statement of the pianist Artur Rubenstein.

> In the past 25 years this country has made more advances than some places in Europe have made in 250 years. Small towns throughout America are more receptive to fine music than old cities in France like Lyon, Marseilles and Bordeaux.[78]

[77] Clement Greenberg, "Avant-Garde and Kitsch," in Rosenberg and White, editors, *op. cit.*, pp. 98–111.
[78] Quoted in *Time*, February 18, 1957, *69*, p. 37.

The evidence for such an assertion has been presented from time to time by a considerable number of writers. For the sake of convenience we will limit ourselves to a few illustrative statistics.[79]

Some of the more startling data are these:

There are 200 symphony orchestras in this country. This is 30 per cent more than 15 years ago and 10 times the number we had in the early 1920s. In the smaller cities many of the symphony orchestras are composed of semi-amateurs. In addition to the 200 symphony orchestras, about 1000 community orchestras have been started in the past 15 years. "Where," writes White, "1916 saw the renowned Diaghilev ballet with Nijinsky come to America and cost its backers about $400,000, by 1954 the Sadler Wells Company of London arrived here and in 20 weeks of a national tour earned more than $2,500,000."[80]

Perhaps baseball *is* our national sport but White points out that in 1955, 35,000,000 persons paid to attend classical music events as against 15,000,000 who attended baseball games. Furthermore, the number attending classical music events was double the comparable figure for 1940. In 1953, Americans spent "for participating arts more than four times as much as was spent on spectator sports."[81]

The "hi-fi" craze is not limited to the listening of esoteric test records. It has been paralleled by a vast increase in buying classical records. In 1934, sales of classical records amounted to about $75,000 a year. Today it exceeds $75,000,000!

We reported previously that TV viewing interferes with reading. But this interference is a relative phenomenon vastly offset by the secular trend toward increased book buying and reading. The paperback publishing business has reached full growth during precisely the period in which TV was coming into its own; however, we know of no single statistic which summarizes the cultural level of the paperbacks. Despite the brief popularity of Mickey Spillane and the proliferation of provocative cover illustrations on prosaic volumes, paperbacks have also produced the unprecedented distribution of books of unquestionably high merit in editions of hundreds of thousands.

Such illustrative data reflect the fact that the traditional arts have prospered while the mass media have been in their heyday.

It may be that consumption of the products of popular culture has grown faster than the consumption of "high cultural products." We know of no assembled data which answer this question. Furthermore, we may

---

[79] These data come mainly from David Manning White's introductory essay in Rosenberg and White, editors, *op. cit.* pp. 13–21, from White's article in the *Saturday Review*, November 3, 1956, *39*, 11–13, and from an editorial in the *Christian Science Monitor*, May 2, 1957, p. 20, quoting a speech of Dean Robert Choate of Boston University.

[80] White, *Saturday Review ibid.*, p. 13.

[81] Dean Choate quoted in *Christian Science Monitor*, May 2, 1957, *loc. cit.*

well anticipate the argument—not entirely without merit—that these data are to some extent spurious since "listening to Bach over a phonograph with one ear closed" isn't "the same" as hearing him played by a live orchestra. And, many of these "new people" approach high art with "inadequate background" and "their experience isn't the same." The fact remains that all quantitative data available seem to point in exactly the opposite direction from that which the theorists of mass society would predict. And what is more, increasing interest in "culture" is not exclusively passive: More Americans are playing music than ever before.

Assessment

Most of the processes of which the theorists of mass society speak do seem to be at work. Some, we don't know how many, writers and actors are bought off into the popular arts. Much, perhaps even most, of the "cultural" products of the mass media are of substandard taste, providing we can agree on standards and providing we do not gloss over the fact that if judged against a comparable range of products from other eras they might not fare badly. There are structural features of the mass media which are inherently limiting on the creative artist: artificial constraints of time, the censorship of a wide range of publics, the necessity of appealing to a large mass, etc.

On the other hand, the mass media has also shown their ability to introduce people to higher art forms—good drama, good music, graphic arts, and intelligent public discussion.

In all probability the increase in cultural interest in the United States is not due primarily or even largely to the mass media but rather to a general increase of educational level, wealth, and social leisure. If the mass media have played an important role, a good portion of this may not be their directly "educational" function, but rather the presentation of life styles which the American people have striven to emulate.

Because of the intricate interrelationship of causal factors, we probably will never be able to say with confidence just what impact the mass media had on popular taste and values.

While the data introduced above indicate an increase in interest in "culture," they do not entirely rule out the possibility of some of the dire consequences which the critics of mass society predict. In all probability the novitiates to higher culture are, on the average, persons of less highly developed cultural tastes. One rather natural assumption would be that these persons, having been introducd to higher artistic experiences, will, in the course of time, acquire the "richer background" that the critic of mass society insists is necessary for "full appreciation" of high culture. The critics, however, would reply that it is more likely that these novitiates, moving in *en masse,* will capture the field of the arts and reduce high culture to *kitsch* (pseudo-high culture). As we pointed out previously, there are no data which permit us to chose between these two predictions. Our observation is that when such a choice is made, it is a function not of any evidence specific to the issue, but rather of the individual's attitude toward the future of American society and his general attitude toward the "masses."

As far as firm evidence of the effects of the mass media themselves is concerned, we cite Klapper's conclusion:

> Whether mass media as a whole raise or lower public taste cannot be definitely stated, nor can the necessary research be looked for in the next several years.[82]

The Mass Media as a Source of Escape

One of the gravest criticisms which the theorists of the "mass society" make of mass communications is that the mass media go beyond the function of providing "healthy" (a question-begging word) recreation, and create a phantom world into which people escape from reality— with resultant "mass apathy," etc. The argument, as the reader will remember, runs thus: Urban, industrial society atomizes the individual, leaves him psychically void and therefore creates a tremendous market for the narcotizing, diversional material of the mass media in which our mass man loses himself.

Since the reader may by now suspect us of having an unduly crotchety attitude toward the theory of mass society, we will offer him the opportunity of listening to another voice for a moment.

Having reviewed the literature, research and conjectural, on the recreational and/or escapist function of the mass media, Klapper concludes:

> Certain psychological and social effects of . . . escape have been observed or conjectured. These include:
> a. the provision of pure relaxation (observed), which has no social effects;
> b. the provision of compensation and prestige (observed), which may have good, bad, or no social repercussions;
> c. The possible development of social apathy (conjectured);
> d. the misuse of escapistic communications as a valid source of information (observed), which is likely to be futile for the individual and perhaps socially deleterious.[83]

His fourth point, the reference to "the misuse of escapistic communications as a valid source of information" refers to the observed fact that some listeners to radio soap operas looked to these programs for guidance in their own life situation.

It is to be noted that of all the posited functions of the recreational content of the mass media, three have been observed, and a fourth—

---

[82] Klapper, op. cit., p. 42.

[83] Ibid, p. 19.

creation of "apathy"—has been conjectured but not observed. We quote Klapper once more:

> Despite the weight and repute of those holding the opposite view, the present author is inclined to believe that the danger of social apathy re- sulting from escapistic communications has been somewhat overempha- sized. . . . there is little reason to believe that (a) plethora of escapistic communications diverts the audience from more serious communication.[84]

The second of the functions which Klapper discusses is "the pro- vision of compensation and prestige." This refers to the tendency of members of the audience to experience vicarious satisfaction from iden- tification with the heroes of the mass media. Various consequences of such identification have been postulated, and at least isolated manifesta- tions of each have been observed. Such identification may serve to chan- nel off aggression via catharsis. It may stimulate anti-social behavior by the example it furnishes. The listener or viewer may experience vicarious prestige, etc. As Klapper says, some of the effects are salutary, and some are undesirable. There is no body of data that permits us to say which effect occurs most often, or whether the summary result is pre- dominantly good or predominantly bad.

Any such inconclusive conclusion as this should not lead to com- placency about the content of the mass media. But neither should it lead to the complacent acceptance of an ingenious insight as an estab- lished fact about the impact of the media.

The Nature of Vicarious Experience and other Side Effects of Mass Communications

It is inherent in the nature of mass communications that the audi- ence learns via the mass media about events beyond its direct experience. This may be, or at least has been, regarded as either a good thing or a bad thing, or both. The immediate arguments *in favor* of this situation are too obvious to be dwelt on for any length of time; the mass media sim- ply enlarge the audience's actual or potential world of experience.

However, this experience is largely indirect and vicarious. The critic of "mass society" contends, in line with the previous argument that mass entertainment is narcotizing, that this vicarious experience becomes a substitute for "real" experience. Whether our society is undergoing any gross reduction in "real," i.e., first-hand, experiences across the board, is not known to us. However, whether or not such a reduction in "real" experiences is occurring, an increase in vicarious experiences is certainly taking place, and this fact is in itself worth looking at.

Intuitively, any psychologist senses that there is a difference in re- lating to the environment via the mediation of symbols and signs, and relating to it via direct sensory impressions. The literature on develop-

---

[84] *Ibid,* p. 12.

mental psychology indicates that the acquisition of language is a crucial stage in the development of the child's personality. The literature of semantics and psychotherapy, however, makes a very good case that the acquiring of so powerful a tool as language is by no means an unmixed blessing. To various degrees one confuses the word with the referent, and this causes both short-run problems and personality difficulties. The situation is similar to that of vicarious or mediated experience in general with, to be sure, vicarious and mediated experience having its distinctive characteristics. The over-all implications of mass communications as a source of vicarious experience are worth exploration. To date, however, we have found little in the literature with which we are acquainted to enable us to proceed beyond identifying this as an interesting problem area.

One exception can be made. Daniel Lerner's study of communications in the Middle East is based upon an interesting theory of the interrelationship of mass communications, individual personality, and social change.[85] Briefly, Lerner identifies the "empathic" individual as the person most responsive to the mass media and to social change. The capacity to "project," to imagine oneself in a situation not bound by his own sense experience, differentiates those persons who read and listen to the mass media and who are least bound to the traditional society. Such a theory is compatible with many of the features of the theory of mass society. However, whereas the "theorists of mass society" regard this relationship negatively, Lerner's position is to put a high value on this "empathic capacity." Furthermore, Lerner views the mass media society as a "participant society," i.e., one in which the populace takes an increasing part in social and political activities. This would seem to fly in the face of the "theory of mass society" which sees the populace as reduced to a state of apathy. Perhaps the two positions are reconcilable and Lerner's "participant society" is merely a transitional phase to the more developed "mass society." On the surface, however, Lerner's position seems to challenge that of the "theorists of mass society," both as to the high value he puts on capacity for "empathic" experience and his view of the "media society" as a "participant society."

For good or ill, experience via the mass media is predominantly vicarious. Looked at from the long-range point of view of the impact of the media on the population, this fact may in itself have more profound implications (which we cannot anticipate) upon the personality of future generations than the actual content of the communications conveyed by the mass media. One could speculate endlessly, plausibly, and in all directions as to what these consequences might be. Some research is in order, and this is an area to which high priority should be given.

---

[85] Daniel Lerner, *The Passing of Traditional Society; Modernizing the Middle East*, Glencoe, Illinois: The Free Press, 1958, 47–52.

Perhaps this is the point at which to deal with the allegation that the mass media produce "passivity." With certain features of the argument, as always there can be no quarrel. Watching a baseball game on TV is less active than playing baseball. Perhaps it is less active than viewing the same game from the grandstand. We do not know what degree of activity to assign to the practice of watching baseball on TV, while typing a manuscript (as one of us is doing at the moment). Without a shadow of doubt the audience or readership of mass communications is more passive in that activity than they might be if indulging in at least some other possible activities. On the other hand, they might also be sleeping, an activity which for most people in most instances is even more passive than attendance to mass communications (in most instances and for most persons). But the key question is again a quantitative one: Are American recreational habits *as a whole* becoming more passive?

What metric should be used? Ideally, the preferred unit of measurement might be the amount of time spent in participant and spectator activities. So far as we know, adequate data are not available. While studies have been made of amount of *time* spent viewing TV, listening to radio, etc., there are no studies of amount of *time* spent in playing golf, fishing, picnicking, swimming, etc. If we accept as our unit of measurement the amount of money spent on various forms of recreation then the evidence and answer is clear. Data released by the U.S. Department of Agriculture show that *over the past few decades the American people have spent an increasing proportion of money on participant as contrasted to spectator recreation,* even though these data cover the period in which American families were making large expenditures on TV.[86] In other words, the trend is in the direction precisely opposite to that predicted by theorists of mass society. The mass media may (as a portion of their effect) incline the population toward passivity, at least in the minimal sense of competing for time with other activities. However, this tendency appears to be offset decisively by other forces in American life.

The Image of Reality

Regardless of the evaluation that one puts on the vicarious nature of the experience derived from the mass media, this vicarious experience does constitute a large portion of modern man's image of the world. This, of course, is the source of a large amount of the complaint about the contents of the mass media. Most of these complaints have dealt mainly with the fanciful material of mass communications. Despite our contention that the effects of such material cannot be *assumed,* we do not think of course for a moment that it has no effect. Here, however, we would like to confine our attention to the non-fictional reporting of the mass media—what may be called "news" in the largest sense, i.e.,

---

[86] Reported in *The New York Times,* April 24, 1957, p. 30.

that material which is most likely to be looked to and accepted as the image of reality.

It stands to reason that news reporting must be selective since "complete reporting" would exceed the physical capacities of both the reporting media and their readers and audiences. Most of the limitations and defects of news reporting are matters of common knowledge; and it is generally accepted, even by practicing communicators, that the image of reality presented by the mass media diverges from the ideal norm of "what the intelligent, interested citizen ought to know." A high proportion of "news" is presented because of its human interest value, i.e., to hold an audience, rather than because of its pertinence to the understanding of the world we live in. Reporting of scientific discoveries are slanted toward "gimmicks" and the basic meaning of the discovery may be totally obscured, etc.

A fuller treatment of this general problem is well warranted, but goes beyond the limits of this essay. For this reason we will restrict ourselves to a few points which have generally not been widely commented on, but which seem to us to be important for the understanding of the role of the mass media.

The mass media make the news as well as report it. Lincoln Steffens made this point well in recounting the "making of a crime wave."[87] By reporting fully the available data on crime in a large city, he personally created the impression of a sudden upsurge in criminal activity. Whether by deliberate intent or by the inevitable decision as to what is "news," the mass media draw attention to some events and away from others. The mere fact of an event being reported tends by itself to elevate this event to a level of importance beyond that of unreported events. This is equally true of the reporting of the behavior of individuals. Lazarsfeld and Merton have referred to this as the "status conferral" function of the mass media.[88] People whose doings are reported are given the status of "important people?"

Assuming no malintent on the part of the communicator, his view of events may diverge from their "true importance." This is particularly the case when communicators as a group overestimate public interest in an issue, and by their concentration on it create the impression of a lively public issue. If we may accept Stouffer's findings on the lack of public interest in communism,[89] the press and other media were guilty of this

[87] Lincoln Steffens, *Autobiography of Lincoln Steffens,* New York: Harcourt, Brace and Company, 1931, Chapter 14, "I Make a Crime Wave."

[88] Paul F. Lazarsfeld and Robert K. Merton, "Mass Communication, Popular Taste, and Organized Social Action," reprinted in Guy S. Swanson, Theodore M. Newcomb, and Eugene L. Hartley, *Readings in Social Psychology,* (2nd ed.), New York: Henry Holt and Co., 1952.

[89] Cf. Samuel Stouffer, *Communism, Conformity, and Civil Liberties,* New York: Doubleday and Company, 1955, Chapter III, "Is There a National Anxiety Neurosis?"

error with respect to Senator McCarthy's escapades.

To some extent, the very mode of reporting tends inevitably to over-dramatize most events. On this point, at least, we have, happily, some data. Lang and Lang found that on-the-spot viewers of a MacArthur Day celebration in Chicago were less impressed by the enthusiasm of the crowds than were TV viewers of the event.[90] The reader can readily see why this is in most cases inevitable. A "world-wide news round-up" of reactions to a given event gives even the most sophisticated reader, listener, or viewer the impression of world-wide interest in the event. In fact, a relatively few people in any one country may actually care about it, even though it may be of crucial importance to the people of the country who are the targets of the communication.

In addition to giving artificial importance to some events, and creating the impression of exaggerated public involvement in most that are reported, the American media (at least) seem to give an appearance of discontinuity to the historical processes which are reported. The concept of "news" which dominates our reporting media dictates that an event is "news" only if it is discontinuous with preceding events *and* if it is relatively recent in occurrence. Apropos the first of these criteria, a story will ordinarily not be printed in an evening newspaper if it has already appeared in the morning paper. Only if there is a "new development" (for example if someone of importance denies the truth of the earlier story) does it have "news value."

Similarly, a story which was missed or which was not included for lack of space will not be printed at a later date. If the reader regards this as a natural phenomenon, we would call his attention to the practice of Soviet newspapers and other media of printing stories which are "several days old." The policy of Soviet journalism is not to report all events as soon as possible, but at the earliest time consistent with over-all policy. Furthermore, if policy dictates, the same event must be reported more than once.

In general, it seems to us that the emphasis of American journalism on novelty and recency must create an image of the process of history as a series of relatively discrete events, proceeding possibly in dialectical negation of each other, i.e., only change is "news." To some extent this notion is contained in the frequently expressed complaint about the lack of background information and interpretation in American news reporting. Whether, in fact, this impression is created, the American media are distinguished from those of other countries, and the mass media are different from other media in this respect, are all of course matters of speculation. These propositions seem, however, at least potentially subject to test.

---

[90] Kurt Lang and Gladys Engel Lang, "The Unique Perspective of Television and Its Effect: A Pilot Study, *American Sociological Review*, February, 1953, *18*, 3–12.

There is a wealth of information that can be brought to bear on the image of reality which is conveyed by the mass media: studies of censorship by formal censors, by advertisers, by interest groups, by publishers, etc.; studies of the flow of news filtered out at various points of transmission; studies of the handling of news by papers of various editorial biases, etc. It is material of this sort which we have identified as beyond the scope of this essay.

We would like however to make one final point in closing this section. A typical study of the flow of information indicates that of the total amount of news (measured in inches of wire copy) available over the wire services, slightly less than 3 per cent of the national and international news was eventually printed in each of four small Wisconsin dailies.[91] Such figures are very often cited as evidence of the failure of the newspapers to do a good job. We are ready to go along with the general feeling that newspapers should include more of the available national and international news. However, we would like to raise a researchable question with respect to whether an increase in amount of available news would or would not increase the reading and assimilation of such news.

At the present time the average person reads only about 20 to 25 per cent of such "heavy" news. Let us consider for a moment the attitude of many (we do not know how many) people toward the "outside world" of national and international affairs. This "outside world" is, to a large extent, an intrusion on his private world. Given his choice he would just as soon not be bothered with Communist China. It is a commonplace observation, verified by psychological experiment, that when a man is overloaded with threatening incoming information he establishes an automatic censor to keep the volume down. It may well be that the American public has established an equilibrium point for the amount of national and international information it will normally absorb. An increase in the flow of such news might well produce sufficient anxiety (assuming that increased importance of the events being reported did not warrant increased attention) that the average reader might actually read *less* rather than more national and international news.

If the above point seems far-fetched, let the reader think of the same problem in terms of radio and TV commercials. If they are short and unobtrusive we may listen to them. If they are long and obtrusive, we may turn to some other business while they are on, or we may "shut them out" psychologically by paying no attention. One of us spent many years learning *not* to hear baseball games over the radio. When later she became interested in the game it took some months of retraining to get over her habit of "not hearing" them.

---

[91] Scott M. Cutlip, "Content and Flow of AP News — From Trunk to TTS to Reader," *Journalism Quarterly*, Fall 1954, *31*, 434–446.

All the above is to say that the image of reality conveyed by the mass media should be studied in close conjunction with the reaction of the audience to that image. It is our guess that, if this is done, many optimistic ideas for reform will have to be abandoned, and that on the other hand many accusations of guilt will be withdrawn. It offers us little comfort to say so, but it may be that the mass media and their audience have established a very efficient symbiotic relationship. To say this is by no means new. However, it is very much worth repeating and worth investigating.

Conformity v.s. Shared Values

Several decades ago Sapir wrote an essay, "Culture, Genuine and Spurious."[92] Our reading of the substance of this essay is that Sapir was pointing out that culture can be internalized to varying degrees by the members of a society. In a stable society, there will be maximal internalization, i.e., culture will become more truly part of the "personality" of the society's members. In a changing society, the culture is relatively "spurious," i.e., it is essentially an external set of rules to which the individual has learned the correct responses. Such a distinction is certainly meaningful and plausible.

Since ours is a rapidly changing society we may expect that our culture is more "spurious" in Sapir's sense than the culture of more stable eras. This seems inevitable. And, the only pose from which one can regard this as wholly lamentable is one which will simultaneously and frankly oppose the economic and social changes which are generating these changes of values and norms.

Here again, we find the "theorists of mass society" standing on undefined ground. Folk societies were blessed with "shared values," whereas the mass media are producing "conformity." What can this mean? As Bell has already pointed out,[93] the critics of "mass society" apply oppositely charged labels to descriptively the same phenomena. Thus, folk societies are "organic," but modern societies are "total," the citizen of the ideal society is "individualistic," but in industrial society he is "isolated." True, these words may have some denotative differences, but what strikes one when reading them in context is the primacy of their connotative intent. One cannot be sure that different phenomena are being referred to, but there is no question that different evaluations are being put on them.

There can be little doubt that the mass media are having an homogenizing influence on American values and norms, and even speech habits. What is apparently objected to is that the mass media are pro-

---

[92] Edward Sapir, "Culture, Genuine and Spurious," *American Journal of Sociology*, 1924, *29*, 401–429.

[93] Daniel Bell, "The Theory of Mass Society," *Commentary*, July, 1956, 22, 75–83.

ducing "conformity." To the extent that there is cultural change involved, these newly acquired values must, by Sapir's definition, be less "genuine" and therefore less internalized. Descriptively it is difficult to distinguish between "conformity" and "shared values" except for the extent to which the relevant values and norms have been internalized. This is neither a theoretical or empirical discovery; merely a tautology.

However, homogenization of the American culture does not *per se* mean more "conformity." Even in a culturally diverse nation, there can be much "conformity" to the values of each of the subcultures. There are two separate problems involved. Unquestionably we are experiencing a reduction of cultural diversity.[94] But, it is more pertinent to ask if this evolving pan-American culture permits less latitude of behavior within its own system of norms and values.

Anyone with a modicum of cross-cultural perspective knows that cultures vary in the areas in which they enforce conformity and in which they permit a relatively wide range of behavior. By selecting the area on which one will focus his interest, it is possible to build a case that any changing society is becoming more "conforming." This point seems to us so obvious that we are appalled at the readiness and lack of critical appraisal with which American intellectuals accept the assertion that we are becoming "a nation of conformists." Again, the critics show their characteristic lack of historical sense. It is our impression that a casual search of the nineteenth century literature[95] would reveal quickly that there was pressure for conformity in the business community at least equal to that exerted on today's employee. Clerks and workers were told directly what to wear, when and where to go to church, whether or not they could smoke, drink, and gamble, or be shaved by a barber; even courting was regulated. We have the impression that these practices extended further down in the organization, to smaller organizations, and were more rigorously enforced than are the controls on today's organization man.

We suggest that the reader make for himself a list of representative areas of behavior and then ask with respect to each whether more or less deviance is permitted *and* exhibited today as compared to the American society of the beginning of the century. May we suggest as a starter: 1) sex; 2) eating habits; 3) marriage stability; 4) parent-child relationships; 5) clothing, (the-man-in-the-grey-flannel-suit-to-the-contrary-notwith-

---

[94] This reduction of intra-national diversity, however, is accompanied by an expanded knowledge of other cultures—via the mass media.

[95] Why, the reader may well ask, have we not made such a search. Our plight on this issue is typical of that on so many related issues. The critics of "mass society" have made casually so many unsubstantiated assumptions on topics subject to empirical investigation that the counter-critic would be completely immobilized if he were to undertake the task that the original writers should have performed initially.

standing); 6) recreation; 7) religion; etc. It is highly doubtful that Americans have become, or are becoming, more conformist in all these areas.

What we suspect is actually happening is the following:

1. American culture is becoming "homogenized" in the sense that a number of subcultures are being blended, mixed into one;

2. Americans as a group are becoming less provincial, more cognizant and accepting of the values of other cultures; and

3. They are probably becoming less "conformist" in the sense that they permit, accept, and practice, more divergence from the new "homogeneous" norms than they did from the norms of the unblended subcultures.

V. 'Mass Society' Re-evaluated

The original intention of this study was to explore the role of mass communications in American society with the view that we might come to a better understanding of the nature of that society. Since the "theory of mass society" came closest among existing statements to a coherent set of propositions about American society and mass communications we took it as a provisional model for our investigation. In this way our efforts were turned in two quite opposite directions, because in the process of looking at the data on mass communications we were also testing the adequacy of the "theory of mass society" as a model of mass communications. Having found it something less than adequate as the latter, we could not avoid also coming to the conclusion that we must enter reservations for its appropriateness as a model of American society. The theory of mass society extends of course well beyond the area of mass communications, and a fair assessment of the "theory" as a whole would demand an exploration well beyond the scope of this essay.

Accordingly the pages which follow must be regarded as an impressionistic effort. Our assumption that this position *is* inappropriate is, of course, based mainly on evidence in the area of communications.

Looking at the "theory of mass society" in perspective, one must grant that it is at many points correct *in detail*. It would be impossible to make so many assertions about American society without being right at least some of the time. But there is major unconfirming evidence for many of its key conclusions.

Does mass society with the aid of mass communications lead to totalitarianism? Other authors have anticipated us in pointing out that the evidence is strongly to the contrary. If one were to rank Western societies according to degree of industrialization and development of mass communications on one hand, and according to susceptibility to totalitarianism on the other, he would find a strong negative correlation between his two rankings. It has been the least developed countries which, in general, have been most susceptible to totalitarianism. Germany is a major exception, and there are several minor reversals (e.g. Czechoslovakia). The over-all data, however, would certainly indicate that *lack* of industrialization and absence of mass communications are correlated with vulnerability to totalitarianism.

We suspect that many of the formulations of the theorists of mass society are based more narrowly on Nazi Germany than they themselves are aware. Not only did communist totalitarianism come to countries in which the mass media were not developed, but when the communists built a system of mass communications they used it in a manner far different from that presented in the theory of "mass society." Communications policy in the Soviet bloc may be soporific but it is not narcotizing in the sense of diverting the citizen's energies into harmless channels. Quite the opposite. It is overly serious, didactic, pedantic, boring. The fact that the "high arts" have had a difficult time under communism is in no sense due to their being perverted to or by the popular taste. For the extent that Soviet painting and music, for example, have approximated "popular culture," we must look mainly to the fact that this is where Stalin's own tastes lay. If he had been aesthetically better educated, we may well guess that the Soviet people would have gotten "high culture" — whether they liked it or not. Similarly, the other scourge of the arts in communist countries, their subservience to political utility, has nothing to do with popular taste and/or desire for narcotic diversion except in the negative sense that popular desires for diversion are frustrated.

Does industrial society increase mental disease? The "theory of mass society" stresses only the "increasing complexity" of modern society, the "breakdown of values," etc., i.e., those factors which presumably increase mental disease. But what about the statistics? Most statistical series would seem on the surface to indicate some increase in mental disease over the past decades. But every source of bias in these series would tend to exaggerate the perceived incidence of mental disorder: (1) More disorders are diagnosed as "mental." (2) Of those diagnosed mental disorders, greater acceptance of mental problems probably results in more cases being reported for what they are. (3) As more families move into the city, home care for "queer" members of the family becomes less tolerable and the rate of hospitalization increases. (4) The population is aging and therefore mental disorders of a later life have more chance to appear. (5) Public acceptance of mental disorders leads to a greater rate of hospitalization (if the beds are available). When scholars have been able to get good statistical series in which they could control such sources of bias, they have found no evidence for an increase in mental disorders in our society.[96]

---

[96] Cf. Herbert Goldhamer and Andrew M. Marshall, *Psychosis and Civilization — Two Studies in the Frequency of Mental Disease* (Glencoe, Ill.: The Free Press, 1953).

We indicated previously our doubts as to whether there is an increase in juvenile or other crime, and as to whether there was evidence for the deterioration of popular taste.

Are Americans becoming passive? If so, how are we to account for the fabulous increases in *participant* sports on the part of Americans (golf, sailing, fishing, hunting, bowling), or for the increased favor of the station wagon as a family car, and the concomitant family traveling and purchase of summer homes (some of them beyond TV reception)? Simultaneous with the rise of TV, America has experienced a "do it yourself" craze. True, the housewife can buy a TV dinner at the store, but in our experience this has been more highly correlated with the energy level and cooking skill of the housewife than with the presence of a TV set in the home. At the same time, of course, there is a revival of "fancy" cooking which offsets in the time required for preparation all the gains that have been made in the pre-preparation of the foods which the housewife buys. At least as much evidence can be introduced against as for the proposition that Americans are becoming more passive.

What we are driving at is that the theorists of mass society, confronted with ambiguous data invariably interpret such data in one predictable direction. When one has a general, overall organizing principle it frequently helps him to make sense out of muddy evidence. This is what we feel is at work here. The motion that American society is running downhill culturally, morally, and politically does not stem from the ordinary type of data against which we would customarily test both the major and minor propositions involved. The general premises could not come from such data because the data do not exist in sufficiently unambiguous form. The over-all schema derives from the values system of the critics of the mass society, and coherence can be found on this level only. Only by taking as a point of departure their values system and a few general notions of social process and organization can we make coherent sense out of their position.

In general the theorists of mass society hold to a relatively mechanistic view of social process and social organization. In the pages which immediately follow this, we shall attempt to indicate this by specific illustration, as well as show that this view of social process and social organization has generally been dropped by social scientists and does not offer a fruitful way of looking at society.

Also, we shall try to indicate by specific illustration the way in which the "theory of mass society" is conditioned by the values system of the theorizers. At this point we would like to make only a few general orienting statements, presenting a few propositions which we feel are the most valuable *entre points* in understanding the theorists of mass society.

The Theorists Of Mass Society Are Elitists

While most of the persons involved are political liberals, the fact remains that they are social elitists. Certain elements of this elitism are explicit, especially the statement of regret that cultural tastes are no longer established by a cultural elite.

Our suspicion — and this can be stated, but hardly can be documented — is that the elements of elitism extend very deeply into the thinking and feeling of the theorists of mass society. Specifically, we suspect that their basic complaint against mass culture is only incidentally that mass taste shall dominate over elite tastes. One might expect that they would be pleased with evidence that the masses were acquiring a genuine taste for high culture. But any evidence of this sort is ignored, explained away, and — we suspect — regarded with some anxiety.

> Shakespeare is dumped on the market along with Mickey Spillane, and publishers are rightly confident that their audience will not feel obliged to make any greater preparation for the master of world literature than for its latest lickspittle.[97]

The reason that evidence for improvement of popular taste is not regarded with favor is that — the major issue — the elite fear the loss of their own distinctiveness. This could occur equally by a lowering of all taste or by a raising of all taste. Our suspicion, therefore, is that the theorists of mass society do not favor but unconsciously resent an improvement in popular taste. The ideal state of affairs would not be one in which a cultural elite would lead the public, but one in which the cultural elite could maintain its distinctiveness and exclude the public from participation in anything smacking of high cultural activities.

The Theorists Of Mass Society Are Intellectuals

They rightly consider it the duty of the intellectual to scrutinize his society with a critical eye, to inveigh against what is wrong, and to suggest improvements. This, however, does not exhaust the picture. Among intellectuals social pessimism is more often and more readily approved than is social optimism. The optimist runs the risk of being regarded as "uncritical," possibly even of having "sold out." Regardless of whether he is right or wrong, the pessimist runs little such risk. True, he may meet with arguments on specific issues, but he will seldom be met with the argument *ad hominem*. As long as he finds things wrong with his society he obviously is not mentally, morally, nor aesthetically sluggish. (We should not ignore also the fact that this adverse criticism of the existing society serves to give the critic and his fellows additional status by drawing a sharp line between themselves and the less desirable elements of the society.)

---

[97] Bernard Rosenberg, "Mass Culture in America," in Bernard Rosenberg and David Manning White (eds.), *Mass Culture* Glencoe, Ill. The Free Press, 1957, 5.

While the above comments may appear to be quite sharp when applied to a group of scholars of obvious integrity and ability, they should not be regarded as unduly critical of the critics of mass society. The truth of the matter is that most optimistic social criticism does tend to be fatuous. It is rare indeed to find a first rate critic who does not "view with alarm" more often than he "views with bright prospect." It is more urgent to alert the public to danger than to lull them to complacency, and it probably does take more brains to challenge rather than approve of the *status quo*.

We may grant then that there is a legitimate reason for the pessimistic orientation of intellectual social analysis. However, we would contend that this pessimism has extended beyond its original function and has become *de rigeur* for "respectable intellectuals" in the same way that long hair became for the bohemians of the twenties, the D.A. haircut for the teenager of the Elvis era, or the beard for the beatnik.

With most of the problems and most of the data with which we have been dealing, the interpretations reached by the critics of mass society can be understood only if it is realized that pessimism operates as a general premise to which ambiguous evidence is assimilated.

The Theorists Of Mass Society Are Opposed To The Protestant Ethic

It is asserted that modern man is "atomized." The crucial step toward the "atomization" of modern man, if the term has any meaning, took place at the time of the Protestant Reformation when the doctrine was advanced that each man must be guided by his individual conscience. The idea of a personal God meant that each individual stood in a direct relationship to the Deity, a relationship unmediated by Church or society. Similarly the conceptions of economic motivation that came out of the Protestant ethic were based on the notion of an isolated individual who pursued his self-interest directly with minimum attention to the societal side-effects of his actions. Protestant society has been egalitarian, and this egalitarianism leads readily to the domination of society by the masses. Protestantism, industrialization, and "the mass society" have been highly correlated.

We are not maintaining that American society conforms closely to the model implied in the Protestant ethic or in the *laissez-faire* doctrine of economics. But we are of the impression that the image of mass society which the "theorists" portray is drawn from the Protestant view of society. In fact, in some instances what is objected to is not American society as it *is,* but American society as it *ought* to be if it conformed to the schematized view of Protestant industrial society.

With these comments we would like to move to the consideration of a number of apparent inconsistencies which can be understood only in view of such considerations as we have just mentioned.

One of the complaints against mass society is that the "mass man" is devoid of "inner resources." But, on the other hand, it is also complained that external signs of status have disappeared; that high culture and "kitsch" become difficult to distinguish; that the individual of highly developed tastes must buy mass products and can not have clothes, furniture, etc., made to his own taste and order. The critic, one would imagine, is making his attack from the vantage point of a person blessed with "inner resources." Why then it it *he* rather than the others who is disturbed by the passing of external signs of distinctions and status?

A Martian, doing a content analysis of this literature, would be forced to record that the group that was most concerned with *other* people being deficient in "inner resources" was the very same group that was decrying the passing of external symbols of status. He might also well conclude that it is the *critics* of mass society who are lacking in "inner resources" — judged by the frequency with which they complain about the disappearance of their own external marks of status and distinction.

If the work of our Martian content analyst happened to be reviewed by one of these people, the reviewer would almost certainly point out that the masses were so "narcotized" that they were not aware of the fact they were lacking in "inner resources." This would leave our Martian in a dilemma, very much like that of a layman trying to understand a psychiatrist's explanation of how a man may be suffering without ever realizing it. The Martian would probably also scurry round looking for data that would help him rule against the troublesome hypothesis that *actually* the critics of mass society were the only people lacking in "inner resources" and were projecting this feeling onto others. Presumably he, just as we, would be reluctant to accept this hypothesis, but the ordinary rules of scientific procedure would compel him to give it a fair shake.

Other inconsistencies seem to stem from the fact that the general notions about mass society were formulated in Europe and are more applicable to European society than to American society. Certainly the folk-urban dichotomy holds up better in the European context, or in Latin America. Considering the vicissitudes and isolation of American rural society of the preceding century it makes little sense to talk about "increasing loneliness" resulting from the urbanization of American society. Furthermore, the critics of mass society can scarcely be talking about *America* at the turn of the century if they contend that there has been an increase in conformity. The American small town was notorious for its insistence on and ability to enforce conformity.

Much of what is seen as worst in industrial society is part and parcel of the "Protestant ethic" as it applies to economic motivation. But the critics fail to recognize the fact that *in America* Protestantism is a rural phenomenon. Eloquent testimony to the importance of this fact is offered by a study of worker motivation reported by William F. Whyte.[98]

The "ratebusters" in the factory under study (i.e., those workers who pursued their individual economic advantage regardless of its repercussions on other workers) were Protestants born in rural areas. The "restrictors" (those who were most likely to hold down production in response to group pressure and interest) were urban-born Catholics. Judged by a series of criteria, the ratebusters were less well integrated into the larger social groups of the factory and neighborhood. The data which Whyte presents are based on too small a number of cases to make one comfortable in accepting these findings on their own merit.[99] However, once Whyte has raised the issue, it is clear that the picture which he paints is much more consistent with what is known of the American scene than is the picture painted by the "theory of mass society."

Another feature of the image of American society that causes difficulties for the critics of mass society is that the model which they employ is outdated by several decades. This is perhaps most clearly illustrated with respect to the work process. The picture of the worker becoming progressively more alienated from the product on which he was working, or retrogressing more and more into routine actions which demanded little skill and creativity and gave the worker little sense of purpose, was still a reasonable description of the status and the trend of American industry of a few decades ago. The onset of automation, however, augurs for a sharp reversal of this trend. In an automized factory the worker will probably still be more concerned with the process than the product, but the scope of his job will be enlarged, the level of training demanded will increase, and he will be given more responsibility and independence. At present we have only limited empirical evidence of workers' response to automation. Such studies as have been made do, however, indicate an increased sense of participation among workers in automated plants.[100]

Another anachronism in the "mass society" view of the work process is that it focuses almost entirely on the production worker in industry.

---

[98] William F. Whyte, *et. al.*, *Money and Motivation* (New York: Harper, 1955), Chapter 4. Whyte reports in this chapter on work done by Donald Roy.

[99] There is the additional possibility that the ratebusters were persons who went to the city because they did not fit into the American rural pattern. James G. Abbeglen in an unpublished study located such a phenomenon in Japanese society. This has since come out as *The Japanese Factory: Aspects of Its Social Organization*, (Glencoe, Ill.: The Free Press, 1958). However, it is our guess that Whyte's ratebusters are not such deviants. Their behavior *conforms* to the idealized norm of the Protestant ethic. Protestantism, Republicanism, independence: all are characteristics of the American rural scene.

[100] Floyd Mann and L. Richard Hoffman, "Individual and Organizational Correlates of Automation," *Journal of Social Issues*, 1956, *12*, 7–17.

This group is no longer the "typical" representative of the evolving work force. A discussion of the job situation of the service worker would be more interesting and pertinent.

We suspect that one of the reasons the critics of mass society hold to an outdated view of the work process arises out of a characteristic confusion between reality and values. The basic opposition of the critics appears to be to the Protestant ethic as statement of how man *ought* to behave with respect to economic motivation. We do not know if the actual behavior of "economic man" ever did correspond closely to the normative model of theologians and economists as to how they thought he should behave. We do know, however, that the outstanding empirical finding of industrial sociology of the past few decades has been such that in our era, at least, workers do *not* behave as the doctrine says they should.

It may well be argued that the formation and activities of informal, primary groups in industry are a compensation for, and therefore a tacit proof of the industrial workers' sense of isolation, etc. This is a reasonable explanation of the origins of primary groups in industry, just as similar explanations would account for the development of neighborhood organizations in urban communities, or the atmosphere of "pseudo-gemeinshaft" in many mass communications. If we accept this explanation, however, the central fact remains that *the compensations have taken place.*

Suppose a man is lonely, isolated, frustrated, or suffers from any ill-feeling we may imagine, and he does something to relieve that feeling. It is true that his compensatory behavior is a documentation of the existence of the original motive but it is not sufficient merely to dismiss this behavior as a symptom. It would seem pertinent also to inquire as to how effective the compensatory behavior is. The seed of psychological and sociological change lies in man's attempts to ease his lot, to solve the problem created by his present situation.

But it is no accident that the theorists of mass society either ignore such processes or dismiss them with labels such as "pseudo," "spurious," "not genuine." Inherently, the theory of mass society has little place for the role of spontaneous processes. This devaluing of spontaneous process stems from two sources: the origins of the "theory," and the elitist predilections of the theorists. As far as the origins of the theory of mass society are concerned, we have already mentioned the fact that the theory of mass society was strongly stimulated by the emergence of conspicuous new formal institutions such as the system of mass communications, the growth of industry and of cities, the development of the modern state, etc. Preoccupation with these formal institutions deflected attention away from informal institutions and spontaneous processes. Such informal institutions and spontaneous processes as were contrary to the theory were regarded as residues of the older society. As most, spontaneous processes were acknowledged to exist but were regarded as deleterious.

By and large, the theory of mass society is a theory of social control *from above* even though it is premised on the necessity for making concessions to mass taste in order that the masses be controlled most effectively. The theorists of mass society approve of control from above. As a matter of fact, one of their central complaints is that a *cultural* elite is no longer in a position to dictate cultural tastes. This elitism seems — in our judgment — to produce a congenital scepticism toward spontaneous, relatively uncontrolled processes, particularly if these processes originate "from below." While the critics of mass society (or at least some of them) exhibit a romantic populist trend when talking about "folk societies," they are strongly anti-populist with respect to modern society (something of an anomaly in view of their generally liberal political orientation). It is our suspicion that in this we are once more encountering a reflection of the European origins and orientation of the theorists of mass society. Not only do they approve of a more highly stratified society, controlled from above, but they seem to find it impossible to believe that a less stratified society can be viable. They view it as an unstable state of affairs that must be moving toward some new form of control from above, namely, a totalitarian dictatorship.

We may be wrong in some or many of the above impressions. They are, however, consistent with the phenomena which we are trying to explain, namely, the fact that the theorists of mass society attribute little importance to spontaneous social process, and exhibit consistent scepticism that "any good" can eventuate in society if it be not originated by a cultural elite.

Basically the so-called "theory of mass society" is a statement of alienation from our own society. A vast portion of the "data" on which this view of mass society ought to be based is absent, contradictory, or completely ambiguous. Furthermore, when an argument, speculation, or "theory" which is essentially two-edged is introduced, only that edge which cuts in the pessimistic direction is employed. Thus, it is asserted that mass communications act as a substitute for desirable participant behavior. It is also asserted that the mass media stimulate anti-social behavior. To the best of our knowledge none of the proponents of these propositions has bothered to explain why he has not entertained the possibility that the mass media may serve as a *substitute* for *anti*-social behavior and *stimulate desirable* participant behavior. (This is not to say for a moment that persons who enjoy mass communications are not equally one-sided in their choice of arguments. However, since they are seldom intellectuals and write books, their views reach the public only if they happen to be caught up in a public opinion poll.)

The focus of this alienation is not strictly our society as it is, but a *view* of that society. We say a *view* of our society because it is abundantly clear that much of the view does not correspond unambiguously to what is known of our society. Our best guess, as we have indicated, is that the true focus of alienation is a stereotyped notion of Protestant industrial society.

There are many features of this model of society to which one might object. We have, however, come to the sour conclusion that the major issue which disturbs the theorists of mass society is the egalitarianism of modern society. While their objections are usually couched in terms of a fear that egalitarianism means "leveling" down; we suspect that they fear equally a leveling up. The basic issue is that whether the leveling be "up" or "down" any sort of leveling would destroy the distinctiveness of the elite, and it is the preservation of this distinctiveness which is what is being fought for.

Let us be frank in admitting that we have been indulging in an argument *ad hominem* of our own. Having come to the conclusion that the view of American society and mass communications reflected in the theory of mass society was certainly not the only scheme of explanation which fitted the available evidence, we were tempted to ask ourselves what there was about these particular people that made this particular scheme of explanation compatible to them. Lest the reader apply a less elegant term to our enterprise, we hasten to point out that such an activity is respectable providing it is called "sociology of knowledge."[101]

It may be equally appropriate to ask why *we* have been so critical of the theory of mass society. We might contend that "all the evidence is on our side." However, that is not so. In at least one instance we have taken a stand on data that seem to argue strongly against us, notably in our contention that there has probably been no rise in juvenile delinquency. We have, it is true, indicated where we would look for the holes in such data. But the fact of the matter is that the data as it is now generally available argues against us. Therefore, we must be doing in our own way something akin to that which we have attributed to the theorists of mass society; i.e., we have projected some general assumption onto these data or employed some personal value in our estimate of it.

We would not pretend to be able to list the full range of motives that colored our approach to this problem. We can, however, identify the one which we believe is central. On preceding pages we commented on the all-pervasive pessimism of social critics. It is on this score that we have perhaps the strongest emotional reaction. The job of the critic

---

[101] If the reader is reminded spontaneously of Tom Lehrer's classic line, "plagarize, only please to call it research," we grant that it was on our mind, too.

should, to a large extent, be one of "viewing with alarm." However, this viewing with alarm can become irresponsible, and this is what bothers us. The critic can indulge himself in masochistic breast beating, or enhance his own status and self-esteem by an indiscriminating blasting of all about him. Taking it all-in-all, there is something a little suspicious in the fact that each generation in recorded history has apparently been convinced that only catastrophe could follow upon its passing. To us it is distressing that intellectuals are so lacking in this rudimentary sense of self-perspective. Unquestionably if we concentrate on making only dire predictions we will be right occasionally, and the predictions will be better remembered than would optimistic ones. However, if we intellectuals make only dire predictions we will lose both our integrity and our influence.

Frankly, the two of us do not know what the long-range prospects for American society are. We have documented in this essay our confusion as to the role of the mass media in present-day America. We are not even convinced with certainty that the theorists of mass society are wrong in their over-all conclusions — merely that there is evidence contrary to specific propositions, and that there are other ways of looking at American society that other scholars have found profitable.

Even though there is need for and prospect of more research which may well resolve many moot points in present speculation about American society and the mass media, there is little prospect that we will ever have adequate evidence for the resolution of the most central propositions involved in such views as those we have been discussing. It seems impossible, for example, to isolate the impact of the mass media on popular taste from all the other social forces that go into the shaping of popular taste. Inevitably, over-all views of society or of our system of communications will necessarily "fit the data loosely." Taking everything into consideration, it looks as though the "theory of mass society" fits a little more loosely than it should.

One could wish that the theorists of mass society had not so confused social analysis and cultural criticism. There is a clear-cut issue — that it is highly desirable to improve the quality of mass communications — which stands by itself apart from any overarching theory of the relationship of mass communications to mass society. Under some circumstances it might be argued that a theory of the relationship of communications to society might help in the changing of the communications system. This argument can not be advanced, however, in favor of the theory of mass society, since it says essentially that *nothing can be done*. One suspects that the comforting feature of such a theory is that it affords its proponent simultaneously the luxury of complaining and criticising, and an iron-clad excuse for not doing anything.

Commentary

I. The Mass Media And The Structure Of American Society

Talcott Parsons and Winston White

Raymond and Alice Bauer have made a careful and informative review of empirical research studies on the determinants and effects of the mass media. Beyond this, the evidence they have adduced has led them into a critique of the so-called theory of mass society, which they speak of as the only available attempt at a generalized interpretation of the phenomena involved. Their findings indicate that there is not only a serious paucity of adequate research findings (which is one of the principal conclusions of this survey) but also an even greater lack of adequate theoretical analysis.

They note that in general the proponents of the theory of mass society operate both as commentators on the empirical state of the society and as evaluative critics of it. We think it extremely important, as do the Bauers, to distinguish between these two problems and that by doing so it is possible to see the theory of mass society as an ideological position congenial to *certain groups* of intellectuals. The Bauers, for example, repeatedly point out the arbitrary ways in which these intellectuals place one of several possible interpretations on items of evidence and tend further to ignore or often distort evidence — in ideological fashion — that does not support their evaluative strictures.

As an alternative to the position of the intellectuals, we wish to suggest a line of theoretical analysis that attempts to fit the evidence on the mass media (and on "mass culture") with that available on other aspects of the society, and that interprets this evidence in the larger context of some of the major features of American social structure and trends of its change. It is only through such a consideration of a wider range of evidence and of the larger social system, we feel, that steps can be taken to reduce the admittedly serious dangers of ideological selectivity and distortion.

Our discussion takes up three main topics. We will first analyze the assumptions underlying the intellectuals' conclusions and then point out the relation between those assumptions and the elements of ideological selectivity that result from them.[1] We will then suggest that the problems involved in the field of communications are analytically simi-

---

[1] This part of the discussion is developed at greater length in Winston White, *Ideology of the Intellectuals*, Doctoral dissertation, Harvard University, 1960.

lar to those in two other fields — the system of economic markets and the system of political power and influence. Finally, we will attempt to state a more generalized formula for the patterns of social structure and sociocultural change into which all three of these problem areas seem to us to fit.

The structure of the intellectual ideology. In an effort to account for the intellectuals' position, the Bauers have suggested that they are at the same time both "cultural elitists" and "social democrats." These labels pinpoint for us two points of reference from which the authors' analysis might be carried further.

On the one hand, there is the problem of cultural values and taste — of cultural standards, if you will. On the other hand, there is the problem of the social structure in which these standards are institutionalized; or put another way, it is the problem of the extent to which a given social structure allows for the expression and development (or frustration and deterioration) of desirable standards. The intellectuals have contended that cultural standards have deteriorated and that social structure has tended to become an aggregate of mass men, alienated from the meaningful ties that would uphold standards. The authors have challenged both of these conclusions with evidence about the upgrading and extension of standards in many areas and with evidence about the viability of primary-group relations.

The intellectuals deplore the "mass man's" alleged vulnerability to exploitation and his exposure to the mediocre. But underlying their discontent, the Bauers suggest, is their reluctance to let the guardianship of cultural standards slip out of their hands into those they consider less qualified. If the intellectuals do in fact hold both of these positions at once, how might one explain this seemingly inconsistent mixture of cultural conservatism and social liberalism?

We would agree with the Bauers that many intellectuals have explicitly or implicitly arrived at this conclusion. We do not feel, however, that all intellectuals have attempted to straddle the cultural and social fence in this manner; many have arrived at less ambiguous — although equally erroneous — conclusions. Behind these conclusions lie three distinct ideological sources, each with its own set of assumptions about social theory — about man's relation to society, to culture, and the like. These assumptions, as the authors point out, must be uncovered in order to understand and assess the intellectuals' positions. Tracing through these ideological patterns may clarify the problem. Two of them lie on the cultural side and one on the social side.

The ideology on the side of social structure assumes that man is essentially good and is only corrupted by social forces. Cultural standards are not seen as problematical but as epiphenomena of social conditions. Given a favorable social environment (e.g., the "right" economic-political institutions, the restoration of community ties, the elimination of "anonymous authority," etc.), desirable cultural standards will spring into efflorescence. But given the unfavorable conditions of a mass society, man is so alienated that he is unable to resist mass culture. He has, so to speak, no consumer sovereignty and is compelled to "buy" whatever supply of culture is at hand. This point of view is more or less Marxian in its assumptions; Erich Fromm is one of its leading spokesmen.

The ideology on the cultural side assumes that man is conditionally good or evil and that his commitments to cultural standards cannot be taken for granted but must be vigilantly maintained. In this version, social structure is a non-problematical epiphenomenon of culture. Given the "right" cultural commitments, appropriate social institutions will follow along in due course. There are two ideological positions within this set of assumptions.

The élitist position, which the authors touch on, is that the highest cultural standards must be maintained by the agency of an élite and that high and folk culture alike should be borne by a gradation of classes. If standards are assured in this way (or, as we would put it, if they are ascribed to class and to region), then the social structure is safe. People know their place and what is expected of them. Without the guardianship of an élite, the demands of the untutored masses for a vulgarized cultural product will take over. T. S. Eliot and Ortega y Gasset have been spokesmen for this point of view.

Another important "cultural" ideology, however, is that held by those we will call the "moralizers." For them, social structure is even less problematical in that buttressing by an elite and by a class structure is no longer felt to be necessary. The moralizers believe that standards must be maintained by individual responsibility. It is up to the individual to maintain his commitments to values, to hold the line on his own, as it were, against the seductions of mass society with its hedonistic flabbiness. It is in the hearts and minds of men that moral heroism (the intellectual's counterpart of the businessmen's rugged individualism) will shape the social fabric. Archibald MacLeish and Joseph Wood Krutch, for example, are notable spokesmen for this point of view. The élitists and the social-structure ideologists tend to regard the moralizers as hopelessly middlebrow, but it seems to us that any definition of "intellectuals" as social critics must include them.

Common to both types of "culture" ideologists — the élitists and moralizers alike — is the assumption that the individual does have "consumer sovereignty." The public gets what it wants (and deserves). Standards deteriorate because of the low quality of mass demand, not because of the low quality of supply.

Finally, those intellectuals whom the Bauers characterize as both cultural elitists and social democrats at the same time are, we suggest, ideologically analogous to, though of course not affiliated with, the Communist Party — an élite group that sets standards where, according to the ideology, there should be no need to. Further, the assertion of cultural autonomy by the mass of men, given favorable social conditions, is analogous to the withering away of the state. Either these intellectuals' beliefs are inconsistent in that they consider élite guidance necessary regardless of what kind of social conditions prevail, or they have embraced élitism as an intermediate means to hold the line until the proper social conditions can be attained, if ever.

None of these points of view is adequate, we believe, for analyzing the relationship between cultural standards and the social structure in which they are institutionalized. We have called them ideologies, for each in its own way is selective in its approach — tending to take for granted or to ignore factors that must be considered for proper analysis. As our further comments will spell out, we see the mass media as a mechanism operating in a "market" between the purveyors of cultural content and the public. And, as the Bauers have emphasized, it is not the only mechanism but one that operates in conjunction with others, such as informal primary-group relationships.

In such a "market,"[2] we maintain, both supply and demand operate without one always being subjugated to the other. Our analysis has tried to show that the intellectuals are by no means in agreement on this issue. The élitists and moralizers believe that low-grade public demand lowers standards; the social-structure ideologists blame the quality of the supply, claiming that the public — or the masses, as they would say — cannot be expected to know better, social conditions being what they are.

It is with respect to standards that the issue comes to a head. The élitists regard standards as ascribed to class, with the highest standards maintained only through their agency. They are like parents who look on the public as their children, believing them incapable of acting responsibly without their surveillance.

The moralizers, on the other hand, tend to ignore the whole problem of the social context in which standards are defined. They believe that each individual, by exercising his autonomous "responsibility," can define his own standards independently of others, by means of "nonconformism" or "individualism." Standards, apparently, are given as in the utilitarian conception of "self-interest." Finally, for the social-structure ideologists, standards are taken for granted. Like autonomy and spontaneity, they spring full-born from the sane society.

Dwight MacDonald's metaphor of Gresham's law represents an interesting combination of the above. For him, the "market" is purely one of runaway inflation which cannot be checked because standards are continually falling. Low-grade demand stimulates low-grade supply, and vice versa — like a reciprocating engine, as he puts it. With no élite in charge of standards, he considers the situation hopeless.

---

[2] When we speak of market here in quotation marks we are generalizing the economic concept to cover several other related types. We hope no confusion results from this usage.

Economic, Political, and Communications Systems

The context in which we wish to place our comparisons between mass communications and economic and political systems is that of the division of labor. Where the functions of units in a social system become sufficiently differentiated, it becomes impossible for the "producers" of an output — be it a commodity, an expression of political support, or a culturally significant message — to be ascriptively bound to the recipients, as would be the case, for example, for custom-made goods, feudal allegiance, or patronage of the arts. The offer of automobiles for sale or party appeals for votes are "broadcast" in a sense analogous to that of soap operas or symphony concerts. Their producers do not know in advance in detail who or how many the recipients will be, or what commitments they will be willing to make as a result of exposure, although market research can in all three cases narrow the range of uncertainty somewhat.

All such processes of differentiation lead to "alienation" — both for the producer from the ultimate use of his product and for the consumer from direct involvement with the source of his supply. Adam Smith's famous generalization about the economic efficiency of the division of labor can, thus — with proper qualifications — be extended to these other two contexts: the "consumer" acquires degrees of freedom that would be impossible without such differentiation. At the same time, certain mechanisms of control become necessary if such a system is to be stable and in fact bring about the degrees of freedom referred to. These controls center on *institutionalized* regulatory patterns — like contract and property in the economic sphere, leadership and authority in the political — and on institutionalized *media* such as money and political power (as exercised, for instance, through the franchise).

Let us consider first the degrees of freedom created by an economic market system and then try to work out the parallels for political and communications systems. In so doing we hope to highlight those features of the latter that are analytically significant for the mass-media problem.

In contrast to a system of economic barter, the consumer who holds money funds in a highly differentiated market system has the following degrees of freedom: 1) in accepting money, e.g. in exchange for labor services, he is not ipso facto committed to buy what he wants to spend it for from any particular source of supply — he can "shop around"; 2) he is not committed to any particular composition of the "package" of items for which he spends it but can select in terms of his wants at the time; 3) he is not committed to any particular terms of exchange but can shop and/or bargain over prices; and 4) he is not committed to any particular time of expenditure of his funds but can extend his expenditures over time (indeed, the availability of interest puts a positive premium on delay).

This classification provides a convenient point of reference for identifying points of strain and certain possibilities of malfunctioning to which a market system is subject to a greater degree than one of ascriptive exchange or barter. All of these deviations have existed in fact in greater and less degree and in particular have figured prominently in critical discussions of "industrial" economies. Particularly prominent among these are the following: 1) Monopoly can restrict to varying degrees (and in the extreme case eliminate) the consumer's freedom of choice with respect to source of supply; indeed, one school of thought has alleged that its increase was an "inevitable" trend of a "capitalistic" economy. 2) Freedom to choose among a wide variety of products may be rendered valueless by an inherent process of product deterioration; the standards of handicraft excellence may give way to the shoddiness of mass-produced products, another point at which a prominent school of thought has alleged inevitability. 3) Freedom with respect to terms of exchange may be cancelled out by the inherently exploitative character of the market structure — a factor partly, but not necessarily wholly, deriving from monopoly. It has thus frequently been alleged that the "real" standards of living of consumers necessarily deteriorate at this point. Finally, 4) the freedom in time can be cancelled out by inflation so that the longer one holds his dollar the greater the disadvantage of his position; inflation again has been held to be an inherent trend. The inference from this syndrome is that the economic welfare of some conceived "typical" individual is inevitably injured by the division of labor, markets and industrialization — unless, as some think, it can be protected by socialism.

The broad answer, of course, is that, though all of these things can and do happen, such trends as have existed have not in general developed cumulatively to extremes in American society (to which present attention is confined). Thus to take one point, contrary to much opinion, it is impossible to prove that the degree of concentration in American manufacturing industry has increased appreciably over the past half century. If these trends have not gone to such extremes, there must be "countervailing" forces that lie in the mechanisms of control mentioned above. The prototypical problem statement here is Gresham's Law and both the Bauers and we must be grateful to Dwight MacDonald for having introduced this conception into the discussion. In the economic case it is simply not true, empirically, that, to paraphrase the Communist Manifesto, "the history of all market and currency systems is a history of galloping inflation" — nor of monopoly, nor of product deterioration, nor of exploitation.

Exactly parallel problems may be identified in the political field. Political differentiation, we suggest, creates degrees of freedom analogous to those of the market as follows: 1) The analogy of economic source of supply is leadership agency, e.g. a party as the agency taking responsibility for collective decision-making if given requisite political support. A "free electorate" has a choice between such agencies and is not ascriptively bound to any one by its legitimacy. 2) The political analogy of products is policies. By virtue of his position in a political system, the individual or group is neither ascriptively committed to favoring particular policies nor committed to them — except in a minority of cases — by "barter deals" but is free to allocate such influence as he has between a significant range of alternatives. 3) Economic price is essentially a determination of *cost*. The political analogy is the obligations entailed by commitment to a collective decision or policy. This means that there must be some balancing between the sharing of the benefits of what "gets done" and allocation of the burdens necessary to get it done, e.g. taxes. Finally, 4) in the political as in the economic case, differentiation makes it possible for leadership and followership both to enjoy greater flexibility with respect to time.

Elements of malfunctioning in such a differentiated political system which parallel those discussed in the economy can be identified as follows: (1) Parallel to economic monopoly is the concentration of political power to the point where effectiveness of choice among leadership elements is eliminated. A typical case of this view is Mills' contention[3] of the existence of a single unified "power elite." (2) The parallel to economic product deterioration is the alleged cumulatively increasing predominance in the political system of special and group interests over the public interest. It is suggested that the public does not get acceptable policies but only the effects of the "selfish" utilization of positions of political advantage to further special group interests. (3) The parallel to economic exploitation through the price system is the conception of progressively increasing exploitation of the "little man" by the "interests." Mills' conception of "cumulative advantage" seems to be the most explicit recent formulation of this view. Finally, (4) there is a political parallel to economic inflation. This is a process of progressive deterioration in the worth of general public commitments to the effective functioning of the political system through leadership. Various elements, that is to say, make "sacrifices," such as military service, only to find that the polity they devoted themselves to is becoming progressively less effective, more interest-dominated, time-serving and the like.

The question of the balance between these disorganizing trends and countervailing factors in the American political system over the last half century, for instance, is clearly a complicated one. There has always been a left-wing school of thought which has given overwhelming preponderance to the former factors, Mills being the most prominent recent exponent. The relative effectiveness in meeting the crises of two world wars and the great depression, however, seem to most observers to indicate the operation of important countervailing factors. It seems

---

[3] Cf. C. Wright Mills, *The Power Elite*. Oxford University Press, New York 1956.

legitimate to consider the theorists of "late monopoly capitalism" and those of the "power elite" as exponents of an ideology in the same sense in which we have attributed this to the theorists of mass culture.

We would like to consider the system of mass communications as a differentiated social system in the same sense that economic and political systems are, and a necessary one in a highly differentiated society of the American type. It involves the same order of specialization of function between "producing" and "consuming" units, and — most importantly — between different kinds of communication output. It also involves relative concentration of resources in the hands of larger producers, though the question of the degree of monopoly is not a simple one. It of course involves "alienation" of the recipient from control over the sources of communications. And it goes without saying that it involves both formal and informal mechanisms of control, the most important of which are institutionalized.

Such a system could be expected to produce degrees of freedom for the typical recipient analogous to those of the economic consumer or the member of the political public.

These may be sketched as follows: 1. Contrasted with the ascriptiveness of tradition is the range of alternative sources of communication output, newspapers, magazines, books, broadcasting stations and programs. This is far from unlimited, but unless restricted by totalitarian types of policies, far wider than in any traditional system. 2. There is a wide range of choice with reference to content, both with reference to types of content and to levels of quality within types. 3. There are freedoms with respect to "cost" — a conception, however, in need of clarification when used in this context. One component, of course, is money cost. Another, which figures in the Bauer study, is time spent by the consumer. Still another is something like "receptivity" to the line of influence suggested. For advertising, purchases can be a measure of this; for political campaigning, actual voting; but where literary tastes are at stake, measures are more difficult. 4. There is freedom with respect to time in the sense of receiving and not receiving communications, and allocation of time between particular kinds. Among the most important points here is the fact that the printed word can, given storage facilities, be preserved for reference at any future time.

It is now our suggestion that the main interpretive contentions of the theorists of mass culture can be fitted into this classification, as modes in which allegedly relevant standards fail to be met. Thus 1. with respect to source, there is much complaint about the concentration of sources, especially with reference to newspapers and broadcasting. This tends to play down the very wide variety available in some fields of communication, e.g. local newspapers and book publishing, especially recently of paperbacks. 2. Perhaps the most prominent single contention is the parallel of economic product deterioration, namely the notion that mass communication inevitably leads to the predominance of *kitsch* over quality items. 3. The analogue of economic exploitation and cumulative advantage in the power system is the idea of the "manipulative" exploitation of the irrational through the mass communication media; the portrayal of violence and its alleged relation to delinquency is a good case in point. Finally, 4. we might suggest that the theme of "apathy" is the analogue of economic inflation, namely the contention that the communication "market" is so flooded with inferior items, from whatever cause, that the standards of the recipient tend to become undermined, his responses becoming automatized and undiscriminating.

Again, as in the previous instances, these malfunctionings can and do occur. The evidence the Bauers have marshalled, however, does not support the contention that such has been the case in American society; at the very least, it compels serious consideration for the position we are advancing that countervailing forces, such as institutionalized standards and favorable "market" conditions, do in fact prevail, to a significant degree.

Summary

In the field of communications, then, we suggest that structural changes have been occurring that are analytically similar to those more familiar in the economic and political systems and that these changes — in all three cases — have the consequences of what we call extension, differentiation, and upgrading.

With respect to communications in particular, fundamental to this process of change is the shaking up of older traditional ascriptions, among the most salient of which are those of stratification. The élitist system confined its audience, by and large, to its peers. It was not expected that the general public would, or could, in any way be interested — except perhaps for a diffuse admiration of the elegance of the upper-class way of life. One major consequence of the breaking down of ascriptive ties is the *extension* of accessibility to cultural content to ever wider circles of the population. In recent Western history, the most conspicuous example of this is the extension of education. Far wider groups than ever before are expected to appreciate elements of the great Western cultural heritage.

The second aspect of change is that of *differentiation*. The term "mass" media itself is misleading, suggesting that the media themselves are undifferentiated with respect to content and audience. Not only do different media (or often the same media) carry qualitatively different content and reach qualitatively different audiences, but the same individual, in many cases, uses a variety of media.

Just as economic and political systems — indeed, social structures in general — become more differentiated, so do the media themselves tend to differentiate. The news coverage, for example, of the newsmagazine and the metropolitan newspaper enables the smaller community paper to specialize in local news. The advent of television has led to more specialization on the part of radio programming, witness the increase in musical programs.

With differentiation and specialization, one might expect, as in other systems, an increase of functional capacity in the communications system with the consequence of *upgrading*. If such is the case, one could expect a proportionately greater spread of the *higher* levels of culture than of the lower. Although the problems of evidence are formidable here, we would suggest, for example, that the advent of television has resulted in the upgrading of other "competing" media, itself coming in at the bottom of the qualitative ladder in certain respects (as successive waves of immigrants came in at the bottom of the occupational ladder, enabling previous arrivals to move up). Anyone watching old motion picture films on TV might well be impressed by their dismal mediocrity when compared with contemporary films, a change that arises from something more than a mere shift in style. The growth of serious music programming on FM stations is also a case in point.

Perhaps one can suggest that both films and radio broadcasting have not only been "kicked upstairs" by TV competition but that differentiation has led to an upgrading of taste. It is surely not too far-fetched to say that certain TV programs now fill a low-grade demand that previously turned to other media for satisfaction. This is not to say, however, that upgrading is *solely* a consequence of changes in the media of the "market" (the fallacy of a social-structure ideology). Upgrading is also dependent on raising the standards of the public in the sense of "building up" the level of their commitments to standards.[4] In addition to the extension of higher levels of education, this process is also effected through primary-group relations, where the individual learns not only to acquire new tastes but helps to define them as well. Even if his motivation arises purely from emulation or "status-seeking" — as some interpreters choose to suggest, brushing aside any realistic desire on the part of the individual to widen his range of experience — the *consequences* of this group interaction cannot be overlooked.

In conclusion, we hope that the combination of our treatment of the ideological problem with the parallel we have drawn between the selectivity of the mass-culture theorists and certain critics of the American economy and political system will serve to broaden the problem raised by the Bauers. By placing the mass-culture issue in a larger perspective, one can perhaps see that it is a special case of more general processes and that there is the same kind of problem in interpretation — not only of mass culture but of American society as a total system.

---

[4] It is essential, in order to avoid ideological traps, to pay attention to both the "demand" and the "supply" sides, rather than explicitly or implicitly assuming that one determines the outcome of the other.

Most fundamental of the fallacies underlying the biases of the mass-culture theorists seems to us to be the assumption that this is an "atomized" mass society where the relations of one individual to another have become increasingly amorphous. Quite the contrary, as Kornhauser[5] has pointed out, American society is one of the preeminent examples of a *pluralist* society in which — through the course of structural differentiation — an increasingly ramified network of criss-crossing solidarities has been developing. Nor is our conclusion to be taken as a defense of the status quo; American society has — in terms of our high expectations for it — many inadequacies. But, we believe, they cannot be "explained," much less confronted with any degree of sophistication, by the currently prominent theory of mass society.

[5] Cf. William Kornhauser, *The Politics of Mass Society,* Free Press, 1960; and Parsons, "Social Structure and Political Orientation," *World Politics,* October 1960.

II. Comments on Bauer and Bauer

Lewis A. Coser

The Bauers have done an excellent job summarizing many recent research findings in the area of mass communications, and for this one cannot but be grateful. But I fear that they failed in the other task they set themselves, the critique of the critics of mass society and mass culture. This, I would suggest, is due mainly to two reasons: 1. their lack of conceptual clarity; and 2. their failure to define the specific targets they attack. In consequence it is hard to know what they are talking about and even harder to find out whom they are talking about. Moreover, since they fail to let the voices of the critics be heard one gets the impression throughout their paper that they try to conduct a dialogue in which one side is from the onset condemned to muteness.

The terms "mass culture" and "mass society" are used interchangeably. This introduces a good deal of confusion. Sociologists generally have agreed that the term *society* refers to a relational system of interaction between individuals or groups, while *culture* refers to the pattern of values, norms, ideas and other symbols which shape human behavior.[1] Hence the term *mass society* properly refers to a type of society in which the relations between individuals have assumed a mass character; whereas mass culture refers to some peculiar characteristic of the system of symbols in use among individuals in a mass society. Failure to observe this elementary distinction accounts for such startling statements as, "the key event in the evolution of mass society . . . was the development of printing," in the fifteenth century!

But more serious than their lack of conceptual clarity is their omission to quote the theorists whom they attack with such calculated ferocity — to the point of imputing their motives. The writings of Karl Mannheim, Ortega y Gasset and other earlier critics of mass society are readily available; the leading contemporary sociological text, Broom and Selznick's *Sociology*,[2] contains a highly sophisticated discussion of the main characteristics of mass society; there have been first-rate monographs and books on the topic, just to mention the work of Philip

---

[1] Cf. A. L. Kroeber and Talcott Parsons, "The Concept of Culture and Social Systems", *American Sociological Review, 23* (1958), 582–3.

[2] Row, Peterson and Co., Evanston, Ill., 1955, 42–44 and passim.

Selznick,[3] William Kornhauser,[4] and C. Wright Mills,[5] but none of this is even mentioned in the Bauers' pages. There are highly informed criticisms of mass culture by such sociologists as Ernest van den Haag, Leo Lowenthal, T. W. Adorno, Bernard Rosenberg[6] and many others, and by literary men such as T. S. Eliot, Richard Blackmur, Q. D. Leavis, Dwight Macdonald, Irving Howe, Clement Greenbreg.[7] These are likewise not given a fair hearing. Instead, the Bauers quote what they consider a summary of the position of the critics by one of their leading adversaries, Daniel Bell, sprinkle a few lines from MacDonald, Lowenthal and Rosenberg through their text, and then go on their way attacking a strawman of their own construction. This leads them to such grotesque affirmations as that "The theorists of mass society [believe] that totalitarianism is the logical extension of industrial society." Mannheim and Ortega y Gasset are dead, but the Bauers owe an apology to the living.

Let me now turn to the last few pages of the Bauers' paper in which they purport to summarize their critique of the critics. It is hard, as I mentioned already, to discuss this critique since the Bauers never say whom they have specifically in mind. There are considerable differences, moral, political, scientific, between, say, Ortega y Gasset and C. Wright Mills, between Ernest van den Haag and Karl Mannheim, between T. S. Eliot and Dwight Macdonald, or Hannah Arendt and Erich Fromm. The Bauers, however, proceed to throw them all in one bag. Moreover, while they document exhaustively every bit of evidence they quote from communication research, they give no evidence whatsoever in support of their charges against the critics; indeed they serve up unproven assertions spiced with a liberal dose of innuendo, *vide* their misuse of psychoanalytic terminology to uncover the "real" motives of the critics. Let me now take up their main assertions seriatim.

(1) "The theorists of mass society are elitists." That some of them are, there can hardly be any doubt. That all of them are is demonstrably untrue. The Bauers fail to consider the fact, recently illuminated by William Kornhauser,[8] that while some theorists of mass society do indeed fear that it destroys the status claims and the prerogatives of

---

[3] *The Organizational Weapon,* McGraw-Hill, New York, 1952.

[4] *The Politics of Mass Society,* The Free Press, Glencoe, Ill., 1959.

[5] *The Power Elite,* Oxford University Press, New York, 1956.

[6] For samples of their work see *Mass Culture* ed. by Bernard Rosenberg and David Manning White, The Free Press, Glencoe, Ill., 1957. This book also has excellent bibliographies.

[7] See ibid. Also, Q. D. Leavis, *Fiction and the Reading Public,* Chatto and Windus, London 1932, and T. S. Eliot, *Notes Toward a Definition of Culture,* Faber and Faber, London, 1948.

[8] Kornhauser, *op. cit.*

traditional elites, others argue from a precisely opposite point of view. These critics aver that mass societies destroy the "public," i.e., those meaningful intermediary groups which mediate between the primary family unit and the nation-state. They claim that by dissolving those proximate units which cushion and envelop the individual and hence make possible a meaningful participation in public affair, mass society destroys the very possibility of a democratic, pluralistic polity. This, in essence, is the point of view of, among many others, Erich Fromm, C. Wright Mills, Seymour Lipset, Philip Selznick; that is, of some of the major contemporary critics of mass society. How do they fit into the Bauers elitist amalgam?

(2) "The theorists of mass society are intellectuals." Yes, and so are most other theorists, one would imagine.

(3) "Adverse criticism of the existing society serves to give the critic and his fellows additional status by drawing a sharp line between themselves and the less desirable elements of the society." This is a rather novel idea; up till now it has been a common assumption among social scientists that high status is achieved by those who conform to the guiding norms of a society rather than by those who deviate from them. Many critics of mass society are conservatives or liberals and their status may indeed be quite high, though I see no evidence that it is derived from their specific type of criticism. But in as far as the critic is a radical it is to be presumed that in general his status in the society at large is not as high as that of the defenders of the *status quo*.

(4) "The theorists of mass society are opposed to the Protestant Ethic." Somehow the Bauers seem to imply that it is a heinous offense to be opposed to the Protestant Ethic; but, apart from this, what do they really have in mind? I have pondered over their pages and the best I can make out is that they want to convey that the critics deplore loneliness, alienation, anomie, the lack of participation, and relate this to their analysis of modern industrial society. How the Bauers manage to equate all this with the Protestant Ethic remains a mystery. I can only conclude that they seem unable to distinguish between individualism and social alienation. Their lack of conceptual clarity again has played them tricks.

(5) "The theory of mass society is a theory [approving] social control from above." Again, whom do the Bauers have in mind? Do Fromm, Lipset, Selznick, Kornhauser want to control society from above? Or are they not rather democrats who believe that there is an urgent need for greater participation from below in a pluralistic social structure? Are Mills or Mrs. Leavis sceptical "toward spontaneous. . . process originating from below?" Ernest van den Haag, perhaps the leading critic of mass culture among social scientists, happens to be an old-fashioned nineteenth-century liberal who wants as much laissez-faire and as little state interference as possible; his mentor, I presume, is

Frederick Hayek. Bernard Rosenberg and Erich Fromm are democratic socialists whose major concern is with the maximization of individual autonomy. Dwight MacDonald considers himself a "conservative anarchist." Of whom, then, are the Bauers talking?

I could continue this listing of dubious assertions, but, frankly, I have little taste for it. Let me instead take up some substantive issues.

I consider a mass society, following Kornhauser's definition, one in which there is a tendency for "the aggregate of individuals [to be] related to one another only by way of their relation to a common authority, especially the state. That is, individuals are not directly related to one another in a variety of independent groups. A population in this condition is not insulated in any way from the ruling group, nor yet from elements within itself."[9] Moreover, the absence of autonomous groups through which individuals may unite to express their political interests and desires leaves the population in an atomized situation and fosters social alienation. Whether American society exhibits features of such a state of affairs, and to which extent, is clearly an empirical question. There is no space here to list detailed evidence — and the Bauers unfortunately failed to mention such evidence — so let me just as an illustration refer the authors to two studies of politics in the Boston area: Bruner and Korchin's well-known investigation of James Curley's amazing hold on a depoliticized Boston population owing to the social support he and his machine provided, and that was otherwise lacking,[10] and the more recent voting study of politics in Boston, *The Alienated Voter* by Murray B. Levin.[11] Levin concludes that Bostonians exhibit "a state of mind characterized by feelings of distrust of politicians and the political process, and a belief that the individual voter is not part of the process, i.e., that he is an alien in the political world." I consider this process of alienation from the political world, the eclipse of meaningful groups intermediary between the state and the citizen, a most serious danger to democratic process. If this be elitism let the Bauers make the most of it.

Mass culture is the cultural correlate of mass society. It emerges with the rise of industrialization and urbanization, the loosening of traditional bonds, and the traditional monopoly of culture on the part of the upper classes. It is distinguished from Folk Culture and from High Culture by its standardized mass production, marketability and parasitic dependence on other forms of art and culture. It embodies a sharp cleavage between the consumer (the audience) and the pro-

---

[9] Ibid., p. 32.

[10] Jerome S. Bruner and Sheldon Korchin, "The Boss and the Vote", *Public Opinion Quarterly*, X, No. 1 (Spring 1946), 1–23.

[11] Murray B. Levin, *The Alienated Voter*, Holt, Rinehart and Winston, New York, 1960.

ducer. The latter exploits and manipulates the former. These characteristics radically distinguish mass culture from other cultural forms. While most past cultures have been the expression of relatively homogeneous communities, mass culture emerges when community, that is groups of individuals linked to each other by concrete values and interests, is eroded. Mass culture, in turn, further undermines community. "When we speak of 'communications' in a [mass] society," wrote Stuart Hall recently, "we have to think less of how we speak to one another, and more of how other people speak *at* us."[12]

All this may appear to the Bauers so much generalization. The fact is, however, that there exists a considerable amount of evidence to this effect. Let them reread Robert K. Merton's *Mass Persuasion*.[13] Let them read some community studies on suburbia, *Crestwood Heights*,[14] for example, or *The Organization Man*.[15] Why not have a look at Maurice Stein's *The Eclipse of Community*,[16] or Vidich and Bensman's *Small Town and Mass Society*,[17] or Hoggart's brilliant study of the erosion of traditional British working class culture by the mass media, *The Uses of Literacy*.[18] Most of these books, by the way, are informed by the authors' humanistic concern for the quality of life which the mass media help to destroy among the common people. No élitists they.

I have no quarrel with most of the findings which are so ably, but also so selectively, reported by the Bauers. I only believe that most of them are of no relevance to a problem which, to me at least, is paramount: the problem of the quality of life in mass society, (There are, of course, empirical studies of this problem. The Bauers, however, do not quote them. In addition to the books just mentioned see *Identity and Anxiety* ed. by Stein, Vidich and White).[19] It is hardly helpful to me if the authors assure me solemnly that most exposure to the mass media take place in a social context and not in isolation, I rather expected that. I am, however, concerned with what Riesman calls the "lonely crowd," that is the loneliness of people who are not hermits but

---

[12] In *Out of Apathy* ed. by E. P. Thompson, Stevens & Sons, London, 1960, p. 86.

[13] *Mass Persuasion*, Harper and Bros., New York, 1946.

[14] John R. Seeley, R. Alexander Sim, and Elizabeth W. Loosley, *Crestwood Heights*, Basic Books, New York, 1956.

[15] William H. Whyte, Jr., *The Organization Man*, Anchor Books, Garden City, N.Y., 1957.

[16] Maurice R. Stein, *The Eclipse of Community*, Princeton University Press, Princeton, 1960.

[17] Arthur J. Vidich and Joseph Bensman, *Small Town in Mass Society*, Princeton University Press, Princeton, 1958.

[18] Richard Hoggart, *The Uses of Literacy*, Chatto and Windus, London, 1958.

[19] The Free Press, Glencoe, Ill., 1960.

rather so highly atuned to the need to adjust to the responses of others, that they lose the ability to be themselves, the ability to act autonomously. I cannot be impressed if I am shown that people in the suburbs have a great deal of social relations with a great many people, because I am concerned with the character, the meaning, and the intensity of their relations rather than with the number of their contacts. (In some cases, because of their understandingly great eagerness to buttress their position, the Bauers distort the very studies they quote. Thus Goldhamer and Marshall reported that they had found no increase in psychosis rates; the Bauers change this into "mental disorders" so that it would appear as if Goldhamer and Marshall include the neuroses — but this they do not! There seems quite general agreement among competent observers that the last few decades have witnessed an increase in the neuroses and the character disorders).

The authors consider that the empirical researchers they quote are somehow "closer to reality" than, say, literary people. Which "reality" are they talking about? With due respect to Professor Lazarsfeld I cannot help but feel that the *Wasteland* or the novels of Kafka get, to say the least, a bit closer to some "reality" than much of the work of the Bureau of Social Research. Moreover, are the reports about middle class neuroses or about drug addiction less close to reality than the findings here reported? And now a word about the moral issues raised:

Rejection of mass culture implies to me concern for the cultural deprivation suffered by ordinary men and women, not a rejection of the masses. It implies revulsion from that cynical manipulation of people which was so starkly revealed in the various TV scandals. It implies, to quote from a recent article by David Riesman and Michael Maccoby that, "when a man is being over-manipulated to the point where his very existence has become unreal, he cannot be 'made' human by more and better manipulation from the 'right' direction, by mere bombardment with pressures and appeals. It is this very habit of ignoring the human qualities of men in order to get them to run smoothly that has caused much of our trouble."[20]

Let us be clear about this: who has contempt for the masses? Those who devise ever more refined instruments to manipulate human beings consciously or subconsciously so that they be made to buy more deodorants, laxatives, cold tablets or athlete's foot remedies, or those who think that such efforts violate human dignity; those who rig the show or those who expose the rigging? Those who ingeniously exploit guilt feelings, fears, anxieties, loneliness, and tension, or those who think that this is contemptible? Those who debase the popular taste and pretend that "this is what the slobs want," or those who fight for the maintenance of high cultural standards?

---

[20] David Riesman and Michael Maccoby, "The American Crisis" *Commentary*, 29, No. 6 (June 1960) 461–472.

Dwight Macdonald reminded us that "The March Hare explained to Alice that 'I like what I get' is not the same thing as 'I get what I like;' but March Hares have never been welcome on Madison Avenue."[21] I submit that Lewis Carrol was considerably "closer to reality" than the Bauers. They believe in an Alice in Wonderland fantasy world where sturdy, individualistic, Protestant Americans happily celebrate their togetherness around the TV set or actively participate in community life on golf courses or around barbecues. Let them take a second look, perhaps they will discover the suburban housewife frantically trying to drown her anxieties with Milltown or cocktails; the fear-ridden lower class mothers narcotizing themselves by vicarious participation in the melodrama of daytime serials; and the boys "growing up absurd"[22] in a world which seems to them without purpose and honor; the beat, the angry, the juvenile delinquents striving for kicks so as to make life meaningful be it only for a short moment of intoxication. The Bauers believe that such substitute gratification may, on balance, be quite beneficial; William Blake writing long before Freud knew better: "Unacted desire breeds pestilence."

The Bauers, I submit, have succumbed to the data they have handled so carefully. They have constructed a pseudo-reality. Let them take a few days off from their academic routines and rove around their city; let them talk to students or to corner boys, to the old men and women in the back wards of nursing homes; let them visit mental hospitals, let them interview a few psychiatrists about their patients; perhaps they will then come closer to social reality.

---

[21] Dwight Macdonald, "Masscult and Midcult", *Partisan Review, 27,* No. 2 (Spring 1960), 203–233.

[22] Cf. Paul Goodman, "Growing Up Absurd", Dissent, *VII,* No. 2 (Spring 1960), 121–136.

III.   Counter-Comment

Raymond A. Bauer and Alice H. Bauer

The comments of Parsons and White we will refer to only briefly. In some instances they strike us as valuable extensions, corrections, or needed amplifications of many points with which we have dealt. More importantly, the reader will have noticed, our own work has served as a springboard for interesting additional contributions of their own.

We would like to talk mostly about Coser's comments. Readers often wonder what lies behind heated academic debate. Sometimes there is no more, as in this instance, than an honest difference of opinion between people who on other grounds find each other quite compatible. We are both admirers of Professor Coser's work and have had the opportunity to discuss with him — with less heat in our voices than in our typewriters — his reaction to our essay.

On one major point, he is probably correct. We have in all likelihood given an inadequate description of the point of view of the critics of mass society. This is no accident, however. We despaired of the task because, as Coser points out, the position is not an entirely coherent one. We chose, therefore, to "construct a model," i.e., to state a coherent position, or actually to adopt Bell's formulation, which we felt represents the "hard core" of the position of the critics. The fact that Bell is a "critic of the critics" does not seem to us to be in point. That he and we have stereotyped the position of the critics, however, is worth talking about. As we have already suggested, we saw no alternative. If qualifications were introduced to take care of the idiosyncracies of each of the critics there would have remained nothing to talk about. Undoubtedly, the readers themselves will feel in a position to judge whether the picture presented is one which is familiar to them.

On some points, however, we do think that Coser has not been fair to us. It is amusing to find ourselves accused in his closing paragraph of being ivory tower types who ought to have closer contact with the realities of the world. One of us (R.B.) feels a little flattered. The other (A.B.) is a little piqued at being told she should visit a mental hospital, having in one fell swoop within the span of a few months visited 10 of the 12 mental hospitals (including the back wards) in the Commonwealth of Massachusetts. She is *active* in at least six state and community committees dealing with mental and social problems. Her first job out of college was to interview venereal disease patients to find out where they acquired the disease and to whom they might have transmitted it. The male of the family has an equally disreputable background: His first job was as a bootblack and cleaner of cuspidors. It is with reluctance that we must reject the accolade of being ivory tower types.

Did we say that we liked the Protestant ethic? Or that there was something wrong with disliking it? Personally we hate it. All we said about the critics is that they were striking out at it, without knowing so. Our general position is that a man ought on the average to know which horse he is beating.

On rereading our reference to the Goldhammer and Marshall study, it seems that our treatment might lead to the interpretation that their work dealt with "mental diseases" rather than with the more limited category of psychoses. We did not so intend. However, we stick to our main point. The Goldhammer and Marshall study presents the only data on *any* type of mental disease which we regard as *adequate* trend data and they found no increase in at least one type of mental disease — psychoses. We cannot accept the popular, but not universally accepted, notion that there has been an increase in neuroses.

Our reasons are spelled out in the text on page III-3. The thrust of our argument is that there are numerous sources of upward bias in virtually all trend statistics on indices of mental disease.[1] This conclusion was forced on A.B. by a number of years of working directly with mental health statistics.

As we said, there are times when Coser is not fair to us. Thus, he ridicules us for saying as though we had discovered something that: "The theorists of mass society are intellectuals." He must really have been angry with us at this point because he missed the fact that our intention in making this statement was to indicate that they react to the sanctions of that sub-group in our society which we call "intellectuals." It is in this context that we said that they were rewarded for criticizing the existing society. Coser is irrelevant, therefore, when he says — as though he is disagreeing with us — ". . . up till now it has been a common assumption among social scientists that high status is achieved by those who conform to the guiding norms of a society rather than by those who deviate from them." Quite obviously we agree with the assumption; but, as Coser himself notes, we said the theorists of mass society are *intellectuals* and they follow the guidelines of the *intellectual* community within which they seek status and not the guidelines of the community at large. By the very same logic, we anticipated that our own attack on the critics would invoke on us censure from at least some segments of the intellectual community. Coser's reaction does not invalidate our prediction.

---

[1] One exception may exist, but it scarcely reflects poorly on our society. It is conceivable that superior medical care for infants may permit a higher proportion of mentally retarded children to survive and thereby increase the incidence of mental retardation.

Most of Coser's darts are aimed at Section III. Please note that we referred to this section as "an impressionistic effort." We made no pretense and had no hope that this impressionistic part of our over-all essay would be immune to criticism. This was a deliberate attempt to stick our necks out. In this we have apparently succeeded.

By the way, we are intrigued with Coser's lament for the destruction of British working class culture by the mass media. Since he is so generous in sharing bibliographies with us, we suggest for him an interesting reference on the state of the British working class a century ago: K. Marx.

Introduction to *Daedalus* **special issue**
'Mass Culture and Mass Media'
Norman Jacobs

from

Daedalus, vol.89 no.2, 1960.

Reprinted by permission of the American Academy of Arts and Sciences and the Editor of *Daedalus*.

Editor's note

This introduction and the following thirteen articles are drawn from a special issue of *Daedalus* devoted to mass media and mass culture. One contribution to this symposium – Edward Shils's paper 'Mass Society and Its Culture' – appears in volume one of *Literary Taste, Culture and Mass Communication*. An excellent summary of that paper is to be found in this introduction.

NORMAN JACOBS

Introduction to the Issue
"Mass Culture and Mass Media"

ALTHOUGH much has been written about mass society and mass culture in the last three decades, this issue of *Dædalus* needs little apology. Beyond the contemporary scene and the transient scandals involving some of the mass media, there is a growing awareness that the problems generated by the development of mass culture are not indigenous to the United States. Throughout the Western world, industrialization, the growth of the mass media, increasing consumer affluence and leisure are introducing the dilemmas of mass culture to older societies. These problems deserve careful consideration.

In the present group of papers, three basic positions emerge, as they did at the conference described in the preface: those of the "optimist," the "pessimist," and the "meliorist." The last is the most complex. While certain meliorists do not disagree with reservations expressed by the pessimists as to mass culture, and are even prepared to concede that mass culture may eventually destroy elite culture, they do not see this as an inevitable course of events. The meliorists argue that what happens depends very much on what individuals are prepared to do, and on how society responds to the problem. Institutional and educational reform, they suggest, may alter the environment sufficiently so that a more cultivated taste develops within the mass society. It is by no means certain, the meliorists say, that elite culture is doomed: it may in fact be approaching a new stage of development.

Edward Shils is perhaps the chief spokesman for the meliorists in this issue. Claiming that contemporary society is a mass society because the mass of the population is incorporated *into* society, Shils finds the distinguishing features of mass society in industrialization, moral equalitarianism, increased social participation, greater individuality, more widely enjoyed personal relationships, and the emergence of an autonomous and affluent youth. Mass society, Shils argues, has witnessed an enormous expansion of the consumption of middle and low culture (in his terminology referred to as "mediocre" and "brutal") as a result of increased affluence, leisure, and literacy. However, this does not mean, Shils says, that high culture ("superior" or "refined") is necessarily threatened. On the contrary, the consumption of such products seems also to be on the increase.

Intellectuals believe that elite culture is declining, and they point to the hostility to elite culture on the part of the mass audience, the wastage of talent through popularization, and other such evidence as proof of their assertion. Shils suggests that comparable conditions prevail in all societies. Creative art has always been long and hard. If in fact high culture has declined, Shils says, the causes may have nothing to do with the impact of mass society. They may be due to such factors as poorer genetic endowment, changes in the distribution of genius, the culmination and exhaustion of a given creative tradition, the flow of genius into new fields of endeavor, and shifts in the standards of measurement. Yet even allowing for these factors, Shils finds the evidence of decline unimpressive. In every field of science and scholarship into which so much of our contemporary genius flows, outstanding work is being done.

Having strongly defended contemporary high culture, Shils seems to reverse himself as he stops to consider what in fact may be its deficiencies. He notes that its position in the United States is insecure, and that the creative life is impoverished in many aspects. The fault, he holds, is not with the mass media, but with the Puritan and provincial traditions of American culture, and, more recently, with the tendency toward educational and professional specialization. Specialization, in producing a technical intelligentsia, has brought about the dissolution of the educated public and intellectual community. This obviously has hurt elite culture, and has provided an opening for the mass media. The prospects for elite culture in this country are nonetheless reasonably promising provided vigorous steps are taken to improve the educational system, and if intellectuals and artists will dedicate themselves to their proper calling: the production and consumption of works of the intellect and art.

Ernest van den Haag is the theoretical spokesman for the pessimists. His attack on Shils's position is an integral one; examining mass society, he finds alienation, conformity, vicarious experience, and invidious leveling its distinguishing characteristics. As for mass culture, this is the half loaf that is worse than none, van den Haag argues. The mass media aim at pleasing the average of consumer tastes; they standardize what they produce, and standardization or homogenization is the death of art. The mass media cannot foster art: they replace it. The temptations of the mass market (money, prestige, and power) seduce and divert potential talent from the creation of art, and contribute further to its decline.

Randall Jarrell and James Baldwin support van den Haag's assault on mass culture, and offer personal testimony to the plight of the creative artist, who works in an environment hostile to creativity, from which he is necessarily alienated. Oscar Handlin suggests that popular art in late nineteenth-century America had a genuine function in the life of the masses—a function it has lost in the contemporary age of mass culture. Hannah Arendt warns that mass culture increasingly utilizes the classics and other genuine works of art, transformed and made digestible, for entertainment. Since the appetites of the entertainment industries are insatiable, they will in time consume the classics, and thereby destroy culture. Stuart Hughes argues that mass culture, with its inherent evils, is the price that has to be paid for democracy.

Leo Rosten is the spokesman for the optimists, though his estimate of the capacity of the mass audience is far from flattering. In Rosten's view, the mass media give the masses what they want, and what they want is largely trashy entertainment. Rosten examines familiar charges against the mass media: that they lack originality; are afraid to step on toes; cannot print or produce the best that is submitted to them; do not deal with the serious problems of our times; sacrifice truth to escapism; corrupt and debase public taste; operate solely for profit; and do not provide an adequate forum for minority views. He suggests that these complaints are not supported by the facts. Rosten insists that the operators of the mass media would be happy to provide superior cultural fare if the audience demands it. If, however, the media move too far ahead of their audience, they may soon have no audience at all. What drags the mass media down to the lowest common cultural denominator is the too common average taste of the masses. Critics of mass culture prefer to ignore these truths for ideological and other reasons, Rosten says, blaming the operators for the deficiencies of the masses, and projecting their own tastes and values on the masses who do not share them.

Frank Stanton argues a more optimistic view of the potentialities of the mass audience and of the role of the mass media. Mass media and intellectuals pursue the same goal: more knowledge and greater understanding. Each, however, employs different techniques to reach his objective. He insists that the television industry is meeting its responsibilities to provide serious information and cultural programs, as well as entertainment, in amounts proportionate to the different areas of audience interest. Stanton disagrees with those who argue that advertisers exercise a pernicious influence in television, but admits that the problem of the advertisers' influence on program content has not been satisfactorily solved.

That the disagreements between the three "schools" are deep, no one would wish to deny. This, however, need not obscure certain areas of agreement. All groups, for example, tend to agree with Shils that the vitality of culture in mass society is dependent finally on the vigor and health of elite culture. That the dilution and weakening of the secondary school has adversely affected the quality of elite and middlebrow culture, everyone admits. The strengthening of the public schools thus becomes an objective of the highest priority. Subsidies from the foundations and from government to support Third Programs or to provide patronage for elite art are also looked upon as a desirable goal. These are some of the tangential agreements reached against the background of large and often perplexing disagreements.

At the conference discussion, Ernest Nagel spoke for many when he expressed his unhappiness with the quality of much of the evidence introduced to support the various positions. Nagel thought too much of it anecdotal. Daniel Bell declared that too many of the generalizations were based on flimsy evidence. Implicit in these criticisms was the suggestion that the conflicting positions were based on all-or-nothing generalizations that went beyond the evidence, and that a more qualified affirmation would produce less disagreement.

Even within a context of qualified affirmation, it would still be essential to determine the direction of developing tendencies in mass culture. Shils and van den Haag, for example, disagreed as to whether mass society is producing a deterioration or an improvement in the qualitative level of the culture consumed by the masses. Both were able to find evidence to support their contentions. Patrick Hazard introduced a new factor into the discussion when he claimed that mass society has opened up new areas of cultural achievement in the fields of industrial design, architecture, landscaping, furniture, and household objects. Stanley Edgar Hyman and others cited the vast increase in the consumption of classical music and serious literature, made possible by the mass production of cheap records and paperbacks. Of course, these arguments do not prove the meliorists' case. But how are they to be weighed in any estimate of the worth of modern culture?

A similar problem bedeviled the discussion of elite culture. Van den Haag said that mass culture tends to destroy elite culture. Hannah Arendt, a pessimist like van den Haag, declared, however, that the twentieth century is a century of great art. This led Sidney Hook to ask whether mass culture has had the corrupting effects suggested by van den Haag. We thus must know how the condition of elite culture is to be measured, and how causal connections accounting for its development are to be established. In the 'twenties and 'thirties American fiction enjoyed one of its great periods; latterly it is in decline. Is this due to the corrosive effects of mass culture, or to some other cause? Meanwhile, since the end of World War II American painting has reached a peak of creativity. How is this development to be weighed, and how is it to be evaluated in the context of generalizations prophesying the demise of high culture?

The resolution of these issues must await the accumulation of more relevant evidence and the development of more refined instruments of social analysis and comparative historical measurement. Even then, perhaps, a resolution may not be forthcoming. It is chastening to note that the debate that raged in the eighteenth century with the appearance of the novel and of lending libraries contains remarkable parallels to the contemporary discussion. Pessimist, optimist, and meliorist may represent basic enduring types of character and attitude that will not yield to the most conclusive evidence or the most refined analysis. If this is so, their debate is one of the perennial debates of the intellect. The following pages present it to the readers of *Dædalus* in its contemporary form.

Society and Culture
Hannah Arendt

from

Daedalus, vol.89, no.2, 1960.

HANNAH ARENDT

Society and Culture

Mass culture and mass society (the very terms were still a sign of reprobation a few years ago, implying that mass society was a depraved form of society and mass culture a contradiction in terms) are considered by almost everybody today as something with which we must come to terms, and in which we must discover some "positive" aspects—if only because mass culture is the culture of a mass society. And mass society, whether we like it or not, is going to stay with us into the foreseeable future. No doubt mass society and mass culture are interrelated phenomena. Mass society comes about when "the mass of the population has become incorporated into society."* Since society originally comprehended those parts of the population which disposed of leisure time and the wealth which goes with it, mass society does indeed indicate a new order in which the masses have been liberated "from the burden of physically exhausting labor."† Historically as well as conceptually, therefore, mass society has been preceded by society, and society is no more a generic term than is mass society; it too can be dated and described historically. It is older, to be sure, than mass society, but not older than the modern age. In fact, all the traits that crowd psychology has meanwhile discovered in mass man: his loneliness (and loneliness is neither isolation nor solitude) regardless of his adaptability; his excitability and lack of standards; his capacity for consumption, accompanied by inability to judge or even to distinguish; above all, his egocentricity and that fateful alienation from the world which, since Rousseau, he mistakes for self-alienation—all these traits first appeared in "good society," where there was no question of masses, numerically speaking. The first mass men, we are tempted to say, quantitatively so little constituted a mass that they could even imagine they constituted an elite, the elite of good society.

Let me therefore first say a few words on the older phenomena of society and its relation to culture: say them not primarily for historical reasons, but because they relate facts that seem to me little known in this country. It may be this lack of knowledge that leads Mr. Shils to say "individuality has flowered in mass society," whereas actually the modern individual was defined and, indeed, discovered by those who—like Rousseau in the eighteenth or John Stuart Mill in the nineteenth century—found themselves in open rebellion against society. Individualism and the "sensibility and privacy" which go with it—the discovery of intimacy as the atmosphere the individual needs for his full development—came about at a time when society was not yet a mass phenomenon but still thought of itself in terms of "good society" or (especially in Central Europe) of "educated and cultured society." And it is against this background that we must understand the modern (and no longer so modern) individual who, as we all know from nineteenth- and twentieth-century novels, can only be understood as part of the society against which he tried to assert himself and which always got the better of him.

The chances of this individual's survival lay in the simultaneous presence within the population of other nonsociety strata into which the rebellious individual could escape; one reason why rebellious individuals so frequently ended by becoming revolutionaries as well was that they discovered in those who were not admitted to society certain traits of humanity which had become extinct in society. We need only read the record of the French Revolution, and recall to what an extent the very concept of *le peuple* received its connotations from a rebellion against the corruption and hypocrisy of the salons, to realize what the true role of society was throughout the nineteenth century. A good part of the despair of individuals under the conditions of mass society is due to the fact that these avenues of escape are, of course, closed as soon as society has incorporated all the strata of the population.

Generally speaking, I think it has been the great good fortune of this country to have this intermediary stage of good and cultured society play a relatively minor role in its development; but the disadvantage of this good fortune today is that those few who will still make a stand against mass culture as an unavoidable consequence of mass society are tempted to look upon these earlier phenomena of society and culture as a kind of golden age and lost paradise, precisely because they know so little of it. America has been only too well acquainted with the barbarian philistinism of the *nouveau riche*, but it has only a nodding acquaintance with the equally annoying cultural and educated philistinism of a society where culture actually has what Mr. Shils calls "snob-value," and where it is a matter of status to be educated.

This cultural philistinism is today in Europe rather a matter of the past, for the simple reason that the whole development of modern art started from and remained committed to a profound mistrust not only of cultural philistinism but also of the word culture itself. It is still an open question whether it is more difficult to discover the great authors of the past without the help of any tradition than it is to rescue them from the rubbish of educated philistinism. And this task of preserving the past without the help of tradition, and often even against traditional standards and interpretations, is the same for the whole of Western civilization. Intellectually, though not socially, America and Europe are in the same situation: the thread of tradition is broken, and we must discover the past for ourselves— that is, read its authors as though nobody had ever read them before. In this task, mass society is much less in our way than good and educated society, and I suspect that this kind of reading was not uncommon in nineteenth-century America precisely because this country was still that "unstoried wilderness" from which so many American writers and artists tried to escape. That American fiction and poetry have so suddenly and richly come into their own, ever since Whitman and Melville, may have something to do with this.

It would be unfortunate indeed if out of the dilemmas and distractions of mass culture and mass society there should arise an altogether unwarranted and idle yearning for a state of affairs which is not better but only a bit more old-fashioned. And the eager and uncritical acceptance of such obviously snobbish and philistine terms as highbrow, middlebrow, and lowbrow is a rather ominous sign. For the only nonsocial and authentic criterion for works of culture is, of course, their relative permanence and even their ultimate immortality. The point of the matter is that as soon as the immortal works of the past became the object of "refinement" and acquired the status which went with it, they lost their most important and elemental quality, which is to grasp and move the reader or spectator, throughout the centuries. The very word "culture" became suspect precisely because it indicated that "pursuit of perfection" which to Matthew Arnold was identical with the "pursuit of sweetness and light." It was not Plato, but a reading of Plato, prompted by the ulterior motive of self-perfection, that became suspect; and the "pursuit of sweetness and light," with all its overtones of good society, was held in contempt because of its rather obvious effort to keep reality out of one's life by looking at everything through a veil of sweetness and light. The astounding recovery of the creative arts in the twentieth century, and a less apparent but perhaps no less real recovery of the greatness of the past, began when good society lost its monopolizing grip on culture, together with its dominant position in society as a whole.

Here we are not concerned with society, however, but with culture —or rather with what happens to culture under the different conditions of society and of mass society. In society, culture, even more than other realities, had become what only then began to be called a "value," that is, a social commodity which could be circulated and cashed in on as social coinage for the purpose of acquiring social status. Cultural objects were transformed into values when the cultural philistine seized upon them as a currency by which he bought a higher position in society—higher, that is, than in his own opinion he deserved either by nature or by birth. Cultural values, therefore, were what values have always been, exchange values; in passing from hand to hand, they were worn down like an old coin. They lost the faculty which is originally peculiar to all cultural things, the faculty of arresting our attention and moving us. This process of transformation was called the devaluation of values, and its end came with the "bargain-sale of values" (*Ausverkauf der Werte*) during the 'twenties and 'thirties, when cultural and moral values were "sold out" together.

Perhaps the chief difference between society and mass society is that society wanted culture, evaluated and devaluated cultural things into social commodities, used and abused them for its own selfish purposes, but did not "consume" them. Even in their most worn-out shapes, these things remained things, they were not "consumed" and swallowed up but retained their worldly objectivity. Mass society, on the contrary, wants not culture but entertainment, and the wares offered by the entertainment industry are indeed consumed by society just as are any other consumer goods. The products needed for entertainment serve the life process of society, even though they may not be as necessary for this life as bread and meat. They serve, as the phrase is, to while away time, and the vacant time which is whiled away is not leisure time, strictly speaking, that is, time in which we are truly liberated from all cares and activities necessitated by the life process, and therefore free for the world and its "culture"; it is rather leftover time, which still is biological in nature, leftover after labor and sleep have received their due. Vacant time which entertainment is supposed to fill is a hiatus in the biologically conditioned cycle of labor, in "the metabolism of man with nature," as Marx used to say.

Under modern conditions, this hiatus is constantly growing; there is more and more time freed that must be filled with entertainment, but this enormous increase in vacant time does not change the nature of the time. Entertainment, like labor and sleep, is irrevocably part of the biological life process. And biological life is always, whether one is laboring or at rest, engaged in consumption or in the passive reception of amusement, a metabolism feeding on things by devouring them. The commodities the entertainment industry offers are not "things"—cultural objects whose excellence is measured by their ability to withstand the life process and to become permanent appurtenances of the world—and they should not be judged according to these standards; nor are they values which exist to be used and exchanged; they are rather consumer goods destined to be used up, as are any other consumer goods.

Panis et circenses truly belong together; both are necessary for life, for its preservation and recuperation, and both vanish in the course of the life process—that is, both must constantly be produced anew and offered anew, lest this process cease entirely. The standards by which both should be judged are indeed freshness and novelty— standards by which we today (and, I think, quite mistakenly) judge cultural and artistic objects as well, things which are supposed to remain in the world even after we have left it.

As long as the entertainment industry produces its own consumer goods, all is well, and we can no more reproach it for the nondurability of its articles than we can reproach a bakery because it produces goods which, if they are not to spoil, must be consumed as soon as they are made. It has always been the mark of educated philistinism to despise entertainment and amusement because no "value" could be derived from them. In so far as we are all subject to life's great cycle, we all stand in need of entertainment and amusement in some form or other, and it is sheer hypocrisy or social snobbery to deny that we can be amused and entertained by exactly the same things which amuse and entertain the masses of our fellow men. As far as the survival of culture is concerned, it certainly is less threatened by those who fill vacant time with amusement and entertainment than by those who fill it with some haphazard educational gadget in order to improve their social standing.

If mass culture and the entertainment industry were the same, I should not worry much, even though it is true that, in Mr. Shils's words, "the immense advance in audibility and visibility" of this whole sector of life, which formerly had been "relatively silent and unseen by the intellectuals," creates a serious problem for the artist and intellectual. It is as though the futility inherent in entertainment had been permitted to permeate the whole social atmosphere, and the often described malaise of the artists and intellectuals is of course partly due to their inability to make themselves heard and seen in the tumultuous uproar of mass society, or to penetrate its noisy futility. But this protest of the artist against society is as old as society, though not older; the great revival of nearly all the arts in our century (which perhaps one day will seem one of the great artistic—and of course scientific—periods of Western civilization) began with the malaise of the artist in society, with his decision to turn his back upon it and its "values," to leave the dead to bury the dead. As far as artistic productivity is concerned, it should not be more difficult to withstand the massive temptations of mass culture, or to keep from being thrown out of gear by the noise and humbug of mass society, than it was to avoid the more sophisticated temptations and the more insidious noises of the cultural snobs in refined society.

Unhappily, the case is not that simple. The entertainment industry is confronted with gargantuan appetites, and since its wares disappear in consumption, it must constantly offer new commodities. In this predicament, those who produce for the mass media ransack the entire range of past and present culture in the hope of finding suitable material. This material, however, cannot be offered as it is; it must be prepared and altered in order to become entertaining; it cannot be consumed as it is.

Mass culture comes into being when mass society seizes upon cultural objects, and its danger is that the life process of society (which like all biological processes insatiably draws everything available into the cycle of its metabolism) will literally consume the cultural objects, eat them up and destroy them. I am not referring to the phenomenon of mass distribution. When cultural objects, books, or pictures in reproduction, are thrown on the market cheaply and attain huge sales, this does not affect the nature of the goods in question. But their nature is affected when these objects themselves are changed (rewritten, condensed, digested, reduced to *Kitsch* in the course of reproduction or preparation for the movies) in order to be put into usable form for a mass sale which they otherwise could not attain.

Neither the entertainment industry itself nor mass sales as such are signs of, not what we call mass culture, but what we ought more accurately to call the decay of culture in mass society. This decay sets in when liberties are taken with these cultural objects in order that they may be distributed among masses of people. Those who actively promote this decay are not the Tin Pan Alley composers but a special kind of intellectuals, often well read and well informed, whose sole function is to organize, disseminate, and change cultural objects in order to make them palatable to those who want to be entertained or—and this is worse—to be "educated," that is, to acquire as cheaply as possible some kind of cultural knowledge to improve their social status.

Richard Blackmur (in a recent article on the "Role of the Intellectual," in the *Kenyon Review*) has brilliantly shown that the present malaise of the intellectual springs from the fact that he finds himself surrounded, not by the masses, from whom, on the contrary, he is carefully shielded, but by these digesters, re-writers, and changers of culture whom we find in every publishing house in the United States, and in the editorial offices of nearly every magazine. And these "professionals" are ably assisted by those who no longer write books but fabricate them, who manufacture a "new" textbook out of four or five already on the market, and who then have, as Blackmur shows, only one worry—how to avoid plagiarism. (Meanwhile the editor does his best to substitute clichés for sheer illiteracy.) Here the criterion of novelty, quite legitimate in the entertainment industry, becomes a simple fake and, indeed, a threat: it is only too likely that the "new" textbook will crowd out the older ones, which usually are better, not because they are older, but because they were still written in response to authentic needs.

This state of affairs, which indeed is equaled nowhere else in the world, can properly be called mass culture; its promoters are neither the masses nor their entertainers, but are those who try to entertain the masses with what once was an authentic object of culture, or to persuade them that *Hamlet* can be as entertaining as *My Fair Lady*, and educational as well. The danger of mass education is precisely that it may become very entertaining indeed; there are many great authors of the past who have survived centuries of oblivion and neglect, but it is still an open question whether they will be able to survive an entertaining version of what they have to say.

The malaise of the intellectual in the atmosphere of mass culture is much more legitimate than his malaise in mass society; it is caused socially by the presence of these other intellectuals, the manufacturers of mass culture, from whom he finds it difficult to distinguish himself and who, moreover, always outnumber him, and therefore acquire that kind of power which is generated whenever people band together and act more or less in concert. The power of the many (legitimate only in the realm of politics and the field of action) has always been a threat to the strength of the few; it is a threat under the most favorable circumstances, and it has always been felt to be more dangerous when it arises from within a group's own ranks. Culturally, the malaise is caused, I think, not so much by the massive temptations and the high rewards which await those who are willing to alter their products to make them acceptable for a mass market, as by the constant irritating care each of us has to exert in order to protect his product against the demands and the ingenuity of those who think they know how to "improve" it.

Culture relates to objects and is a phenomenon of the world; entertainment relates to people and is a phenomenon of life. If life is no longer content with the pleasure which is always coexistent with the toil and labor inherent in the metabolism of man with nature, if vital energy is no longer fully used up in this cycle, then life may reach out for the things of the world, may violate and consume them. It will prepare these things of the world until they are fit for consumption; it will treat them as if they were articles of nature, articles which must also be prepared before they can enter into man's metabolism.

Consumption of the things of nature does no harm to them; they are constantly renewed because man, in so far as he lives and labors, toils and recuperates, is also a creature of nature, a part of the great cycle in which all nature wheels. But the things of the world which are made by man (in so far as he is a worldly and not merely a natural being), these things are not renewed of their own accord. When life seizes upon them and consumes them at its pleasure, for entertainment, they simply disappear. And this disappearance, which first begins in mass culture—that is, the "culture" of a society poised between the alternatives of laboring and of consuming—is something different from the wear and tear culture suffered when its things were made into exchange values, and circulated in society until their original stamp and meaning were scarcely recognizable.

If we wish to classify these two anticultural processes in historical and sociological terms, we may say that the devaluation of culture in good society through the cultural philistines was the characteristic peril of commercial society, whose primary public area was the exchange market for goods and ideas. The disappearance of culture in a mass society, on the other hand, comes about when we have a consumers' society which, in so far as it produces only for consumption, does not need a public worldly space whose existence is independent of and outside the sphere of its life process. In other words, a consumers' society does not know how to take care of the world and the things which belong to it: the society's own chief attitude toward objects, the attitude of consumption, spells ruin to everything it touches. If we understand by culture what it originally meant (the Roman *cultura*—derived from *colere*, to take care of and preserve and cultivate) then we can say without any exaggeration that a society obsessed with consumption cannot at the same time be cultured or produce a culture.

For all their differences, however, one thing is common to both these anticultural processes: they arise when all the worldly objects produced by the present or the past have become "social," are related to society, and are seen in their merely functional aspect. In the one case, society uses and exchanges, evaluates and devaluates them; in the other, it devours and consumes them. This functionalization or "societization" of the world is by no means a matter of course; the notion that every object must be functional, fulfilling some needs of society or of the individual—the church a religious need, the painting the need for self-expression in the painter and the need of self-perfection in the onlooker, and so on—is historically so new that one is tempted to speak of a modern prejudice. The cathedrals were built *ad majorem gloriam Dei;* while they as buildings certainly served the needs of the community, their elaborate beauty can never be explained by these needs, which could have been served quite as well by any nondescript building.

An object is cultural to the extent that it can endure; this durability is the very opposite of its functionality, which is the quality which makes it disappear again from the phenomenal world by being used and used up. The "thingness" of an object appears in its shape and appearance, the proper criterion of which is beauty. If we wanted to judge an object by its use value alone, and not also by its appearance (that is, by whether it is beautiful or ugly or something in between), we would first have to pluck out our eyes.

Thus, the functionalization of the world which occurs in both society and mass society deprives the world of culture as well as beauty. Culture can be safe only with those who love the world for its own sake, who know that without the beauty of man-made, worldly things which we call works of art, without the radiant glory in which potential imperishability is made manifest to the world and in the world, all human life would be futile and no greatness could endure.

A Dissent from the Consensual Society
by
Ernest van den Haag

from

Daedalus, vol.89, no.2, 1960.

Reprinted by permission of the American Academy of Arts and Sciences and the Editor of *Daedalus*.

ERNEST VAN DEN HAAG

A Dissent from the Consensual Society

EDWARD SHILS replaces Van Wyck Brooks' high, middle, and lowbrow classification (lately elaborated fruitfully by Richard Chase[1]) with his own: "refined," "mediocre," and "brutal" culture. The old terminology was unsatisfactory; but the new one is much more so. The evaluative element inherent in both should be formulated independently.[2] It is stronger in the new notation. Further, this notation is misleading in its implications. "Refined" has a genteel connotation, which I find hard to apply to such highbrows as Joyce, Kafka, Dostoyevsky, Céline, or Nathanael West. Nor are lowbrow and "brutal" equivalent; indeed, the belief that they are is a middlebrow cliché, a projection of ambivalent desire and fear that identifies vitality and brutality. Actually, much lowbrow culture is maudlin and sentimental rather than brutal.[3] Even the term "mediocre" culture, though less misleading than the others, is not satisfactory and provides a criterion that would be hard to apply.

In my opinion, emphasis on cultural objects misses the point. A sociologist (and to analyze mass culture is a sociological enterprise) must focus on the function of such objects in people's lives: he must study how they are used; who produces what for whom; why, and with what effects. To be sure, value judgments cannot be avoided, but the qualities of the product become relevant only when related to its social functions. Middlebrow culture objects are not necessarily "mediocre." To be a middlebrow is to *relate* to objects, any objects, in a certain way, to give them a specific function in the context of one's life. A middlebrow might, for example, use a phrase, whatever its origin, as a cliché—i.e., in such a way that it loses its emotional impact and specific concrete meaning and no longer communicates but labels or stereotypes and thus avoids perception and communication. The phrase is not middlebrow (or "mediocre"); he is. Beethoven does not become "mediocre," even though he may become a favored middlebrow composer and function as part of middlebrow culture. Mozart may "tinkle" for the middlebrow; it is not Mozart but the audience that is mediocre. Indeed, it is characteristic of much middlebrow culture to overuse highbrow cultural objects of the past without understanding them and thus both to honor and debase them. Mr. Shils's terminology precludes the description of cultural dynamics in these terms and thus disregards one of the most important aspects of mass culture: the corruption and sterilization of the heritage of the past.

Mass culture is not the culture of a class or group throughout history. It is the culture of nearly everybody today, and of nearly nobody yesterday; and because of production, market, and social changes, it is quite a new phenomenon which cannot be reduced to quantitative changes nor identified with timeless categories. Mr. Shils dismisses the conditions under which mass culture is produced and consumed with some descriptive phrases but does not relate mass production to the qualities of the cultural objects he discusses. His categories remain ahistorical, even though garnished with familiar historical references. Thus, the problem of mass culture is defined away, instead of being analyzed.

Mr. Shils hopefully maintains that "refined" culture now has become available to more people than ever before. This is true, but it constitutes the problem—not the solution. What are people making of the cultural heritage that is becoming available to them? What impact does it have on them? What are they doing to it? Mass culture involves a change in the conditions in which objects are produced, consumed, and related to on all levels, a change in the role each level plays, and a change finally in the way people relate to each other. At times Mr. Shils seems to recognize this change; but his categories preclude analysis of it. The destruction of folk culture by mass culture is apparently denied and then explained by the hypothesis that the proportion of gifted people remains "fairly constant" in any population and that they are now "diverted into other spheres." This is, of course, what is meant by the destruction of folk culture, in addition to other effects of increased mobility and communication. It is remarkable that Shils also says that, if high culture has declined (which he denies) possibly "our neural equipment is poorer than that of our ancestors." Neither of the two inconsistent hypotheses—unchanged or changed "neural equipment"—can be proved. Does this mean that we can use both? Since we know so little about neurological change, would it not be sensible to look for social changes to explain cultural changes? Mr. Shils recognizes social changes but refuses to relate them to cultural changes, which he denies, asserts, deplores, and approves. He cannot be wrong since he has left all possibilities open.

Mr. Shils suggests that anyone critical of mass culture must be a *laudator temporis acti;* I see no basis for this, nor for his own temporal chauvinism. We have no measurements; and history is not a homogeneous stream; hence, comparisons with the past depend largely on the period selected as standard. Comparison of specific aspects and levels of culture may be instructive or, at least, illustrative; but wholesale judgments seem futile.[4]

The crucial issue is fully comprised in the question with which Rostovtzeff concludes his *magnum opus*: "Is it possible to extend a higher civilization to the lower classes without debasing its standard and diluting its quality to the vanishing point? Is not every civilization bound to decay as soon as it begins to penetrate the masses?"

Mr. Shils describes mass society as one in which there is "more sense of attachment to society as a whole . . . more sense of affinity with one's fellows." According to him, the mass stands in a closer relationship to the center; there is a "dispersion of charisma" with "greater stress on individual dignity"; "the value of sensation has come to be widely appreciated"; individuality has been "discovered and developed," as has the value of personal relationships; the masses begin to "become capable of more subtle perception and judgment" as their "moral responsiveness and sensibility are aroused."

The society which Mr. Shils describes is not the one in which I live. I am forced to conjecture that the generosity of his wishes has relaxed the customary strictness of his methods and blunted the accuracy of his perception.[5]

Progress toward the fulfillment of Mr. Shils's wishes is implied by the terms he uses. Yet there are some material doubts. Is the value of sensation more widely appreciated than it was in antiquity, the Renaissance, or even the nineteenth century? I find American society singularly antisensual: let me just mention the food served in restaurants, preprandial cocktails intended, often charitably, to kill sensation. The congested seating arrangements in restaurants, the way cities, suburbs, exurbs, and resorts are built do not support the hypothesis of increased value placed on privacy. Even sex is largely socialized and de-sensualized. Do we stand in closer relationship to the center—or are we alienated, suffering from what Wordsworth described as "perpetual emptiness, unceasing change" because in Yeats' words, "Things fall apart; the centre cannot hold"? Has there actually been a "dispersion of charisma"?[6] Or has there been a shift from real to Hollywood queens? Does our society foster "personal relationships," "individuality," "privacy," or marketability, outer-directedness, pseudo-personalizations parasitically devouring the genuine personalities of those who assume them? Could Jesus go into the desert today to contemplate? Wouldn't he be followed by a crew of *Life* photographers, cameramen, publishers' agents, etc.? What of the gossip columns, of people's interest in other people's private lives and particularly their personal relations—don't these phenomena suggest a breakdown of reserve, vicarious living—indeed, pseudo-life and experience?

Statistical data reveal that there is now higher income, more education, and more equally distributed leisure, increased mobility, travel, and communication. Undoubtedly there is more material opportunity for more people than ever before. But if so many people are so much better off in so many respects, is culture better than ever? The lowered barriers, the greater wealth, the increased opportunities are material achievements but only cultural promises. Mr. Shils appears to have taken all the promises of the age and confused them with fulfillments. It is as though one were to take the data of the Kinsey report and conclude that since there seems to be so much intercourse, people must love each other more than ever. I have nothing against Mr. Kinsey's entomological enterprise (though it makes me feel waspish). But even though it may furnish raw data, we must distinguish it from sociological enterprise.

If people address each other on a first-name basis when they meet, do they really love and esteem each other more than people who do not use first names? Or does equal familiarity with all suggest a lack of differentiation, the very opposite of personal relations, which are based on discriminating among perceived individualities? "In America," de Tocqueville wrote, "the bond of affection is extended but it is relaxed." Mr. Shils notes the extension but not the dilution. Yet extension can only be bought at the price of lessened intensity, depth, and stability.

Of course we have more communication and mobility than ever before. But isn't it possible that less is communicated? We have all the opportunities in the world to see, hear, and read more than ever before. Is there any independent indication to show that we experience and understand more? Does not the constant slick assault on our senses and minds produce monotony and indifference and prevent experience? Does not the discontinuity of most people's lives unsettle, and sometimes undo them? We surely have more external contacts than ever before. But most people have less spontaneous and personal (internalized) relationships than they might with fewer contacts and opportunities.

We have more equality of opportunity. But the burden of relative deprivations is felt more acutely the smaller they are and the greater the opportunities. [7] People become resentful and clamor for a different kind of equality, equality at the end rather than the beginning, in short, invidious leveling. Does not the comminution of society alienate people from one another—as the discontinuity of their existence fragments them—and replace a sense of purpose with a sense of meaninglessness? Is the increased "conviviality" Mr. Shils hails more than the wish for "togetherness" which marks the lonely crowd?

Mr. Shils contends that we have more intellectuals, consumers, and producers of "refined" culture than before. In one sense, he is quite right. But these are intellectuals by position (university teachers, authors, etc.), and having more of them tells us nothing about the number of intellectuals by ability, interest, and cultivation. Mr. Shils almost concedes as much. But he remains on the phenomenal level, and never goes to the root of the phenomenon: [8] the marginal role, the interstitial life, of intellectuals in a mass culture society. And I mean those who remain engaged in intellectual life and do not allow themselves to be reduced to the status of technicians or manufacturers of middlebrow entertainments.

Similarly, Mr. Shils mentions the possibility that intellectual and artistic creators may be seduced into more remunerative pseudo-creative activities only to dismiss it by pointing out that "the mere existence of opportunity will not seduce a man of strongly impelled creative capacities once he has found his direction." Of course, no one is impelled *only* by "creative capacities." The trouble is that the lure of mass media (and of foundation money and prestige) and the values that go with them are internalized long before the potential creator "has found his direction."

Mr. Shils declares that "the heart of the revolution of mass culture" is "the expanding radius of empathy and fellow feeling" which "have given to youth opportunities never available before." These opportunities, Mr. Shils concedes, are utilized mainly through "mediocre and brutal culture." But he does not point out (though noting the effect) that the appalling ignorance of educated youth is produced by reliance on the equally ignorant charisma-endowed peer group; by belief, in short, that there is little to learn from the past and its representatives. The loss of respect for learning and tradition, particularly in its less tangible aspects, is not independent of the leveling dear to Mr. Shils; it is not unrelated to the widely held view that obsolescence automatically overtakes aesthetic and moral values, as it does technological invention. It should be evident that this notion is generated by the pragmatic nature of mass culture and by the high mobility that Mr. Shils extolls.[9]

To object to some of Mr. Shils's views is to agree with others. For he starts by praising and ends by deploring mass culture. This nice balance is achieved, I feel, at the expense of a coherent theory of mass culture. Let me suggest a few prolegomena to such a theory.

The most general characteristics of mass culture are deducible from premises on which there is no disagreement: they are concomitants of any industrial, mass production society. Included among these are increased income and mobility, more equally distributed leisure, egalitarianism, wider communication and education,[10] more specialization and less scope for individuality in work. The consequences that I deduce from these premises are consistent and fit my impressions. But there is no strict empirical proof, although I do believe it may be possible to test some of these hypotheses after appropriate reformulation. Further, other hypotheses may be consistent with these premises, and the real question turns on their relative importance and their relevance. With these qualifications, I submit that this quasi-deductive method which relates the ascertainable to the less tangible is the only one that can yield a "theory" of mass culture deserving the name.

Let me outline some of the most important characteristics of mass culture.[11]

(1) There is a separation of the manufacturers of culture from the consumers, which is part of the general separation of production and consumption and of work and play. Culture becomes largely a spectator sport, and life and experience become exogenous and largely vicarious. (Nothing will dissuade me from seeing a difference between a young girl walking around with her pocket radio listening to popular songs and one who sings herself; nor am I persuaded that the tales collected by the brothers Grimm remain the same when enacted on television or synthetically reproduced by Walt Disney.)

(2) Mass production aims at pleasing an average of tastes and therefore, though catering to all to some extent, it cannot satisfy

any taste fully. Standardization is required and necessarily de-individualizes—as do the techniques required by mass production and marketing.

(3) Since culture, like everything else in a mass society, is mainly produced to please an average of consumer tastes, the producers become (and remain) an elite by catering to consumer tastes rather than developing or cultivating autonomous ones. Initiative, and power to bestow prestige and income, have shifted from the elite to the mass. The difference may be seen by comparing the development of ritual dogmatic beliefs and practices in the Protestant denominations and in the Roman Catholic church. The latter has minimized, the former maximized dependence on consumers. In the Protestant churches, there is, therefore, no body of religious (as distinguished from moral) beliefs left, except as an intellectual curiosity.

(4) The mass of men dislikes and always has disliked learning and art. It wishes to be distracted from life rather than to have it revealed; to be comforted by traditional (possibly happy and sentimental) tropes, rather than be upset by new ones. It is true that it wishes to be thrilled, too. But irrational violence or vulgarity provides thrills, as well as release, just as sentimentality provides escape. What is new here is that, apart from the fact that irrelevant thrills and emotions are now prefabricated, the elite is no longer protected from the demands of the mass consumers.

(5) As a result of the high psychological and economic costs of individuality and privacy, gregariousness has become internalized. People fear solitude and unpopularity; popular approval becomes the only moral and aesthetic standard most people recognize. This tendency is reinforced by the shrinkage in the importance and size of primary groups, which have also become looser; by a corresponding increase in the size and importance of secondary groups and publics; and finally, by the shift of many of the functions of primary to secondary groups.

(6) The greatly increased lure of mass markets for both producers and consumers diverts potential talent from the creation of art. (Within the arts, the performing do better than the creative ones.) Here interesting empirical questions arise: to what extent is talent bent endogenously and exogenously; to what extent can it be?

(7) Excessive communication serves to isolate people from one another, from themselves, and from experience. It extends bonds by weakening them. People become indifferent and indiscriminately

tolerant; their own life as well as everything else is trivialized, eclectic, and styleless.

(8) Mass media for inherent reasons must conform to prevailing average canons of taste.[12] They cannot foster art; indeed, they replace it. When they take up classics, they usually reshape them to meet expectations. But even when that is not the case, they cannot hope to individualize and refine taste, though they may occasionally supply an already formed taste for high culture. Half a loaf, in these matters, spoils the appetite, even with vitamins added, and is not better than none. The technical availability of good reproductions and the paperback editions of noncondensed books are unlikely to change this situation; they often add alien elements which merely decorate lives styled by mass culture.[13]

(9) The total effect of mass culture is to distract people from lives which are so boring that they generate obsession with escape. Yet because mass culture creates addiction to prefabricated experience, most people are deprived of the remaining possibilities of autonomous growth and enrichment, and their lives become ever more boring and unfulfilled.

This very brief sketch of the general features of mass culture should make it clear that I do not agree with those mass culture optimists who favor the wide presentation of "refined" culture through the mass media. I do not think this desirable or desired. Nor, for that matter, practicable. People get what they wish and I see no way of imposing on them anything else. I have to disagree with those who appear to think that the issue is to improve the culture offered the mass of men and to try to reach the masses in greater and greater numbers. My conclusion is different: high or refined culture, in my opinion, is best preserved and developed by avoiding mass media. I should go further and give up some advantages of mass production for the sake of greater individualization. This would reverse many present policies. For instance, I should favor fairly high direct taxes on most mass media, or a tax on advertising. Perhaps we might still be capable of replacing the noise that would be thus eliminated with conversation.

REFERENCES

1 Richard Chase, *The Democratic Vista*, Garden City: Doubleday, 1958.
2 Unless it is contended that everything (and everybody) "refined" is morally and aesthetically superior to everything (and everybody) "brutal" or "mediocre," etc. Yet the possibility of excellence *sui generis* must not be excluded

by definition—unless, instead of social and cultural, purely aesthetic categories are to be discussed. On this score—and in the whole taxonomic scheme —Mr. Shils is confusing.

3 See *True Romances*, various soap operas, and lowbrow religious and familial piety. "Kitsch," which is part of low and of middle-lowbrow culture, means corny sentimentalization and, contrary to Mr. Shils, it does not "represent aesthetic sensibility and aesthetic aspiration, untutored . . ." but a synthetic, an *Ersatz* for both. Paper flowers, however real they look, will never grow.

4 Elsewhere Mr. Shils has suggested that critics of mass culture are sour ex-Marxists. Possibly. Ex-Marxists are likely to be critical minds. That is what made them first Marxists and then ex. But though ex-Marxists may incline to be critics of mass culture (and only some, by no means all), the converse certainly does not follow. At any rate, I am tempted to paraphrase advice attributed to Lincoln: abstemious sociologists might benefit by a draught of radical ex-Marxism.

5 John Stuart Mill (*On Liberty*, ch. 3) concludes his discussion of the power of public opinion in egalitarian societies by pointing out that as leveling proceeds, "there ceases to be any social support for nonconformity . . . any substantive power in society which . . . is interested in taking under its protection opinions and tendencies at variance with those of the public." From de Tocqueville to David Riesman, the dangers of "cultural democracy" have been considered. I do not believe that Mr. Shils comes seriously to grips with these dangers.

6 I am not convinced even that the greater inclusiveness of our society can quite be taken for granted. The fate of the Jews in Germany cannot be that easily dismissed. Nazism was political Kitsch as well as a rise of "brutal culture."

7 "The more complete this uniformity the more insupportable the sight of such a difference becomes," de Tocqueville notes.

8 Even on that level, one might quarrel with Mr. Shils. England is not yet as much imbued with mass culture as we are. The class system and selective education have not been entirely overcome; nor have the traditions of elite culture. With only a quarter of our population—not to speak of wealth—England publishes more books every year than we do. And it has at least as many economists, philosophers, and novelists of the first rank as we do.

9 The phenomenon is part of mass culture everywhere, but the ignorance and rejection of the past were particularly fostered in America because of the immigrant background of many parents, the melting-pot nature of the school system, and the rapid rate of change which makes the experience of the old seem old-fashioned and diminishes their authority.

10 Note that more has to be learned through formal instruction, partly because less culture is transmitted informally and individually. This is no advantage because our school system helps bring about the spread of a homogenized mass culture intentionally and unintentionally.

11 For a fuller exposition of my views, see Ralph Ross and Ernest van den Haag, *The Fabric of Society* (New York: Harcourt, Brace and Company, 1957), ch. 15.

12 In Frank Stanton's words, "Any mass medium will always have to cater to the middle grounds . . . the most widely held, or cease to be."

13 Joseph Bram has called my attention to the several distinct phases of mass culture. It often begins with a rather moving attempt of the uneducated to become seriously educated. One sees this in countries beginning their industrial development. The adulteration of, and disrespect for, education comes with full industrialization, when the mass culture market is created and supplied with goods manufactured for it.

Comments on Mass and Popular Culture
Oscar Handlin

from

Daedalus, vol.89, no.2, 1960.

Reprinted by permission of the American Academy of Arts and Sciences and the Editor of *Daedalus*

OSCAR HANDLIN

Comments on Mass and Popular Culture

THE QUESTION of the uses of culture, raised in this discussion, offers a strategic point for analysis of the differences between those forms of expression communicated by the mass media and all other popular varieties of art. For, although no society has been devoid of culture, that which we now associate with the mass media appears to be unique in its relationship to the way of life of the people. A brief consideration of the function of culture will illuminate the character of that uniqueness.

Until the appearance of those phenomena which we now associate with the mass media, culture was always considered incidental to some social end. Men did not build architecture or compose music in the abstract. They constructed churches in which to worship or homes in which to live. They composed masses and cantatas as parts of a sacred service. The forms within which they built or composed were important in themselves, but they were also intimately related to the functions they served for those who used them.

Hence the significance of Miss Arendt's suggestive statement which pointed out that in the eighteenth and nineteenth centuries in Europe, culture acquired another kind of utility: that is, it became a means by which the bourgeoisie sought to identify itself with aristocratic society. I would add that an analogous development occurred in the United States in the last quarter of the nineteenth century, complicated by the fact that here the aristocracy was putative only and had to improvise its own standards. The difficulty of doing so brought the whole process to the surface and as a result it was much more open and visible in America than in Europe.

In any case, by 1900 almost everywhere in the Western world the term culture had acquired a distinctive connotation, just as the term Society had. Society no longer referred to the total order of the populace in a community, but only to a small self-defined segment of it. And culture no longer referred to the total complex of forms through which the community satisfied its wants, but only to certain narrowly defined modes of expression distinguished largely by their lack of practicality.

In the process of redefinition, culture lost all connection with function other than that of establishing an identification with that narrow society which had made itself the custodian of the values attached to the arts. The châteaux of Fifth Avenue were not erected to meet men's needs for homes, any more than the rare books of the tycoons were assembled to satisfy their desire for reading matter. Architecture, literature, art, and music, as defined by society and its intermediaries, became, rather, primarily the symbols of status.

That very fact, indeed, served Society as the justification of its aristocratic pretensions. "Changes in manners and customs," an influential manual explained, "no matter under what form of government, usually originate with the wealthy or aristocratic minority, and are thence transmitted to the other classes. . . . This rule naturally holds good of house-planning, and it is for this reason that the origin of modern house-planning should be sought rather in the prince's mezzanine than in the small middle-class dwelling."*

By the end of the nineteenth century, therefore, Americans could readily identify a miscellaneous congeries of artistic forms as their culture. The citizens of the Republic and foreign observers had no difficulty in recognizing what was American music, literature, or painting, for an elaborate apparatus of critical institutions—museums, orchestras, journals, and universities—existed to pass judgment on what belonged and what did not. These institutions and the impresarios who controlled them had the confidence and support of Society, that segment of the community which assumed that wealth or birth gave it leadership.

Outside the realm of the official culture as defined by Society there persisted other, but excluded, modes of action and expression. The peasants of Europe, the workers of the industrial cities, the ethnic enclaves of the United States did not share the forms of behavior, the tastes and attitudes of the would-be or genuine aristocracy, although they often acknowledged the primacy of the groups above them. But peasants, laborers, and foreigners did retain and employ in their own

---

* Edith Wharton and Ogden Codman, Jr., *The Decoration of Houses* (New York: Charles Scribner's Sons, 1897), p. 5.

lives a complex of meaningful forms of expression of their own. At the time these were commonly characterized as popular or folk culture. Thus in the early decades of this century, it was usual to refer to popular music, popular literature, and popular art, set off and distinct from *the* music, *the* literature, and *the* art of Society.

That designation was misleading, in so far as it carried the implication that popular culture was as coherent and uniform as the official culture. In actuality, popular culture, in America at least, was composed of a complex of sub-cultures. The mass of the population of the metropolitan cities, the Negroes, the farmers of the Great Plains, and other groups which together constituted the bulk of the American population had no taste for the music played by the Philharmonic or the novels approved by Thomas Bailey Aldrich or the paintings certified by Duveen. These people sang and danced, they read, and they were amused or edified by pictures. Only, what they sang or read or looked at was not music or literature or art in the sense defined by Society, and therefore was explained away by the general designation, popular.

Superficially, popular culture differed from the defined culture in the lack of an accepted set of canons or of a normative body of classics. A vaudeville song or a piece of embroidery or a dime novel was accepted or rejected by its audience without comparison with or reference to standards extraneous to itself. But this surface difference sprang from a deeper one. Popular, unlike defined, culture retained a functional quality in the sense that it was closely related to the felt needs and familiar modes of expression of the people it served. Popular songs were to be danced to, vaudeville to be laughed at, and embroidery to be worn or to cover a table.

The development of mass culture—or more properly speaking of the culture communicated through the mass media—has had a disturbing effect upon both popular and defined cultures. The consequences for the latter are the easier to distinguish, for it left not only vestiges but a record of its past which makes possible ready comparisons with the present.

It is far more difficult to make similar comparisons in the case of popular culture. Precisely because it lacked a canon, it also lacked a history. It was not only displaced by later forms; its very memory was all but obliterated. As a result we know very little about the culture that until recently served the people who now consume the products of the mass media. And that gap in our information has given rise to the misconception that the "mass culture" of the present is but an extension of the popular culture of the past.

Yet if that popular culture did not produce its own record, it can be pieced together from fragmentary historical materials which reveal that the mass media have had as deep an impact upon popular as upon official culture. The Ed Sullivan show is not vaudeville in another guise any more than "Omnibus" is a modernized Chautauqua. Television, the movies, and the mass-circulation magazines stand altogether apart from the older vehicles of both popular and defined culture.

An examination of the popular theater, of vaudeville, of the popular newspapers, especially in the Sunday supplements, and of the popular literature of the 1890's reveals four significant elements in the difference between the popular culture of that period and that communicated by the mass media of the present.

In the first place, popular culture, although unstructured and chaotic, dealt directly with the concrete world intensely familiar to its audience. There was no self-conscious realism in this preoccupation with the incidents and objects of the everyday world. Rather, this was the most accessible means of communication with a public that was innocent in its approach to culture, that is, one that looked or listened without ulterior motive or intent.

In the second place, and for similar reasons, popular culture had a continuing relevance to the situation of the audience that was exposed to it. That relevance was maintained by a direct rapport between those who created and those who consumed this culture. The very character of the popular theater, for instance, in which the spontaneous and the "ad lib" were tolerated, encouraged a continuous and highly intimate response across the footlights. So too, the journalism of the American ethnic sub-groups maintained an immediate awareness of the needs and problems of their readers. In general, furthermore, in all media, the writers and actors sprang from the identical milieu as their audience did, and maintained a firm sense of identification with it.

In the third place, popular culture was closely tied to the traditions of those who consumed it. A large part of it was ethnic in character, that is, arranged within the terms of a language and of habits and attitudes imported from Europe. But even that part of it which was native American and which reached back into the early nineteenth and eighteenth centuries, maintained a high degree of continuity with its own past.

Finally, popular culture had the capacity for arousing in its audience such sentiments as wonder and awe, and for expressing the sense of irony of their own situation which lent it enormous emotional power. Men and women shed real tears or rocked with laughter in the playhouses of the Bowery, as they could not in the opera or the theater uptown. The acrobats and the animals of the circus evoked wonder as the framed pictures of the museum could not. The difference was the product of the authenticity of the one type of culture and the artificiality of the other.

Out of American popular culture there emerged occasional bursts of creativity of high level. Instances may be found in the work of Charlie Chaplin, in some of the jazz music of the decade after 1900, and in that strain of literary realism developed by novelists and dramatists whose experience in journalism had brought them into direct contact with popular culture.

In total perspective, however, popular culture was not justified by such by-products so much as by the function it served. Millions of people found in this culture a means of communication among themselves and the answers to certain significant questions that they were asking about the world around them. Indeed, it was the perception of this function that attracted the avant-garde in the opening decades of the twentieth century. Those creative spirits, repelled by the inert pretensions of official culture, often found refreshing elements of authenticity in the popular culture of their times. Bohemia, too, was a kind of ghetto in which the artist, equally with the Italian or Negro laborer, was alien, cut off from respectable society. In fact some of the Bohemians were inclined to idealize popular culture in revulsion against the inability of the official culture to satisfy their own needs.

In the light of these considerations, it is possible to begin to assess the effects of the mass media on the character of popular culture. To some extent the impact of the new media is simply a product of their size. The enormous growth of these media has been of such an order as to involve immediate qualitative changes. The transformation of an audience, once numbered in the thousands, to one of millions profoundly altered all the relationships involved. More specifically, the impact of the mass media has altered the earlier forms of control; it has deprived the material communicated of much of its relevance; and it has opened a gulf between the artist and the audience.

A good deal of the familiar talk about the degree to which advertisers or bankers or interest groups control the mass media is irrelevant. There has been a genuine change in the character of the control of these media as contrasted with the situation of fifty or sixty years ago. But it has taken a more subtle form than is usually ascribed to it.

What is most characteristic of the mass media today is precisely the disappearance of the forms of control that existed in the popular culture of a half-century ago. No one can decide now (as Hearst or Pulitzer could in 1900) to use a newspaper as a personal organ. Nor could any TV or movie executive, advertiser, agent, or even a large sector of the audience dictate the content of what is transmitted through these media. The most they can do is prevent the inclusion of material distasteful to them.

The only accurate way of describing the situation of the mass media is to say they operate within a series of largely negative restraints. There are many things they cannot do. But within the boundaries of what they may do, there is an aimless quality, with no one in a position to establish a positive direction. In part this aimlessness is the product of the failure to establish coherent lines of internal organization; in part it flows from the frightening massiveness of the media themselves; but in part also it emanates from a lack of clarity as to the purposes they serve.

The inability to exercise positive control and the concomitant inability to locate responsibility heighten the general sense of irrelevance of the contents of the mass media. It would, in any case, be difficult for a writer or performer to be sensitive to the character of an unseen audience. But the problems are magnified when the audience is numbered in the millions, in other words, when it is so large that all the peculiarities of tastes and attitudes within it must be canceled out so that all that remains is an abstract least common denominator. And those problems become insoluble when no one has the power or the obligation to deal with them.

In the world of actuality, Americans are factory workers or farmers, Jews or Baptists, of German or Irish descent, old or young; they live in small towns or great cities, in the North or the South. But the medium which attempts to speak to all of them is compelled to discount these affiliations and pretend that the variety of tastes, values, and habits related to them do not exist. It can therefore only address itself to the empty outline of the residual American. What it has to say, therefore, is doomed to irrelevance in the lives of its audience; and the feedback from the consciousness of that irrelevance, without effective countermeasures, dooms the performer and writer to sterility.

The critics of the mass media are in error when they condemn its products out of hand. These media can tolerate good as well as bad contents, high as well as low art. Euripides and Shakespeare can perfectly well follow the Western or quiz show on TV, and the slick magazine can easily sandwich in cathedrals and madonnas among the pictures of athletes and movie queens.

What is significant, however, is that it does not matter. The mass media find space for politics and sports, for science and fiction, for art and music, all presented on an identical plateau of irrelevance. And the audience which receives this complex variety of wares accepts them passively as an undifferentiated but recognizable series of good things among which it has little capacity for choice, and with which it cannot establish any meaningful, direct relationship.

The way in which the contents of the mass media are communicated deprives the audience of any degree of selectivity, for those contents are marketed as any other commodities are. In our society it seems possible through the use of the proper marketing device to sell anybody anything, so that what is sold has very little relevance to the character of either the buyers or of the article sold. This is as true of culture as of refrigerators or fur coats. The contents of the magazine or the TV schedule or the newspaper have as little to do with their sales potential as the engine specifications with the marketability of an automobile. The popularity of quiz shows no more reflects the desires of the audience than the increase in circulation of *American Heritage* or *Gourmet* reflects a growing knowledge of American history or the development of gastronomic taste, or, for that matter, than the efflorescence of tail fins in 1957 reflected a yearning for them on the part of automobile buyers. All these were rather examples of excellent selling jobs.

The mass media have also diluted, if they have not altogether destroyed, the rapport that formerly existed between the creators of popular culture and its consumers. In this respect, the television playlet or variety performance is far different from the vaudeville turn, which is its lineal antecedent. The performer can no longer sense the mood of his audience and is, in any case, bound by the rigidity of his impersonal medium. The detachment in which he and they operate makes communication between them hazy and fragmentary. As a result, the culture communicated by the mass media cannot serve the function in the lives of those who consume it that the popular culture of the past did.

Yet the latter was no more able to withstand the impact of the mass media than was official culture. The loose, chaotic organization of popular culture, its appeal to limited audiences, its ties to an ethnic past attenuated with the passage of time, all prevented it from competing successfully against the superior resources of the mass media. Much of it was simply swallowed up in the new forms. What survived existed in isolated enclaves, without the old vitality.

The most important consequences of this change were the destruction of those older functional forms of popular culture, the separation of the audience from those who sought to communicate with it, and the paradoxical diminution of the effectiveness of communication with the improvement of the techniques for communication. Thus far the result has been a diffusion among the audience of a sense of apathy. The intense involvement of the masses with their culture at the turn of the century has given way to passive acquiescence. Concomitantly, the occasional creative artist who wishes to communicate with this audience has lost the means of doing so. At best his work will be received as one of the succession of curious or interesting images that flicker by without leaving an enduring impression upon anyone's consciousness.

Thus there is passing a great opportunity for communication between those who have something to say and the audiences who no longer know whether they would like to listen to what there is to be said.

The Intellectual and the Mass Media
Leo Rosten

from

Daedalus, vol.89, no.2, 1960.

Reprinted by permission of the American Academy of Arts and Sciences and the Editor of *Daedalus*

LEO ROSTEN

The Intellectual and the Mass Media

MOST INTELLECTUALS do not understand the inherent nature of the mass media. They do not understand the process by which a newspaper or magazine, movie or television show is created. They project their own tastes, yearnings, and values upon the masses—who do not, unfortunately, share them. They attribute over-simplified motivations to those who own or operate the mass media. They assume that changes in ownership or control would necessarily improve the product. They presume the existence of a vast reservoir of talent, competence, and material which does not in fact exist.

A great deal of what appears in the mass media is dreadful tripe and treacle; inane in content, banal in style, muddy in reasoning, mawkish in sentiment, vulgar, näive, and offensive to men of learning or refinement. I am both depressed and distressed by the bombardment of our eyes, our ears, and our brains by meretricious material designed for a populace whose paramount preferences involve the narcotic pursuit of "fun."

Why is this so? Are the media operated by cynical men motivated solely by profit? Are they controlled by debasers of culture—by ignorant, vulgar, irresponsible men?

Many intellectuals think so and say so. They think so and say so in the face of evidence they either do not examine or cannot bring themselves to accept: that when the public is free to choose among various products, it chooses—again and again and again—the frivolous as against the serious, "escape" as against reality, the lurid as against the tragic, the trivial as against the serious, fiction as against fact, the diverting as against the significant. To conclude otherwise is to deny the data: circulation figures for the press, box-office receipts for the movies and the theater, audience measurement for radio and television programs.

The sad truth seems to be this: that relatively few people in any society, not excluding Periclean Athens, have reasonably good taste or care deeply about ideas. Fewer still seem equipped—by temperament and capacity, rather than education—to handle ideas with both skill and pleasure.

The deficiencies of mass media are a function, in part at least, of the deficiencies of the masses. Is it unfair to ask that responsibility for mental laziness and deplorable taste be distributed—to include the schools, the churches, the parents, the social institutions which produce those masses who persist in preferring pin-ball games to anything remotely resembling philosophy?

Intellectuals seem unable to reconcile themselves to the fact that their hunger for more news, better plays, more serious debate, deeper involvement in ideas is not a hunger characteristic of many. They cannot believe that the subjects dear to their hearts bore or repel or overtax the capacities of their fellow citizens. Why this is so I shall try to explore later. At this point, let me remark that the intellectual, who examines his society with unyielding and antiseptic detachment, must liberate himself from the myths (or, in Plato's term, the royal lies) by which any social system operates. It is ironic that intellectuals often destroy old myths to erect and reverence special myths of their own. A striking example is found in the clichés with which they both characterize and indict the mass media. Let us consider the principal particulars in that indictment.*

"The mass media lack originality."

They certainly do. Most of what appears in print, or on film, or on the air, lacks originality. But is there any area of human endeavor of which this is not true? Is not the original as rare in science or philosophy or painting as it is in magazines? Is not the original "original" precisely because it is rare? Is it not self-evident that the more that is produced of anything, the smaller the proportion of originality is likely to be? But is the absolute number of novel creative products thereby reduced? Are we dealing with Gresham's Law—or with imperfect observation?

* For the best general summary, and critical comment, see Chapter XV in *The Fabric of Society*, by Ralph Ross and Ernest van den Haag (Harcourt, Brace & Co., 1957), a work of remarkable lucidity and good sense.

The mass media are not characterized by endless inventiveness and variation. But they are considerably more varied and inventive, given their built-in limitations, than we give them credit for. Consider these limitations: neither life nor truth nor fiction offers infinite choices: there is only a limited number of plots or stories or themes; there is only a limited number of ways of communicating the limited body of material; audiences develop a cumulative awareness of resemblances and an augmented resistance to the stylized and the predictable; and even the freshest departures from routine soon become familiar and routine. Besides, originality is often achieved at the price of "balance" or proportion: the most arresting features in, say, *The New Yorker* or *Time* often incur the displeasure of scholars precisely because they prefer vitality to a judicious ordering of "all the facts."

The artist, of course, wrests freshness and new insight from the most familiar material; but true artists, in any field at any given time, are so rare that their singularity requires a special word—"genius."

The mass media are cursed by four deadly requirements: a gargantuan amount of space (in magazines and newspapers) and time (in television and radio) *has* to be filled; talent—on every level, in every technique—is scarce; the public votes, i.e., is free to decide what it prefers (and it is the deplorable results of this voting that intellectuals might spend more time confronting); and a magazine, paper, television or radio program is committed to periodic and unalterable publication. Content would be markedly improved if publications or programs appeared only when superior material was available. This applies to academic journals no less than to publications or programs with massive audiences.

"The mass media do not use the best brains or freshest talents."

Surely the burden of proof is on those who make this assertion. The evidence is quite clear that talent in the popular arts is searched for and courted in ways that do not apply in other fields: seniority is ignored, tenure is virtually nonexistent, youth is prized. In few areas is failure so swiftly and ruthlessly punished, or success so swiftly and extravagantly rewarded.

And still—talent is scarce. It is a woeful fact that despite several generations of free education, our land has produced relatively few first-rate minds; and of those with first-rate brains, fewer have imagination; of those with brains and imagination, fewer still possess judgment. If we ask, in addition, for the special skills and experience involved in the art of communicating, the total amount of talent available to the media is not impressive.

"The best brains" in the land do not gravitate to the media—if by brains we mean skill in analyzing complexities, or sustaining abstract propositions for prolonged intellectual operations. But the best brains would not necessarily make the best editors, or writers, or producers, or publishers—at least they would not long survive in a competitive market.

The media are enterprises, not IQ tests. They feed on inventiveness, not analytic discipline. They require creative skills and non-standardized competences. Their content has, thus far at least, resisted the standardized and accumulative statement of propositions of a Euclid or an Adam Smith.

"The mass media do not print or broadcast the best material that is submitted to them."

To edit is to judge; to judge is, inevitably, to reward some and disappoint others.

The assumption that a vast flow of material pours into the editorial offices of the media—from which publishers or producers simply select the worst—is simply incorrect. A huge proportion of what finally appears in magazines, radio, and television was "dreamed up" inside the media offices, and ordered from the staff or from free-lance writers. And as often as not, even when the best talent is employed, at the highest prices, and given complete freedom, the results disappoint expectations. Excellence is not necessarily achieved because it is sought.*

"The mass media cannot afford to step on anyone's toes."

The following recent articles in popular magazines most conspicuously stepped on quite powerful toes: What Protestants Fear About Catholics; Cigarettes and Lung Cancer; Birth Control; The Disgrace

---

* Yet consider that the mass media have recently presented to the public such indubitable highbrows as, say, Jacques Maritain, Reinhold Niebuhr, Robert Oppenheimer, Edith Hamilton, Aldous Huxley, Warren Weaver, Edith Sitwell, Jacques Barzun, James Bryant Conant, and Julian Huxley.

of Our Hospitals; Fee-Splitting by Doctors; Agnosticism; Financial Shenanigans and Stock Manipulations; A Mercy Killing; The Murder of Negroes in the South.

The movies and television recently offered all but the deaf and blind these scarcely soporific themes: miscegenation; adultery; dope addiction; white-Negro tensions; the venality of television; the vulgarity of movie executives; the cowardice of a minister, a banker; hypocrisy in business and advertising; big business and call girls; the degeneracy of Southern whites.

It was long assumed that the most sacred of sacred cows in a capitalist society is the Businessman or Big Business as an institution. But in recent years we have been exposed to a striking number of revelations about Business. Advertising men and methods, presumably too "powerful" to expose, much less deride, have been raked with coals of fire—in media which depend upon advertisers and advertising. "The Man in the Grey Flannel Suit" became a symbol of conformity to the masses, no less than the intellectual, through the mass media.

It is worth noticing that the sheer size of an audience crucially influences the content of what is communicated to it. Taboos, in movies or television, are not simply the fruit of cowardice among producers (though their anxiety is often disproportionate, and their candor unnecessarily hampered by pessimistic assumptions of what public reaction will be). Taboos are often functions of audience size, age-range, and heterogeneity. Things can be communicated to the few which cannot be communicated (at least not in the same way) to the many.

Books, magazines, and newspapers can discuss sex, homosexuality, masturbation, venereal disease, abortion, dope addiction, in ways not so easily undertaken on television or film. The reader reads alone— and this is a fact of great importance to those who write for him.

"The mass media do not give the public enough or adequate information about the serious problems of our time."

Never in history has the public been offered so much, so often, in such detail, for so little. I do not mean that Americans know as much as intellectuals think they ought to know, or wish they did know, about the problems which confront us. I do mean that the media already offer the public far more news, facts, information, and interpretations than the public takes the trouble to digest. I find it impossible to escape the conclusion that, apart from periods of acute crisis, most people do not want to be *involved*, in precisely those areas which the intellectual finds most absorbing and meaningful.

Consider these recent authors and subjects in popular journalism: Winston Churchill on the war; Harry S. Truman on the presidency; Geoffrey Crowther on United States-British relations; William O. Douglas on Russia; Dean Acheson on Berlin; Joseph Alsop on Suez; George Kennan on Europe; Henry Kissinger on nuclear weapons; Adlai Stevenson on nine different countries and their problems; Nehru on India and the West; Ben-Gurion on the Middle East.

I wonder how many academic journals have been more relevant or edifying.

Do intellectuals find it unnoteworthy that, year after year, four to five times as many citizens in New York City choose the *Daily News* as against the New York *Times* or *Herald Tribune?* Or that for decades the citizens of Chicago have preferred the Chicago *Tribune* to competitors closer to the intellectuals' heart? Or that for decades the people of Los Angeles have voted in favor of the Los Angeles *Times*, at the expense of less parochial competitors?

"The aesthetic level of the mass media is appalling: truth is sacrificed to the happy ending, escapism is exalted, romance, violence, melodrama prevail."

The mass media do not attempt to please intellectuals, on either the aesthetic or the conceptual plane. Some commentators believe that if the media offered the public less trivia, the taste of the public would perforce be improved. But if the media give the public too little of what they want, and too much of what they don't want (too soon), they would simply cease to be mass media—and would be replaced by either "massier" competitors or would drive the public to increased expenditures of time on sports, parlor games, gambling, and other familiar methods of protecting the self from the ardors of thought or the terrors of solitude.

The question of proportion (how much "light stuff" or staple insipidity to include as against how much heavy or "uplifting" material) is one of the more perplexing problems any editor faces. It is far from uncommon to hear an editor remark that he will run a feature which he knows will be read by "less than 5 per cent of our readers."

I suspect that intellectuals tend to judge the highbrow by its peaks and the nonhighbrow by its average. If we look at the peaks in both cases, how much do the mass media suffer by comparison? American movies, for instance, caught in staggering costs (and, therefore, risks), have produced, in a short span of time, such films as *The Bridge on the River Kwai, Marty, The African Queen, Twelve Angry Men, The Defiant Ones, High Noon, The Sheepman, Seven Brides for Seven Brothers,* etc.

Television, beset by the problem of a heterogeneous audience, and submitting to the disgraceful practice of advertisers permitted to exercise editorial censorship, has produced some extraordinary news and documentary programs, and such dramas as: *Middle of the Night, Patterns, Little Moon of Alban, Days of Wine and Roses, The Bridge of San Luis Rey, The Winslow Boy, Requiem for a Heavyweight.* CBS's "Camera Three" recently presented, with both skill and taste, three programs dramatizing Dostoevski's *Notes from the Underground, A File for Fathers* (scenes from Lord Chesterfield, Lewis Carroll, Oscar Wilde), *Père Goriot,* Chekhov's *The Proposal.*

In my opinion, some of the more insightful work of our time can be found in the mass media, for example, the comic strip *Peanuts,* which throws an original and enchanting light on children; the comic strip *Li'l Abner,* which is often both as illuminating and as savage as social satire should be; the movies of, say, William Wyler, George Stevens, Jules Dassin, John Huston, David Lean, Delbert Mann.

Intellectuals generally discover "artists" in the popular arts long after the public, with less rarefied aesthetic categories, has discovered them. Perhaps there is rooted in the character structure of intellectuals an aversion, or an inability, to participate in certain sectors of life; they do seem blind to the fact that the popular can be meritorious. This changes with time (e.g., consider the reputations of Twain, Dickens, Dumas, Balzac, Lardner). And a Jack Benny or Phil Silvers may yet achieve the classic dimension now permitted the Marx Brothers, who—once despised as broad vaudevillians—have become the eggheads' delight.

"The mass media corrupt and debase public taste; they create the kind of audience that enjoys cheap and trivial entertainment."

This implies that demand (public taste or preference) has become a spurious function of manipulated supply. Here the evidence from

Great Britain is illuminating: for years the government-owned BBC and the admirable Third Program offered the British public superior fare: excellent music, learned talks, literate discussions. For years, the noncommercial radio defended the bastions of culture. Yet when the British public was offered choices on television, it dismayed Anglophiles by taking to its heart the same silly quiz shows, panel shows, Westerns, melodramas, and "situation comedies" which the critics of daily newspapers deplore both in London and New York.

Or consider what happened in March 1959 when the Granada TV network, a British commercial chain, presented *The Skin of Our Teeth* with no less a star than Vivien Leigh—and in her first appearance on television. The noncommercial BBC ran, opposite the Wilder play and Lady Vivien, a twenty-five-year-old American movie, *Follow the Fleet*, with Ginger Rogers and Fred Astaire. The English critics sang rare hosannahs for Thornton Wilder's play, its glamorous star, the script, the direction, the production. But for every seventeen homes in London that chose the Pulitzer Prize play, sixty-six preferred the twenty-five-year-old musical. Outside of London, the ratio was even more depressing. Viewers by the millions, reported Reuters, switched their dials away from Wilder and Leigh to Fred and Ginger. The head of the Granada network even castigated the BBC in the press, urging that it be "ashamed of itself" for seducing a public that might have adored Art by offering it Entertainment. (A similar *contretemps* occurred on American television when the magnificent production of *Green Pastures* lost viewers by the millions to the ghastly *Mike Todd Party* in Madison Square Garden.) The final and crushing irony lies in the fact that *Follow the Fleet* put a BBC program among the first ten, in popularity, for the first time in the year.

Doubtless the mass media can do more, much more, to elevate what the public reads, sees, and hears. But the media cannot do this as easily or as rapidly as is often assumed. Indeed, they cannot get too far in front of their audiences without suffering the fate of predecessors who tried just that. There is considerable evidence to support the deflating view that the media, on the whole, are considerably *ahead* of the masses—in intelligence, in taste, in values, e.g., the vocabulary in almost any popular journal, not excluding fan magazines, is often too "highbrow" for its readers.

It seems to me a fair question to ask whether the intelligence or taste of the public is really worse today than it was before the mass media came along.

"The mass media are what they are because they are operated solely as money-making enterprises."

Publishers and producers are undoubtedly motivated by a desire for profits. But this is not *all* that motivates them. Publishers and producers are no less responsive than intellectuals to "ego values"; they are no less eager to win respect and respectability from their peers; they respond to both internalized and external "reference groups"; they seek esteem—from the self and from others.

Besides, producers know that a significant percentage of what they present in the mass media will not be as popular as what might be substituted—but it is presented nonetheless. Why? Partly because of nonpecuniary values, and partly because of what critics of the crass profit-motive seem blind to: the fact that part of the competitive process involves a continuous search for products which can win favor with audiences not attracted to, or satisfied by, the prevailing output. New and minority audiences are constantly courted by the media, e.g., the strictly "egghead" programs on television, the new magazines which arise, and flourish, because they fill a need, as *Scientific American, American Heritage.*

Whenever profits, used as either a carrot or a stick, are criticized, it is tacitly assumed that reliance on other human impulses would serve man better. Is this so? Do virtue, probity, self-sacrifice guarantee excellence? It seems to me that most of the horrors of human history have been the work not of skeptical or cynical or realistic men, but of those persuaded of their superior virtue.

To replace publication for profit by publication via subsidy would of course be to exchange one set of imperfections for another.* The postal system offers scant support to those who assume that nonprofit enterprise is necessarily better than private competition (I hasten to add that in some fields, e.g., public health, it clearly is).

It should be noted, parenthetically, that anyone who enters the magazine or newspaper field in the expectation of high profits is either singularly naïve, extremely optimistic, or poorly informed: few

---

* It is unthinkable, for instance, that any open competitive system would have barred from the air someone like Winston Churchill—who was not given access to BBC, for his then-maverick opinions, from 1934 to 1939. Nor is it likely that a government-controlled network would be able to withstand the furore that followed CBS's initial interview with Nikita Khrushchev. Nor would a governmentally supervised program dare to present a' show such as *The Plot to Kill Stalin.*

areas of American business show so high a mortality rate, are plagued by such unpredictabilities, promise so many headaches, and return so low a net profit. Successful magazines earn as modest a profit as three percent on invested capital. To the purely profit-minded, business has long offered innumerable opportunities outside of publishing which far surpass it in profitability, security, or potential.

"The mass media are dominated—or too much influenced —by advertisers."

The influence of advertising is often too great—even if that influence is one-tenth as potent as many assume it to be. The editorial function should be as entirely free of non-editorial influences as possible.

But publishers, producers, and editors would respond to power or influence *even if all advertising were abolished.* It is an inescapable fact of human organization that men adjust to power (that, indeed, is one of power's attributes); that men consider, or try to anticipate, the effect of their acts on those who hold most of whatever is most prized in a society.

There is a reverse and paradoxical angle to advertising: when a newspaper or magazine, a radio or television station becomes successful, the advertiser needs it as much as the other way around. Revenues from many advertisers increase the capacity to resist pressure from individual advertisers. Organs which can be "bought" nearly always decline in prosperity and influence.

Purely professional calculations often override vested interest. Some news or stories are so significant that it is impossible to prevent their publication.

The instance of the cigarette industry, mentioned above, is worth notice. Tobacco companies represent one of the largest and most consistent sources of national advertising revenue. Yet within an hour after medical reports appeared linking cigarette smoking to lung cancer, they were fully and dramatically presented to the public—not only on the front pages of newspapers but in radio and television reporting as well. The news was simply too big, too "newsworthy" to be suppressed (even though several discussion programs shied away from the subject). The deficiencies of automobiles, where safety is concerned, have been analyzed in magazines which receive huge advertising revenues from automobile companies.

This is not to say that all truths which threaten power—in business, in the arts, even in the groves of academe—always gain as swift and public an airing as they deserve. They often do not. They do not because men, even men in power, are often timid, or weak, or frightened, or avaricious, or opportunistic, or unwise, or short-sighted. Some media operators, like some politicians, some clergymen, some labor leaders, some economists, are overly sensitive to the side on which their bread is buttered.

There is another and telling body of evidence about advertising on which no one, so far as I know, has commented: motion pictures accept no advertisements, never did, never depended on it, and were never "at the mercy of advertisers."* Yet of all the mass media, it is the movies which have been most parochial and timorous. Is it because movies do depend entirely on box-office receipts, and have no advertising revenues to subsidize independnce?

Advertisers seem to me to exercise their most pernicious influence in television. For in television, advertisers are permitted to decide what shall or shall not appear in the programs they sponsor. This seems to me insupportable. An advertiser in a newspaper or magazine buys a piece of space in which to advertise his product. He does not buy a voice on the news desk or at the editorial table. But the television advertiser buys time both for his commercials and for *the time between commercials*; he becomes a producer and publisher himself. I am convinced that this is bad for the public, bad for television, and (ultimately) bad for the sponsors.†

"The mass media do not provide an adequate forum for minority views—the dissident and unorthodox."

Producers and publishers give more space and time to minority views (which include the *avant-garde*) than numerical proportions require. They feel that it is the function of specialized journals to carry specialized content. The popular media carry far more material of this kind than anyone would have predicted two decades ago.

The democratic society must insure a viable public forum for the dissenter—in politics, morals, arts. That forum will never be as large as the dissenters themselves want. But I know of no perfect way to determine who shall have what access to how many—at the expense

---

* Some movie theaters show advertisements on their screens before and after a feature, but advertising is not to be found *in* movies.

† When I wrote a similar criticism in *Harper's Magazine* in 1958, certain television executives hotly denied this. That was eighteen months before the recent and sensational revelations of advertiser-control over quiz shows.

of whom else—except to keep pressing for as free a market as we can achieve.

It may seem to some readers that I have substituted an indictment of the masses for an indictment of the mass media; that I have assigned the role of villain to the masses in a social drama in which human welfare and public enlightenment are hamstrung by the mediocrity, laziness, and indifference of the populace. I hope that detachment will not be mistaken for cynicism.

I should be the first to stress the immensity of the social gains which public education and literacy alone have made possible. The rising public appreciation of music, painting, ballet; the growth of libraries; the fantastic sales of paperback books (however much they are skewed by *Peyton Place* or the works of Mickey Spillane), the striking diffusion of "cultural activities" in communities throughout the land, the momentous fact that popular magazines *can* offer the public the ruminations of such nonpopular minds as Paul Tillich or Sir George Thomson—the dimensions of these changes are a tribute to the achievements of that society which has removed from men the chains of caste and class that hampered human achievement through the centuries. I, for one, do not lament the passing of epochs in which "high culture" flourished while the majority of mankind lived in ignorance and indignity.

What I have been emphasizing here is the inevitable gap between the common and the superior. More particularly, I have been embroidering the theme of the intellectual's curious reluctance to accept evidence. Modern intellectuals seem *guilty* about reaching conclusions that were once the *a priori* convictions of the aristocrat. It is understandable that twentieth-century intellectuals should dread snobbery, at one end of the social scale, as much as they shun mob favor at the other. But the intellectual's snobbery is of another order, and involves a tantalizing paradox: a contempt for what *hoi polloi* enjoy, and a kind of proletarian ethos that tacitly denies inequalities of talent and taste.

The recognition of facts has little bearing on motivations and should surely not impute preferences. The validity of an idea has nothing to do with who propounds it—or whom it outrages. The author is aware that he is inviting charges of Brahminism, misanthropy, a reactionary "unconscious," or heaven knows what else. But is it really heresy to the democratic credo for intellectuals to admit, if only in the privacy of professional confessionals, that they are, in fact, more literate and more skillful—in diagnosis, induction, and generalization, if in nothing else—than their fellow-passengers on the ship of state?

Perhaps the intellectual's guilt, when he senses incipient snobbery within himself, stems from his uneasiness at being part of an elite, moreover, a new elite which is not shored up by ancient and historic sanctions. For intellectualism has been divorced from its traditional *cachet* and from the majesty with which earlier societies invested their elites: a classical education, Latin or Greek (in any case, a language not comprehensible to the untutored), a carefully cultivated accent, the inflection of the well born, the well bred, or the priestly. One of the painful experiences spared intellectuals in the past was hearing Ideas discussed—with profundity or insight—in accents which attest to birth on "the other side of the tracks."

It may be difficult for shopkeepers' sons to admit their manifest superiority over the world they left: parents, siblings, comrades. But the intellectual who struggles with a sinful sense of superiority, and who feels admirable sentiments of loyalty to his non-U origins, must still explain why it was that his playmates and classmates did not join him in the noble dedication to learning and the hallowed pursuit of truth. The triumph of mass education is to be found not simply in the increment of those who can read, write, add, and subtract. It is to be found in a much more profound and enduring revolution: the provision of opportunities to express the self, and pursue the self's values, opportunities not limited to the children of a leisure class, or an aristocracy, or a landed gentry, or a well-heeled bourgeoisie. The true miracle of public education is that no elite can decide where the next intellectual will come from.

Each generation creates its own devils, and meets its own Waterloo on the heartless field of reality. The Christian Fathers blamed the Prince of Darkness for preventing perfectible man from reaching Paradise. Anarchists blamed the state. Marxists blame the class system. Pacifists blame the militarists. And our latter-day intellectuals seem to blame the mass media for the lamentable failure of more people to attain the bliss of intellectual grace. This is a rank disservice to intellectuals themselves, for it dismisses those attributes of character and ability—discipline, curiosity, persistence, the renunciation of worldly rewards—which make intellectuals possible at all. The compulsive egalitarianism of eggheads even seems to lure them into a conspicuous disinterest in the possible determinism of heredity.

Responsibility increases with capacity, and should be demanded of those in positions of power. Just as I hold the intellectual more responsible than others for the rigorous exploration of phenomena and the courageous enunciation of truths, so, too, do I ask for better and still better performance from those who have the awesome power to shape men's minds.

Parallel Paths
Frank Stanton

from

Daedalus, vol.89, no.2, 1960.

Parallel Paths

THE MASS MEDIA are tempting targets: they are big, they are conspicuous, they are easily distorted, they invite bright and brittle condemnations—and they do have built-in limitations of their virtues. They have shown themselves inefficient warriors, and on the whole have tended to be too little concerned with what the intellectuals have had to say.

On the other side, the fondest attachment of the intellectuals is to theory not to practice; more importantly, there is among many intellectuals an uncongeniality with some of the basic ingredients of a democratic society and, in many cases, a real distrust of them. Democratic procedures, to some extent even democratic values, necessarily involve quantitative considerations, about which intellectuals are always uneasy. This uneasiness is not restricted to cultural matters. For example, it influences their view of the legislative processes and of economic interplays in our society. The intellectual is highly impatient of much that is imperfect but also inevitable in democracies. But despite these differences between intellectuals and the mass media, I think that they have something in common, that their efforts are fundamentally going toward the same general goal but along different paths.

I take it to be the distinguishing characteristic of civilized man that he is concerned with the environment and destiny of himself and his kind. The end of all scholarship, all art, all science, is the increase of knowledge and of understanding. The rubrics of scholarship have no inherent importance except in making the expansion of knowledge easier by creating system and order and catholicity. The freedom of the arts has no inherent value except in its admitting unlimited comments upon life and the materials of life. There is no *mystique* about science; its sole wonder exists in its continuous expansion of both the area and the detail of man's comprehension of his physical being and his surroundings.

The ultimate use of all man's knowledge and his art and his science cannot be locked up into little compartments to which only the initiate hold the keys. It cannot be contemplated solely by closeted groups, or imposed from above. If vitality is to be a force in the general life of mankind, it must sooner or later reach all men and enter into the general body of awarenesses. The advancement of the human lot consists in more people being aware of more, knowing more, understanding more.

The mass media believe in the broad dissemination of as much as can be comprehended by as many as possible. They employ techniques to arrest attention, to recruit interest, to lead their audiences into new fields. Often they must sacrifice detail or annotation for the sake of the general idea.

Although it may be presumptuous, perhaps I can suggest a general contrast in the position of the professional intellectual: he feels that knowledge, art, and understanding are all precious commodities that ought not to be diluted. He believes that if things were left to him this dilution would not happen, because the doors of influence would be closed to the inadequately educated until they had earned the right to open them, just as he did. His view is that if standards remain beyond the reach of the many, the general level will gradually rise.

In this respect, I dissent from Mr. Rosten's conclusion that the intellectuals "project their own tastes, yearnings, and values upon the masses."* I do not believe there is such an irreducible gap between the tastes, yearnings, and values of the intellectuals and those of the masses. The difficulty is that the intellectuals do not project at all to the uninitiated. Their hope is to attract them, providing that it is not too many, too fast. They would wait for more and more people to qualify to the higher group, although they themselves want to stay a little ahead of the new arrivals.

This accounts, I believe, for the intellectuals' fear of popularization. The history of the Book-of-the-Month Club illustrates this point. Intellectuals have repeatedly made statements (not entirely characterized by a disciplined array of evidence), that the book club would bring about an "emasculation of the human mind whereby everyone loses the power of his determination in reading,"[1] and that the club's selections were "in many cases, not even an approximation to what the average intelligent reader wants."[2] Yet a study by a Columbia University researcher found that over an eighteen-year span the reaction of reviewers, critics, and professors to the Book-of-the-Month Club selections was far higher in terms of approval than their reaction to random samples of nonselections.[3]

By comparing the two heaviest book selections of the club in 1927 to their two lightest ones in 1949 (without other evidence) Stanley Edgar Hyman suggests that the standards of selection are deteriorating.* Yet he makes no mention of the fact that in 1949 the Book-of-the-Month Club for the first time in its history distributed a serious contemporary play, *Death of a Salesman*, that it distributed a serious discussion of a vital issue in Vannevar Bush's *Modern Arms and Free Men*, that it put into hundreds of thousands of homes William Edward Langer's *Encyclopedia of World History*, that it brought to its subscribers George Orwell's *Nineteen Eighty-four*, Winston Churchill's *Their Finest Hour*, and A. B. Guthrie's Pulitzer-Prize novel, *The Way West*.

Let me press what Mr. Hyman regards as evidence of "deterioration" of the Book-of-the-Month Club selections to the conclusion at which he himself arrived, that in the decade since 1949 "the selections seem to have continued to deteriorate." Even a glance at the evidence would refute this slashing generality. Indeed, the books distributed by the club throughout the 1950's suggest some high levels of excellence: in fiction there have been three books by William Faulkner, three by James Gould Cozzens, two by John Hersey, seven plays by Shaw, six by Thornton Wilder, Eugene O'Neill's *Long Day's Journey into Night*, novels by Feuchtwanger, Salinger, Thomas Mann, Hemingway, John Cheever, and James Agee; there have been eight historical works by Churchill, two by Schlesinger, two by Van Wyck Brooks, others by Morison and Nevins, Dumas Malone, Bernard DeVoto, Catherine Drinker Bowen's life of John Adams, Toynbee's *Study of History*, two of Edith Hamilton's studies of ancient Greece, and Max Lerner's *American Civilization*; in poetry, Stephen Vincent Benet, and *The Oxford Book of American Verse*; from the classics, Bulfinch's *The Age of Fable*, Frazer's *The Golden Bough*, the Hart edition of Shakespeare, a new translation of *The Odyssey*, works by

Dostoevsky, Gustave Flaubert, and Mark Twain; in art, Francis Henry Taylor's *Fifty Centuries of Art*, John Walker's *Masterpieces of Painting from the National Gallery*, and *Art Treasures of the Louvre*; in reference works, Fowler's *Modern English Usage*, Palmer's *Atlas of World History*, Audubon's *Birds*, and Evans' *Dictionary of Contemporary American Usage*.[4]

To turn to television, I hear over and over such generalities as, "There is nothing but Westerns on television," or "Television is all mysteries and blood and thunder." Such charges usually come from people who do not look at television, but that does not modify their position. As in the case just cited, there is no uncertainty about this exaggeration; one can look at the actual record.

Let us take by way of example the week of February 15 to 21, 1959, on the CBS Television Network, because that week had nothing exceptional about it. During the preceding week, there were such outstanding broadcasts as Tolstoy's *Family Happiness* and a repetition of the distinguished documentary, *The Face of Red China*. In the following week, the programs included the New York Philharmonic and the Old Vic Company's *Hamlet*. Returning to the unexceptional week of February 15, about 4½ hours, or ⅟₁₈ of CBS Television's total program content of 75½ hours, were devoted to Westerns; about 5 hours, or ⅟₁₅, were taken up by mysteries. On the other hand, 7¾ hours, or about ⅟₁₀ of the total number of hours, were devoted to news and public affairs. Altogether, some 78 percent of the evening programing was occupied by drama, fairly evenly divided among serious, comedy, mystery, Westerns, and romance-adventure.

Looking at the record for the first five months of 1959, I find on the CBS Television Network alone four Philharmonic concerts; 90-minute-long productions of plays by Shakespeare, Barrie, and Saroyan, adaptations of Shaw and Ibsen, full-length productions of *The Browning Version*, Melville's *Billy Budd*, Henry James' *Wings of the Dove*, Hemingway's *For Whom the Bell Tolls*, and many distinguished original dramas; thirteen conversations with people of such diverse minds and talents as James Conant, Sir Thomas Beecham, and James Thurber; nine historic surveys of great personalities or developments of the twentieth century; and nine specially scheduled programs inquiring into major issues in public affairs, such as the Cuban revolution, the closing of integrated high schools, statehood for Hawaii, and the Geneva Conference.

I am citing these for two purposes. One is to show how, by using selected examples, it can be as easily proved that television is exclusively instructive as that it is exclusively diverting. My other purpose is by way of considering a practical response to the complaints that the intellectuals voice about all the mass media.

What do the intellectuals really want? Do they want us to do *only* serious programing, only programs of profound cultural value? Or do they just want us to do more? And if so, what is more? Do they want the Book-of-the-Month Club to distribute only heavy reading, or just more? Does the club do harm because it has included books of humor among the thirty to forty selections, alternates, and dividends it distributes each year? Is there any serious belief anywhere that among the paperback books we ought to censor what we consider culturally insignificant and allow only what we consider culturally enriching? Or do not the intellectuals really want to stake out reserves, admission to which would be granted only on their terms, in their way, at their pleasure?

Television occupies the air waves under the franchise of the American people. It has a threefold function: the dissemination of information, culture, and entertainment. There are different levels and different areas of interest at which these are sought by a hundred and fifty million people. It is our purpose—and our endlessly tantalizing task—to make certain that we have enough of every area at every level of interest to hold the attention of significant segments of the public at one time on another. Therefore we do have programs more likely to be of interest to the intellectuals than to others. We can try to include everybody somewhere in our program planning, but we cannot possibly aim all the time only at the largest possible audience.

The practice of sound television programing is the same as the practice of any sound editorial operation. It involves always anticipating (if you can) and occasionally leading your subscribers or readers or audience. The "mass of consumers" does not decide, in the sense that it initiates programs, but it does respond to our decisions. A mass medium survives when it maintains a satisfactory batting average on affirmative responses, and it goes down when negative responses are too numerous or too frequent. But so also does the magazine with a circulation of five thousand—as the high mortality rate of the "little magazines" testifies. Success in editing, whether a mass medium or an esoteric quarterly, consists in so respecting the audience that one labors to bring to it something that meets an interest, a desire, or a need that has still to be completely filled. Obviously, the narrower and the more intellectually homogeneous your audience, the easier this is to do; and conversely, the larger it is and the more heterogeneous, the more difficult.

I must dissent from the unqualified charge that "advertisers today . . . exercise their most pernicious influence in television." The basis of this charge is that, while an advertiser buys space in a magazine with no power of choice as to the editorial content of the magazine, on television he allegedly controls both the commercials and what program goes into the time space. The matter is not so simple.

In the first place I categorically assert that no news or public-affairs program at CBS, however expensive to the sponsor, has ever been subject to his control, influence, or approval. There is a total and absolute independence in this respect.

An advertiser in magazines does have the power to associate his advertising with editorial content by his choice of a magazine. If he makes a household detergent, he can choose a magazine whose appeal is to housewives. In television, he can achieve this association only by seeking out kinds of programs, or, more properly, the kinds of audience to which specific programs appeal. This is of course why a razor blade company wants to sponsor sports programs. But this does not mean that the company is going to referee the game or coach the team. In television, for the most part, advertisers are sold programs by networks or by independent producers, somewhat in the sense that space in the magazines is sold by sales efforts based on the kind of audience the magazine reaches. At the same time, we are perfectly aware that in the rapid growth of television the problem of the advertiser's relationship with program content has not yet been satisfactorily solved. It is an area to which we are going to have to devote more thought and evolve new approaches.

I return to a central point: that some sort of hostility on the part of the intellectuals toward the mass media is inevitable, because the intellectuals are a minority, one not really reconciled to some basic features of democratic life. They are an articulate and cantankerous minority, not readily given to examining evidence about the mass media and then arriving at conclusions, but more likely to come to conclusions and then select the evidence to support them. But they are an invaluable minority. We all do care what they think because they are a historic force on which our society must always rely for self-examination and advancement. They constitute the outposts of our intellectual life as a people, they probe around frontiers in their splendid sparsity, looking around occasionally to see where—how far behind—the rest of us are. We are never going to catch up, but at least we shall always have somewhere to go.

As for the mass media, they are always in the process of trying, and they never really find the answers. They also are the victims of their pressing preoccupations, and can undoubtedly improve their performances, better understand their own roles, learn more rapidly. I feel that intellectuals and the media could really serve one another better if both parties informed themselves more fully, brought somewhat more sympathy to each other's examinations, and stopped once in a while to redefine their common goals. We in the mass media have probably been negligent in not drawing the intellectuals more intimately into our counsels, and the intellectuals, by and large, have not studied the evidence carefully enough before discussing the mass media. The mass media need the enlightened criticism, the thorough examination, of the intellectuals. When the latter are willing to promise these, we shall all make progress faster and steadier.

REFERENCES

1 Edward F. Stevens, cited in Charles Lee, *The Hidden Public* (Garden City: Doubleday, 1958), p. 51.

2 *Ibid.*

3 Joseph W. Kappel, "Book Clubs and the Evaluation of Books," *Public Opinion Quarterly*, 1948, *12*: 243-252.

4 For complete selections for 1926-1957, see Lee, *op. cit.*, pp. 161-194.

The Artist and the Museum in Mass Society
James Johnson Sweeney

from

Daedalus, vol.89, no.2, 1960.

Reprinted by permission of the American Academy of Arts and Sciences and the Editor of *Daedalus*. .

JAMES JOHNSON SWEENEY

The Artist and the Museum
in Mass Society

ONE SHOULD PUT ASIDE at the outset the notion that there is any essential threat in the mass media to the genuinely creative artist or to genuine art. The artist, qua artist, is an individualist, and the quality of his art lies in its individuality. A work of art is the concrete record of an artist's discovery of himself, first to himself, then at a second remove to the world around him. In this sense, what may from one point of view be seen as a "monologue" may also be regarded as a hypothetical duologue or conversation.

The true artist does not feel the need to address a mass meeting to have the sense of conversing with his fellow man. He speaks to an ideal audience, but what speaker succeeds in envisaging his audience otherwise? Consequently, for the advantages of audience the mass media may offer, the true artist will not be tempted, nor will the true artist's work suffer, in a culture given its broad color by those advantages. Only the current equivalents of pseudo-artists who in the past have sacrificed their individuality to other temptations will suffer from the seductions of mass media.

Any suggested threat to the creative artist through mass culture does, however, serve very frequently to obscure the true issue. For the real present danger is not to the creative artist or to creative art, but to the conditioning of the public in its response to creative art, particularly in the field of painting and sculpture. As S. E. Hyman has pointed out: "The technological revolution does not yet seem to have brought the plastic arts into mass culture. . . . Mass-produced copies of pictures and sculptures have been around for a long time and make all but the most contemporary work cheaply available in reproduction, but they seem to have had little of the impact on taste of paperbacks and long-playing records."*

Whether or not long-playing records have had any profound effect on musical discrimination, if the test is not merely one of recognizing accepted works, is difficult to say. It seems evident that an ear educated only by long-playing records would be as far from the real experience of a musical work as any eye trained by color reproductions would be from the sensuous experience of actual painting. In Hyman's linking the influences of paperbacks and long-playing records, it seems to me he has slightly mixed his categories of reproduction. The paperback is merely a less luxurious form of book, for the text is, or should be, the same; but between a long-playing record and a live rendition there is a difference in sense stimuli, just as there is between a painting and a printed reproduction of a painting—perhaps not a wide difference, but an essential one.

What both long-playing records and color reproductions basically provide is "information" about the works of art in question, not an immediate experience of either the music as played or the actual painting. In painting and sculpture the danger lies in the confusion which can so readily develop between information about a work of art and the experience an immediate sensuous contact with a work of art provides. And a true appreciation of works of art in these fields can only come through direct experience.

Reproductions of painting and sculpture speak to the eye of the observer through materials different from those of the original. The material in which an artist works is an essential element of his expression. Materials different from those employed in the original must provide different relationships in the result. At best, the reproduction can only resemble or suggest the original, although at times it misleads the uncritical observer by its pretension to do more.

Reproduction in the mass media will never supply a truly adequate equivalent for the immediate experience of a painting or a sculpture. What might be achieved is an equivalent expression within the limitations of the medium, much as one had hoped (and still hopes) for a color cinema which would set out, not to reproduce effects, but to exploit the potentialities of creating new forms through color and light effects—fresh expressions of visual order rather than the imitation of already existent expressions. But because the technological

* Stanley E. Hyman, from an earlier draft of his article, as delivered to the participants of this symposium.

revolution has not yet found a way either to bring the pictorial and sculptural arts into mass culture, or to create a fresh expression within the various media which might be analogous, information is offered as a substitute, and the indolent public is readily led to accepting it, with the resultant danger of eventual confusion between the two.

The general educational approach to the appreciation of painting and sculpture is in part a consequence of mass culture and the influence of mass media; in part, it is a result of indolence. I refer to a general emphasis on the informational approach in schools and even in museums where there is so little excuse for it. It is easier to approach painting or sculpture through the ears than through the eyes: our temptation today is to lean on the accepted authority, rather than to look for ourselves and respond directly to the sensory stimuli of the work of art. Yet when we speak of accepted authority with regard to a work of art, this can only refer to a work of the past. The viewer who leans on accepted authority can never depend on such a crutch in the case of a truly fresh work, nor can he ever experience a direct communication between a work of art and himself: it must always be at second hand.

The indolent approach to the visual arts is now generally encouraged as a result of the hasty democratization of education of the past century. Everyone has a right to know and appreciate all; therefore, everyone ought to know and appreciate all, and if one does not, it is cause for shame, and one should pretend to be a connoisseur. Art is long; time is short; therefore, any means toward creating this impression of familiarity is welcome, whether it actually interferes with a true, direct appreciation of a work or not.

Museums and educational institutions in general for the past three or four decades (those in which mass media have been developing apace) have fallen deep into this betrayal of the public in the field of the visual arts. Perhaps museums, as looked upon by certain museum trustees, are primarily intended as instruments of popular education along mass media lines. The interest of museum trustees in popular attendance would point this way. Attendance statistics would readily show them that an exhibition of painting or sculpture in an idiom familiar to the public and by an artist or artists whose name it knows will draw crowds. By contrast, the attendance at an exhibition of work by a less known or less publicized artist, or artists, even though more interesting in quality and freshness to the exploring gallery-goer or connoisseur, will suffer. To catch and hold the attention of the indolent visitor, elaborate biographical, critical, explanatory labels, even canned lectures over earphones, are provided, like aesthetic water wings, so one may dabble about without getting too deep into the water. Art should never be spoon-fed nor offered in capsule, digested form. Yet this is what is being essayed in our museums today, simply because museum trustees or perhaps even museum directors are ambitious to embrace the broadest possible public and, in our democratic age, have not the courage to face the fact that the highest experiences of art are only for the elite who "have earned in order to possess."

In the case of a commercial television station, one can adopt a degree of leniency toward this attitude: profits are involved. To a certain extent, the public is bound to dictate the editorial policies if the station is to succeed financially. But in the case of a museum there is no such ground for exculpation. A museum is a nonprofit organization which should be responsible only to its own standards. There is no comparison between the freedom which a museum or a publication like *Partisan Review* should enjoy in maintaining these standards and the responsibility of a television network to its consumers.

The function of a museum is the encouragement of the enjoyment of art and through this the indirect encouragement of the creative artist. Visual art is basically a sensory experience, one of relationships of form, of colors, and of associations, physical, unconscious, or representational. Therefore, the first step in a museum's educational process is the confrontation of the spectator with the actual work of art, so that the artist can speak directly to the spectator. The immediate sensory experience of a work of art is the only direct approach to the artist's communication. Mass media cannot provide this experience, but the museum can and should. On this foundation of a direct sensory acquaintance, the experience of a work of art may be soundly enriched by its peripheral associations. It is the responsibility of the museum to stimulate the indolent public to approach art directly through aesthetic experience, pleasurable and enjoyable, and to incite the visitor to make the effort, always more or less arduous, which is necessary for him to enter into communication with the artist through the artist's personal expression. For it is this interaction between the observer and the creative artist that makes it possible to maintain or raise standards of judgment and appreciation.

A lowering of standards would appear inevitable when all or most energies are expended toward raising the lowest or broadest common denominator. In turn, this will encourage a broadening and a dilution of culture, as indeed has been the case over the past thirty years, not only in our own country, but in others where the mass media have developed.

If the general trend lies in this direction, and if even such non-profit institutions as museums widen their embrace to attract the broadest possible number (fit or unfit as the case may be), where are we to look for standards of aesthetic quality in this new culture? Here is where the creative artist must play his part. For if the mass media have no influence on the true artist, who by his essential nature is a seeker, an explorer, always apart and in advance of his fellows, it is he who provides what the mass media fail to give: standards of quality and integrity for our culture as a whole.

A Sad Heart at the Supermarket
Randall Jarrell

from

Daedalus, vol.89, no.2, 1960

Reprinted by permission of the American Academy of Arts and Sciences and the Editor of *Daedalus*.

A Sad Heart at the Supermarket

THE EMPEROR AUGUSTUS would sometimes say to his Senate: "Words fail me, my Lords; nothing I can say could possibly indicate the depth of my feelings in this matter." But I am speaking about this matter of mass culture, the mass media, not as an Emperor but as a fool, as a suffering, complaining, helplessly nonconforming poet-or-artist-of-a-sort, far off at the obsolescent rear of things: what I say will indicate the depth of my feelings and the shallowness and one-sidedness of my thoughts. If those English lyric poets who went mad during the eighteenth century had told you why the Age of Enlightement was driving them crazy, it would have had a kind of documentary interest: what I say may have a kind of documentary interest.

> The toad beneath the harrow knows
> Exactly where each tooth-point goes;

if you tell me that the field is being harrowed to grow grain for bread, and to create a world in which there will be no more famines, or toads either, I will say, "I know"—but let me tell you where the tooth-points go, and what the harrow looks like from below.

Advertising men, businessmen, speak continually of "media" or "the media" or "the mass media"—one of their trade journals is named, simply, *Media*. It is an impressive word: one imagines Mephistopheles offering Faust media that no man has ever known; one feels, while the word is in one's ear, that abstract, overmastering powers, of a scale and intensity unimagined yesterday, are being offered one by the technicians who discovered and control them—offered, and at a price. The word, like others, has the clear fatal ring of that new world whose space we occupy so luxuriously and precariously; the world that produces mink stoles, rockabilly records, and tactical nuclear weapons by the million; the world that Attila, Galileo, Hansel and Gretel never knew.

And yet, it's only the plural of "medium." "Medium," says the dictionary, "that which lies in the middle; hence, middle condition or degree. . . . A substance through which a force acts or an effect is transmitted. . . . That through or by which anything is accomplished; as, an advertising *medium*. . . . *Biol.* A nutritive mixture or substance, as broth, gelatin, agar, for cultivating bacteria, fungi, etc." Let us name *our* trade journal *The Medium*. For all these media (television, radio, movies, popular magazines, and the rest) are a single medium, in whose depths we are all being cultivated. This medium is of middle condition or degree, mediocre; it lies in the middle of everything, between a man and his neighbor, his wife, his child, his self; it, more than anything else, is the substance through which the forces of our society act upon us, make us into what our society needs.

And what does it need? For us to need . . . Oh, it needs for us to do or be many things—to be workers, technicians, executives, soldiers, housewives. But first of all, last of all, it needs for us to be buyers; consumers; beings who want much and will want more —who want consistently and insatiably. Find some spell to make us no longer want the stoles, the records, and the weapons, and our world will change into something to us unimaginable. Find some spell to make us realize that the product or service which seemed yesterday an unthinkable luxury is today an inexorable necessity, and our world will go on. It is the Medium which casts this spell— which is this spell. As we look at the television set, listen to the radio, read the magazines, the frontier of necessity is always being pushed forward. The Medium shows us what our new needs are—how often, without it, we should not have known!—and it shows us how they can be satisfied: they can be satisfied by buying something. The act of buying something is at the root of our world: if anyone wishes to paint the beginning of things in our society, he will paint a picture of God holding out to Adam a checkbook or credit card or Charge-A-Plate.

But how quickly our poor naked Adam is turned into a consumer, is linked to others by the great chain of buying!

> No outcast he, bewildered and depressed:
> Along his infant veins are interfused
> The gravitation and the filial bond
> Of nature that connect him with the world.

Children of three or four can ask for a brand of cereal, sing some soap's commercial; by the time that they are twelve they are not children but teen-age consumers, interviewed, graphed, analyzed. They are on their way to becoming that ideal figure of our culture, the knowledgeable consumer. I'll define him: the knowledgeable consumer is someone who, when he goes to Weimar, knows how to buy a Weimaraner. He has learned to understand life as a series of choices among the things and services of this world; because of being an executive, or executive's wife, or performer, or celebrity, or someone who has inherited money, he is able to afford the choices that he makes, with knowing familiarity, among restaurants, resorts, clothes, cars, liners, hits or best-sellers of every kind. We may still go to Methodist or Baptist or Presbyterian churches on Sunday, but the Protestant ethic of frugal industry, of production for its own sake, is gone. Production has come to seem to our society not much more than a condition prior to consumption: "The challenge of to-day," writes a great advertising agency, "is to make the consumer raise his level of demand." This challenge has been met: the Medium has found it easy to make its people feel the continually increasing lacks, the many specialized dissatisfactions (merging into one great dissatisfaction, temporarily assuaged by new purchases) that it needs for them to feel. When, in some magazine, we see the Medium at its most nearly perfect, we hardly know which half is entertaining and distracting us, which half making us buy: some advertisement may be more ingeniously entertaining than the text beside it, but it is the text which has made us long for a product more passionately. When one finishes *Holiday* or *Harper's Bazaar* or *House and Garden* or *The New Yorker* or *High Fidelity* or *Road and Track* or—but make your own list—buying something, going somewhere seems a necessary completion to the act of reading the magazine. Reader, isn't buying or fantasy-buying an important part of your and my emotional life? (If you reply, *No,* I'll think of you with bitter envy as more than merely human; as deeply un-American.) It is a standard joke of our culture that when a woman is bored or sad she buys something to make herself feel better; but in this respect we are all women together, and can hear complacently the reminder of how feminine this consumer-world of ours is. One imagines as a characteristic dialogue of our time an interview in which someone is asking of a vague gracious figure, a kind of Mrs. America: "But while you waited for the Intercontinental Ballistic Missiles what did you *do*?" She answers: "I bought things."

She reminds one of the sentinel at Pompeii—a space among ashes, now, but at his post: she too did what she was supposed to do. . . . Our society has delivered us—most of us—from the bonds of necessity, so that we no longer need worry about having food enough to keep from starving, clothing and shelter enough to keep from freezing; yet if the ends for which we work, of which we dream, are restaurants and clothes and houses, consumption, possessions, how have we escaped? We have merely exchanged man's old bondage for a new voluntary one. But *voluntary* is wrong: the consumer is trained for his job of consuming as the factory worker is trained for his job of producing; and the first is a longer, more complicated training, since it is easier to teach a man to handle a tool, to read a dial, than it is to teach him to ask, always, for a name-brand aspirin—to want, someday, a stand-by generator. What is that? You don't know? I used not to know, but the readers of *House Beautiful* all know, and now I know: it is the electrical generator that stands in the basement of the suburban houseowner, shining, silent, until at last one night the lights go out, the freezer's food begins to—

Ah, but it's frozen for good, the lights are on forever; the owner has switched on the stand-by generator.

But you don't see that he really needs the generator, you'd rather have seen him buy a second car? He has two. A second bathroom? He has four. He long ago doubled everything, when the People of the Medium doubled everything; and now that he's gone twice round he will have to wait three years, or four, till both are obsolescent—but while he waits there are so many new needs that he can satisfy, so many things a man can buy.

> Man wants but little here below
> Nor wants that little long,

said the poet; what a lie! Man wants almost unlimited quantities of almost everything, and he wants it till the day he dies.

We sometimes see in *Life* or *Look* a double-page photograph of some family standing on the lawn among its possessions: station wagon, swimming pool, power cruiser, sports car, tape recorder, television sets, radios, cameras, power lawn mower, garden tractor, lathe, barbecue set, sporting equipment, domestic appliances—all the gleaming, grotesquely imaginative paraphernalia of its existence. It was hard to get them on two pages, soon they will need four. It is like a dream, a child's dream before Christmas; yet if the members of the family doubt that they are awake, they have only to reach out and pinch something. The family seems pale and small, a negligible appendage, beside its possessions; only a human being would need to ask, "Which owns which?" We are fond of saying that something-or-other is not just something-or-other but "a way of life"; this too is a way of life—our way, the way.

Emerson, in his spare stony New England, a few miles from Walden, could write:

> Things are in the saddle
> And ride mankind.

He could say more now: that they are in the theater and studio, and entertain mankind; are in the pulpit and preach to mankind. The values of business, in an overwhelmingly successful business society like our own, are reflected in every sphere: values which agree with them are reinforced, values which disagree are cancelled out or have lip-service paid to them. In business what sells is good, and that's the end of it—that is what *good* means; if the world doesn't beat a path to your door, your mousetrap wasn't better. The values of the Medium (which is both a popular business itself and the cause of popularity in other businesses) are business values: money, success, celebrity. If we are representative members of our society, the Medium's values are ours; even when we are unrepresentative, non-conforming, our hands are (too often) subdued to the element they work in, and our unconscious expectations are all that we consciously reject. (Darwin said that he always immediately wrote down evidence against a theory because otherwise, he'd noticed, he would forget it; in the same way we keep forgetting the existence of those poor and unknown failures whom we might rebelliously love and admire.) *If you're so smart why aren't you rich?* is the ground-bass of our society, a grumbling and quite unanswerable criticism, since the society's nonmonetary values *are* directly convertible into money. (Celebrity turns into testimonials, lectures, directorships, presidencies, the capital gains of an autobiography *Told To* some professional ghost who photographs the man's life as Bachrach photographs his body.) When Liberace said that his critics' unfavorable reviews hurt him so much that he cried all the way to the bank, one had to admire the correctness and penetration of his press-agent's wit: in another age, what mightn't such a man have become!

Our culture is essentially periodical: we believe that all that is deserves to perish and to have something else put in its place. We speak of "planned obsolescence," but it is more than planned, it is felt

—is an assumption about the nature of the world. The present is better and more interesting, more real, than the past; the future will be better and more interesting, more real, than the present. (But, consciously, we do not hold against the present its prospective obsolescence.) Our standards have become, to an astonishing degree, those of what is called "the world of fashion," where mere timeliness—being orange in orange's year, violet in violet's—is the value to which all other values are reducible. In our society "old-fashioned" is so final a condemnation that a man like Norman Vincent Peale can say about atheism or agnosticism simply that it is old-fashioned; the homely recommendation of "Give me that good old-time religion" has become after a few decades the conclusive rejection of "old-fashioned" atheism.

All this is, at bottom, the opposite of the world of the arts, where commercial and scientific progress do not exist; where the bone of Homer and Mozart and Donatello is there, always, under the mere blush of fashion; where the past—the remote past, even—is responsible for the way that we understand, value, and act in, the present. (When one reads an abstract expressionist's remark that Washington studios are "eighteen months behind" those of his colleagues in New York, one realizes something of the terrible power of business and fashion over those most overtly hostile to them.) An artist's work and life presuppose continuing standards, values stretched out over centuries or millennia, a future that is the continuation and modification of the past, not its contradiction or irrelevant replacement. He is working for the time that wants the best that he can do: the present, he hopes—but if not that, the future. If he sees that fewer and fewer people are any real audience for the serious artists of the past, he will feel that still fewer are going to be an audience for the serious artists of the present, for those who, willingly or unwillingly, sacrifice extrinsic values to intrinsic ones, immediate effectiveness to that steady attraction which, the artist hopes, true excellence will always exert. The past's relation to the artist or man of culture is almost the opposite of its relation to the rest of our society. To him the present is no more than the last ring on the trunk, understandable and valuable only in terms of all the earlier rings. The rest of our society sees only that great last ring, the enveloping surface of the trunk; what's underneath is a disregarded, almost hypothetical foundation. When Northrop Frye writes that "the preoccupation of the humanities with the past is sometimes made a reproach against them by those who forget that we face the past: it may be shadowy, but it is all that is there," he is saying what for the artist or man of culture is self-evidently true; yet for the Medium and the People of the Medium it is as self-evidently false—for them the present (or a past so recent, so quick-changing, so soon-disappearing, that it might be called the specious present) is all that is there.

In the past our culture's frame of reference, its body of common knowledge (its possibility of comprehensible allusion) changed slowly and superficially; the amount added to it or taken away from it in any ten years was a small proportion of the whole. Now in any ten years a surprisingly large proportion of the whole is replaced. Most of the information people have in common is something that four or five years from now they will not even remember having known. A newspaper story remarks in astonishment that television quiz programs have "proved that ordinary citizens can be conversant with such esoterica as jazz, opera, the Bible, Shakespeare, poetry and fisticuffs." You may exclaim, "Esoterical If the Bible and Shakespeare are esoterica, what is there that's common knowledge?" The answer, I suppose, is that Elfrida von Nardoff and Teddy Nadler (the ordinary citizens on the quiz programs) are common knowledge; though not for long. Songs disappear in two or three months, celebrities in two or three years; most of the Medium is lightly felt and soon forgotten. What is as dead as day-before-yesterday's newspaper, the next-to-the-last number on the roulette wheel? and most of the knowledge we have in common is knowledge of such newspapers, such numbers. But the novelist or poet or dramatist, when he moves a great audience, depends upon the deep feelings, the live unforgotten knowledge, that the people of his culture share; if these have become contingent, superficial, ephemeral, it is disastrous for him.

New products and fashions replace the old, and the fact that they replace them is proof enough of their superiority. Similarly, the Medium does not need to show that the subjects that fill it are timely or interesting or important—the fact that they are its subjects makes them so. If *Time, Life,* and the television shows are full of Tom Fool this month, he's no fool. And when he has been gone from them a while, we do not think him a fool—we do not think of him at all. He no longer exists, in the fullest sense of the word "exist": to be is to be perceived, to be a part of the Medium of our perception. Our celebrities are not kings, romantic in exile, but Representatives who, defeated, are forgotten; they had always only the qualities that we delegated to them.

After driving for four or five minutes along the road outside my door, I come to a long row of one-room shacks about the size of kitchens, made out of used boards, metal signs, old tin roofs. To the people who live in them an electric dishwasher of one's own is as much a fantasy as an ocean liner of one's own. But since the Medium (and those whose thought is molded by it) does not perceive them, these people are themselves a fantasy: no matter how many millions of such exceptions to the general rule there are, they do not really exist, but have a kind of anomalous, statistical subsistence; our moral and imaginative view of the world is no more affected by them than by the occupants of some home for the mentally deficient a little farther along the road. If, some night, one of these outmoded, economically deficient ghosts should scratch at my window, I could say only, "Come back twenty years ago." And if I, as an old-fashioned, one-room poet, a friend of "quiet culture," a "meek lover of the good," should go out some night to scratch at another window, shouldn't I hear someone's indifferent or regretful, "Come back a century or two ago"?

When those whose existence the Medium recognizes ring the chimes of the writer's doorbell, fall through his letter slot, float out onto his television screen, what is he to say to them? A man's unsuccessful struggle to get his family food is material for a work of art—for tragedy, almost; his unsuccessful struggle to get his family a stand-by generator is material for what? Comedy? Farce? Comedy on such a scale, at such a level, that our society and its standards seem, almost, farce? And yet it is the People of the Medium, those who long for and get, or long for and don't get, the generator, whom our culture finds representative, who are there to be treated first of all. And the Medium itself—one of the ends of life, something essential to people's understanding and valuing of their existence, something many of their waking hours are spent listening to or looking at— how is it to be treated as subject matter for art? The writer cannot just reproduce it; should he satirize or parody it? But often parody or satire is impossible, since it is already its own parody; and by the time the writer's work is published, the part of the Medium which is satirized will already have been forgotten. Yet isn't the Medium by now an essential part of its watchers? Those whom Mohammedans speak of as the People of the Book are inexplicable, surely, in any terms that omit it; we are people of the magazine, the television set, the radio, and are inexplicable in any terms that omit them.

Oscar Wilde's wittily paradoxical statement about Nature's imitation of Art is literally true when the Nature is human nature and the

Art that of television, radio, motion pictures, popular magazines. Life is so, people are so, the Medium shows its audience, and most of the audience believe it, expect people to be so, try to be so themselves. For them the People of the Medium are reality, what human beings normally, primarily are: and mere local or personal variations are not real in the same sense. The Medium mediates between us and raw reality, and the mediation more and more replaces reality for us. In many homes either the television set or the radio is turned on most of the time the family is awake. (Many radio stations have a news broadcast every half hour, and many people like and need to hear it.) It is as if the people longed to be established in reality, to be reminded continually of the "real," the "objective" world—the created world of the Medium—rather than be left at the mercy of actuality, of the helpless contingency of the world in which the radio receiver or television set is sitting. (And surely we can sympathize: which of us hasn't found a similar refuge in the "real," created world of Cézanne or Goethe or Verdi? Yet Dostoievsky's world is too different from Wordsworth's, Piero della Francesca's from Goya's, Bach's from Hugo Wolf's, for us to be able to substitute one homogeneous mediated reality for everyday reality in the belief that it *is* everyday reality.) The world of events and celebrities and performers, the Great World, has become for many listeners, lookers, readers, the world of primary reality: how many times they have sighed at the colorless unreality of their own lives and families, sighed for the bright reality of, say, Lucille Ball's—of some shadow dyed, gowned, directed, produced, and agented into a being as equivocal as that of the square root of minus one. The watchers call the celebrities by their first names, approve or disapprove of "who they're dating," handle them with a mixture of love, identification, envy, and contempt—for the Medium has given its people so terrible a familiarity with everyone that it takes great magnanimity of spirit not to be affected by it. These celebrities are not heroes to us, their valets.

Better to have these real ones play themselves, and not sacrifice too much of their reality to art; better to have the watcher play himself, and not lose too much of himself in art. Usually the watcher is halfway between two worlds, paying full attention to neither: half distracted from, half distracted by, this distraction—and able for the moment not to be affected too greatly, have too great demands made upon him, by either world. For in the Medium, which we escape to from work, nothing is ever *work*, nothing ever makes intellectual or emotional or imaginative demands which we might find it difficult to satisfy. Here in the half-world everything is homogeneous —is, as much as possible, the same as everything else: each familiar novelty, novel familiarity, has the same texture on top and the same attitude and conclusion at bottom; only the middle, the particular subject of the particular program or article, is different. (If it *is* different: everyone is given the same automatic "human interest" treatment, so that it is hard for us to remember, unnecessary for us to remember, which particular celebrity we're reading about this time—often it's the same one, we've just moved to a different magazine.) Heine said that the English have a hundred religions and one sauce; so do we; and we are so accustomed to this sauce or dye or style, the aesthetic equivalent of Standard Brands, that a very simple thing can seem perverse, obscure, without it. And, too, we find it hard to have to shift from one art form to another, to vary our attitudes and expectations, to use our unexercised imaginations. Poetry disappeared long ago, even for most intellectuals; each year fiction is a little less important. Our age is an age of nonfiction; of gossip columns, interviews, photographic essays, documentaries; of articles, condensed or book length, spoken or written; of real facts about real people. Art lies to us to tell us the (sometimes disquieting) truth; the Medium tells us truths, facts, in order to make us believe some reassuring or entertaining lie or half truth. These actually existing celebrities, of universally admitted importance, about whom we are told directly authoritative facts—how can fictional characters compete with them? These *are* our fictional characters, our Lears and Clytemnestras. (This is ironically appropriate, since many of their doings and sayings are fictional, made up by public relations officers, columnists, agents, or other affable familiar ghosts.) And the Medium gives us such facts, such photographs, such tape recordings, such clinical reports not only about the great, but also about (representative samples of) the small; when we have been shown so much about so many—*can* be shown, we feel, anything about anybody—does fiction seem so essential as it once seemed? Shakespeare or Tolstoy can show us all about someone, but so can *Life;* and when *Life* does, it's someone real.

The Medium is half life and half art, and competes with both life and art. It spoils its audience for both; spoils both for its audience. For the People of the Medium life isn't sufficiently a matter of success and glamor and celebrity, isn't entertaining enough, distracting enough, *mediated* enough; and art is too difficult or individual or

novel, too restrained or indirect, too much a matter of tradition and
the past, of special attitudes and aptitudes: its mediation sometimes
is queer or excessive, and sometimes is not even recognizable as
mediation. The Medium's mixture of rhetoric and reality, which
gives people what we know they want in the form we know they like,
is something more efficient and irresistible, more habit-forming, than
any art. If a man all his life has been fed a sort of combination
of marzipan and ethyl alcohol—if eating, to him, is a matter of being
knocked unconscious by an ice cream soda—can he, by taking
thought, come to prefer a diet of bread and wine, apples and well-
water? Will a man who has spent his life watching gladiatorial
games come to prefer listening to chamber music? And those who
produce the bread and wine and quartets for him—won't they be
tempted either to give up producing them, or else to produce a
bread that's half sugar, half alcohol, a quartet that ends with the
cellist at the violist's bleeding throat?

The Medium represents to the artist all that he has learned not
to do: its sure-fire stereotypes seem to him what any true art, true
spirit, has had to struggle past on its way to the truth. The artist sees
the values and textures of this art substitute replacing those of his art
with most of society, conditioning the expectations of what audience
he has kept. Any outsider who has worked for the Medium will have
noticed that the one thing which seems to its managers most unnat-
ural is for someone to do something naturally, to speak or write as
an individual speaking or writing to other individuals, and not as a
subcontractor supplying a standardized product to the Medium.
It is as if producers, editors, supervisors were particles forming a
screen between maker and public, one that will let through only
particles of their own size and weight (or, as they say, the public's);
as you look into their bland faces, their big horn-rimmed eyes, you
despair of Creation itself, which seems for the instant made in their
own owl-eyed image. There are so many extrinsic considerations
about everything in the work, the maker finds, that by the time it is
finished all intrinsic considerations have come to seem secondary.
It is no wonder that the professional who writes the ordinary commercial success, the ordinary script, scenario, or article, resembles
imaginative writers less than he resembles advertising agents, columnists, editors, and producers. He is a technician who can supply
a standard product, a rhetorician who can furnish a regular stimulus
for a regular response, what has always made the dog salivate in this
situation. He is the opposite of the imaginative artist: instead of

stubbornly or helplessly sticking to what he sees and feels, to what seems right for him, true to reality, regardless of what the others think and want, he gives the others what they think and want, regardless of what he himself sees and feels.

Mass culture either corrupts or isolates the writer. His old feeling of oneness, of speaking naturally to an audience with essentially similar standards, is gone; and writers do not any longer have much of the consolatory feeling that took its place, the feeling of writing for the happy few, the kindred spirits whose standards are those of the future. (Today they feel: the future, should there be one, will be worse.) True works of art are more and more produced away from, in opposition to, society. And yet the artist needs society as much as society needs him: as our cultural enclaves get smaller and drier, more hysterical or academic, one mourns for the artists inside them and the public outside. An incomparable historian of mass culture, Ernest van den Haag, has expressed this with laconic force: "The artist who, by refusing to work for the mass market, becomes marginal, cannot create what he might have created had there been no mass market. One may prefer a monologue to addressing a mass meeting. But it is still not a conversation."

Even if the rebellious artist's rebellion is whole-hearted, it can never be whole-stomached, whole-Unconscious'd. Part of him wants to be like his kind, is like his kind; longs to be loved and admired and successful. Our society (and the artist, in so far as he is truly a part of it) has no place set aside for the different and poor and obscure, the fools for Christ's sake: they all go willy-nilly into Limbo. The artist is tempted, consciously, to give his society what it wants, or if he won't or can't, to give it nothing at all; is tempted, unconsciously, to give it superficially independent or contradictory works which are at heart works of the Medium. (Tennessee Williams' *Sweet Bird of Youth* is far less like Chekhov than it is like Mickey Spillane.) It is hard to go on serving both God and Mammon when God is so really ill-, Mammon so really well-organized. Shakespeare wrote for the Medium of his day; if Shakespeare were alive now he'd be writing *My Fair Lady*; isn't *My Fair Lady*, then, our *Hamlet*? shouldn't you be writing *Hamlet* instead of sitting there worrying about your superego? I need my *Hamlet*! So society speaks to the artist; but after he has written it its *Hamlet*, it tries to make sure that he will never do it again. There are more urgent needs that it wants him to satisfy: to lecture to it; to make public appearances; to be interviewed; to be on television shows; to give testimonials; to make trips abroad for the State Department; to judge books for contests or Book Clubs; to read for publishers, judge for publishers, be a publisher for publishers; to be an editor; to teach writing at colleges or writers' conferences; to write scenarios or scripts or articles, articles about his home town for *Holiday,* about cats or clothes or Christmas for *Vogue,* about "How I Wrote *Hamlet*" for anything; to . . .

But why go on? I once heard a composer, lecturing, say to a poet, lecturing: "They'll pay us to do *anything,* so long as it isn't writing music or writing poems." I knew the reply that, as a member of my society, I should have made: "So long as they pay you, what do you care?" But I didn't make it—it was plain that they cared. . . . But how many more learn not to care, love what they once endured! It is a whole so comprehensive that any alternative seems impossible, any opposition irrelevant; in the end a man says in a small voice, "I accept the Medium." The Enemy of the People winds up as the People—but where there is no Enemy, the people perish.

The climate of our culture is changing. Under these new rains, new suns, small things grow great, and what was great grows small; whole species disappear and are replaced. The American present is very different from the American past: so different that our awareness of the extent of the changes has been repressed, and we regard as ordinary what is extraordinary (ominous perhaps) both for us and the rest of the world. For the American present is many other peoples' future: our cultural and economic example is, to much of the world, mesmeric, and it is only its weakness and poverty that prevent it from hurrying with us into the Roman future. Yet at this moment of our greatest power and success, our thought and art are full of troubled gloom, of the conviction of our own decline. When the President of Yale University writes that "the ideal of the good life has faded from the educational process, leaving only miscellaneous prospects of jobs and joyless hedonism," are we likely to find it unfaded among our entertainers and executives? Is the influence of what I have called the Medium likely to make us lead any good life? to make us love and try to attain any real excellence, beauty, magnanimity? or to make us understand these as obligatory but transparent rationalizations, behind which the realities of money and power are waiting?

Matthew Arnold once spoke about our green culture in terms that have an altered relevance (but are not yet irrelevant) to our ripe one. He said: "What really dissatisfies in American civilization is the want of the *interesting*, a want due chiefly to the want of those two great elements of the interesting, which are elevation and beauty." This use of *interesting* (and, perhaps, this tone of a curator pointing out what is plain and culpable) shows how far along in the decline of the West Arnold came; it is only in the latter days that we ask to be interested. He had found the word in Carlyle. Carlyle is writing to a friend to persuade him not to emigrate to the United States; he asks, "Could you banish yourself from all that is interesting to your mind, forget the history, the glorious institutions, the noble principles of old Scotland—that you might eat a better dinner, perhaps?" We smile, and feel like reminding Carlyle of the history, the glorious institutions, the noble principles of new America, that New World which is, after all, the heir of the Old. And yet . . . Can we smile as comfortably, today, as we could have smiled yesterday? listen as unconcernedly, if on taking leave of us some tourist should say, with the penetration and obtuseness of his kind:

I remember reading somewhere: that which you inherit from your fathers you must earn in order to possess. I have been so much impressed with your power and possessions that I have neglected, perhaps, your principles. The elevation or beauty of your spirit did not equal, always, that of your mountains and skyscrapers: it seems to me that your society provides you with "all that is interesting to your mind" only exceptionally, at odd hours, in little reservations like those of your Indians. But as for your dinners, I've never seen anything like them: your daily bread comes *flambé*. And yet—wouldn't you say?—the more dinners a man eats, the more comfort he possesses, the hungrier and more uncomfortable some part of him becomes: inside every fat man there is a man who is starving. Part of you is being starved to death, and the rest of you is being stuffed to death. . . . But this will change: no one goes on being stuffed to death or starved to death forever.

This is a gloomy, an equivocal conclusion? Oh yes, I come from an older culture, where things are accustomed to coming to such conclusions; where there is no last-paragraph fairy to bring one, always, a happy ending—or that happiest of all endings, no ending at all. And have I no advice to give you, as I go? None. You are too successful to need advice, or to be able to take it if it were offered; but if ever you should fail, it is there waiting for you, the advice or consolation of all the other failures.

Mass Culture and the Creative Artist
James Baldwin

from

Daedalus, vol.89, no.2, 1960.

Reprinted by permission of the American Academy of Arts and Sciences and the Editor of *Daedalus*.

JAMES BALDWIN

Mass Culture and the Creative Artist

Some Personal Notes

SOMEONE once said to me that the people in general cannot bear very much reality. He meant by this that they prefer fantasy to a truthful re-creation of their experience. The Italians, for example, during the time that De Sica and Rossellini were revitalizing the Italian cinema industry, showed a marked preference for Rita Hayworth vehicles; the world in which she moved across the screen was like a fairy tale, whereas the world De Sica was describing was one with which they were only too familiar. (And it can be suggested perhaps that the Americans who stood in line for *Shoe Shine* and *Open City* were also responding to images which they found exotic, to a reality by which they were not threatened. What passes for the appreciation of serious effort in this country is very often nothing more than an inability to take anything very seriously.)

Now, of course the people cannot bear very much reality, if by this one means their ability to respond to high intellectual or artistic endeavor. I have never in the least understood why they should be expected to. There is a division of labor in the world—as I see it— and the people have quite enough reality to bear, simply getting through their lives, raising their children, dealing with the eternal conundrums of birth, taxes, and death. They do not do this with all the wisdom, foresight, or charity one might wish; nevertheless, this is what they are always doing and it is what the writer is always describing. There is literally nothing else to describe. This effort at description is itself extraordinarily arduous, and those who are driven to make this effort are by virtue of this fact somewhat removed from the people. It happens, by no means infrequently, that the people hound or stone them to death. They then build statues to them, which does not mean that the next artist will have it any easier.

I am not sure that the cultural level of the people is subject to a steady rise: in fact, quite unpredictable things happen when the bulk of the population attains what we think of as a high cultural level, i.e., pre-World War II Germany, or present-day Sweden. And this, I think, is because the effort of a Schönberg or a Picasso (or a William Faulkner or an Albert Camus) has nothing to do, at bottom, with physical comfort, or indeed with comfort of any other kind. But the aim of the people who rise to this high cultural level—who rise, that is, into the middle class—is precisely comfort for the body and the mind. The artistic objects by which they are surrounded cannot possibly fulfill their original function of disturbing the peace —which is still the only method by which the mind can be improved —they bear witness instead to the attainment of a certain level of economic stability and a certain thin measure of sophistication. But art and ideas come out of the passion and torment of experience; it is impossible to have a real relationship to the first if one's aim is to be protected from the second.

We cannot possibly expect, and should not desire, that the great bulk of the populace embark on a mental and spiritual voyage for which very few people are equipped and which even fewer have survived. They have, after all, their indispensable work to do, even as you and I. What we are distressed about, and should be, when we speak of the state of mass culture in this country, is the overwhelming torpor and bewilderment of the people. The people who run the mass media are not all villains and they are not all cowards —though I agree, I must say, with Dwight Macdonald's forceful suggestion that many of them are not very bright. (Why should they be? They, too, have risen from the streets to a high level of cultural attainment. They, too, are positively afflicted by the world's highest standard of living and what is probably the world's most bewilderingly empty way of life.) But even those who are bright are handicapped by their audience: I am less appalled by the fact that *Gunsmoke* is produced than I am by the fact that so many people want to see it. In the same way, I must add, that a thrill of terror runs through me when I hear that the favorite author of our President is Zane Grey.

But one must make a living. The people who run the mass media and those who consume it are really in the same boat. They must continue to produce things they do not really admire, still less, love, in order to continue buying things they do not really want, still less, need. If we were dealing only with fintails, two-tone cars, or programs like *Gunsmoke*, the situation would not be so grave. The trouble is that serious things are handled (and received) with the same essential lack of seriousness.

For example: neither *The Bridge On the River Kwai* nor *The Defiant Ones*, two definitely superior movies, can really be called serious. They are extraordinarily interesting and deft: but their principal effort is to keep the audience at a safe remove from the experience which these films are not therefore really prepared to convey. The kind of madness sketched in *Kwai* is far more dangerous and widespread than the movie would have us believe. As for *The Defiant Ones*, its suggestion that Negroes and whites can learn to love each other if they are only chained together long enough runs so madly counter to the facts that it must be dismissed as one of the latest, and sickest, of the liberal fantasies, even if one does not quarrel with the notion that love on such terms is desirable. These movies are designed not to trouble, but to reassure; they do not reflect reality, they merely rearrange its elements into something we can bear. They also weaken our ability to deal with the world as it is, ourselves as we are.

What the mass culture really reflects (as is the case with a "serious" play like *J.B.*) is the American bewilderment in the face of the world we live in. We do not seem to want to know that we are *in* the world, that we are subject to the same catastrophes, vices, joys, and follies which have baffled and afflicted mankind for ages. And this has everything to do, of course, with what was expected of America: which expectation, so generally disappointed, reveals something we do not want to know about sad human nature, reveals something we do not want to know about the intricacies and inequities of any social structure, reveals, in sum, something we do not want to know about ourselves. The American way of life has failed—to make people happier or to make them better. We do not want to admit this, and we do not admit it. We persist in believing that the empty and criminal among our children are the result of some miscalculation in the formula (which can be corrected), that the bottomless and aimless hostility which makes our cities among the most dangerous in the world is created, and felt, by a handful of aberrants, that the lack, yawning everywhere in this country, of passionate conviction, of personal authority, proves only our rather appealing tendency to be gregarious and democratic. We are very cruelly trapped between what we would like to be, and what we actually are. And we cannot possibly become what we would like to be until we are willing to ask ourselves just why the lives we lead on this continent are mainly so empty, so tame and so ugly.

This is a job for the creative artist—who does not really have much to do with mass culture, no matter how many of us may be interviewed on TV. Perhaps life is not the black, unutterably beautiful, mysterious, and lonely thing the creative artist tends to think of it as being; but it is certainly not the sunlit playpen in which so many Americans lose first their identities and then their minds.

I feel very strongly, though, that this amorphous people are in desperate search for something which will help them to re-establish their connection with themselves, and with one another. This can only begin to happen as the truth begins to be told. We are in the middle of an immense metamorphosis here, a metamorphosis which will, it is devoutly to be hoped, rob us of our myths and give us our history, which will destroy our attitudes and give us back our personalities. The mass culture, in the meantime, can only reflect our chaos: and perhaps we had better remember that this chaos contains life—and a great transforming energy.

Ideals, Dangers and Limitations of Mass Culture
Stanley Edgar Hyman

from

Daedalus, vol.89, no.2, 1960.

Reprinted by permission of the American Academy of Arts and Sciences and the Editor of *Daedalus*.

STANLEY EDGAR HYMAN

Ideals, Dangers, and Limitations
of Mass Culture

I SHALL ASSUME that we all know what mass culture is, and that we all more or less agree that its technological revolution is the major transformation that has happened to the arts (including literature, the art I profess) in our lifetime. I should like to discuss some of the ideals, dangers, and limitations of mass culture. In my opinion, the most important ideal is pluralism, making a wide variety of aesthetic goods available, rather than lifting us all half an inch by the great collective bootstrap. That is why paperbacks and long-playing records seem so hopeful a tendency despite their defects: *Peyton Place* and *Witch Doctor* are available in their millions, but *Finnegans Wake* and *Don Giovanni* (not to speak of *Fat Mama Blues*) are available in their thousands. Even the magazine situation is dreary and discouraging but still triumphantly pluralist; there is a magazine, however tiny, subsidized, or absurd, to publish every kind of writing, to furnish any sort of reading or looking (within the limits of the law) that any few readers or lookers want. One has only to compare the situation with that of England, which has one little magazine to every fifty of ours, or of Russia, which has not had one since Maya-kovsky's day, to see the virtues of pluralism. It is only when the expenses of production become prohibitive, with a newspaper or film company, a radio or television station, that a wide variety of aesthetic goods becomes impossible, and only ventures that will satisfy many thousands or millions are feasible. Then it is necessary to talk of improving standards, raising levels, educating public taste, taking the initiative for better quality, and such functions more proper to a benign tyranny than to our anarchic cultural democracy.

The second ideal, about which I am somewhat more dubious but still hopeful, is the natural evolution of taste, given a variety of possibilities. (In other words, it depends on pluralism, although pluralism, as a good in itself, would make sense even if taste were known to be static.) This is the assumption that a certain number of those who read and enjoy *The Subterraneans* will go on to read, and prefer, *The Possessed*; that some will comparably graduate from rock 'n roll to traditional blues. This naturally happens at school age (although not in every case), and the ideal assumes its happening at every age. Here the evidence is rather mixed. William Phillips, in an article in the *Partisan Review* (Winter 1959) describes the question as "the old senseless argument about whether a man who listens to popular tunes has taken the first step to Schönberg." This may, however, be a very important question for the future of our culture.

A decade ago the Book-of-the-Month Club sent around a circular listens to popular tunes has taken the first step to Schönberg." This It clearly made the point (which I do not think it was designed to make) that these had worsened annually, from books like Sylvia Townsend Warner's *Lolly Willowes* and Elinor Wylie's *Orphan Angel* in 1926 to Frances Gaither's *Double Muscadine* and the Gilbreths' *Cheaper by the Dozen* in 1949. Over the decade since, despite (or because of) the presence of such learned fellows as Gilbert Highet on the board of judges, the selections seem to have continued to deteriorate. If someone had subscribed and taken the selections over the past thirty years, *his* taste would not have evolved onward and upward. But the turnover is very high; how could we find out about those who learned to read books for pleasure as subscribers, then resigned from the club to read better books on their own?

The BBC radio, with its three programs designed for three levels of taste, would seem a perfect device for encouraging this sort of cultural mobility. Yet I wonder what percentage of listeners of mature years graduated from family comedy on the Light to sea chanteys on the Home to translations of Bulgarian poetry on the Third? How many slid slowly downward? Now, unfortunately, the Third has been curtailed, and with the increased cost of television production and a competing commercial channel, it has not been possible for the BBC to set up anything of the sort for television. Here for the first time some planned range of availability was created in a mass medium, but we know too little about its cultural results.

The third ideal of mass culture I take from a letter Patrick D.

Hazard wrote to me in 1958 in connection with some remarks I had published about the ironic mode. He wrote: "Now it seems to me that a great many intellectuals in America have achieved a viable irony, but I wonder how the great mass who are no longer folk and not yet people can find a footing for their ironic stance. Do any of the following seem to you footholds?" He then proceeded to list such newer comic performers as Mort Sahl and Jonathan Winters, such older comic performers as Groucho Marx and Fred Allen, and such miscellaneous phenomena as Al Capp, *The Threepenny Opera*, and *Humbug* magazine. His comment on the list was: "These things seem to question in one way or another some aspect of flatulence in popular culture, its sentimentality, fake elegance, phony egalitarianism, or its perennial playpen atmosphere."

I did not know the answer to the question then and do not know it now, but I present Hazard's question and comment to raise the possibility of a third ideal. This is that mass culture throws up its own criticism, in performers of insight, wit, and talent, and in forms of irony and satire, to enable some of the audience to break through it into a broader or deeper set of aesthetic values. Again, I much prefer this sort of evolutionary possibility to types of patronizing enlightenment. We do well to be wary when a *Time* editor like Thomas Griffith writes *The Waist-High Culture* to ask whether we haven't sold our souls "for a mess of pottage that goes snap, crackle, and pop," or television producer David Susskind tells *Life*:

I'm an intellectual who cares about television. There are some good things on it, tiny atolls in the oceans of junk. . . . You get mad at what you really care about—like your wife. I'm mad at TV because I really love it and it's lousy. It's a very beautiful woman who looks abominable. The only way to fix it is to clean out the pack who are running it and put in some brainy guys.

We assume that if Griffith ran *Time* it would crackle less, that Susskind is the sort of brainy lover TV needs. I would sooner rest my hopes in Groucho Marx, who does not describe himself as an intellectual, or the late Fred Allen, who had a cleansing bitterness and despair about the media themselves, and wasn't campaigning for David Sarnoff's job. If there are such footings as Hazard suggests for an ironic stance in mass culture, let them not crusade under our feet.

The dangers of mass culture are much easier to define than the ideas. The foremost one, which may negate all the ideals, is an overpowering narcotic effect, relaxing the tired mind and tranquilizing the anxious. Genuine art is demanding and difficult, often unpleasant, nagging at the mind and stretching the nerves taut. So much of mass culture envelops the audience in a warm bath, making no demands except that we all glow with pleasure and comfort. It is this that may negate the range of possibility (the bath is pleasanter at the shallow end), keep taste static or even deteriorate it a little, muffle the few critical and ironic sounds being made. That premature cultural critic Homer knew all about this effect, at various times calling it Lotus Eaters, Calypso, Circe, and the Sirens, and he just barely got our hero through intact.

An obvious source of danger is the cults. In one direction we have the cult of the folk. Some ten years ago I published an article called "The American Folksy" in *Theatre Arts* (April 1949), protesting that we were being overwhelmed by an avalanche of pseudo-folk corn. I turn out not to have been very prophetic. What I then took to be the height of something like the great tulip craze can now be seen to have been only the first tentative beginnings of something so vast and offensive that it dwarfs historical parallels. I named half a dozen folksy singers of the time, but could not have guessed that a decade later there would be hundreds if not thousands, that magazines would be devoted to guitar and banjo styles, that the production of washtub basses would be an American industry. I certainly could not have predicted Elvis Presley. I mention this failure of imagination now only to explain why the ramifying vertical combine that lives by falsifying America's cultural past seems to me a major deterrent to any of the hopes for mass culture.

Opposed to the cult of the folk, which identifies (however falsely) with a tradition, and blows hot, or passionate, is the cult of the hip which denies (however falsely) having any tradition, and blows cool. (At the juvenile end it tells sick jokes, glorying in the impassivity of: "Mrs. Brown, can Johnny come out and play ball?" "But you children know he has no arms or legs." "That's O.K. We want to use him for second base.") At higher levels it admits wryly to Jules Feiffer's truths, professes Zen, or joins Norman Mailer in making what he called in *Dissent*,* "the imaginative journey into the tortured marijuana-racked mind and genitalia of a hipster daring to live on the edge of the most dangerous of the Negro worlds." At this point, obviously, cool has become pretty hot, an outlaw folk

* "The White Negro (Superficial Reflections on the Hipster)," *Dissent*, Summer 1957, 4:276-293.

tradition has been established, and perhaps both these polar cults are recognizable as the same sort of fantasy identification. To the extent that mass culture permits, encourages, and thrives on these adolescent gratifications, it is as spurious and mendacious as its harshest critics claim.

One more danger inherent in mass culture, and perhaps the most menacing one, is the existence of a captive audience with no escape. In regard to art, it is not much of a problem; many will sit through worse than they expected, and a few will sit through better than they desire. As a machinery for selling us consumer goods, using all the resources of a prostituted psychology and sociology, it becomes more menacing, although here too mass culture seems to throw up its counterstatements. Against a million voices stridently shouting "Buy!" the tiny neo-Thoreauvian voice of J. K. Galbraith whispers, "Reduce your wants," and is immediately amplified by a book club and blurbs from a number of magazines that would not last a week if his advice were heeded. It is when the same technique is used to sell us politics that our status as a captive audience to mass media becomes menacing, an Eisenhower or a Nixon today but a Big Brother or a Big Daddy tomorrow.

At this point we are informed that the fashionable cult of New Conservatism, with its scorn for our worship of the mob and the mob's brittle toys, will save us, if only we elect to follow Burke and Calhoun instead of those demagogues Jefferson and Paine. The corrective here is reading the tribute to Roy Campbell that Russell Kirk published in *The Sewanee Review* (Winter 1956) and discovering that Kirk's heart's vision is not Edmund Burke orating nobly in the House of Commons, but Roy Campbell spanking a small, effeminate Marxist poet on a public lecture platform. In short, New Conservatism yearns masochistically for its fantasy storm troopers, and Kirk and his fellows are less the doctor than the disease.

Some of the limitations of mass culture have already been suggested. One absolute limitation is the Law of Raspberry Jam, that the wider you spread it the thinner it is. Another is the nature of art itself. As genuine art, advancing sensibility, stretching the limits of form, purifying the language of the tribe, it is always for an elite of education (which does not mean a formal education), sensibility, and taste. When its freshness has grown somewhat stale, diluted by imitators and popularizers, its audience widens, although if it is true art it will always continue to demand more than a mass audience cares to give it.

A special limitation, not inevitable and not universal, is the timidity of those in positions of authority in the mass media. Jerry Lewis, of all people, wrote in the *New York Times Magazine* for 7 December 1958:

Unfortunately, TV fell into the well-manicured hands of the Madison Avenue bully boys, who, awed by the enormousness of the monster, began to "run scared." They were easy prey for the new American weapon —the pressure group.

Steve Allen's reply in the same symposium suggests that we confront no simple matter of pressure or censorship, that here horses break themselves with alacrity and great civic responsibility. Allen writes:

There are, frankly, a few things I joke about in private that I do not touch upon on the air, but this implies no feeling of frustration. I realize that some tenets of my personal philosophy would antagonize the majority without educating them; hence, no good could come of experimenting with such subjects.

Matching the timidity of the producers is the ignorance of the consumers. Who knows what they might want if they knew what there was to want, if they knew what they didn't know? This again is a special and perhaps transitory limitation. As education spreads and leisure increases, some of our mass audiences may acquire, if not what we call "taste," at least a wider knowledge of cultural possibility. The well poisoner is an unlovely figure, but the responsibility of those poisoning *these* reservoirs from which millions drink is comparably greater. What defense has an ignorant and eager reader, buying *The Origin of Species* in the Everyman edition, against its introductory assurance that authoritative scientists no longer believe these things? He has scarcely heard of Darwin, how is he to know that W. R. Thompson is not the voice of modern science? If he happens to read T. H. Robsjohn-Gibbings' book attacking modern architecture and design, it is the confession of a contemporary designer to what he has always rather suspected; he is not apt to have encountered Mr. Robsjohn-Gibbings' hi-fi unit with Doric columns in a decorator's studio. Because it knows no better, in short, the mass audience is condemned to the fate of never knowing any better.

We come finally to the matter of taking a stand or stands. Each of us confronts mass culture in a number of roles. My own include customer, parent, journalist, critic, teacher of literature. The role of teacher seems the best one from which to tackle the problem, since the college teacher of literature is not only assumed to be a custodian of traditional values, but must deal with the new values in his day-to-day contact with what students read and write. He cannot entirely ignore them or wash his hands of them. I would propose that there are at least six different things he must do about mass culture, varying with the quality and promise of the specimen involved, the differing needs of students, and his own needs and perhaps moods. I list them by the operative verbs, using literary examples as much as possible.

Reject. This is a traditional function of the critic of mass culture, and it can be performed in a variety of moods, from the high good fun of H. L. Mencken whacking one or another fatuosity of the booboisie to the owlish pomposity of recent *American Mercury* pundits. The best current example of rejection is Leslie Fiedler, who told a symposium at Columbia not long ago that the writer's proper role is a nay-saying and destructive one, that he should not hesitate to bite the hand which feeds him. Fiedler's slogan for Hollywood and TV was, "We must destroy their destructiveness." As a teacher, I would reserve this rejection for the real junk, Mickey Spillane and *Peyton Place.* Here, it seems to me, any sort of undercutting or resistance is legitimate, short of actually snatching the book out of the student's hands and pitching it into the garbage. Let the teacher rant and rave, appeal to his authority, the student's shame, or the ghost of Henry James. Let him expose and deride this pernicious trash in every way possible. The really hopeless is only a small percentage of the total output of mass culture, however, which allows the teacher to save some of his energy for other operations, and to contribute a small sum to a subscription to replace Leslie Fiedler's teeth when they wear out.

Embrace. This too is a traditional function, and we have had intellectual cults of the popular arts, of Chaplin or Keaton, Krazy Kat or Donald Duck, since there were popular arts. Reuel Denney's article on Pogo, reprinted in his book, *The Astonished Muse,* is a fine example of the passionate professorial embrace. Denney shows learnedly that the strip is "a study in the disintegration of the New Deal phase of the Democratic party," that "if the political stance of the strip is Democratic and Steffens-like, the literary stance is post-Joycean, and the psychological stance is post-Freudian." Poor Albert Alligator becomes a parataxis of oral aggression, although at this point I begin to suspect that Denney is having a pull at the reader's leg. It was very shrewd of George P. Elliott to make his impossible sociologist in *Parktilden Village* the creator, as the result of his researches, of a cartoon strip that appealed to every cultural level. George Orwell was in something of this position, studying boys' books with loving attention, then himself writing a superior boys' book in *1984*, which sold its million copies in paperback. The products of mass culture one can wholeheartedly welcome and embrace are probably as small a percentage as those one ought wholeheartedly to reject. I would suggest such rare best-sellers as *Catcher in the Rye*, hovering on the edge of serious literature, such sparkling musical comedies as *Guys and Dolls* and *Pajama Game*, and comedians and comic strips to taste.

Ignore. This is perhaps more a teacher's dodge than any other. Several years ago at Bennington, David Riesman made some remarks (which I dare say he has since published) about the tyranny of the curricular. When he was an undergraduate, he said, his intellectual solace was that he could read Marx and Freud, which *they* (his teachers) didn't know about or didn't approve, and thus have an area of his mind and life that Harvard could not regiment. At a place like Bennington, he said, Marx and Freud would immediately be made the subject of courses, as would anything else in which the students showed interest.

I sat in the audience trying to get the arrow out of my throat, since that year I was teaching a course in Marx and Freud (along with Darwin and Frazer), and I had just organized a lively faculty seminar on rock 'n roll, at which we told the students what it was all about. The only comfort I had was that however tyrannous the curricular, there was always *something* the students could block off privately; if they were being taught Marx and "Fats" Domino, perhaps they were pursuing Racine and Mozart on the sly. In any case, they had some underground culture the faculty would do best not to know about. I find this tactic of ignoring very useful in regard to West Coast poetry (I suspect that that book of verse called *Howl* circulates surreptitiously at Bennington, but I have never made any attempt to find out), in regard to the intricacies of modern cool jazz ("He doesn't dig *Mulligan!*"), and most particularly in regard to any combination of the two. Probably I would be better off, we would all be better off, ignoring more, letting them keep private whatever current work speaks to their condition, letting education grow up without daily watering and all those infernal sunlamps.

Improve. Here we have the traditional pedagogic tactic of using what the student likes as a guidepost to something better. Ah, one can sigh in relief, at last some *constructive* criticism, not that irresponsible ignoring. It is this attitude of exploring mass culture for signs of hope and maturity that has distinguished *Commentary* over the years. I think of such articles as Robert Warshow's "Paul, the Horror Comics, and Dr. Wertham," reprinted in Rosenberg and White's *Mass Culture*, and Norman Podhoretz's "Our Changing Ideals, as Seen on TV," reprinted in Brossard's *The Scene before You*. A sign of the awareness of the problem by a group of English teachers is the recent organization of a new section of the Modern Language Association, dealing with Literature and General Culture. An organizing statement that was circulated before the meeting expressed the hope that by studying mass culture "we may come to learn what clearly separates the best-seller from the work of distinction, and, if our aims become in part educational, offer our students the necessary exercises in discrimination." Again, I am wary of the big battalions. Teaching this sort of discrimination has always been the teacher's function, as it has always been the critic's. The works that call for it are those mixed bundles that cannot be rejected or embraced and should not be ignored, works of genuine imagination flawed by crassness, hokum, or sheer want of craft. I think of the novels of Jack Kerouac and the plays of Tennessee Williams. What attracts the student or reader to them is better available in Dostoevsky and Chekhov, in Fielding and Shakespeare, but they may be precisely the bridges to get there, and in any case are worth study in their own terms.

Replace. Beyond all this, the college teacher of literature as a custodian of traditional value has to remember what he has in his custody. John Crowe Ransom, in his 1958 Phi Beta Kappa address, "Our Age among the Ages," reprinted in the *Kenyon Review* (Winter 1959), came to a civilized and pluralist but deeply pessimistic conclusion. He wrote:

At any rate, the old ways of life have been disappearing much too rapidly for comfort, and we are in a great cultural confusion. Many millions of underprivileged persons now have income and leisure which they did not have before. They have the means to achieve the best properties of a culture, if they know how to spend their money wisely. And it is a fact that they spend handsomely on education. Now, I am in the education business, and I can report my own observations on that. It is as if a sudden invasion of barbarians had overrun the educational institution; except that the barbarians in this case are our neighbors and friends, and sometimes they are our own children, or they are ourselves, they are some of us gathered here on this very fine occasion. We should not fear them; they are not foreigners, nor our enemies. But in the last resort education is a democratic process, in which the courses are subject to the election of the applicants, and a course even when it has been elected can never rise above the intellectual passion of its pupils, or their comparative indifference. So, with the new generation of students, Milton declines in the curriculum; even Shakespeare has lost heavily; Homer and Virgil are practically gone. The literary interest of the students today is ninety percent in the literature of their own age; more often than not it is found in books which do not find entry into the curriculum, and are beneath the standard which your humble servants, the teachers of literature, are trying to maintain. Chaucer and Spenser and Milton, with their respective contemporaries, will have their secure existence henceforth in the library, and of course in the love and intimate acquaintance of a certain academic community, and there they will stay except for possible periods when there is a revival of the literature of our own antiquity. Our literary culture for a long time is going to exist in a sprawling fashion, with minority pockets of old-style culture, and some sort of a majority culture of a new and indeterminate style. It is a free society, and I should expect that the rights of minorities will be as secure as the rights of individuals.

Ransom's prediction may be exactly accurate, yet the teacher cannot reconcile himself to a minority status for his values in his own classroom, however reconciled he is to it everywhere else. He must ceaselessly bring to the attention of his students the greatest literature he knows. It is not easy for an ill-educated man to teach Homer and Virgil, Greek drama and the Bible, Milton and Shakespeare, as I can testify, but it is essential, and in our curricula Darwin and Marx, ballads and blues, must have a place, but not the primary place. "The best that has been thought and known," as Arnold somewhat pompously put it, is even more vital for college students these days when they seem to come already knowing the worst.

Warn. Here the teacher as critic of mass culture needs a good stout voice, along with the prescience of Ortega y Gasset and the bitterness of Randolph Bourne. The evidence, from Q. D. Leavis' *Fiction and the Reading Public* in 1939 to Margaret Dalziel's *Popular Fiction 100 Years Ago* in 1959, suggests that in some significant respects the standards of mass culture are deteriorating over the centuries, and that instead of flying the kites of our hopes for evolution and awakening, we had better dig in and try to keep things from getting worse than the Victorian penny dreadful. The notable voice here is Randall Jarrell's, and in "The Appalling Taste of Our Age" in the *Saturday Evening Post*'s Adventures of the Mind series, he warned us in the most violent terms that the digest and the revised simplified version menace not only high literary culture but the art of reading itself, the use of the written word. In the most terrifying chapter of *Das Kapital*, "The Working Day," Marx told us of English laboring children so brutalized and degraded by working twelve and sixteen hours a day in the mills that they did not know the name of the Queen, or the story of Noah, or where London was. Now Jarrell tells us of our own children, raised in comfort and love, getting the most expensive education in the world, who do not know who Charlemagne was, or the story of Jonah, or what comes before E in the alphabet. Warn? One should bellow and curse and call down doom, like the prophet Jeremiah.

Yes, but of course also reject and embrace, ignore, improve, and replace. The teacher and the critic of mass culture cannot simply reduce himself to one attitude, but must keep varying the attack, like a young pitcher learning to supplement his high-school fast ball with a curve and a change of pace. Among the dangers of mass culture is the danger to the critic of atrophy, not to call it *rigor mortis*, of hardening in one fixed position. The comparable danger to the writer or artist is being squeezed dry too fast, like a television comedian, or brought up into the big time too soon, like a young fighter. The defense in both cases is wariness, and periodic rites of withdrawal. The ultimate ideal of mass culture is the ideal of the whole culture (to return to the anthropologists' term), something nearer the good life for all mankind. Here Homer and the Athenian tragic dramatists are useful in reminding us of basic limitation, of man's flawed, blind, and mortal nature, and of the ironies of hope and expectation.

We are not the good society, but we do have a vision of it, and that vision is a pluralist one, in which many different forms of satisfaction, including clearly spurious ones, can coexist peacefully. Mass culture is here to stay, but so, I hope, are those of us who want another sort of culture for ourselves and for anyone else who wants it, or who can be educated, led, or cajoled into wanting it. In so far as all of mass culture represents someone's organization of experience into what he intends as meaningful and pleasurable patterns, it is all a kind of shabby poetry, but we dare not forget that there are other kinds of poetry too.

Mass Culture and Social Criticism
H. Stuart Hughes

from

Daedalus, vol.89, no.2, 1960.

Reprinted by permission of the American Academy of Arts and Sciences and the Editor of *Daedalus*.

Mass Culture and Social Criticism

CONTEMPORARY CRITICS of mass culture have gotten themselves into inextricable difficulties by refusing to admit to their own "snobbery." The original critics of the phenomenon, from de Tocqueville to Ortega y Gasset and Irving Babbitt, were frankly aristocrats who never thought of apologizing for the special and exclusive nature of their own standards. Indeed, it was precisely the fastidious distaste of the well born and the carefully educated that prompted the identification of mass culture at all. Culturally privileged elites have always resisted the invasion of the vulgar; there was no particular novelty in the fact that in the late nineteenth and early twentieth centuries people of humanistic education reacted so sharply against the unfamiliar standards of the "half-educated." The novelty appeared only when (as Edward Shils[1] has explained) the intellectual leaders began to identify themselves with democracy or socialism and sought virtue in the cultural pursuits of the common man. From this latter point of departure, a bewildered disappointment could be the only result.

For our contemporary critics have been trying to apply two incompatible standards at the same time. They have clung to the special cultural definitions of a narrow elite—the insistence on a common core of "humanist" reading or artistic enjoyment, on the importance of foreign languages, ancient or modern, and on the elegant manipulation of one's own—maintaining all the while that these things are perfectly capable of mass dissemination. They have tried to combine elitism and democracy—things compatible perhaps in a Periclean or Jeffersonian sense of popular government led by "the best," but, under contemporary conditions, radical opposites.

In a word, I believe that contemporary democracy and contemporary mass culture are two sides of the same coin, and that our discussions of the latter phenomenon, now and in the future, will get nowhere until we recognize this simple equation and the corollaries that stem from it. Few of us, I think, would be prepared to jettison democracy and to substitute some sort of aristocratic regime in its place. All sorts of reasons, both moral and technical, spring to our minds as counter-arguments. Hence, if we want to live in our world with some degree of equanimity, it is incumbent on us to make our peace with mass culture in at least a few of its more bearable manifestations.

By now it should be obvious that I agree with Messrs. Rosten and Shils that the mass media cannot be held responsible for "corrupting" popular taste. The taste of the masses, I believe, has always appeared more or less "corrupt" to the better educated, and I see no reason why this situation should change. I am also impressed with Mr. Rosten's argument that the media frequently produce or print things that are over the heads of their audience, and that the most serious limitation on them is the absence of talent to cope with the totally unprecedented demand for copy. At the same time (even under the most favorable conditions) I do not believe the media capable of performing the task of general education that their would-be reformers want to entrust to them. Or, more precisely, I think that only certain cultural values are susceptible of large-scale dissemination, and that certain other values, traditionally regarded as distinguishing features of the educated man, when subjected to such a process simply become diluted beyond recognition.

About twenty years ago I was first struck by Henry Adams' observation that the United States in 1800 possessed a cultural equipment that was almost exclusively restricted to theology, literature, and oratory. While these were frequently cultivated with intensity and finesse, the realm of the visual arts and music (the more sensuous gratifications of old Europe) were practically nonexistent.[2] As the years have passed since I first read those lines—and as our country has undergone the most profound social and cultural change in its history—I have watched Adams' words turn into their very opposite. Today it is the arts of language that have passed into disrespect: even the man of reasonable education can no longer handle English with any sureness of touch; we have become a nation of nongrammarians admirably represented by the curious syntax of our chief executive. At the same time, the enjoyment of music, the semiprofessional theater, and even painting has become diffused in a fashion almost nobody anticipated a generation ago. The arts of sensuous consumption are prospering everywhere. In the sphere of traditional music and the less difficult forms of the drama and the visual arts, popular taste has never been so well developed.

Now what the arts of sensuous consumption have in common (as opposed to reading, speaking, logical argument, or the more intellectualized forms of painting or music) is, of course, the passivity of their reception. This passive quality has been lamented again and again by the critics of our contemporary culture; they have repeatedly called for a return to the strenuous effort that they find characteristic of all true artistic or intellectual attainment. Here, I think, the critics have become impractical visionaries. For it is precisely the active, acute, finely perceptive elements of traditional culture that, *under contemporary conditions,* are incapable of mass dissemination. If spread too widely, they become unrecognizable. Or, perhaps more commonly, they produce boredom and a weary sensation of irrelevance.

Why is it that so much of what to us may seem the best parts of our cultural heritage strikes the majority of our countrymen, and even our students, as supremely irrelevant? The question is not as foolish as it sounds. And it is not to be answered merely by angry assertions of the greatness of a Virgil or a Milton. If almost no one cares to read Milton today, it is not just because we have lost our feeling for traditional culture. It is because most of what an author like Milton has to say has in simple truth become irrelevant to our contemporary lives.

The passivity of our cultural response mirrors the passivity of the society in which we live. Ours is a world without issues—or rather with one issue, so vast and so frightening that people prefer not to talk about it at all. If our students yawn over the classics, it is not just that they are boorish and obtuse; on the contrary, many of them may be acute enough to realize that the subject matter of these great works has very little to do with their own lives. Heroic endeavor, "purity" and chastity, poverty and pestilence, the fine distinctions of theology, the duties of kingship, the perfect society— all these noble old subjects seem muted and remote to contemporary Americans. The hardest task of the historian of ideas is to convince his students or his readers that at one time people cared, even to the point of dying for them, about notions that today seem hopelessly arid and scholastic.

And so we have come to social criticism. Without it, I maintain, any analysis of mass culture is shallow and unprofitable. For I think that there is in fact a qualitative difference between the cultural attitude of the ordinary man today and the plebeian standards within an earlier society. Both, of course, have been concerned primarily with sensual enjoyment. But in past ages the more perceptive and sensitive of the plebs had an uneasy awareness that their lives and standards were far from perfect: their consciences were not clear— at the very least, they felt excluded from the great stage where the major dramas of their time were being enacted. Today the ordinary man does not have the same sense of exclusion. Indeed, he is given a front-row seat: the media see to that. The only trouble is that nothing particularly exciting is going on, on the stage.

Hence there is no incentive to learn the fine points of the drama. If the audience is basically convinced that the great traditional issues of human life, both social and private, no longer have much meaning, if the public senses (as well it may) that the actors them- selves are playing their roles mechanically and without putting much conviction into their lines, then its reception of the play will quite naturally be that of lazy-minded and passive spectators. How dif- ferent things were a couple of generations ago! One has only to con- jure up the image of half-literate European workers patiently listen- ing to the exegesis of Marxian texts for hours at a stretch (a common scene around 1900) to realize the difference in cultural climate. These workers were obviously more poorly educated than their American counterparts of today: they had less capacity to follow a closely reasoned argument. But their inclination to do so was greater. For they were convinced that the lengthy and largely incompre- hensible speeches of their leaders and teachers were of moment to them. The complex reasoning of these people from a loftier cultural sphere really mattered to their listeners: at some point (perhaps a very far-distant point), their auditors believed, it would make a differ- ence in their own lives, or at least in the lives of their descendants.

Today most people have lost this conviction. They do not think that their own lives will get much better or even that their children will be happier than they are. Indeed, they suspect that the contrary may be true. At the conscious level, they repeat to themselves that they are already living in the promised land. Deeper down, they fear that the vision of such a land has vanished forever.

Unless we realize the full import of this loss of the vision of utopia, we shall never be able to understand properly our country and its culture—and along with these, the more general characteristics of twentieth-century society in the Western world. Without such a realization, we shall not be able to express what it is about mass culture that we find so peculiarly depressing. For, as so many of our contributors have asserted, it is not its *mass* character as such that is novel and threatening: it is rather its slackness and meaninglessness. And this flaccid quality springs precisely from the wider nature of the society of which mass culture is simply the most obvious and flamboyant manifestation.

Let me reiterate that I do not think this to be exclusively an American question. The same socio-cultural complex has recently begun to appear in Western and Central Europe, perhaps with a certain time lag, but still with unmistakably familiar features. And this not through what the defenders of the old culture angrily attack as "Americanization": rather than being primarily an importation from outside, the vast social and cultural change that Europe has been undergoing since the Second World War gives every evidence of indigenous and spontaneous origin; the direct copying from America seems to be relatively superficial.

As I look over the social and ideological scene today, I am impressed with the great similarity among the dominant views in the major Western nations—with the possible exception of Britain, which shows remnants of an earlier pattern of clearly marked and significant differences of opinion. Elsewhere one encounters a kind of gray uniformity. The ideologies that call themselves Christian Democracy in Germany and Italy, Gaullism in France, and the bipartisan consensus in our own country, on closer inspection, turn out to be very much the same thing. They stand for an ideology that is the negation of ideology—and of utopia also. In name and in formal organization they are liberal and democratic, but in fact they seem dedicated to draining liberal democracy of its content. No longer do they have any particular enthusiasm behind them. They rest, rather, on material prosperity, and beyond that, and more important than that, on weariness, on apathy, on passive acceptance, on a tacit agreement not to discuss potentially "divisive" issues—on what still needs to be called "conformity," despite the excessive use of that term during the past half-decade of post-McCarthy breast-beating.

I am not surprised, then, that Mr. Shils has referred to this situation as a "culture of consensus." That is exactly what it is—with all the virtues and all the defects that the term implies. I do not want to be misunderstood: I find this culture more tolerant, gentler, and more humane than anything that the Western world knew before; it provides a setting in which the artist, however marginal and irrelevant he may feel himself to be, is seldom mistreated, and almost never starves. One of our contributors has referred to the price we pay for democracy. I think that is a good expression—provided we recognize both that the price is worth paying and that it is a heavy price indeed.

A generation ago Karl Mannheim warned us of what it would mean to live without utopia—without any notion of transcendence in social and cultural pursuits.[3] He held up to us the vision of a cold, bleak world, a world drained of meaning. More recently writers like Lewis Mumford and Erich Fromm have echoed the warning. I do not agree with Mr. Hyman that we still have a vision of the good society. In fact, I could scarcely disagree more strongly. I believe we have lost that vision: most of us are quite satisfied with the ugliness of our cities, the waste in our economy, the cheerful incompetence of our leaders, the meaninglessness of public discourse, the general insensibility to the overwhelming danger that threatens us. Along with our vision, we have lost our capacity for indignation, our ability to feel a cosmic anger with what we see going on around us. And until we regain this vision, these capacities, our culture will continue to be what it is today—"weary, flat, stale, and unprofitable."

REFERENCES

1 "Daydreams and Nightmares: Reflections on the Criticism of Mass Culture." *The Sewanee Review*, LXV (1957).

2 *History of the United States during the Administrations of Jefferson and Madison*, I (New York, 1889), Chapters 3, 4, 5.

3 *Ideology and Utopia* (London and New York, 1936), pp. 230, 236.

Notes on a National Cultural Policy
Arthur Schlesinger, Jr.

from

Daedalus, vol.89, no.2, 1960.

Reprinted by permission of the American Academy of Arts and Sciences and the Editor of *Daedalus*.

ARTHUR SCHLESINGER, JR.

Notes on a National Cultural Policy

TOO MUCH DISCUSSION of the problems of mass culture takes the form of handwringing. The point to be understood, I would think, is that these problems, while complicated and often discouraging, are by no means insuperable, unless we ourselves make them so. Things can be done in all sorts of ways to counteract the more depressing tendencies in our mass civilization. I would like in this brief note to call particular attention to possibilities in the field of public policy.

Let me begin with something both important and specific—that is, the problem of television. There are now over 50 million television sets in the country, covering almost 90 percent of American households. From its inception, television has been in a downward spiral as an artistic medium; but it has taken recent disclosures of fraud in quiz programs to awaken the nation to the potentialities locked up in the tiny screen. The question is: what, if anything, can be done to improve the honesty and the quality of our television programing?

The first point is that television is an area in which there can be no question concerning the direct interest of the national government. No one has a divine right to a television channel. The air belongs to the public; and private operators can use the air only under public license. Why therefore should the national government stand helplessly by while private individuals, making vast sums of money out of public licenses, employ public facilities to debase the public taste? Obviously there seems no reason in law or prudence why this should be so. Government has not only the power but the obligation to help establish standards in media, like television and radio, which exist by public sufferance.

It has this obligation, among other reasons, because there seems no other way to rescue television from the downward spiral of competitive debasement. There are responsible and enlightened men managing television networks and stations; but they are trapped in a competitive situation. The man who gives his audience soap opera and give-away shows will make more money for his stockholders than the man who gives his audience news and Shakespeare. In consequence, the tendency is almost irresistible for television programs to vie with each other, not in elevating the taste of their audiences, but in catering to the worst side of the existing taste. As *Fortune* recently summed up the situation, it seems "that television has reached a kind of ceiling, that mediocrity is increasing, and that only *through some drastic change in the medium's evolution* will the excitement and aspiration of, say, 1954 return to our TV screens" (my italics). *Fortune's* analysis was, as usual, better than its solution, which was Pay TV. Pay-as-you-see TV would be no more exempt from the passion to maximize its audiences than is free TV; and, in due course, it would doubtless undergo the same evolution. (See *Fortune*, December 1958.)

Still "some drastic change in the medium's evolution" remains necessary. But what? Actually there is nothing new about the situation of responsible TV people; they are in precisely the position that responsible businessmen were in twenty-five years ago when they wanted, for example, to treat their workers better but could not afford to do so because of the "competitive situation." Thus many employers disliked sweatshops and child labor but knew that raising wages and improving working conditions would increase their costs and thereby handicap them as against their more callous competitors. Private initiative was impotent to deal with this situation: gentlemen's agreements within an industry always broke down under pressure. There was only one answer—public action to establish and enforce standards through the industry. Finally the Wages and Hours Act required all employers in interstate commerce to meet certain specifications and thus abolished the economic risks of decency.

What television needs is some comparable means of equalizing the alleged competitive disadvantages of enlightened programing. Fortunately the machinery for this is already at hand. According to the Communications Act of 1934, the Federal Communications Commission is to grant licenses to serve the "public convenience, interest, or necessity." A television channel is an immensely lucrative thing; and those lucky enough to secure an FCC license ought to be regarded, not as owners of private property with which they can do anything they want, but as trustees of public property under the obligation to prove their continuing right to the public trust.

It is up to the FCC, in short, to spell out the equivalent of minimum wages and maximum hours for television. What would this imply? It would surely imply the following:

1. A licensing system which would cover networks as well as individual stations.

2. The writing into each license of a series of stipulations which the grantee pledges himself to fulfill in order to retain the license.

3. A major stipulation would be the assumption by the networks and stations of full control over their programing—which means that sponsors and advertising agencies would no longer influence the content of programs. Other media live off advertisements without letting advertising agencies and sponsors dictate and censor content as they do in television. So long as television permits this, it will be fourth-rate. We should go over to the British and Canadian systems, in which the advertiser purchases time on the air as he purchases space in a newspaper, and has to leave editorial matters alone.

4. Other stipulations might include the allocation of stated portions of broadcast time to cultural and educational programs, to programs dealing with public issues, to local live programs; the limitation of advertising (the House of Commons has currently under consideration a bill prohibiting advertising on British TV for more than six minutes in any hour); the allocation of free time during presidential campaigns to all parties polling more than 10 percent of the vote in the previous election.

5. Licenses should come up for annual renewal; and stations which have not met their obligations should expect to have their licenses revoked (the FCC has not refused a request for license renewal since 1932).

6. All this implies, of course, a revitalization of the FCC, which once had chairmen and commissioners of the caliber of Paul Porter, James Lawrence Fly, and Clifford Durr, but has become in recent years the preserve of complaisant political hacks.

Back in 1946, the FCC proposed in its famous Blue Book doing much this sort of thing for radio; but the industry issued the standard lamentations about governmental control, the public remained indifferent, and nothing came of it. One can expect to hear the same wail of "censorship" raised now against proposals for the establishment of federal standards. The fact is that we already have censorship of the worst kind in television. As John Crosby has written, "So long as the advertiser has direct personal control over programs, or direct ownership of programs, it's silly to talk about [government] censorship. The censorship is already stifling. The government should step in not to censor broadcasting but to free it."

The setting of federal standards does not mean government domination of the medium, any more than the Wages and Hours Act meant (as businessmen cried at the time) government domination of business. But the rejection of the Blue Book in 1946 emphasizes the difficulty of the problem. The FCC, even reconstituted as it would have to be in another administration, could not tighten up federal standards by itself. If the FCC proposes to buck the industry, it will require organized public support; it is perhaps a mistake that public energy which might have gone into establishing general standards was diverted into setting up separate facilities for educational television. And the FCC would also probably require some form of administration supplementation—perhaps a National Citizens' Advisory Board, of the kind proposed some years ago by William Benton,[1] or a National Broadcasting Authority, financed by rentals on the licenses, of the sort recently suggested by John Fischer in *Harper's*.[2]

The measures proposed above represent a minimum program. Walter Lippmann and others have recently argued for the establishment of a public network to be "run as a public service with its criterion not what will be most popular but what is good." Lippmann does not suppose that such a network would attract the largest mass audience. "But if it enlisted the great talents which are available in the industry, but are now throttled and frustrated, it might well attract an audience which made up in influence what it lacked in numbers. The force of a good example is a great force, and should not be underrated." Proposals of this sort still horrify many Americans, though fewer now than in the days when Charles Van Doren was a community hero. But clearly, if television cannot clean its own house and develop a sense of responsibility commensurate with its influence, we are bound to come to a government network. If, as Dr. Frank Stanton of the Columbia Broadcasting System insists (*his* italics), "*The strongest sustained attention of Americans is now, daily and nightly, bestowed on television as it is bestowed on nothing else*,"[8] then television is surely a proper subject for public concern. If the industry will not undertake to do itself what is necessary to stop the drift into hopeless mediocrity (and, far from showing any signs of so doing, its leaders deny the reality of the problem and even justify the present state of things by pompous talk about "cultural democracy"), then it must expect public intervention.

The case for government concern over television is indisputable because government must control the air. The case for government concern over other arts rests on a less clear-cut juridical basis. Yet, as John Quincy Adams said one hundred and thirty-five years ago, "The great object of the institution of civil government is the improvement of the condition of those who are parties to the social compact, and no government, in whatever form constituted, can accomplish the lawful ends of its institution but in proportion as it improves the condition of those over whom it is established." Adams added that this applied no less to "moral, political, intellectual improvement" than to internal improvements and public works.

The American government has acknowledged this responsibility variously and intermittently since its foundation. But the problem of government encouragement of the arts is not a simple one; and it has never been satisfactorily solved. In order to bring some coherence into its solution, Congressman Frank Thompson, Jr., of New Jersey has been agitating for some time for the establishment of a Federal Advisory Council on the Arts, to be set up within the Department of Health, Education, and Welfare and charged with assisting the growth of the fine arts in the United States. "A major duty of the Council," the bill (H.R. 7656) reads, "shall be to recommend ways to maintain and increase the cultural resources of the United States."

There is no automatic virtue in councils. Congressman Thompson and Senator Fulbright, for example, got through Congress a year ago an act establishing a National Cultural Center in Washington. After a protracted delay, President Eisenhower named the thirty-four members of the new Center's board of trustees. Of the whole group, only a handful had shown any evidence of knowing or caring anything about the arts; the typical members include such cultural leaders as the former football coach at West Point, the President's minister (balanced, of course, by Catholic and Jewish clerics), his television adviser, representatives of labor, etc. A Federal Advisory Council on the Arts, appointed on such principles, would be worse than useless. But in due course some President will seek our genuine leaders of the arts and ask them to think through the issues of the government relationship.

Let no one mistake it: there are no easy answers here. But also there has been, in this country at least, very little hard thought. Government is finding itself more and more involved in matters of cultural standards and endeavor. The Commission of Fine Arts, the Committee on Government and Art, the National Cultural Center, the Mellon Gallery, the poet at the Library of Congress, the art exhibits under State Department sponsorship, the cultural exchange programs—these represent only a sampling of federal activity in the arts. If we are going to have so much activity anyway, if we are, in addition, worried about the impact of mass culture, there are strong arguments for an affirmative governmental policy to help raise standards. Nor is there reason to suppose that this would necessarily end up in giving governmental sanction to the personal preferences of congressmen and Presidents—e.g., making Howard Chandler Christy and Norman Rockwell the models for American art. Congressmen have learned to defer to experts in other fields, and will learn to defer to experts in this (one doubts, in any case, whether the artistic taste of politicians is as banal as some assume; certainly the taste of the two most recent governors of New York is better than that of most professors).

Certain steps are obvious. Whereas many civilized countries subsidize the arts, we tend to tax them. Let us begin by removing federal taxes on music and the theater. Then we ought to set up a Federal Advisory Council on the Arts composed, not of presidential chums and other hacks, but of professional and creative artists and of responsible executives (museum directors, presidents of conservatories, opera managers, etc.). This Council ought to study American precedents in the field and, even more important, current experiments in government support of the arts in Europe. A program of subsidies for local museums and galleries, for example, would be an obvious possibility.

There is a considerable challenge to social and administrative invention here. As the problems of our affluent society become more qualitative and less quantitative, we must expect culture to emerge as a matter of national concern and to respond to a national purpose. Yet the role of the state can at best be marginal. In the end the vitality of a culture will depend on the creativity of the individual and the sensibility of the audience, and these conditions depend on factors of which the state itself is only a surface expression.

REFERENCES

1 William Benton, in his testimony before the Senate Interstate Commerce Committee, printed in the 31 May 1951 issue of the *Congressional Record* (A3313-7).

2 John Fischer, "Television and Its Critics," *Harper's Magazine*, July 1959, *219*: 10-14.

3 Frank Stanton, "The Role of Television in Our Society," an address of 26 May 1955.

De Tocqueville on Democracy and the Arts

from

Daedalus, vol.89, no.2, 1960.

Reprinted by permission of the American Academy of Arts and Sciences and the Editor of *Daedalus*.

Documents

De Tocqueville on Democracy and the Arts

In What Spirit the Americans Cultivate the Arts

IT WOULD BE to waste the time of my readers and my own if I strove to demonstrate how the general mediocrity of fortunes, the absence of superfluous wealth, the universal desire for comfort, and the constant efforts by which everyone attempts to procure it make the taste for the useful predominate over the love of the beautiful in the heart of man. Democratic nations, among whom all these things exist, will therefore cultivate the arts that serve to render life easy in preference to those whose object is to adorn it. They will habitually prefer the useful to the beautiful, and they will require that the beautiful should be useful.

But I propose to go further, and, after having pointed out this first feature, to sketch several others.

It commonly happens that in the ages of privilege the practice of almost all the arts becomes a privilege, and that every profession is a separate sphere of action, into which it is not allowable for everyone to enter. Even when productive industry is free, the fixed character that belongs to aristocratic nations gradually segregates all the persons who practice the same art till they form a distinct class, always composed of the same families, whose members are all known to each other and among whom a public opinion of their own and a species of corporate pride soon spring up. In a class or guild of this kind each artisan has not only his fortune to make, but his reputation to preserve. He is not exclusively swayed by his own interest or even by that of his customer, but by that of the body to which he belongs; and the interest of that body is that each artisan should produce the best possible workmanship. In aristocratic ages the object of the arts is therefore to manufacture as well as possible, not with the greatest speed or at the lowest cost.

When, on the contrary, every profession is open to all, when a multitude of persons are constantly embracing and abandoning it, and when its several members are strangers, indifferent to and because of their numbers hardly seen by each other, the social tie is destroyed, and each workman, standing alone, endeavors simply to gain the most money at the least cost. The will of the customer is then his only limit. But at the same time a corresponding change takes place in the customer also. In countries in which riches as well as power are concentrated and retained in the hands of a few, the use of the greater part of this world's goods belongs to a small number of individuals, who are always the same. Necessity, public opinion, or moderate desires exclude all others from the enjoyment of them. As this aristocratic class remains fixed at the pinnacle of greatness on which it stands, without diminution or increase, it is always acted upon by the same wants and affected by them in the same manner. The men of whom it is composed naturally derive from their superior and hereditary position a taste for what is extremely well made and lasting. This affects the general way of thinking of the nation in relation to the arts. It often occurs among such a people that even the peasant will rather go without the objects he covets than procure them in a state of imperfection. In aristocracies, then, the handicraftsmen work for only a limited number of fastidious customers; the profit they hope to make depends principally on the perfection of their workmanship.

Such is no longer the case when, all privileges being abolished, ranks are intermingled and men are forever rising or sinking in the social scale. Among a democratic people a number of citizens always exists whose patrimony is divided and decreasing. They have contracted, under more prosperous circumstances, certain wants, which remain after the means of satisfying such wants are gone; and they are anxiously looking out for some surreptitious method of providing for them. On the other hand, there is always in democracies a large number of men whose fortune is on the increase, but whose desires grow much faster than their fortunes, and who gloat upon the gifts of wealth in anticipation, long before they have means to obtain them. Such men are eager to find some short cut to these gratifications, already almost within their reach. From the combination of these two causes the result is that in democracies there is always a multitude of persons whose wants are above their means and who are very willing to take up with imperfect satisfaction rather than abandon the object of their desires altogether.

The artisan readily understands these passions, for he himself partakes in them. In an aristocracy he would seek to sell his workmanship at a high price to the few; he now conceives that the more expeditious way of getting rich is to sell them at a low price to all. But there are only two ways of lowering the price of commodities. The first is to discover some better, shorter, and more ingenious method of producing them; the second is to manufacture a larger quantity of goods, nearly similar, but of less value. Among a democratic population all the intellectual faculties of the workman are directed to these two objects: he strives to invent methods that may enable him not only to work better, but more quickly and more cheaply; or if he cannot succeed in that, to diminish the intrinsic quality of the thing he makes, without rendering it wholly unfit for the use for which it is intended. When none but the wealthy had watches, they were almost all very good ones; few are now made that are worth much, but everybody has one in his pocket. Thus the democratic principle not only tends to direct the human mind to the useful arts, but it induces the artisan to produce with great rapidity many imperfect commodities, and the consumer to content himself with these commodities.

Not that in democracies the arts are incapable, in case of need, of producing wonders. This may occasionally be so if customers appear who are ready to pay for time and trouble. In this rivalry of every kind of industry, in the midst of this immense competition and these countless experiments, some excellent workmen are formed who reach the utmost limits of their craft. But they rarely have an opportunity of showing what they can do; they are scrupulously sparing of their powers; they remain in a state of accomplished mediocrity, which judges itself, and, though well able to shoot beyond the mark before it, aims only at what it hits. In aristocracies, on the contrary, workmen always do all they can; and when they stop, it is because they have reached the limit of their art.

When I arrive in a country where I find some of the finest productions of the arts, I learn from this fact nothing of the social condition or of the political constitution of the country. But if I perceive that the productions of the arts are generally of an inferior quality, very abundant, and very cheap, I am convinced that among the people where this occurs privilege is on the decline and that ranks are beginning to intermingle and will soon become one.

The handicraftsmen of democratic ages not only endeavor to bring their useful productions within the reach of the whole community, but strive to give to all their commodities attractive qualities that they do not in reality possess. In the confusion of all ranks everyone hopes to appear what he is not, and makes great exertions to succeed in this object. This sentiment, indeed, which is only too natural to the heart of man, does not originate in the democratic principle; but that principle applies it to material objects. The hypocrisy of virtue is of every age, but the hypocrisy of luxury belongs more particularly to the ages of democracy.

To satisfy these new cravings of human vanity the arts have recourse to every species of imposture; and these devices sometimes go so far as to defeat their own purpose. Imitation diamonds are now made which may be easily mistaken for real ones; as soon as the art of fabricating false diamonds becomes so perfect that they cannot be distinguished from real ones, it is probable that both will be abandoned and become mere pebbles again.

This leads me to speak of those arts which are called, by way of distinction, the fine arts. I do not believe that it is a necessary effect of a democratic social condition and of democratic institutions to diminish the number of those who cultivate the fine arts, but these causes exert a powerful influence on the manner in which these arts are cultivated. Many of those who had already contracted a taste for the fine arts are impoverished; on the other hand, many of those who are not yet rich begin to conceive that taste, at least by imitation; the number of consumers increases, but opulent and fastidious consumers become more scarce. Something analogous to what I have already pointed out in the useful arts then takes place in the fine arts; the productions of artists are more numerous, but the merit of each production is diminished. No longer able to soar to what is great, they cultivate what is pretty and elegant, and appearance is more attended to than reality.

In aristocracies a few great pictures are produced; in democratic countries a vast number of insignificant ones. In the former statues are raised of bronze; in the latter, they are modeled in plaster.

When I arrived for the first time at New York, by that part of the Atlantic Ocean which is called the East River, I was surprised to perceive along the shore, at some distance from the city, a number of little palaces of white marble, several of which were of classic architecture. When I went the next day to inspect more closely one which had particularly attracted my notice, I found that its walls were of whitewashed brick, and its columns of painted wood. All the edifices that I had admired the night before were of the same kind. . . .

Literary Characteristics of Democratic Times

In an aristocratic people, among whom letters are cultivated, I suppose that intellectual occupations, as well as the affairs of government, are concentrated in a ruling class. The literary as well as the political career is almost entirely confined to this class, or to those nearest to it in rank. These premises suffice for a key to all the rest.

When a small number of the same men are engaged at the same time upon the same objects, they easily concert with one another and agree upon certain leading rules that are to govern them each and all. If the object that attracts the attention of these men is literature, the productions of the mind will soon be subjected by them to precise canons, from which it will no longer be allowable to depart. If these men occupy a hereditary position in the country, they will be naturally inclined, not only to adopt a certain number of fixed rules for themselves, but to follow those which their forefathers laid down for their own guidance; their code will be at once strict and traditional. As they are not necessarily engrossed by the cares of daily life, as they have never been so, any more than their fathers were before them, they have learned to take an interest, for several generations back, in the labors of mind. They have learned to understand literature as an art, to love it in the end for its own sake, and to feel a scholar-like satisfaction in seeing men conform to its rules. Nor is this all: the men of whom I speak began and will end their lives in easy or affluent circumstances; hence they have naturally conceived a taste for carefully chosen gratifications and a love of refined and delicate pleasures. Moreover, a kind of softness of mind and heart, which they frequently contract in the midst of this long and peaceful enjoyment of so much welfare, leads them to put aside, even from their pleasures, whatever might be too startling or too acute. They had rather be amused than intensely excited; they wish to be interested, but not to be carried away.

Now let us fancy a great number of literary performances executed by the men, or for the men, whom I have just described, and we shall readily conceive a style of literature in which everything will be regular and prearranged. The slightest work will be carefully wrought in its least details; art and labor will be conspicuous in everything; each kind of writing will have rules of its own, from which it will not be allowed to swerve and which distinguish it from all others. Style will be thought of almost as much importance as thought, and the form will be no less considered than the matter; the diction will be polished, measured, and uniform. The tone of the mind will be always dignified, seldom very animated, and writers will care more to perfect what they produce than to multiply their productions. It will sometimes happen that the members of the literary class, always living among themselves and writing for themselves alone, will entirely lose sight of the rest of the world, which will infect them with a false and labored style; they will lay down minute literary rules for their exclusive use, which will insensibly lead them to deviate from common sense and finally to transgress the bounds of nature. By dint of striving after a mode of parlance different from the popular, they will arrive at a sort of aristocratic jargon which is hardly less remote from pure language than is the coarse dialect of the people. Such are the natural perils of literature among aristocracies. Every aristocracy that keeps itself entirely aloof from the people becomes impotent, a fact which is as true in literature as it is in politics.*

Let us now turn the picture and consider the other side of it; let us transport ourselves into the midst of a democracy not unprepared by ancient traditions and present culture to partake in the pleasures of mind. Ranks are there intermingled and identified; knowledge and power are both infinitely subdivided and, if I may use the expression, scattered on every side. Here, then, is a motley multitude whose intellectual wants are to be supplied. These new votaries of the pleasures of mind have not all received the same education; they do not resemble their fathers; nay, they perpetually differ from themselves, for they live in a state of incessant change of place,

---

* All this is especially true of the aristocratic countries that have been long and peacefully subject to a monarchical government. When liberty prevails in an aristocracy, the higher ranks are constantly obliged to make use of the lower classes; and when they use, they approach them. This frequently introduces something of a democratic spirit into an aristocratic community. There springs up, moreover, in a governing privileged body an energy and habitually bold policy, a taste for stir and excitement, which must infallibly affect all literary performances.

feelings, and fortunes. The mind of each is therefore unattached to that of his fellows by tradition or common habits; and they have never had the power, the inclination, or the time to act together. It is from the bosom of this heterogeneous and agitated mass, however, that authors spring; and from the same source their profits and their fame are distributed.

I can without difficulty understand that under these circumstances I must expect to meet in the literature of such a people with but few of those strict conventional rules which are admitted by readers and writers in aristocratic times. If it should happen that the men of some one period were agreed upon any such rules, that would prove nothing for the following period; for among democratic nations each new generation is a new people. Among such nations, then, literature will not easily be subjected to strict rules, and it is impossible that any such rules should ever be permanent.

In democracies it is by no means the case that all who cultivate literature have received a literary education; and most of those who have some tinge of belles-lettres are engaged either in politics or in a profession that only allows them to taste occasionally and by stealth the pleasures of mind. These pleasures, therefore, do not constitute the principal charm of their lives, but they are considered as a transient and necessary recreation amid the serious labors of life. Such men can never acquire a sufficiently intimate knowledge of the art of literature to appreciate its more delicate beauties; and the minor shades of expression must escape them. As the time they can devote to letters is very short, they seek to make the best use of the whole of it. They prefer books which may be easily procured, quickly read, and which require no learned researches to be understood. They ask for beauties self-proffered and easily enjoyed; above all, they must have what is unexpected and new. Accustomed to the struggle, the crosses, and the monotony of practical life, they require strong and rapid emotions, startling passages, truths or errors brilliant enough to rouse them up and to plunge them at once, as if by violence, into the midst of the subject.

Why should I say more, or who does not understand what is about to follow before I have expressed it? Taken as a whole, literature in democratic ages can never present, as it does in the periods of aristocracy, an aspect of order, regularity, science, and art; its form, on the contrary, will ordinarily be slighted, sometimes despised. Style will frequently be fantastic, incorrect, overburdened, and loose, almost always vehement and bold. Authors will aim at rapidity of execution more than at perfection of detail. Small productions will be more common than bulky books; there will be more wit than erudition, more imagination than profundity; and literary perform- ances will bear marks of an untutored and rude vigor of thought, frequently of great variety and singular fecundity. The object of authors will be to astonish rather than to please, and to stir the passions more than to charm the taste.

Here and there, indeed, writers will doubtless occur who will choose a different track and who, if they are gifted with superior abilities, will succeed in finding readers in spite of their defects or their better qualities; but these exceptions will be rare, and even the authors who so depart from the received practice in the main sub- ject of their works will always relapse into it in some lesser details.

The Trade of Literature

Democracy not only infuses a taste for letters among the trading classes, but introduces a trading spirit into literature.

In aristocracies readers are fastidious and few in number; in democracies they are far more numerous and far less difficult to please. The consequence is that among aristocratic nations no one can hope to succeed without great exertion, and this exertion may earn great fame, but can never procure much money; while among democratic nations a writer may flatter himself that he will obtain at a cheap rate a moderate reputation and a large fortune. For this purpose he need not be admired; it is enough that he is liked.

The ever increasing crowd of readers and their continual craving for something new ensure the sale of books that nobody much esteems.

In democratic times the public frequently treat authors as kings do their courtiers; they enrich and despise them. What more is needed by the venal souls who are born in courts or are worthy to live there?

Democratic literature is always infested with a tribe of writers who look upon letters as a mere trade; and for some few great authors who adorn it, you may reckon thousands of idea-mongers.

Some Observations on the Drama Among Democratic Nations

The Puritans who founded the American republics not only were enemies to amusements, but they professed an especial abhorrence for the stage. They considered it as an abominable pastime; and as long as their principles prevailed with undivided sway, scenic performances were wholly unknown among them. These opinions of the first fathers of the colonies have left very deep traces on the minds of their descendants.

The extreme regularity of habits and the great strictness of morals that are observable in the United States have as yet little favored the growth of dramatic art. There are no dramatic subjects in a country which has witnessed no great political catastrophes and in which love invariably leads by a straight and easy road to matrimony. People who spend every day in the week in making money, and Sunday in going to church, have nothing to invite the Muse of Comedy.

A single fact suffices to show that the stage is not very popular in the United States. The Americans, whose laws allow of the utmost freedom, and even license of language in all other respects, have nevertheless subjected their dramatic authors to a sort of censorship. Theatrical performances can take place only by permission of the municipal authorities. This may serve to show how much communities are like individuals; they surrender themselves unscrupulously to their ruling passions and afterwards take the greatest care not to yield too much to the vehemence of tastes that they do not possess.

Editing for 13,000,000 Families
William I. Nichols

from

Daedalus, vol.89, no.2, 1960.

WILLIAM I. NICHOLS

Editing for 13,000,000 Families

THE FOLLOWING ARTICLE by William I. Nichols provides a rare glimpse of how and where much of mass culture is being produced, and by whom. It is a condensed (and approved) version of a talk given last year by Mr. Nichols, the Editor-in-Chief of *This Week* magazine. The occasion was the annual meeting of the representatives of the forty-two newspapers that actively participate in setting editorial policy and help distribute that magazine, as a supplement, to more than one-fourth of all the families in the United States every Sunday. Some of the comments on Mr. Nichols' talk on the part of these working editors are also given. This material, therefore, is an authentic document, as it were, a set of data that will help give an operational meaning to terms such as mass communication, mass media, and mass culture.—Ed.

I WANT TO SAY a few words that will help set the mood of our meeting in terms of what I feel to be the mood of the country, and how we at *This Week* should try to break into our job of producing a magazine which will supplement your efforts and help your organizations during the year ahead.

The past year can be summed up in two words, *very competitive!* A natural sequence to this statement is this: the minute anything becomes very competitive, it also becomes very imitative. That is our biggest problem and our biggest danger.

It is a fallacy to assume that competition always produces original-ity and enterprise. Sometimes competition produces nothing but copying, and I have here a wonderful exhibit on that score.

Not long ago I was out in Minneapolis making a talk to the execu-tives of one of our principal advertisers, and I was wondering just how I would describe this copycat problem that was so much on my mind. As I went into the hotel I took one look at the newsstand and there, as usual, was a dazzling array of magazines, including three of "pocket" book size: *Reader's Digest, Pageant,* and *Coronet.* I will now read to you two sets of titles of the stories that each magazine chose to promote on its cover. The *Reader's Digest* was saying, "Is it true what they say about husbands?" *Pageant* made a bolder departure with "Why do some men fail their wives?" *Coronet* went still further over this forbidden frontier and talked about "A marriage counselor tells the truth about sex in marriage."

The *Reader's Digest* also carried a big article about "Your amazing glands," *Pageant,* one called "An amazing pill that will prolong life," and *Coronet* came out with "A new pep-up diet for middle-age vitality."

If you take these three magazines, all the same size, all featuring the same articles, virtually the same headlines, then I think you begin to have an idea of what we are up against. And wherever you turn in this competitive world, it seems to me you run into the same phenomenon. It isn't peculiar to us. Wherever you go, you find people complaining about it, whether in terms of TV programs, detergents, or toothpaste.

Wherever you are, you have a feeling that this is where you came in. The fact is that we are surrounded by what you might call "homogenized" journalism. Everything has been whipped up and put into the mixer and it comes out tasting very much the same. In a recent article run in the *Saturday Evening Post's* distinguished series on "Adventures of the Mind," Randall Jarrell took advantage of the diplomatic immunity that was given to writers in this series and made a nice swing right at the mid-rib of the *Saturday Evening Post,* and the press in general. He talked not about "homogenized journalism" but about "Instant Literature," and said, "The makers of Instant Literature, whether it is a soap opera, a *Saturday Evening Post* serial, or a historical sexual best seller, humor us—flatter our prejudices and show us that they know us for what they think us to be: Impressionable, emotional, ignorant, somewhat weak-minded Common Men." And then comes a sentence which underlines this point, "Each year *Harper's,* the *Saturday Evening Post* and the Sunday supplements seem more nearly the same magazine."

Well, that is our problem—competition breeds imitation, and the bigger you get the more acute that problem becomes. And that is one of the things that has haunted me during this past year.

This Week has reached a circulation of 13 million copies every

Sunday. If you were to take a statistical profile of *This Week* and superimpose it on the population of the United States, you would find that the readership of *This Week* represents the public of the United States as a whole. And that brings us face to face with the problem of homogenization. The bigger you get the more you tend to gravitate toward talking about the big, common-denominator subjects; and the more you talk about the big, common-denominator subjects, the more danger there is of being just like everybody else— just like the big television programs, just like the other Sunday magazines, just like every other aspect and manifestation of mass journalism. And if you are not careful you are going to find that instead of producing something new, original, different, distinctive, important, memorable, or valuable, you are simply in a struggle where you are fighting for a plus or minus point in the readership surveys, so you can say, "My article about American husbands is better than your article about American husbands."

Frankly, I think that that isn't good enough. It isn't good enough in terms of my conception of what *This Week* should be, and it shouldn't be good enough in terms of what your conception of what *This Week* should be. You remember the joke in the *New Yorker* where one little Quaker boy says to another: "My father is meeker than thine." If we are not careful we are going to end up with our promotion men saying, "My Sunday magazine is blander than thine."

We have got somehow within our limitations—and very real limitations they are—to find some way of being something that has an edge to it, so that when people talk about *This Week* you know that they mean they are talking about *This Week*, and not talking about the *American Weekly*, and not talking about *Parade*, and not talking about *Family Weekly*; they are talking about something that is something, that brings something, that does something in its own name.

Now, how do you do that? The answer, I think, is first of all to stop imitating and decide what service you can render. You know the old rule for success, whether it is a business, or an invention, or anything else—to find a need and fill it. Well, it seems to me that applies to us. You have to find a service we can render—a service supplementary to the very real service which newspapers already render—and stick to it.

What is our need? That is the key question of our meeting, and I am taking my time now to talk deliberately on this rather general problem, because it seems to me if I can establish this, then all our other discussions about articles, subjects, layout, and everything else will fall into place and have a little bit of extra purpose.

The problem that concerns us all is that of trying to have an affirmative attitude, of trying to give some sense of purpose and importance to people, in a world which is spinning so dizzily that it leaves us all not only sometimes car-sick and air-sick but often heart-sick and soul-sick, too.

I have brought along three quotations which, out of all the things I have read in the course of this year, somehow seem to give a picture of what the problem of our time is, what the mood of the period is—the need which we can fill. The first is a story that appeared in the *New York Times.* It is a quotation from Boris Pregel, the President of the New York Academy of Sciences.

> The average industrial work week will be reduced, "probably very soon," to twenty hours, the retiring president of the New York Academy of Sciences predicted last night. Dr. Boris Pregel told 250 scientists that a world re-altered by automation and the abundance of cheap nuclear energy would bring about a class of "leisure-stricken" individuals who would replace the "poverty-stricken." He foresaw downgraded skilled industrial workers, beset by boredom. . . . Because technical developments outrun social progress, he said, resources of entertainment will be "grievously insufficient" to accommodate the needs of a growing number of "leisure-stricken."

That is a good phrase to remember, "leisure-stricken."

The next quotation comes from a report that has had a wonderfully strong response. It has been quoted up and down the land and has generally precipitated a new phrase into our vocabulary. That is the Rockefeller Report on Education called "The Pursuit of Excellence," prepared by a group headed by John Gardner, a director of the Carnegie Foundation. Embodied in this report is a statement you may know because we used it on our Page 2 on October 26th.

> What most people, young or old, want is not merely security, or comfort, or luxury—although they are glad enough to have these. *They want meaning in their lives.* If their era and their culture and their leaders do not or cannot offer them great meanings, great objectives, great convictions, then they will settle for shallow and trivial meanings.

> People who live aimlessly, who allow the search for meaning in their lives to be satisfied by shallow and meretricious experiences have simply not been stirred by any alternative meanings—religious meanings, ethical values, ideas of social and civic responsibility, high standards of self-realization.

This is a deficiency for which we all bear a responsibility. It is a failure of home, church, school, government—a failure of all of us.

But it is also an opportunity for us, too.

Now we come to the third quotation, published at Christmas in *Time Magazine* in a much-talked-about critique of Rollo May, the psychiatrist, whose ideas seem to be challenging the older and more traditional forms of psychiatry. I will read a quotation or two which somehow seem to interrelate the things I have been talking about, the "leisure-stricken" aspect of our society, and the hunger for meaning, purpose, and significance.

> Since World War II, Dr. May contends, there has been another change: most of the anxiety that he sees in practice comes from the fact that *too many people feel that life has lost its meaning* for them. This, he argues, brings anxiety to the surface.
>
> Nowadays, when people first sense this normal anxiety they may still repress it and consequently develop an ultra-modern form of neurotic anxiety with symptoms of depression, blocking in regard to work, despair, and melancholy, summed up in the cry "What I do isn't worth anything." The trouble lies, says May, in dammed-up potentialities, rather than repressed instincts.
>
> Americans, says May, use perpetual work as a defense against anxiety. They cannot face life itself, because life as such has lost its meaning. In the U. S. this despondency has been sharply intensified by the realization that a hydrogen-bomb war could wipe out all life; so the threat of it brings man abruptly face to face with . . . non-existence and . . . nothingness.

What is the relationship of these quotations to our problem? I think any publication has to have a conception of the frame of reference in which it is operating. Any good editor has to have a philosophy, and I think that our challenge now is to see if we can't recognize the fact that the public as a whole is hungry for some form of leadership, inspiration, guidance, which will help fill the vacuum of this "leisure-stricken" age, and give a sense of purpose and direction in a time when too many people feel rootless, leaderless, and rudderless.

Recently I saw this function fulfilled at a lunch given in honor of Commander Anderson and the crew of the missile sub *Nautilus*, just after the historic cruise under the North Pole. In all the years of going to "civic functions" I have never seen such a turnout. It was the most distinguished gathering of New Yorkers I have ever seen.

And never have I seen the air so full of excitement and enthusiasm. Never have I heard great words spoken so spontaneously, old words that suddenly took on new meaning. It took you back to the days of Winston Churchill when he talked about blood and sweat and tears. Again, old words came to life again, words like *"valor,"* *"the adventurous spirit,"* *"enterprise,"* *"excellence,"* *"competence,"* *"imagination,"* *"courage,"* and *"skill."*

Now those are all old words, but suddenly they seemed to take on meaning. And why? Because something had happened to make them real and to make that group, each member of it, proud to be an American. Something had happened to give back a sense of meaning and purpose and worthwhileness to life.

Now, somehow my concept is that this is where our job lies. The imitative field is still there. We have still got to keep up with the Joneses, as you will see if you read the list of the year's major promotable articles. We still need hard-news promotables. We want the best names, and we want to have the strongest statements. We still need to cover entertainment, in the field of television and sports and movies and everywhere else. We still need to do our very best to get the best fiction, the best cartoons, and so on. But as to all these other things, let's just remember that however good we are, we never, never can completely dominate the field. You all know the old rule, "Never do anything that anybody else can do better." And I still carry several sample magazines around which underline that point. For example: a copy of the magazine *Europeo,* which I picked up in Rome the day after the new Pope was elected, had his picture on the cover—in full color! We go to press six weeks early. We are never going to beat that.

When it comes to sex and sensation pick up any issue of *Playboy* (I don't carry it publicly) and you will find that you are not going to beat that.

And when it comes to service, we never can or will tell people how to cook hamburger in as many billions of words as *Good Housekeeping* or *Better Homes and Gardens.*

But what we can do, it seems to me, thanks to the character we have built up at *This Week,* and thanks to the character that you have built up in your papers, and thanks to the kind of people that we have gathered together in our family of 13 million readers—what we can do is to represent a steady, healthy vibration in American life. We can give people a renewed sense of meaning and purpose and importance. That is where our special section on Page Two comes in. And through our main articles we can give them a sense of opening up gateways of opportunity to new and better ways for people to use their free time, their leisure time, to be better members of the family and of the community and of our country as a whole, and thus share personally in the building of A Better America. On every page we can concentrate on the individual reader, look him in the eye, speak to him directly as a human being, let him participate in the fun and excitement of building this great magazine. That happens through such features as "I've Got A Question," or "Dick Clark Speaking," or "How America Eats," or "Quiz 'Em," and all the other person-to-person features in which we seek to achieve, not just reader interest, but reader intimacy and reader response and—most important of all—reader participation. That is the basis of *This Week*'s "friend and neighbor" approach which underlies all our editorial thinking, and which causes us, in all we do, to think and act in terms of the individual.

Now there, it seems to me, is a mission and a job. If we do it right we are not going to find ourselves confused and confounded by our imitators.

Later on, during our working sessions we shall be talking about all this in greater detail—our plans for the "Words To Live By" page, the new "Meaning of Life" series, our new plan for "Gateway" articles, each one opening the door and leading the way to some new hobby, recreational activity, or home-study project which will help the reader to grow as an individual. But at this point, all I want to do is to state my deep and firm conviction that this is our job, our area, that we must move into it, that we must continue to fill it with such a sense of leadership and inspiration that nobody, anywhere, can catch up with us on it.

What I have said is not impractical because this, I know, is what people want more than anything. If we are successful in meeting this want, it is going to rub off in terms of circulation, in terms of advertising revenue, in terms of response, and, therefore, from every standpoint it is the biggest thing there is.

Key quotations from the ensuing discussion among the editors of distributing newspapers follow.

Mr. T: We even liked a lot of your mistakes this year. (Laughter) When we get telegrams from you that there is a mistake in a recipe or something, instead of apologizing for it, we capitalize on it and write a promotion ad that makes people look for the mistake that you did make. After all, you are supposed to be perfect. When you do make a minor error it just proves that you are human. People do not like perfect things.

Mr. S: I think part of your problem as an editor is that you perhaps respect too much the little prejudices that we as individual editors have, and I think if we are going to make this thing move in the direction it has got to move in, all of us around the table have got to agree that you are going to select some material during the next year which will not conform to our local prejudices and our local needs and our local narrowness and our local restrictions, so that you can in effect give *This Week* the edge you are talking about. And if you can't do that you are just consigned to blandness. That is the greatest editorial challenge you have got this year.

Mr. O: I have the feeling, listening to everyone here, that everything is oversurveyed and overresearched; I am not completely convinced that that is the way to get a proper magazine, or one that will appeal to me.

Mr. L: Why not stand on your own ideas? I can imagine *Parade* and *American Weekly* might have a meeting like this, and give the same questions out and say, "Help us out. Tell us what to do," and the result probably would be very much the same. You would come out with the same articles and wonder why you did it. Why not have a list of subjects that no other paper will have, no other magazine of this type will have?

Mr. F: With *This Week* magazine I don't find any fault. We have three or four magazines and *This Week* is one of them. Maybe I like it because we made some money last year out of it.

Mr. H: I think the purpose of inspiration and entertainment is about all that *This Week* has to have. Surveys may tend to make you a little too conscious of competition with magazines that you are really not in competition with.

I would like to support what you said about your purpose and inspirational qualities as something that is very much needed. In the news section, we can, and will, and do scare the pants off our readers. We would like you to give them a pleasant Sunday afternoon and an inspirational lift.

Mr. W: I subscribe very heartily to what has been said about the people approach. If I may, I would like to read a quote because I think it is constructive. "Don't write about ideas or things, but about *the people* who have the ideas or who build or break the things.

Let the ideas and the things be described but by all means make them incidental."

Mr. F: One of the reasons I came is that we are faced with a price increase for the Sunday edition, and I believe we are going to have to do a bit more selling than we have before. I personally believe in strong promotion. We have done it on the newspaper as a whole, and particularly on our daily, but we haven't done it as much as we should on *This Week* magazine.

Mr. P: There have been a lot of good ideas expressed. Mainly, the idea is that you don't have to agree with us editors all the time. The hell with us. Give us some rows. It is wonderful. I realize you have got to avoid religion and a few of those things. I am afraid with your staff of editors you are more and more letting survey experts edit it. I would be much more satisfied to distribute a magazine that ran a piece as a result of Bill Nichols' having said, "That is a damn interesting story," than one that fits all the elements of a survey.

Mr. Nichols: Needless to say, I subscribe to what P. says. On the other hand, when it comes to the advertising side, and to some extent the newspaper side, people like to be convinced that you are not just dealing with pie-in-the-sky, that what you do is not good just because you think so, but because other people think so, and they want proof.

I have always felt that the answer to that comes not just in surveys, which can always be self-serving, but *in results*. My pride is that *This Week* produces more book advertising than any other publication. My pride is that when *This Week* goes out to get coupons we get more coupons-per-dollar than any other publication does. I don't think we can deny that Madison Avenue is just loaded with people who need and want proof, and you are in a position of weakness unless you can produce it. And that is where the need for research comes in.

Cultural Change and Changes in Popular Literature
Harold H. Punke

from

Social Forces, vol.15, no.3, March 1937.

CULTURAL CHANGE AND CHANGES IN POPULAR LITERATURE

HAROLD H. PUNKE

Georgia State Womans College

THERE has been frequent comment as to the social importance of the increasing body of popular literature, especially periodical literature, and the rôle of this literature in shaping the opinions of the average citizen. Casual observation might lead one to suppose that there had always been in this country an abundance of popular literature available to the adult public. The student of American society, of course, knows that this is not the case, although he may not know how widely the rates of growth in such reading material have varied, or how the material has changed in character. The present article traces the growth in amount and change in character of periodical material, and points out certain relations between that material and the changing intellectual life of the country.

GROWTH IN CIRCULATION OF PERIODICAL LITERATURE IN GENERAL

The growth in circulation of newspapers and periodicals, and the relation of that growth to the growth in population, is shown numerically in Table I and graphically in Figure I.

For nearly 120 years there was a continuous per capita increase in the number of copies of newspapers and periodicals. The increase was much more rapid from 1880 to 1927 than in earlier times, although a significant upward trend is apparent from 1830 to 1880. So great has been the total increase, that at the end of the period studied more than fifty times as many copies of newspapers and periodicals appeared per capita as in 1810. The increased availability of periodical material for the average person is of

TABLE I

POPULATION, NUMBER OF COPIES OF NEWSPAPERS AND PERIODICALS OF ALL CLASSES ISSUED PER YEAR, AND NUMBER OF COPIES PER PERSON, FOR CERTAIN YEARS FROM 1810 TO 1929

YEAR	POPULATION (IN THOUSANDS)	COPIES ISSUED ANNUALLY (IN THOUSANDS)	COPIES PER PERSON
1810	7,240	22,322[a]	3.1
1828	12,220E	68,118[a]	5.6
1840	17,069	195,839[a]	11.5
1850	23,192	426,410[a]	18.4
1860	31,443	927,952[b]	29.5
1870	38,558	1,508,548[b]	39.1
1880	50,156	2,067,848[b]	41.2
1890	62,948	4,681,114[b]	74.4
1900	75,995	8,168,149[c]	107.5
1909	90,374E	11,591,354[d]	128.3
1919	104,338E	15,729,203[e]	150.7
1923	110,487E	16,715,481[f]	151.3
1927	118,468E	19,741,829[f]	166.7
1929	121,394E	20,141,020[g]	165.9

E—estimated. For 1828 the figure indicated is the census figure for 1820, plus $\frac{4}{5}$ of the increase from 1820 to 1830, for 1909 the census for 1910 minus $\frac{1}{10}$ of the increase from 1900 to 1910, for 1919 the census for 1920 minus $\frac{1}{10}$ of the increase from 1910 to 1920. The 1923 figure is the 1924 estimate (Biennial Survey of Education, 1922–24, Bulletin 1926, No. 23, Table 1, p. 350) minus $\frac{1}{4}$ of the increase from 1920 to 1924. The 1927 figure is the 1928 estimate (Biennial Survey of Education, 1926–28, Bulletin 1930, No. 16, Table 1, p. 452) minus $\frac{1}{3}$ of the increase from 1925 to 1928. The 1929 figure is the 1928 estimate plus half the difference between that estimate and the 1930 census count.

[a] *Compendium of Seventh Census:* 1850, Table CLXIV, p. 158.

[b] *Eleventh Census of the United States:* 1890, Report on Manufacturing Industries, Part III, p. 652.

[c] *Twelfth Census of the United States:* 1900, Manufactures, Part III, Vol. 9, Table 5, p. 1043.

[d] *Thirteenth Census of the United States:* 1910, Manufactures, Report for Principal Industries, Vol. X, Table 40, p. 788.

[e] Calculated from data presented in *Fourteenth Census of the United States:* 1920, Manufactures,

Reports for Selected Industries, Vol. X, Table 19, p. 581.

ᶠ Calculated from data presented in United States Department of Commerce, Bureau of Census, *Census of Manufactures:* 1927, "Printing and Publishing and Allied Industries," Table 9, p. 16.

ᵍ Do: 1929, Table 9, p. 13.

The calculations mentioned in footnotes e, f, and g were made by multiplying the average circulation of publications of different frequency of issue (daily, weekly, quarterly, etc.) by the number of issues per year, and adding the products. The sources indicate a small miscellaneous group, "other Classes." Calculations on this group for earlier intervals for which census data for all classes, including the miscellaneous group, are given, indicated that the average per publication of this group was then seventy-five copies per year. This figure was used in making the calculations for the group, as entered in items covered by footnotes e, f, and g.

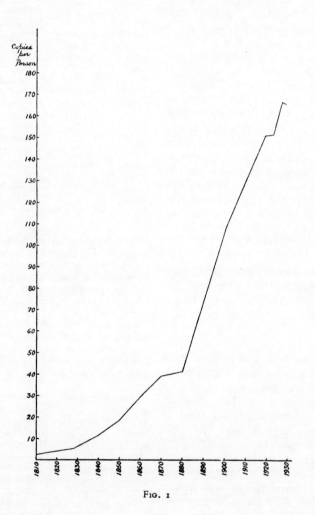

Fɪɢ. ɪ

course greater than the increase in number of copies per person, because people have come to live in cities where libraries make a few copies of a publication available to several persons.

Passing reference may be made to the two plateaus shown on the graph, 1870–80 and 1919–23. Each plateau followed the close of a war, and apparently reflects a decreased interest in reading and intellectual activity often thought to follow such disturbances. The decrease in circulation between 1927 and 1929 should here be noted. Perhaps this decrease is a result of unfavorable economic conditions, in the same sense as are the plateaus.

About 1880, then, a rate of increase in circulation of current literature began, which has been maintained with little change since that time.

TYPE OF PUBLICATION ACCORDING TO FREQUENCY OF ISSUE

Marked increase in the total volume of current literature does not necessarily mean that the increase is proportional for all types of publications. Table II indicates changes in relative status from 1850 to 1929 of different types of current literature, classified according to frequency of issue.

A steady increase in circulation of daily publications is shown for the entire period. The percentage increase was greater before 1900 than since that time,[1] but in recent pre-depression years the absolute increases greatly exceeded those of earlier years. Between 1904 and 1929 the circulation of Sunday publications more than doubled. The increase in cir-

[1] Some writers feel that circulation data for these early periods are not very reliable, and it is no doubt well to use caution in interpreting them. See Malcolm M. Willey and Stuart A. Rice, *Community Agencies and Social Life*, p. 156.

culation of monthly publications has also been marked, particularly in recent years.

It seems that the American people are gradually but definitely becoming readers of two types of current literature; daily and Sunday newspapers and monthly magazines. The circulation of tri-weeklies and semi-weeklies in recent years has not expanded in proportion to increases in population, the status of semi-monthly publications fluctuates somewhat, and quarterlies seem to be on a decline.

TYPE OF LITERATURE ACCORDING TO INTEREST SERVED

Circulation data, classified according to subject matter, are available for only part of the period thus far considered. Data on the number of publications in different fields, however, give some index of character of interest of the reading public. Table III presents data of this kind.

From 1880 to 1919 the great majority of all publications were in the field of "News, politics, and family reading." Religious publications held second place, and publications in the general field of "Commerce, finance, insurance, railroads, and trade" ranked third. Other classes have varied in ranking from time to time.

It is obvious that fundamental changes occurred in the number of publications in different fields between 1919 and 1927. By 1927 certain periodicals had built up wide circulations, while others were eliminated. Hence the number of publications is in 1927 perhaps less indicative of circulation for particular classes, than it is at earlier intervals. Chief interest in the data for 1927, as compared with earlier data, is in the separate listing of fields relating to automobiles, sports, and motion pictures.

Where available, circulation figures are a better index of relative importance of

TABLE II

Relative Change, between Certain Dates from 1850 to 1929, in Aggregate Circulation per Issue of Newspapers and Periodicals, Classified According to Frequency of Issue

(In Thousands)

FREQUENCY OF ISSUE	1850[a]	1860[a]	1870[a]	1880[a]	1890[a]	1899[b]	1904[c]	1909[d]	1914[d]	1919[d]	1923[e]	1925[e]	1927[e]	1929[e]
Daily (except Sunday)	758	1,478	2,602	3,566	8,387	15,102[f]	19,633	24,212	28,777	33,029	35,733	38,040	42,343	42,948
Sunday							12,022	13,347	16,480	19,369	24,512	25,630	27,696	29,012
Triweekly	76	107	155	68	50	229	296	335	549	492	432	401	469	312
Semi-weekly	54	175	247	265	562	2,833	2,937	2,313	2,484	2,020	2,025	1,934	2,027	2,982
Weekly	2,945	7,582	10,595	16,267	28,955	34,242[f]	36,217	40,823	50,337	51,902	47,861	50,815	55,985	53,378
Semi-monthly											5,532	6,773	5,956	9,168
Monthly	741	3,412	5,651	8,140	19,624	37,870	64,306	63,281	79,191	91,682	91,654	111,876	120,693	133,048
Quarterly	26	101	212	1,944	8,125	11,067	11,710	16,058	18,854	18,921	22,198	22,840	21,247	20,605
Other Classes	543	808	1,381	1,379	3,437	5,546	2,879	4,094	8,923	5,068	2,097	1,677	2,201	2,346
Aggregate no. of copies per issue—all classes	5,143	13,663	20,843	31,629	69,140	106,889	150,010	164,463	205,595	222,483	232,044	259,986	278,617	293,799

[a] *Twelfth Census of the United States*, (1900), Manufactures: Part III, Table 15, p. 1046.
[b] *Thirteenth Census of the United States*, (1910), Manufactures: Reports for Selected Industries, Vol. X, Table 41, p. 788.
[c] Ibid., also Table 44, p. 789.
[d] *Fourteenth Census of the United States*, (1920), Manufactures: Reports for Selected Industries, Vol. X, Table 19, p. 581.
[e] United States Department of Commerce, Bureau of Census, *Census of Manufactures*, 1929, "Printing and Publishing and Allied Industries," Table 9, p. 13.
[f] For 1899 the "Daily" line includes Sunday editions of daily papers, and the "Weekly" line includes exclusively Sunday issues.

different reading interests, than are numbers of publications. Circulation figures for 1927 and 1929 appear in Table IV.

the number of religious publications (Table III), however, are not reflected in circulation increases (Table IV). The

TABLE III

NUMBER OF PUBLICATIONS, ACCORDING TO INTEREST SERVED, APPEARING DURING CERTAIN YEARS FROM 1880 TO 1929 INCLUSIVE

INTEREST OR CHARACTER OF PUBLICATION	NUMBER OF PUBLICATIONS BY YEARS								
	1880[a]	1890[a]	1900[a]	1904[b]	1909[b]	1914[c]	1919[c]	1927[d]	1929[e]
1. News, politics, family reading......	8,863	11,326	14,867	17,032	17,698	17,574	15,746	206[y]	300[y]
2. Religion.........................	553	1,025	952	1,287	1,251	1,421	1,162	1,368	1,436
3. Commerce, finance, insurance, railroads, trade....................	363	671	710	991	949	1,196	1,061	1,171	1,227
4. Agriculture, horticulture, dairying stock raising...................	173	263	307	360	316	346	334	243	257
5. General literature, including magazines.........................	189	291	239	328	340	284	220		
6. Medicine, surgery...............	114	123	111	192	197	178	185	145[z]	154[z]
7. Law..........................	45	47	62	81	56	65	59		77
8. Science, mechanics..............	68	83	66	83	139	135	246	109[m]	176[m]
9. Fraternal organizations..........	149	216	200	450	419	312	314	126	168
10. Education, history, including college and school periodicals......	248	256	259	351	473	534	599	222[x]	330
11. Society, art, music, drama, fashion..	72	152	88	155	164	212	227	130	162
12. Labor............................					w	163	182	172	172
13. Reform and social science.........					v	179	85		
14. Automobiles, motor boats, etc......								77	103
15. Sports, games, amusements........								103	122
16. Motion Pictures..................								35	47
17. Miscellaneous...................	477	448	365	538	139	164	69	552	424
Total—all kinds...............	11,314	14,901	18,226	21,848	22,141	22,763	20,489	4,659	5,155

[a] *Twelfth Census of the United States*, (1900), Manufactures, Part III, Table II, p. 1045.

[b] *Thirteenth Census of the United States*, (1910), Manufactures, Vol. X, Tables 36 and 37, pp. 786–87.

[c] *Fourteenth Census of the United States*, (1920), Manufactures, Vol. X, Table 18, p. 580.

[d] United States Department of Commerce, Bureau of Census. *Census of Manufactures*, 1927, "Printing and Publishing and Allied Industries," Table 22, pp. 27–29.

[e] Do. 1929, Table 21, pp. 19–20.

[x] Includes only college and school periodicals.

[z] Includes dentistry.

[m] Science and technology.

[y] Includes also line five.

[w] Included in "fraternal."

[v] Included in lines 2, 6, 10, and 17.

News summaries and general literature easily heads the list, as might be expected from the scope of the category. That "Religion" should come second might not be quite so expected. Recent increases in

third group, catering to women's interests, ranks above agriculture—a field which once represented our outstanding vocational interest. The marked decrease in circulation of society and fashion magazines and of labor publications might be noted, as well as the increase in circulation of publications dealing with science and technology. The short span of time represented, however, should be kept in mind.

TABLE IV

Circulation per Thousand People in 1927 and 1929, of Publications Classified According to Interest Served[1]

INTEREST SERVED	CIRCULATION PER THOUSAND PEOPLE	
	1927	1929
1. News summaries, gen. literature, family, fiction..........	483	518
2. Religion.....................	342	343
3. Society, fashion, beauty culture, etc.....................	254	186
4. Agriculture, stock raising, etc..	154	167
5. Fraternal organizations........	74	78
6. Labor......................	72	28
7. Trade.......................	70	64
8. Commerce, finance, insurance...	23	26
9. Sports, games, amusement......	17	19
10. Motion pictures...............	14	19
11. Science and technology........	11	25
12. Automobiles, motor boats, etc...	11	17
13. Medicine, surgery, dentistry....	8	16
14. Art, music, drama.............	7	11
15. College and school.............	6	8
16. Educational...................		23
17. Law.........................		1.4

[1] The data are calculated from data presented in United States Department of Commerce, Bureau of Census, *Census of Manufactures*, 1927, "Printing and Publishing and Allied Industries," Table 22, pp. 27–29; and do. 1929, Table 21, pp. 19–20.

The population data used are those indicated for Table I.

INTERESTS SERVED BY MOST WIDELY CIRCULATED PUBLICATIONS

A study of the interests served by most widely circulated publications yields further evidence concerning adult reading interest. Such a study can be made from Table V.

The table shows a steady decrease since 1881 in number of persons per copy of the most widely circulated periodical. In 1870 over half of our leading periodicals were news reviews or weekly newspapers. Periodicals fostering the interests of particular groups appeared, but the literature represented by leading periodicals was not dominated by group interests at that time. Much the same situation existed in 1881, although religious publications were gaining in prominence—largely at the expense of literary publications and news reviews. During this decade the number of persons in the United States per copy of the most widely circulated periodical more than doubled. By 1890 religious and agricultural publications clearly dominated the field. With the passing of another decade thirty-five of the leading fifty periodicals fostered these two interests. This domination is even clearer when it is noted that the upper limit of circulation of the fifty leading periodicals was more than twice as high in 1890 as in 1881, and that it practically doubled between 1890 and 1900.

Between 1900 and 1910 there was a distinct change in the character of reading represented by leading periodicals. Women's periodicals which showed a significant upward trend by 1900, continued this trend. By 1910 religion and agriculture had definitely retreated from the interests of foremost ranks among leading periodicals. In fact agriculture had already begun the retreat in 1900. The unmistakable reappearance of literary periodicals and news reviews is also seen by 1910.

In general the period 1910–1930 seems to have been a period of carrying forward developments begun earlier. Women's and agricultural periodicals maintained their 1910 status, religious periodicals continued the decline begun sharply between 1900 and 1910, publications of fraternal organizations gained somewhat, and juveniles remained out of the list after appearance of travel and sport magazines; and of a motion-picture magazine. These periodicals reflect the growth of recent interests in American culture.

TABLE V

CLASSIFICATION OF THE LEADING FIFTY PERIODICALS AT INTERVALS FROM 1870 TO 1930, INDICATING LARGEST AND SMALLEST CIRCULATIONS, NUMBER OF PERSONS IN THE UNITED STATES PER COPY OF THE MOST WIDELY CIRCULATED PERIODICAL, AND NUMBER OF PERIODICALS FOSTERING DIFFERENT INTERESTS[1]

CIRCULATIONS AND INTERESTS FOSTERED	INTERVALS						
	1870	1881	1890	1900	1910	1920	1930
Highest circulation (in thousands)	350	200	442	846	2,036	2,021	2,908
Lowest circulation (in thousands)	35	33	45	92	300	428	576
Persons per copy of most widely circulated periodical[2]	110	251	142	89	45	52	42
Interest fostered:							
Religion	6	9	16	23	8	4	1
Agriculture	2	4	17	12	6	6	7
Women, family, fashion	7	8	6	10	17	18	18
Juvenile	5	4	5	1	3		
Literary and news reviews	14	8			13	12	10
Weekly newspapers	12	15			1	2	1
Fraternal				3	2	4	5
Fictional							3
Travel and sport	1		2				2
Motion pictures							1
Mech., tech., voc., trade	1	1	2	1	1	3	2
Humor		1					
Prohibition			2				
Not classified	2					1	
Total	50[a]	50[a]	50[a]	50	51[b]	50	50

[1] The data for Tables V–VII are from newspaper annuals. Those for the years 1881–1930 are from the corresponding volumes of Ayer's *Directory of Newspapers and Periodicals*. Those for 1870 are from Geo. P. Rowell and Co., *The American Newspaper Directory*, for 1870.

The term "periodical" as here used does not include daily or Sunday newspapers, publications available for free distribution, or series of several publications when only the total of the series falls within the limits of the leading fifty.

[2] Census data of population are from *Fifteenth Census of the United States*, (1930), Population Bulletin, First Series, Table 3, pp. 4–5.

[a] In 1870 two of the fifty leading periodicals were printed in German, in 1881 and in 1890 one was so printed.

[b] The last three publications included for this year had the same circulation; all three were therefore listed in order to make the proportion in different fields more comparable.

1910. The chief innovations for 1930 are the appearance of fictional periodicals, represented by such publications as *True Story Magazine, True Romance*, etc.; the

CONTINUITY IN PROMINENCE OF SPECIFIC PERIODICALS

As a further index of change in the character of adult reading interests and of periodical literature, a study was made of the length of time during which specific periodicals were among the prominent ones. Data indicating the number of decades during which certain publications were among the leading fifty, are presented in Table VI.

inclusive a nucleus of between one-fourth and one-third of the fifty persisted. The last three decades, however, show a distinct change from preceding decades. Twenty-three periodicals listed for 1910 were also listed for at least two other decades. The corresponding figures for

TABLE VI

NUMBER ACCORDING TO INTEREST FOSTERED, OF PERIODICALS WHICH WERE AMONG THE LEADING FIFTY FOR THREE OR MORE DECADES, AND THE NUMBER FOR TWO DECADES ONLY, WITH THE RESPECTIVE DECADES FOR WHICH SUCH PERIODICALS WERE IN THE LEAD

INTEREST FOSTERED	INTERVALS						
	1870	1881[a]	1890	1900	1910	1920	1930
Three or more intervals:							
Religious	1	3	4	3	1	1	
Agricultural	1	4	5	4	4	4	2
Women's	2	3	4	4	9	9	9
Literary	1	2			4	5	4
Juvenile	1	1	1	1	1		
Fraternal				2	1	2	2
Fictional					1	1	1
Weekly Newspapers					1	1	1
Unclassified			1		1	1	1
Two intervals only:							
Religious	2	4	6	8	5	2	
Agricultural			1	2	1	1	1
Women's					3	7	4
Literary	1	3			1	4	2
Juvenile	1	1	1				
Fraternal				1	1	1	1
Mechanical, technical, vocational	1	1				2	2
Weekly Newspapers	6	6					
Sub-totals—two intervals only	11	15	8	11	11	17	10
Sub-totals—three or more intervals	6	13	15	14	23	24	20
Grand totals	17	28	23	25	34	41	30

[a] This interval was treated as a decade, the same as the other intervals used.

Only six of the leading periodicals in 1870 were among the leading ones for two or more other decades. The corresponding figure for 1881 is thirteen, or roughly one-fourth of the fifty.[2] From 1881 to 1900

1920 and 1930 were twenty-four and twenty respectively. This means that a large proportion of the particular periodicals listed for 1910 were also listed for the two subsequent decades, rather than for two or more preceding decades; that

[2] If data for periods previous to 1870 had been included, the figure for 1870 would likely have been more nearly that for 1881, because periodicals which had earlier been prominent but which were just passing off the scene would then have been included. For the opposite reason, what is true of 1870 is also true of 1930.

is, during the three decades of this century rather than during the last decades of the preceding century. This is clearly illustrated in the case of women's periodicals, which as a group more than doubled between 1900 and 1910 in the number listed. Moreover, the nine listed for 1910 *were the same periodicals* as those listed for 1930, whereas only a few of the nine were the same as were listed earlier. In all but five cases, the decades for which periodicals were among the leading fifty were consecutive decades; that is, when a periodical once appeared in the list it stayed there until crowded out, subsequently to stay out.

The kind of periodical prominent at one time in a particular field of interest is, then, different in character from that prominent at another time. The most distinct breaks appeared between 1881 and 1890, and between 1900 and 1910. The first two decades represent the end of one period in American intellectual life, toward the end of which the circulation of periodical literature remained about on a level. The next two decades represent a period of transition and some confusion, with the appearance of several periodicals the prominence of which was of short duration. Agriculture and religion represented the two most stable fields of interest during this time. Beginning about 1910 new interests became more prominent.

PROMINENCE OF PERIODICAL IN RELATION
TO DATE OF ESTABLISHMENT

The gradual growth of new intellectual interests can further be traced by a study of the dates of establishment of particular periodicals. Table VII presents the essential data.

As one might expect, in recent decades periodicals have become prominent which were established only a few decades earlier. This fact, however, does not explain why

periodicals established much earlier should almost entirely disappear from the list during recent decades. Of the twenty-three listed as having been prominent in 1890 and at least one other decade, only six are listed for 1870; one agricultural, one juvenile, two religious, and two women's publications. The four literary periodicals in the 1870 list, failed to appear in the 1890 list, as did all weekly newspapers. Over half of the twenty-three periodicals listed for 1890 were established between 1870 and 1890, and five within the period 1881–1890.

Of the thirty-four periodicals among the leading fifty for 1910 and at least one other decade, only three were established before the close of the Civil War: *Youths Companion* (1827), *Saturday Evening Post* (1728), and *Sunday School Advocate* (1841). Of the thirteen women's periodicals listed for 1910, only two appeared for 1890: *Delineator* and *Ladies' Home Journal*. The *Saturday Evening Post* is the only periodical appearing in the list for 1930 which was established before 1870, and it has experienced "re-birth" since its original establishment.

During the period 1871–1890 an especially large number of periodicals, which later became prominent, were established. Over half of the women's periodicals listed for 1910 or for 1930 were established during this period, as were approximately half of the literary periodicals. The period 1871–1890 also witnessed the first establishment of publications of fraternal organizations, of such character as later to gain wide circulation. Hence, as in an earlier connection, the period 1870–1890 appears to be one of change and transition in American periodical literature.

SUMMARY AND CONCLUSIONS

The circulation of literature during the first third of the preceding century was

TABLE VII

DATES OF ESTABLISHMENT OF PERIODICALS WHICH RANKED AMONG THE LEADING FIFTY FOR TWO OR MORE DECADES BETWEEN 1870 AND 1930, CLASSIFIED BY ALTERNATE DECADES AND BY CHARACTER OF INTEREST FOSTERED

DECADE AND INTEREST FOSTERED	TOTAL BY DECADE AND INTEREST	DATE OF ESTABLISHMENT									
		Before 1840	1841–50	1851–60	1861–70	1871–80	1881–90	1891–1900	1901–10	1911–20	1921–30
(A) 1870: Religious	2	1		1							
Agricultural	1		1								
Literary	4	1		1	2						
Juvenile	1	1									
Women's	2		1		1						
Fraternal											
Mech., tech., etc.	1		1								
Fictional											
Weekly newspaper	6	3	1	2							
Totals for 1870	17	6	4	4	3						
(B) 1890: Religious	10	2		1	3	2	2				
Agricultural	6		1			4	1				
Literary	1						1				
Juvenile	2	1				1					
Women's	4		1		1	1	1				
Fraternal											
Mech., tech., etc.											
Fictional											
Weekly newspaper											
Totals for 1890	23	3	2	1	4	8	5				
(C) 1910: Religious	5		1			1	3				
Agricultural	5					4			1		
Literary	6	1					4	1			
Juvenile	1	1									
Women's	13					3	4	5	1		
Fraternal	2						2				
Mech., tech., etc.	1								1		
Fictional											
Weekly newspaper	1						1				
Totals for 1910	34	2	1			8	14	6	3		
(D) 1930: Religious											
Agricultural	3					1		1	1		
Literary	7	1				1	3	1	1		
Juvenile											
Women's	13					3	5	2	3		
Fraternal	3						2			1	
Mech., tech., etc.	2						1		1		
Fictional	1								1		
Weekly newspaper	1						1				
Totals for 1930	30	1				5	12	4	7	1	

small and showed little increase. Between this period and 1880 there was a distinct upward trend in circulation, followed by a much sharper upward trend after 1880. Only minor interruptions in this trend have appeared, and these during periods of economic disturbance.

Distinct changes have appeared from time to time in the interests dominating our periodical literature. In 1870 publications of general literary character predominated. Beginning a decade or two after the close of the Civil War, new influences for social change appeared in American culture and continued their operation into the early part of the present century. Industrialization, the rise of labor organizations, strikes, monopolies, adulterated products, etc., became factors in American life. Women were employed in gainful occupations in increasing numbers. Later on expansion occurred in elementary education, and agitation for reform and extension of secondary education came to be heard. The war with Spain also made its contribution to the general atmosphere of shift, change, and expansion. In an environment of such unsettling forces, it was impossible for periodical literature to remain in status quo. Not only was there a demand for more literature, but also for a different kind. During the last two decades of the century, there was considerable experimentation regarding the type of literature necessary to meet the new demand. While other interests were growing, religion and agriculture, as stable and conservative elements of American society, dominated the field. With increased urbanization and the growth of different vocational interests, however, agricultural interests naturally came to occupy a less prominent place among American periodicals. Religion, too, rapidly lost most of its representation among leading periodicals.

Although the American people, judging from their periodical literature, were rural and religious in the eighties and nineties, it appears that a large portion of the population which was reading agricultural publications at that time is now reading literary periodicals and news reviews, and a large portion which was reading religious publications at that time is now reading women's magazines.

The fact that juvenile publications have disappeared from the list of leading periodicals, may be due in part to a decrease in the number of children per thousand population, but the extension for many children of the period of school attendance beyond the period of juvenile interest, and the meeting of such interests through various school activities, is no doubt a factor.

With the second quarter of the present century, evidence is appearing of types of literature not prominent during the first quarter of the century; magazines of fiction, travel, sport, and motion pictures. These publications reflect a change in abundance as well as in the use made of the wealth and leisure afforded by present society, as contrasted with that of earlier times.

There are two direct educational implications of the foregoing study. One relates to the increasing use of current literature as material for instruction in public schools. It is quite commonly accepted that the particular interests of a publisher, economic or otherwise, influence the color of material which appears in his publications. If it were not expected that this coloring would influence the reader, there would be no object in the coloring. The extent to which a child will be influenced by such coloring is in many instances greater than the extent to which an adult would be influenced. If the child is to arrive at sane judgments regarding current topics of public importance, the school has the task of supplying him with a comprehensive basis of civic training in regard to the purpose and development of those social functions and institutions which are frequent topics of comment in current literature; government, schools, police force, public health, public utilities, transportation, etc. This means that while the increasing abundance of periodical literature makes available more current material on specific civic functions, it also places a heavier obligation on the schools to train maturing children for evaluating the material.

The second implication grows out of the same difficulty, evaluating material, but pertains to the adult level. When periodical literature increases at the rate that it has in this country since 1880, authors of articles, reviews, and news stories are increasingly interested in rendering a service that will sell, and commonly one that will sell to publications which carry advertising. In treating controversial issues, the author is therefore not likely to be guided entirely by a desire to present an unbiased analysis, but partly by the desire to present such an "analysis" as is approved by publishers and advertisers, and such as seems to readers to be within broad limits of plausibility. Hence the adult reader is often puzzled by attacks of organized interests, and lacks the basic civic understanding necessary for interpreting what he reads. Some aid to adult readers may be expected through organized adult education, but in the long run most of it will probably have to come through the schools—before adulthood is reached. In societies in which decision on matters of general public concern is not supposed to rest with the average citizen, there need not be as much direct concern over matters of this kind, as in a country which attempts to operate on democratic principles.

Mass Communication, Power and Influence
Nature Editorial

from

Nature, vol. 174, no.4433, October 1954.

NATURE

No. 4433   SATURDAY, OCTOBER 16, 1954   Vol. 174

CONTENTS

Editorial and Publishing Offices of " NATURE "
MACMILLAN & CO., LTD.,
ST. MARTIN'S STREET, LONDON, W.C.2.
Telephone Number: Whitehall 8831. Telegrams: Phusis Lesquare London

Annual subscription £6, payable in advance,
postage paid to any part of the world

Advertisements only should be addressed to
T. G. Scott & Son, Ltd., Crown House, 143–147 Regent Street, London, W.I
Telephone Number : Regent 3891

MASS COMMUNICATION, POWER AND INFLUENCE

NOW that the Television Act is on the statute book and the chairman and director-general of the Independent Television Authority have been appointed, it should be possible to continue the public discussion of the real issues free from the heat engendered by the decision to make commercial television a party political matter. The composition of the governing body of the Independent Television Authority encourages confidence that every effort will be made to see that the development of television is fostered with due regard to the public interest, though it has yet to be seen whether in practice the high standards of public service established by the British Broadcasting Corporation can be maintained. Meanwhile, it should be apparent that the misgivings which are entertained on that score are due not to poor opinions of business interests or of advertisers, but rather to doubts whether the Authority possesses sufficient powers and independence to make the public interest prevail if a clash with commercial interests should arise. To insist that the public interest must prevail, or that the question of what is the public interest is not to be determined by those whose interests are immediately concerned, is no more to impute bad faith to such persons than to maintain that government departments should not be left to judge the public interest in matters in which they are immediately concerned is to impeach the integrity of the Civil Service.

It is only too easy to attack the motives of those whose belief that broadcasting and television represent instruments of immense power over the minds of men, the social and economic implications of which are not yet apparent, leads them to urge that both broadcasting and television should be treated in the same way and on the same plane as questions of education and other matters which profoundly affect the life and thought of whole communities. When the dust of party political conflict has subsided, attacks on the integrity of men like Lord Halifax and Lord Waverley, for example, can be seen for what they are worth ; and the genuineness of the concern of such men that television and broadcasting may profoundly affect the character of our people for good or ill is unquestionable. It is indeed the belief that we need all the help we can get from this new instrument, of which science has made us masters, that has led to such stress being laid on the principle of public service—the principle that such power should be exercised responsibly for the public good. Broadcasting and television are necessarily and above all, as the Archbishop of Canterbury said in the debate on July 1, instruments of education. They provide ideas and information in such a way as to evoke, create, and contribute to mental, moral and spiritual reactions in the hearer or viewer. As with the cinema, their function as entertainment cannot be separated from this process of stimulus and reaction, even when it amounts to no more than passive acceptance. Indeed, the gravest danger of television appears to be that, instead of encouraging the process of education, it will foster a sluggish torpidity of mind which will render many incapable of being educated at all.

Even so, it would be going too far to consider the system created under the Television Act solely or even primarily as an educational instrument, though that aspect cannot be disregarded in considering any aspect of the system. What needs to be remembered is that this is a matter of influence, not of power, and its effect should be considered along with that of such other public influences as the Press and the cinema, and not in isolation. Failure to do so has encouraged the mistaken belief that the British Broadcasting Corporation possesses great power, whereas in fact it possesses little or no power but great influence.

Even so the summary of the report of the Drogheda Committee* of inquiry into British Overseas Information Services, which the Government published last April, should help to remove that belief and to put broadcasting in its proper perspective as a vehicle for the communication of ideas and information. The Drogheda Committee could not avoid the conclusion that a modern government has to concern itself with public opinion abroad and be properly equipped to deal with it, and it followed accordingly that overseas information services play an important and indeed an essential part in support of foreign, Commonwealth and Colonial policies. The report faces fairly and squarely the implications of propaganda and counter-propaganda as a means of influencing public opinion in other countries, which the development of methods of mass communication has made possible.

It is obvious from the Government's treatment of the report, and the negative attitude which the Government spokesman, Mr. H. A. Nutting, had to reveal, particularly his denunciation of co-ordination, in the debate on July 6, that some, at any rate, of the findings of the Committee, and particularly its recommendations for a concerted and long-term policy, are unpalatable. But to the impartial observer, those findings, on the evidence published, are the more impressive because of the moderation with which they are presented. The case is not over-stated. Although the need for official information services is argued convincingly, it is never suggested that propaganda is a substitute for policy or for military strength, economic efficiency or financial stability. Its effect on the course of events is unlikely to be more than marginal; but in certain circumstances it could be a decisive factor in determining diplomatic success or failure. Even in this supplementary role, it can, however, make a contribution of outstanding importance to the efficiency with which Great Britain's resources are used to further policy.

The Drogheda Committee presents a case for the support of overseas information services, including

* Overseas Information Services. Miscellaneous No. 12 (1954): Summary of the Report of the Independent Committee of Enquiry into the Overseas Information Services. Pp. 56. (Cmd. 9138.) (London: H.M. Stationery Office, 1954.) 1s. 9d. net.

broadcasting, with adequate resources for objectives which are broadly but clearly defined. No attempt has been made to refute that case, or to deny the Committee's assertion that the resources at present provided are entirely inadequate to meet those purposes. The increased expenditure of some two million pounds recommended by the Drogheda Committee, bringing the total to some twelve and a half million a year, is insignificant in comparison with its importance to the military and economic strength of Britain, and any political party which shirks finding the necessary funds because unpopular economies are involved elsewhere is clearly guilty of dereliction of public duty.

The published summary of this report shows how carefully the Drogheda Committee examined broadcasting as a means of influencing public opinion in relation to other means of promoting an understanding of the British way of life and point of view, such as books, periodicals and newspapers. It is admitted that it is difficult to assess the effectiveness of any information service, whether spoken or printed, and that broadcasting as a means of influencing opinion is always in danger of falling between the two stools of the mass audience and the influential minority. Nevertheless, the Committee holds that the high reputation of the British Broadcasting Corporation External Service for objective and honest news-reporting is a priceless asset which sets that service apart from all other broadcasting systems. This high reputation for objectivity must be maintained at all costs, and the concern with which the Government's attitude to commercial broadcasting and television is regarded arises, at least to some extent, from the belief that the Government is unwilling to put at the disposal of the new Authority sufficient resources to make it independent of influences which could destroy that objectivity.

It is perhaps unlikely that any attempt will be made by the Government to use the British Broadcasting Corporation for anything in the way of direct propaganda; but, apart from indirect effects which commercial broadcasting might have, and also commercial television, measures which entail financial stringency threaten more than the scale of the Corporation's factual presentation to other countries of the news and of British views concerning the news. The Government must make up its mind either to provide sufficient support for overseas information services to enable them to be planned as a whole on a long-term basis, safeguarded against the changes which destroy efficiency, or see that the British Broadcasting Corporation itself is provided with sufficient resources to provide the services required without risk of their magnitude or content being subjected to sectional interests or pressure. Once the reputation for objectivity is lost or the opportunities for presenting the British point of view are missed, they are not easily recovered.

These related problems are internal as well as external, and they were considered by Sir William Haley in the Clayton Memorial Lecture delivered before the Manchester Literary and Philosophical

Society last March*. That penetrating lecture, on the theme of the part which the Press and broadcasting play in building up public opinion and thus, in a democracy, in shaping public policy, deserves to be read widely. It is a valuable contribution to the clear thinking which is required on the problems arising out of the interplay of the means of information, education and entertainment in the world to-day and their bearing on wise government. The reception of the Drogheda Report itself is sufficient evidence of the dangers which arise if a government feels itself insufficiently secure to take steps imperative in the public interest because to do so may involve other unpopular measures the necessity for which could not perhaps be clearly explained to the public in the conditions of party political debate.

What Sir William Haley said bears closely on this vital matter of securing an alert, informed and intelligent public opinion. First, he explained the difference in the nature of broadcasting and the Press. Apart from its comparative novelty, though geographically the most pervading form of communication yet devised, broadcasting has limitations. Compared with the Press, it is comparatively inaccessible, being limited by time both in range and in space. Against the advantage of immediacy, especially on great occasions, has to be set its complexity and comparative inflexibility of operation compared with the Press. The Press, said Sir William, is far freer and less inhibited in political matters : because each individual reader can comprehend its output, a newspaper can have an impact which no broadcasting station can possess. It is not merely free to have a policy, an attitude, a way of thought : it can also make these things felt. Moreover, the printed word is more enduring than the spoken word, and while much of the best broadcasting is aimed at the emotions, most of the best journalism is aimed at the head.

Sir William Haley here makes a point which has received little attention in the debates over television and broadcasting of the past few years. The limitations to which he refers arise not out of the nature of the British Broadcasting Corporation and its monopoly ; they apply to any system of broadcasting and are inherent in the nature of the medium. The use we make either of broadcasting or of television and the influence they exert in our own or any other community depend not only on technique and on the way in which we use them, but also on the nature of the medium. Ultimately, practical and physical considerations must determine what is done, and Sir William's comments on television in this connexion are shrewd and disturbing.

He emphasizes what is often overlooked—that over the programme field as a whole television, from its nature, cannot have the same range as sound broadcasting. Moreover, although television robs broadcasting of the great stimulus of the listener's imagination, for whole sections of the population television threatens to become the whole of broad-

* "The Public Influence of Broadcasting and the Press". By Sir William Haley. (Clayton Memorial Lecture.) (Manchester : Literary and Philosophical Society, 1954.)

casting. Because thereby passivity instead of co-operation is encouraged, the whole educational purpose of broadcasting is at stake.

This is true whatever the outcome of the struggle between the idea of public purpose and commercial interest in television and broadcasting, and the picture Sir William gives of how much is at stake, particularly in politics and news, is disturbing. He pays a tribute to the way in which in the past the combined wisdom of Parliament, of the early committees on broadcasting, of the political party leaders and elder statesmen in both Houses of Parliament and of responsible directors and governors of the British Broadcasting Corporation, have given us a panoply of political broadcasting which has led the nation to be informed, persuaded, fairly exhorted, and given the requisite facts or opinions upon which to make up its mind, while simultaneously defending it against irresponsibility, demagogy and abuse. These same experienced forces, he believes, will bring wisdom and judgment to bear on the use of television, but they cannot ignore the nature of the medium with which they are working ; and Sir William regards the coming of the television screen into every home, and the visual presentation of political affairs and politicians in this way, as a major sociological influence of our time.

Sir William Haley is disturbed because much news, particularly the most significant and important news, has no visual quality. The nature of the medium, accordingly, is likely to be continually at war with the real values of the news, and though he is confident that the B.B.C. will make an imaginative, courageous and thoroughly honest attempt to reconcile this conflict, he is less confident as to the outcome. On its outcome the future influence of both broadcasting and the Press may well depend ; but it is difficult to feel as sure as Sir William that if the televized news bulletin proves a failure, the ordinary man or woman will revert to the printed word. There is the effect of television on the viewer, on education, and on literacy to be considered. Lord Reith was right at least in asserting that in the Television Act social, political, intellectual and ethical issues of incalculable gravity are at stake. He did not believe that its supporters would wittingly or willingly suborn moral responsibility or do moral hurt to their country at any one's dictation ; but he may not have been so very wide of the mark in suggesting the possibility that the Government has surrendered a fundamental principle, moral values and intellectual and ethical objectives that should be cherished.

The reality of such dangers appears more clearly as we reflect upon Sir William Haley's observations on the inter-relations of the Press and broadcasting and the way their influence is exerted in the society of to-day. He believes that the Press still has great influence, but the character of its influence has changed ; it is now not so much political as informative and interpretative, and while the great masses of the people may, as Sir William suggests, eschew opinions on the bewildering range of our manifold problems to-day and leave it to their representatives, we cannot entirely ignore the outlook and opinions of the general population. The serious Press is undoubtedly able to inform those representatives on hosts of important matters, and has sources of information and of informed judgment which in total are not available to the ordinary member of Parliament and can often supplement the knowledge of Ministers. Its influence on serious public opinion can be powerful, constructive, widespread and continuous.

Nevertheless, leaders of thought and action inside and outside Parliament, those of all classes in industry, the universities and schools, the professions, the churches and every walk of life who take an intelligent interest in events, still form only a fraction, though probably a greater part than formerly, of the nation. As voters in the electorate their influence could be ineffective, and Sir William Haley is clearly disturbed that the national temper may be such that the judgment and wisdom of the informed minority may fail to avert disaster. The symptoms and tendencies which he notes, moreover, may well be fostered as television encourages further both passivity and the expectancy that the individual can and should receive everything of the nation without contributing in return.

Sir William's own conclusion is not too pessimistic. He says quite frankly that certain daily and weekly newspapers with huge circulations among the less discerning and discriminating section of the community are indirectly and cumulatively building up an attitude of mind in the new generation which can be disastrous unless it is counteracted, and he points out that the Press has missed some opportunities which broadcasting has given it ; but he recognizes that much of the Press has done and is doing fine work. He regards the Press and broadcasting as complementary, not inimical to each other. The Press, he suggests, could have concentrated on what broadcasting could not at one time do, namely, providing the background, explanation, opinion, exegesis and illustration, and maintaining a sense of values.

It does not appear, however, that Sir William is over-confident that should television take over the major part of the broadcasting audience and the televized news bulletins prove a failure, the popular Press will return to its proper role and again become an educative force. That might happen, he thinks, under the influence of public opinion, and he reminds us of the short time since we created a nation that can read. We have yet to make it a literate nation ; whether television will assist or hinder that step remains to be seen.

Sir William suggested in this lecture that the most significant influence of the popular Press is now on what he calls morals, whereas the influence of British broadcasting has been mostly on manners. That influence could equally continue in television, but the arguments against commercial television indicate that widespread doubts are entertained as to whether in such a context television or broadcasting can raise standards of conduct or taste, or even maintain them. However that may be, Sir

William's contention that the Press as well as broadcasting should resume their role as leaders rather than followers of public opinion is indeed timely. Unless they remain true to their earliest ideals and seek to guide and uplift and not debase public opinion, we are on the way to an essentially uneducated nation, with all that is thereby implied in the abandonment of democracy and the growth of regimentation and intolerance.

What needs to be emphasized is that for the Press, no less than for broadcasting and television, the educational purpose cannot, without danger to the whole basis of the British way of life, be subordinated to the entertainment function. The two purposes must be harmonized and reconciled, but it must not be by the abdication of leadership and the disregard of the responsibility for the accurate and fair presentation of facts, opinions and events. Sir William Haley denounces rightly as humbug and nonsense the doctrine that the public should be given nothing but what it wants, and that any design to give it or to lead it to want something better is highly dangerous and anti-democratic.

If, however, the Press and broadcasting are to exercise their role of leadership, they must recognize that their roles are complementary, and must respect each other's functions. Largely, broadcasting, perhaps even television, can be a stimulator, and the Press can satisfy the stimulated appetite. But how effectively that educative function is discharged depends also on whether informed public opinion cares enough to maintain and advance standards, and to see that vigour and openmindedness are brought to the discussion of values and that no shibboleth goes unchallenged ; and to speak out to that end, with vision, with care and with courage.